FROM BERGEN-BELSEN TO THE OLYMPIC GAMES

Shaul P. Ladany

KING
OF THE
ROAD

**The Autobiography of an Israeli Scientist
and a World Record-Holding Race Walker**

gefen 🍇 גפן
publishing house בית הוצאה לאור
JERUSALEM • NEW YORK

Translated from the Hebrew by Sara Kitai
Layout: Marzel A.S. — Jerusalem
Cover Design: S. Kim Glassman

ISBN: 978-965-229-421-0
Edition 1 3 5 7 9 8 6 4 2

Gefen Publishing House Ltd.   Gefen Books
6 Hatzvi St.   600 Broadway
Jerusalem 94386, Israel   Lynbrook, NY 11563, USA
972-2-538-0247   1-516-593-1234
orders@gefenpublishing.com   orders@gefenpublishing.com
www.israelbooks.com
Printed in Israel   *Send for our free catalogue*

Contents

For my family and friends,
and for race walkers and sport lovers everywhere

| Preface

In 1974, while in New York on my first sabbatical from Tel Aviv University, I wrote to a distinguished American publishing house regarding publication of a scientific text I had written. As usual, I included a résumé of my professional career along with the manuscript. They did not accept my book (later put out by another publisher), but instead had a proposition of their own to put to me. Having noticed the mention of several athletic achievements in my résumé, they wondered whether I would be interested in writing an autobiography focusing mainly on my life as a race walker, and asked me to prepare an outline.

During my years as an athlete, I had religiously collected all the papers, photographs, documents, and newspaper clippings relating to my achievements and arranged them in weighty albums. Since my mother was planning a visit to New York, I asked her to bring them with her. Relying on these sources, I prepared an outline for a book in English. In some twenty thousand words, I organized the dozens of events into chapter headings, in some cases including my thoughts and detailed descriptions of the race. The editor I was in contact with read my lengthy outline and responded enthusiastically. He informed me he would try to get approval for a contract and an advance. About two weeks later he reported that his superiors did not share his unreserved enthusiasm, and would only be willing to offer a contract after they read a completed chapter or two and were convinced I would actually be able to put my stories in writing.

I've held on to that outline for a long time. I didn't like the idea of writing only a chapter or two, and I'm not sure I even know how to, so I never wrote those sample chapters. Over the years I have written or edited six scientific texts and a book about another hobby of mine that has nothing to do with sports. The outline sat on my desk, both in my office and at home, for years. I took it with me each time I went abroad on sabbatical, and whenever I spent more than a couple of weeks away from home. But with everything else I was involved in, I never even had the time to make a start. Still, the idea intrigued me and I wanted very much to tell my story. Sometimes I would relate bits and pieces of it to my training companions. This was the way things stood until 1995 when, again on sabbatical, I found myself in Singapore, the ideal place to write a book; after two or three days, a week at most, there is nothing more to do there. So after completing six studies, writing them up and sending the papers off to the appropriate scientific journals, I decided to attack the book and finished it in a relatively short time. The book was published in Hebrew in 1997, and now appears for the first time in English.

I wanted my autobiography to make it clear that sport is a way of life you have to love and it has to give you pleasure. It is not something you do for a while when the circumstances demand physical activity. I also wanted to stress that the road to glory is long, very long, but that anyone can get there through hard work, even if not endowed with extraordinary natural abilities. My story is also proof that you can achieve that glory not only because of an athletic establishment but even, as in my case, despite it.

My assessments of the people I have met are obviously subjective, reflecting my own feelings. If I think someone is an idiot — and I never use that word in this book — I do not mean to say that he is a certified graduate of idiot school. I only mean that that is how he appears to me, and that if other people were to offer their subjective opinions, they might not describe him as a complete idiot — maybe only semi-idiotic, just as a glass may be half-full or half-empty.

The book describes a period of time, an atmosphere, and real people. I would therefore like to dedicate it with gratitude to my mentors Henry Laskau and Elliott Denman; my coaches Michael Igloi, Edna Medalia, and Pino Dordoni; my Israeli walking companions, Yoram Cohen and Moshe Arieli; my defender as I tilted with windmills, General Aharon Doron; the man who promoted the sport of race walking in Israel and helped organize competitions, Justice Itzhak Braz; the referee whose name is synonymous with the word "volunteer," former runner Israel Assoulin; the friends who trained with me and constantly gave me their help: John Kelly, Dr. John Shilling, the late Don Johnson, Howie Jacobson, Dr. Bill Omelchenko, Ron Kulik, Noah Gurock, Gary Westerfield, Steve Hayden, Ron Laird, Colin Young, and Alfred Badel; my fellow competitor Reuven Peleg; my colleagues

Michael Sklar and Arnold Reisman who devoted enormous effort to bring my story to the English-reading audience, and the dozens of people around the world who volunteered their assistance and who appear in this book. The list is simply too long for me to name them all here. Last but not least, I dedicate this book to my wife, Dr. Shoshana Ladany, who bore the burden of my unusual athletic activities. As she read the manuscript, she offered her comments, corrected my mistakes, improved on the phrasing, and fought ferociously as servant and defender of the language to ensure that every *i* was dotted and *t* crossed.

June 2008

Part 1

Starting Out

■ Chapter One | Tour du Var

I can hear the footsteps, quick, barely discernible. The road is smooth, and instead of the familiar sound of feet on gravel I can just make out the squeaking of shoes on the hard asphalt surface, striking it regularly. They're behind me. It's hard to tell if it's only one person back there or a whole group. The pace is fast, but I can't hear breathing — neither the sound of air being drawn in through the nostrils nor the rush as it is expelled through the mouth. It's early, and what with the haze and the fog I can only see a few yards up the road, maybe a little more. The droplets of water in the thin mist cool my head. A pleasant sensation. It's hard to make out any details. On the sides of the road everything is still veiled in shades of gray and blue, and my eyes can't distinguish the clear outline of any tree or object. It's all blurred. I sense the white of a building going by. I can also make out the border between the edge of the road and the shoulder. It's not marked, but the smooth gray asphalt gleams uniformly while the uneven gravel in the plowed earth to my right looks entirely different. I stick to the right side of the road, using the difference in colors as a guide.

I'm worried about the footsteps behind me. "Who's back there?" I wonder. "Is he catching up or am I pulling away from him?" I want very much to know. I could turn my head and look back; it would only slow me down by a few tenths of a second at most. But I don't. I don't want to lose even that minimal time, because you can never tell if a wasted moment is going to be critical and give someone a chance to get ahead of you. And if he's on my heels, turning my head will be a clear signal that I'm tired and worried, so he'll redouble his efforts to pass me. I can't make that kind of mistake. I'll pick up the pace instead. I can still hear the footsteps. By the sound of the shoes on the road I try to assess whether the distance between us has grown. I'm not sure, but I do know it hasn't gotten shorter. That's a relief, but I know the race isn't over yet. I'm tense, but not alarmed.

I wonder how much longer I can keep up this pace. Should I step it up even more? If I speed up now, the competitors behind me might not be able or not want to catch up, and the immediate threat would seem to be taken care of. But it would demand a greater exertion and I could collapse pretty soon. Then I'd be lost. There are no free lunches, as I well know. If I put a lot of distance between me and the men behind me now, I might have to pay dearly for it later. The question of which tactic to employ is weighing on my mind, but I can't seem to find the answer. "How did I get into this?" I ask myself again. "I'm an intelligent human being, and I know that the difference between wise and clever is that clever people can get out of situations wise people would never have gotten into in the first place. So where did it all begin?

I don't like the Bernard Baruch College of the City University of New York, where I'm spending my sabbatical. The events of the Yom Kippur War are still fresh in my mind, even though it's all behind me now. I still train, even train hard, in my spare time and I'm getting fitter. It shows in the competitions too. I'm up to my ears in a research project that's beginning to pay off. Every month I produce a paper with the latest findings and submit it for publication. They're on a variety of subjects: optimal hotel booking confirmation policies, optimal calibration of machine tooling processes, the development of a program for economically efficient sampling of destructible items. They all involve the design of mathematical-statistical models for practical problems in the field of management and engineering and finding their optimal solution. I've even found time to invent a humidity-sensitive thermostat for use in air conditioners and toasters so that fresh bread will brown and dry bread won't burn, and I have already applied for a US patent.

In the middle of all this intense activity, I fly to Boston on a Monday in late April 1974 for the joint semi-annual conference of the Institute of Management Sciences (TIMS) and the Operations Research Society of America (ORSA), where I present two new papers. I have to pay my own way because the university isn't willing to cover any of my expenses. When I get back to New York on Wednesday night there's a surprise waiting for me: a telegram from the French Sports Federation. God only knows how they got

my address, but the fact is the telegram was sent to my apartment in
Riverdale. The real surprise is inside: an all-expense-paid invitation to a two-
day 183-kilometer walk in Toulon that coming Friday and Saturday.

In the previous ten years I'd been invited to lots of competitions. Each
invitation was accompanied by a form that had to be filled out and returned
to the organizers together with a registration fee. In every single case, the
entrant had to cover his own expenses, and only rarely were we offered free
accommodation. In my entire career there were only three times when I'd had
some of the expenses paid, but never before had I received an invitation that
promised to cover everything. Under ordinary circumstances I would have
jumped for joy. None of the walkers I knew, including myself, received any
compensation for our training, races, or even for winning. We were amateurs
in every sense of the word, professionals only in terms of the time, effort,
talent, and dedication we devoted to the sport. The invitation was the answer
to a prayer, and made it possible for me to take part in an event I could not
otherwise attend. It gave me the chance to win honor, a cup, and a medal that
had no monetary value whatsoever, but that I could show off and decorate my
home with.

My excitement was short-lived. It was late Wednesday night and I realized
I would have to leave New York the next day and would only be back on Tues-
day. I had classes to teach at the university on Friday and Monday. I didn't
think it would be right to ask to miss classes for a sporting event when this
non-Israeli institution, unconcerned with the needs of the State of Israel, had
granted me a month's leave so I could return home for the Yom Kippur War
not very long before.

I got to the university early on Thursday. When I saw my colleague John
Humes, I told him about the race and why I had decided, under the circumstances, not to go. John is a warm, genuinely nice person who instead of
spending his time at Baruch College doing research and publishing, wasted it
on administrative chores whose results other people took the credit for. As a
true sportsman at heart and a member of the prestigious New York Athletic
Club, he had the use of the impressive facility on 59th Street opposite Central
Park — a place where I, as a Jew, could not set foot. He begged me not to turn
down the invitation. He volunteered to fill in for me, perhaps also in return
for the fact that a few months before I had added his name as co-author of an
article I wrote. I hesitated not only because I hadn't trained enough for the

event, but also because I hadn't followed the high-carbohydrate diet I should
have started a week before the long and exhausting race that was to begin in
about thirty-six hours. Eventually I was swayed by John's argument that this
was an opportunity that might never come again and I would be a fool to pass
it up. Actually, it wasn't all that hard to convince me.

That same night I took the red-eye to Marseilles. From the time I got
home to the time I left for the airport, I had barely ten minutes to pack all my
gear and say good-bye to my wife Shosh and my daughter Danit. It's a good
thing I'd called Shosh earlier and told her I'd decided to go. I landed in
Marseilles on Friday morning and got to Toulon, totally drained and
exhausted, just before noon.

The telegram had instructed me to meet the organizers at the train station
at one o'clock. When I arrived at 11:30, there was no one there. I had no idea
where in that relatively large station we were supposed to meet, and I didn't
know the sponsors' names or what they looked like. For some reason, it never
occurred to me that someone might be playing a practical joke on me. Nothing like that had ever happened to me before, and the invitation seemed
authentic. After I'd sat there for a few minutes and watched the station fill up
again with passengers and people waiting for them, I caught sight of a solid-
looking athletic type holding an Adidas bag and wandering around as if he
were looking for someone, just as I had done. I went over and asked him in
my broken French if he had come for the race-walking event. My question
and his "yes" made us both feel better and laid to rest any suspicions we may
have had.

By one o'clock there were a few more walkers there, all Frenchmen I had
never met before. At 1:15 two jovial guys showed up and drove us to their
headquarters at a local restaurant. I learned that the race, called the Tour du
Var, would have three parts: ninety-eight kilometers the first day and a sixty-
five-kilometer stretch followed by another twenty-kilometer walk the next.
The route passed through the Var region, starting and ending in Toulon and
making its way through some of the celebrated towns of the French Riviera. It
was organized by the race-walking commission of the French Sports Federation as an international qualifying meet for the traditional annual Strasbourg
to Paris race. A local paper, the *Journal du Var* published in Toulon, was the
main sponsor of the event; they were paying for it and publicizing it. They
had invited a number of European walkers who had distinguished themselves

in long distances, people from England, Italy, Belgium, West Germany, Holland, Luxembourg, and Switzerland. I was the only non-European, included because I had won the world title at the 100-kilometer walking championship in Lugano in October 1972. We foreigners were there to spice up the competition for the numerous French contenders, and to draw the crowds.

I was very curious about my competition, but I didn't see any of them at the restaurant. Since I was dying to get some sleep, I decided not to waste my time trying to find out who they were, but to take care of what seemed most important at the moment: getting a local assistant and a hotel room. They introduced me to a very French-looking, fifty-year-old gentleman in a black beret and told me he would follow me in his car, together with the rest of his family, for the duration of the race. He had a stationery store, and in typical French fashion was taking advantage of this opportunity to volunteer his services by a huge sign with the name of the store on the roof of his long Peugeot alongside the official event logo. He was friendly, effusive, and eager to help in a way that only Latins can be. I sensed he was a sports lover and had experience supplying the needs of competitors. I knew France was the home of the Tour de France, and that a convoy of vehicles runs alongside the cyclists throughout the race. His first question to me was: "*Monsieur le docteur*, what drink do you want for the race?"

I don't know what impressed him the most, my degree and the fact that I was a university professor, that I was world champion and could earn him a great deal of reflected glory, the excitement of the competition, or the fact that I didn't make him break his teeth in German or English and appeased his French chauvinism by my efforts to make myself understood in broken French. Whatever the reason, he promised to provide me with Coca-Cola, water, and paper cups. I didn't want to overtax him by asking for ice cubes or chips, and I didn't think there was any point in going into lengthy explanations of how high to fill the cups or how to hold them out to me. If after he did it the first time he didn't understand what I wanted, then my explanations now wouldn't do much good. From experience I knew that the most important thing was for the assistant to try to identify with the competitor and ask himself what he needed and how he could best help. So I decided to wait for the next day to mention the glucose and the salt.

He took me to the hotel and promised to be there the next morning at five to drive me to the race. Before he left, I managed to elicit some information that was vital in terms of planning my tactics and my outfit: the weather forecast — cool in the early morning and hot during the day. The hotel was about six stars short of a five-star accommodation. I'm not too particular about such things, especially in this case when I had no say in the matter. After flying all night, all I wanted to do was sleep. I set the alarm for two a.m., and took out the banana, four slices of bread, jam, and salt shaker I had brought with me from New York, leaving them on the table. A few minutes later I was sound asleep.

The alarm goes off and I silence it. I don't bother looking at the clock; I know it's right. This isn't the time I usually get up, but I have to eat four hours before the race to give my stomach time to digest the food. Otherwise, at best I'll be uncomfortable and at worst I'll throw up during the walk and certainly won't be able to do as well as I could. Using a spoon, I spread the jam on so generously that it looks like I'm eating bread on jam rather than the other way around. This way I supply my body with a source of energy that will be released gradually during the race. I sprinkle salt liberally over the jam. No, I don't like salty jam, but this is my ounce of prevention. Because I'm going to sweat profusely, my muscles will ache if I don't take salt both now and during the race, and I might as well sweeten the pill.

From start to finish, the meal takes less than ten minutes. I set the alarm for 4:15 and go back to sleep. I inherited this ability to fall asleep instantly almost anywhere from my father. Unfortunately, I also do it in lectures, unless they are particularly interesting and I've gotten a good night's sleep, or unless I'm the one giving them. Even as a student at the Technion, where I used to sit in the front row, I had to wear prescription sunglasses so as not to incur the lecturers' envy...

The alarm goes off again. Regrettably, I know the clock isn't fast. I have to get up. I pull back the curtain and look outside. Pitch black. I open the window and stick my hand out. A light misty rain is falling. Using well-practiced motions, I start rubbing myself with Vaseline: in the armpits, under the upper arms, in the crotch. I don't like the feel of that thick sticky goo and don't generally use it in training. But if I didn't put it on before a race, when the arms and legs are moving so hard and so fast, I would get badly chafed and suffer miserably. I spread it on my nipples too. I could stick tape over them, like many athletes do. I did that a few times, until once when the edge of the tape came loose, twisted around and got stuck to my shirt. During the race it started pulling at the end still sticking to my chest. The pain was horrendous. Ever since, I've used Vaseline. I learned from the Hungarian marathon runner Sütö, who finished fifth in the Tokyo Olympics and with whom I shared a room at the classic marathon in Athens in 1965, that it's also a good idea to rub Vaseline on the folds and seams of my racing clothes.

Over the white shirt — on which I had the word *ISRAEL* printed several years ago — and the light blue gym shorts, I put on the old green spandex track suit made by the Swiss company Nabholtz. I bought it in 1966 and it has seen hundreds of races and two Olympics since then, but I've never been able to find anything like it for comfort and softness. Unlike other products where concerns of elegance and fashion are paramount, this was designed to be a functional garment without any seams or folds that could come into contact with the moving body and cause chafing, and with large ventilation holes under the arms. I put my white lightweight waterproof Canadian parka on over the track suit. I've had it as long as the suit and I'm just as attached to it.

My EB shoes were a gift from Brütting of Nuremberg, a small company that specializes in shoes for race walkers and marathon runners. Their shoes are so good that most of the walkers in the Munich Olympics wore them for the race, even though all the big shoe companies handed their products out to everyone for free. I make sure to tighten the laces evenly, so as not to put too much pressure on any one part of the foot. You have to remember that your foot is going to swell. I finish the job with a double knot, one bow on top of the other. That way I'm sure they won't come undone during the race. It also makes the floppy loops smaller, so I don't have to expend unnecessary energy.

I shove my white beanie — the kind they call a *tembel* hat that's considered an Israeli trademark — into the pocket of my jacket. I expect to need it during the race. "I'm ready," I say to myself. "Not yet," I remember. I roll up some toilet paper and stuff it into my back pocket. You never know if there'll be any in the toilet near the starting line — if they have a toilet there at all. I feel in my pocket for the two large dextrose pills and small salt pill I put there the night before.

I go down to the lobby and wait for my assistant. It's 4:58. He arrives on time. A few minutes later we're at the starting line near the entrance to the port. It's still raining. I take a sip from one of the bottles of Coke he brought, and we arrange a meeting place near the starting line where I can give him my extra clothing. I get out of the car. It's still dark, but under the streetlights I can make out some strange shapes — figures like myself milling about every-where. Some are standing around in small groups talking, others are doing all sorts of weird stretching exercises, and still others are warming up by walking or running. I decide not to join any of the groups. If I do, I'll waste time chat-ting and that won't leave enough time to warm up and go to the bathroom.

Taking small rhythmic steps, I start moving away from them along the street leading out of the port. After about five minutes, I turn around and come back, picking up the pace a little. When I get back to the starting line, I turn around again, this time alternating — ten yards fast, twenty yards slow — repeating the pattern about ten times. I'm getting warm, but not enough to break a sweat. I want to avoid that at this stage. I feel my bowels starting to loosen up and think I could go to the bathroom. I look around for one. There's no dressing room or toilet at the starting line. I already noticed a coffee shop, actually just a lunch counter, about a hundred yards away. They must open it at this ungodly hour for the dockworkers. I can see a dim light through the open door. I walk over there quickly, go in, see a Moroccan or Algerian cleaning up, and blurt out "Toilet." He points to a cubbyhole with a door and I hurry inside. It's a primitive affair. I haven't seen anything like it in years, but it'll do. It's a good thing I put the toilet paper in my pocket. I'm also glad the word *Israel* on my shirt is hidden under the track suit. Otherwise I might not be able to use even this facility.

I'm back on the street again. It's 5:30. I take the salt pill from my pocket, crush it between my teeth and throw my head back, forcing myself to swallow it in one go. Then I take out a dextrose pill and chew it slowly. It not only neutralizes the taste of the salt in my mouth, it also ensures a high blood sugar level for the start. I go through part of my daily exercise routine in order to loosen and lengthen a number of critical muscles that are still tense: all sorts of arm movements, neck movements, back movements, circular hip move-ments, and finally leg movements. I feel loose and just about ready. Again I start walking, first slowly then alternating with a quicker pace, but I take care not to tire myself out during the rapid segments. I decide it's time to find out who the competition is.

I go back to the starting line and the athletes standing around. I recognize a lot of them, but not everyone. Shaking hands, I say alternately, "*Wie geht's?*" "*Comment ça va?*" "How are you?" or "*Ciao,*" as the situation demands. I see Ludwig, the German walker, and we embrace. We competed three times at the world championships in Lugano so I don't suppose I have too much to fear from him. Nor am I concerned about the Belgians, the Dutch, or the Swiss. Charles Sowa from Luxembourg is also there. He's around my age and a tougher competitor. He came in ahead of me at two Olympics. But they were 50-kilometer walks, and the longer the race, the more I have the edge on him. Nonetheless, he can still pose a threat. Standing nearby is the legendary José Simon. He's also from Luxembourg, but due to the rivalry between them, they're not on very good terms. Simon was in several of the Strasbourg-to-Paris races, and the last time he won his entourage included ten cars and three doctors paid for by his sponsor, Radio Luxembourg. He's best at very long distances. When the walk is "only" fifty kilometers, he's relatively slow, which is why they never sent him to the Olympics. I don't think I'll have to worry about him at a hundred kilometers either. "After all," I say to myself, "I do a hundred kilometers more or less at the same speed as I do fifty."

I don't think any of the walkers I know there could beat me on a good day. On the other hand, the ones I never met before, especially the French, are an unknown quantity. There are a lot of ultra-long-distance events in France, and some of them might have trained well, might be in first-rate condition, and might pose a serious threat. I can't dismiss that possibility. All in all, I feel pretty good about the race. By winning the 100-kilometer world championships and setting a world record for fifty miles, I proved I was the best in the world at these distances a year and half ago. That's why I was invited, the only competitor the organizers brought over from so far away and at such expense. I also won the US 100-mile championship the past October, the 100-kilometer title a month ago, and the 75-kilometer championship that same month, setting a new US record. So I'm pretty confident. "I may not be in the shape I was last year," I pump myself up, "but I'm certainly not out of condition and I have a good chance of winning."

Considering these facts, and the weather, I work out my strategy for the race. As a walker whose basic speed isn't that great but who has outstanding consistency and stamina for extreme exertions day after day, I decide to disregard the two legs awaiting me the next day. In other words, on the first day I'd do the ninty-eight kilometers at close to top speed for that distance, without giving too much thought to the need to leave myself enough energy for the second day. As for my tactics, since the race is starting in the early morning when it's still cool, I'll set out at a somewhat faster pace because I won't be losing much fluid at that speed in the cold. Later, when it heats up, the greater loss of fluids that comes with higher speeds will make us all go a little slower. By then, I hope, I'll have put a big enough gap between myself and the others, and if not, at least I will have set my speed so that the effort is evenly spaced. By starting out at a fast pace in the cooler hours, I'll also be able to get rid of my track suit and windbreaker before I start, so I won't waste precious time removing layers of clothing along the route.

"Five minutes to start time," they announce over the loudspeakers. I go back to the starting line and locate my personal coach. I take the glucose pill from my pants pocket and hold it while I take off my watch and shove that into the pocket. Why waste energy wearing it for the race? Without taking off my shoes, I get out of my pants and hold them in three fingers of my right hand; I'm still grasping the pill with two fingers. Then I quickly pull the parka over my head, followed by the top of the track suit. As the pill dissolves in my mouth, I hand my clothes to my assistant. At the same time, I get the hat out of the jacket pocket and make him promise to hand it to me as soon as the sun begins to heat my head. He doesn't ask when that will be and I don't make any effort to define the precise moment. I also ask him to keep close after the first half hour, not to drive in front of me and choke me with the exhaust fumes from his car, and to hold out small quantities of Coke at fairly short intervals. Next, I explain that in the bag I gave him at the hotel there's a plastic bottle of glucose powder with a spoon inside and a small bottle of salt pills. At my instructions, and only then, he is to mix a little glucose in with the Coke.

I try to explain all this in my meager French, miming and using my hands in the hope that he is taking it all in and trusting him to have the will and ingenuity to consider it a worthy goal to look out for me. I have spelled out his functions clearly, and done everything I can by way of preparations and explanations. I am very well aware that winning depends on two factors: my ability and willingness to make the extra effort on the one hand, and the quality and constancy of the help I get on the other. If I don't get what I need when I need it, I won't be able to reach my full potential. From this moment on, I have to rely on the good graces of my local assistant, and can only hope for the best.

It's two minutes to the starting gun. It's still raining lightly. Like most of the other competitors, I go through my last warm-up exercises, a few quick steps. We line up for the start. Standing there, I lean forward locking my knees and slowly stretching the muscles at the back of the calf and the knee tendons. They put me in the first row. I swivel my pelvis left and right a few times. My body is still warm. I feel as if I've been standing there a long time, but it's only been a few seconds. I stick out my right leg and bend over it with my right arm out, stretching several times as my hand moves back and forth over the toes. I can feel the leg muscles stretching. If I had the room I'd do a full split, but here at the front of the line-up I can only stick one leg out in front of me. There's no room to stretch the other leg back. I switch feet and stretch again. "That's it," I say to myself, "it's time," and straighten up. But there are still a few seconds to go. I get in another couple of pelvis swings, although the radius has to be smaller than usual because of the people standing so close to me. I just have to keep my body warm. I shake hands with my two neighbors and wish them luck. The starter positioned at the right raises his gun. I stop moving my hips, inch my left foot up to the edge of the starting line, bring my right foot back and rise up on the toes. I'm tensed and ready. So are all the others. The starter puts a whistle in his mouth, a back-up option in case the gun doesn't go off.

I hear the whistle. The gun didn't fire. My rear leg moves powerfully forward and we're off. The whole body of walkers lined up in parallel rows behind the starting line begins to move. I estimate there are about two hundred of us. The fastest entrants, myself included, all in the front row, shoot ahead, followed by the rest. We cover the first ten meters at more or less the same speed. The pace is quick, very quick, but I can easily go faster. Some of the walkers are already starting to pick it up. "Fools," I think to myself. "Either they're just trying to show off or they don't have enough experience. A few hundred meters more and they'll have to slow to below their cruising speed." I'm not even tempted to catch up to them. I learned that from sad experience when I made the same mistake at the Munich Olympics and suddenly found myself in the leading pack at the end of the first lap around the stadium. It's still dark and rainy. There's a slight headwind. Although we only took off about a minute ago, my breathing is already regular and I can feel the heat throughout my body. I'm not panting or exerting myself too much. This is a comfortable pace to walk at under these conditions. If it weren't so cool and wet, I'd already be covered in sweat.

There are five walkers about ten yards ahead of me. I'm not familiar with the route, so if I stay behind I can follow them and not waste unnecessary steps. There have already been three turns. Each time I managed to plan the angle I'd take them well in advance and thus saved steps by walking the hypotenuse, rather than the sides, of an imaginary right triangle.

About five minutes later, we cross the main road at an intersection with a large traffic island in the middle. I know from the briefing they gave us that from here on the route is straight. I can also see that the leaders have slowed down. They must have tired themselves out, just as I predicted. Without having to alter my speed, the gap between us has shortened. "It's time to make my move," I say to myself, picking up the pace. I leave the other walkers behind. In about half a minute I catch up to the leaders. But I don't slow down again, not yet. If I move at their speed or just a little faster, they'll try to keep up with me while I'm attempting to pass them. So I step it up even more — I'm still way below my fastest speed and I can keep up this pace for another few kilometers — and glide past them.

First I overtake the one slightly behind the four leaders. Then I leave behind the four bunched up at the head of the race. The whole business takes maybe twenty seconds. I don't recognize anyone as I go by. Charles Sowa is an old warhorse who's adopted similar tactics to mine. Once I overtake the first walker, who managed to keep pace with me for around thirty yards, I'm on my own at the front. I pick it up even more, but I'm still going at a speed I can maintain for several kilometers. I want to increase the gap so no one will be tempted to try to get ahead of me. The sound of the footsteps behind me is getting fainter, proof that I'm pulling away from them. I still don't want to go back down to my slower cruising speed. "After another two or three kilometers," I plan in my head. I know this is just the beginning, no great effort so far. The real fight, particularly the inner struggle to fight the exhaustion, will come much later. "I've done it plenty of times before," I pump myself up, my thoughts returning to the circumstances that forged my strength.

■ Chapter Two | The Forge

The writing was on the wall, but like most Jews in Europe at that time, my parents couldn't read it. They saw it, but apparently failed to grasp the message.

Middle-class Austro-Hungarian Jews, they were married in Yugoslavia in 1932. In response to the Emancipation movement and the pressures of anti-Semitism, my father's father had changed his name from Leopold to the Hungarian "Ladany" at the end of the previous century. In the first decade of the new century, he was appointed manager of the freight train station in the Hungarian town of Sabadka, a major railway depot. Even way back then he had his own car. My father was born in 1903 and went to the classical Hungarian Gymnasium, graduating with honors in 1921. Three years before, control of the town had passed from Hungary to Yugoslavia, and the name was changed to Subotica.

Father decided to study chemistry, following in the footsteps of his young uncle Yani — who had earned a PhD in chemistry at the start of the century and, unusually for a Jew, had risen to the rank of major in the Austro-Hungarian army during World War I. Their policy of *numerus clausus*, a quota system limiting the number of Jewish students to a token figure, closed the doors of Hungarian universities to him, so he was very pleased when he was accepted by the chemical engineering department of the prestigious German university at Karlsruhe. With anti-Semitism rampant among a large part of the student population, he joined the Zionist student organization and became an activist.

After graduation he returned to Yugoslavia where he worked first with his uncle, who had a pharmaceutical factory in Zagreb, and then moved to Belgrade where he helped to set up another pharmaceutical plant. Being a dynamic and enterprising individual, he later started his own liquid glass factory. Liquid glass is made by a process similar to that for making regular glass and is a raw material used primarily in the production of glue and paper. Taking advantage of his writing skills and his training in engineering, he established the first patent attorney office in Belgrade. He managed the office and the factory simultaneously, and was very proud to be the first chemical engineer admitted to the Yugoslavian Engineers Association and later to be elected co-chairman of the organization.

My mother was born in the Hungarian town of Ujvidék in 1912, one of five daughters of Max Kassovitz, a gentleman with commercial training who established and managed a bank and was one of its chief stockholders. Although he didn't have a car, there was a telephone line between his office and his home. The connection had to be made through an operator, so they had to be on very good terms with her if they wanted to talk. When Yugoslavia took over the town in 1918, the name was changed to Novisad and the bank became the biggest in the city.

Mother graduated from high school in 1930, having learned Serbian among other things. The Kassovitzes were assimilated Reform Jews, observing the Jewish holidays and fired by Zionism. My grandfather traveled to Palestine in 1929 for the first Levant Fair in Tel Aviv, and even bought land there (a purchase no record of which, unfortunately, survives). In 1935 he returned to Palestine with one of his daughters for the Second Maccabiah Games, but he never took his spiritual Zionism to the obvious conclusion by moving to Israel. Neither did my parents. When they got engaged, however, my mother donated money to the Jewish National Fund to have a grove planted in the Holy Land in my father's name.

I was born in Belgrade in 1936, two and a half years after my sister. I had a typical middle-class childhood in a large modern home with central heating that my father built in one of the better suburbs of Belgrade, not far from the royal residence. Father's parents lived on the first floor and we lived upstairs. We spoke Hungarian at home. My nanny was called Laila, a Tot woman, not Jewish, and I spoke German with her and Serbian with the maid. They were both live-in domestics. The laundress came once a week. Father had a car, a Czech Skoda, that was kept in a locked garage in the basement. I was showered with toys, irritating my mother by trading them with the neighborhood children for bits of colored porcelain or glass.

In late 1940 my father was called up to the army reserves for an indefinite period. A lieutenant in the Yugoslavian engineering corps, he was sent to the south, stationed first in Montenegro. Later, during the fighting between Yugoslavia and Italy, he advanced with the army into Albania. His uncle Yani came to visit us on April 1, 1941, while Father was still in the army. I wasn't particularly impressed by the commotion he caused and his long arguments with his older brother, my grandfather. Nor was I aware that Germany had almost completed implementation of its "salami" policy, slicing through one country after another, and that it had already occupied Holland and Norway. Political analysts were undoubtedly worried that Germany, after signing pacts with Italy, Hungary, Romania, and Bulgaria, was planning to invade Yugoslavia through Austria (which had been annexed in the Anschluss in 1938), thereby taking the pressure off its Italian ally, on the run in Albania, and preparing the way to march into Greece.

My only happy concern was the wondrous mechanical toy Yani had brought me for my fifth birthday the next day. I don't know whether my grandfather refused to leave Yugoslavia immediately. There's no question he was unwilling to leave as long as my father was in the army somewhere in the south. The fact is, however, that Yani managed to get out of Yugoslavia in time. He slipped out at the eleventh hour, taking his family to Italy and from there to Brazil.

April 6 started like any other day. Then the storm broke out suddenly. The Germans made a surprise attack on Yugoslavia, offering no reason, or even pretext, for their action. It began with a massive aerial bombing of strategic targets. We could hear the bombs going off all around us, but not right nearby. In the morning, during a break in the bombing, people from the neighboring houses came to seek shelter in our basement where they thought they'd be safer. My mother's cousin Trude, whose husband was also in the army, showed up for the same reason. The whole family, along with Laila and the maid, squeezed into the tiny basement laundry room that was made of reinforced concrete, while the neighbors occupied the large cellar next door.

The lull was broken by a new barrage of bombs exploding with a horrendous and terrifying noise. Suddenly the building shook and the noise was excruciating. My grandmother grabbed me and fell to the ground, covering me with her body in an attempt to protect me. The heavy door to the laundry room was torn off its hinges and fell onto Grandmother. We were covered in thick dust. Next we heard groans and screams. None of us in the laundry room was hurt, except for being struck by the falling door. But on the other side of the wall, in the cellar, the situation was grim. Apparently the Germans considered our house a strategic target — it suffered a direct hit. The shell entered at an angle from the rear, toppling the exterior walls on the first and second floors and landing in the cellar where it exploded. Two people were killed and several critically wounded.

We stayed in the basement until the sound of the bombing died down. Grandfather tried to start my father's long-idle car, but to no avail. Mother went upstairs, collected her money and jewelry, and we fled the house at a run — five women and two children led by my sixty-five-year-old grandfather — taking advantage of the lull in the shelling. We raced through a large field to the Berger house at the top of the street leading to the Avala district near the royal residence. Djiga Berger, a doctor, had been my father's best friend since childhood, and the same architect had even designed the two houses. We stayed in their large cellar, where several other families had already gathered, until nightfall. The bombardment went on, starting and stopping all day.

After lengthy arguments, it was decided that under cover of darkness we would try to get as far away from Belgrade as possible. We set out at nightfall, joining other groups making their way to the mountains. We walked all night, even me, a five-year-old child. But I didn't cry. Early on in our trek we ran into a convoy of soldiers moving on foot in the same direction. They shouted to my mother to hide my white sweater before it gave us away to the Germans. The noise of airplanes and exploding shells went on even at night. By morning we had reached a small village, Shremchica, and stopped there.

For an exorbitant sum of money, a peasant couple agreed to allow the eight of us the use of their barn and to supply us with food. We heard the bombs falling on Belgrade for a second day, and then the noise stopped. After five days, Mother sent the non-Jewish maid back to Belgrade — on foot, naturally — to check out the situation there and bring us some essential clothing from the house. She came back the next day with our clothes and reported that the Yugoslavian government had surrendered to the Germans after two days of fighting, and that Belgrade was teeming with German soldiers but things were quiet. After debating the issue, on the seventh day the family decided to return to Belgrade on foot in daylight. If there was any chance of seeing my father again, they knew it was only there.

Since our house was now unlivable, we went straight to Father's large office in the city center, one street over from the royal palace, and settled in there. I was given the most luxurious accommodation: an upholstered "bed" made from pushing two soft chairs together. When Grandfather went out the next morning, he found notices ordering the Jews to report to the exhibition grounds and promising: "Anyone not complying will be shot." For the meanwhile, we stayed where we were, waiting for Father to turn up somehow.

When Yugoslavia surrendered, my father found himself near the Albanian border. His military unit disintegrated, and like the rest of the soldiers, he tried to make his way home. He started out on horseback and later got hold of a truck, until it ran out of gas. When he got near Nish, the locals informed him that German soldiers were taking all the officers prisoner and killing the Jews on the spot. Getting rid of his uniform, he changed into civilian clothes he bought from a peasant and continued northward, succeeding in getting on a train for Belgrade without being recognized.

Then he heard that the Gestapo was closely checking all the arrivals. Fearing that his cultured mien would give him away as an officer, and that further examination would reveal him to be a Jew, he jumped from the train under cover of darkness — together with several other people — as it was entering the suburbs of Belgrade on its way to the central station. They waited for it to slow down to take a curve. From there he went to our house on foot. He found it bombed out and deserted, and burst into tears. One of the neighbors saw him and comforted him with her assurances that we were alright and waiting at his office. Because of the curfew, he had to wait until morning when he suddenly appeared in the office door. Our joy was unimaginable.

Father and Grandfather decided right then and there that we had to get out of occupied Yugoslavia immediately. Hungary seemed to be the natural choice. Although it was an ally of Germany, there were no Germans there. We all spoke Hungarian and had a Hungarian name. The day after the occupation of Yugoslavia, the Hungarians reannexed the territories they had lost to Yugoslavia in 1918, including the towns where my parents were born. The only thing now separating us from Hungary was the Danube outside Belgrade. We decided to try to cross the new border that very night.

We persuaded the maid and Laila not to put themselves at risk by coming with us, especially since as Christians, and particularly Laila as a member of the German minority in Yugoslavia, they would be in no danger if they stayed behind. Trude was well aware of the risk of staying, but decided to nevertheless in the hope that her husband would also somehow manage to find his way back home. Then they would sneak across the border together. The problem was that all the bridges over the Danube had been blown up. The only way to make the crossing was by boat or impromptu ferry.

Throughout the day, my sister and I were repeatedly instructed not to open our mouths in Serbian or to say we were Jewish. Just before dark we approached one of the ferries, led by Grandfather, who announced authoritatively to the Hungarian officers in charge in perfect Hungarian: "I'm a pensioner of the Royal Hungarian Railway taking my family home." His confident bearing, along with his emphasis on our Hungarian surname, made him appear legitimate, and they let us through without checking any papers at all. The next night we were in Novisad, now known again as Ujvidék.

We stayed with Mother's parents. Seeing them and my three aunts once more was an emotional experience. They pampered us extravagantly. Somehow, the authorities got word of our arrival and my father was arrested. Grandfather Kassovitz used his influence and contacts to arrange his release two days later. The whole family conferred and decided it would be best for us to put more distance between ourselves and the Serbian border and move on to Sabadka. The next day we boarded the train, accompanied by a gentile friend of my grandfather's whose job it was to cover for us if the authorities made trouble.

Two of Grandfather's sisters lived in Sabadka in adjacent houses he owned that were connected by a large inner courtyard, creating a compound closed off from the outside. We stayed there for about two months. I was hardly ever allowed out, but Father and Grandfather ventured outside in an attempt to procure papers for us that made no mention of our ever having been in Yugoslavia. Father was picked up twice by the police as a Jewish refugee from Serbia and interned in a nearby detention camp to await transfer to the Germans. Each time he was released thanks to the intervention of a schoolmate from the Gymnasium who was now a high-ranking police officer.

After his second arrest, when he was held for over a week, the family decided to slip away to the capital where we would be inconspicuous in the big city. Again accompanied by a gentile hired to escort us, the six of us fled by train to Budapest. Grandfather and my parents rented two apartments in different parts of the city and got hold of false papers for us. Although they stated that we were Jewish, there was no reference to any time spent out of

Hungary or of our being Serbian refugees subject to extradition. Father got a job as a research engineer in a huge pharmaceutical concern, and after office hours worked illegally until late at night for two patent attorney offices where he had previous contacts. With the help of his two jobs, money was no problem. In October that same year, my parents bought a large apartment in a good section of Buda.

One morning I was awakened by the sound of Mother crying. Father had already left for work. She was weeping bitterly, the tears streaming from her eyes, her head hanging low and now and then letting out a deep sigh. She went on this way for the longest time. I tried to comfort her, but to no avail. I brought her my favorite teddy bear and stroked the delicate fair skin on her face and hand. She looked at me and clutched me to her, the tears still flowing. She cried all that day, even after Father came home. The next day too. Then little by little her tears dried up.

Later I found out why. A Hungarian general charged with crushing the Serbian resistance to annexation that had broken out in several isolated farms in the reclaimed territories had marched into Ujvidék and placed it under curfew. On his own authority, he had issued orders to his soldiers to round up all the Jews, transport them to the bathhouses on the bank of the Danube, and shoot every last one of them. Their bodies, riddled with bullets, fell into the river amid the blocks of broken ice. Mother's two sisters, Peery (who looked so much like her that it is hard for me to distinguish between them in photographs) and Margo were married to two brothers, Bela and Dezsö Zemanek, and lived together with their sister-in-law and her family in a large house. Before the three couples were dragged from their home, they managed to hide their four children. The six adults were slaughtered in the bathhouses along with seventeen hundred other Jews.

The massacre began in the morning. The news reached Budapest in the afternoon, delivered to a liberal member of the Hungarian nobility, Graf Bajcsy-Zsilinszky, who approached the Hungarian strongman, Admiral Horty, demanding that he stop the killing. Horty gave the order and it was conveyed to Ujvidék. It was received as Grandmother and Grandfather Kassovitz, together with their third daughter Ila and her husband Laci Lampel, were lined up awaiting their death. (There was no chance of help or rescue, and the men refused to abandon their wives and attempt to make a break for it on their own.) The entire affair is known as the *Razia* of Ujvidék. Grandfather later found the children huddled in their hiding place.

He kept twelve-year-old Olga, the Zemaneks' niece, with him, placed Peery's four-year-old Robert with Ila, and hired a gentile to bring Margo's Evi, a girl my age, and Peery's six-month-old baby Marta to us in Budapest. By the time they arrived, Mother had stopped crying. Since Evi knew what had happened, they had to tell me too. Half the time Evi behaved like a perfectly normal child, singing and laughing, and then suddenly, without any warning or apparent reason, she would burst out crying inconsolably.

About two weeks later we were visited by Marica, Grandfather Kassovitz's favorite niece for whom he had provided the dowry for her marriage to Eugen Türkel. They had no children, and begged Grandfather's permission to adopt Evi. Evi went with them for a trial period and stayed. Today she is a doctor like her late father. Marta cried too when she came to us, but it was baby tears. She remained with us. Today she is my sister. My parents instructed me not to tell her anything. I was only five and a half. I didn't tell. I kept it to myself all those years. It was only after Father died, when Marta was a twenty-three-year-old student, that some "well-intentioned" people starting dropping hints that made her suspect Mother was really her step-mother. Only then did I tell her the truth. She's still my sister.

Like most of the Jewish men in Hungary, Father was conscripted for forced labor, but he always managed to arrange his release because of his essential job in the pharmaceutical industry. A large number of Jews were sent to dig trenches on the Russian front where they met their death. Like us, Trude and her husband Oscar found their way to Budapest. When Oscar was conscripted for forced labor, Trude came to live with us and took care of my sisters and me until her husband was released. Ever since, even today at the age of sixty, I have called her "Trude tanti" — Aunt Trude.

In the summers of 1942 and 1943, I was sent to spend a few weeks with my father's sister Lily and her husband Dr. Imre Rosinger, a Jewish attorney whose affability and help to the needy made him very popular with the peasants in the town of Monor where they lived. It was there, while playing with my cousins Peti and Vera, that I came up against the anti-Semitism rooted so deeply in many layers of Hungarian society. Every now and then the local children would call us "stinky Jews," throw stones at us, and pick up mounds of horse manure they called "horse lemons" — I was disgusted by the very thought of even touching such a thing — and hurl them at us, too. Covered by Vera, then a teenager, armed with a broomstick, we would retreat into our courtyard protected by a high wall, closing the heavy iron gate behind us.

Those events had a profound impact on me, one that made itself known forty-five years later when I was in Australia for a scientific conference. Hearing my name, a man turned to me in Hungarian and asked if I was Hungarian. I answered spontaneously, as if from somewhere deep inside, "I'm Israeli. In Hungary I was only a stinky Jew."

In September 1942 I started primary school near our home. I went to first and second grade there, the only Jew in the class. I had no friends at school. For religious lessons (most of the pupils were Catholic, although there were some Protestants among them), the other Jews in school and I, around ten of us in all, were taught by a rabbi who tried to instruct us in the Torah and the Hebrew alphabet. Since I was learning the Latin alphabet at the same time, and I was never given Hebrew lessons after those two years, if I learned anything from him at all I soon forgot it. There were two other Jewish children in our building with whom I played. Then our games, and my schooling, came to an abrupt end.

After the beating they took on the Russian front, the defeat at El Alamein and retreat from Africa, and the entrance of the Allied forces into Sicily and Italy, the Germans feared that Hungary would withdraw from the Axis and ally itself with the enemy. Consequently, on March 19, 1944, the German army marched into Hungary. The Hungarian government was left in place, with the German presence designed to ensure its fealty. They chose not to conduct themselves like conquerors, with one exception: implementation of the "Final Solution" was to be extended to Hungary. Eichmann arrived to plan and supervise the operation. Things moved very quickly.

We were immediately ordered to wear the yellow star. The Jews in the provinces began to be picked up and transported to camps. Grandmother and Grandfather Kassovitz, Olga, and my cousin Roby (who had been sent back to stay with Grandfather while Ila was in hospital), all of whom had survived the massacre of the *Razia* of Ujvidék two years earlier, were packed into sealed freight cars and carted away along with the other Jews remaining in Novisad, supposedly to be relocated in work camps.

Grandfather, who traveled a lot and had most likely heard rumors of the mass exterminations at Auschwitz, was apparently able to identify the route they were taking through the cracks in the wall. He scribbled a note in pencil reading: "We are all still together, but are being taken to our death." He stuck it in an envelope addressed to Eugen Türkel in Budapest, and before tossing it by some extraordinary means from the moving train, added: "If you find this letter, please perform an act of humanity and convey it to my family so they will know what happened to me." My uncle Eugen told me about the letter when I visited him in Vienna fifteen years ago. When I told my mother, she responded sadly: "I also got a letter like that." Hungary can boast of at least two righteous men who did the humanitarian thing and stuck a stamp on an envelope and mailed it.

During the same time, the Hungarian provincial police arrested Trude and Oscar, who had tried to find sanctuary outside Budapest using false Aryan papers. They were separated. Trude was sent to Auschwitz, and as a young healthy woman was marked by Dr. Mengele, who determined the fate of all the newcomers, as fit for work and not doomed to instant death. She was assigned to sort the items confiscated from the new arrivals, and was shocked to find Grandfather's valise among them. She didn't need to have it spelled out for her. Oscar was murdered at Mauthausen.

When news reached us of the deportations of the Jews from the provinces, my parents tried to figure out how to save the children. They heard that the Salerzian monastery had an orphanage, and that the monks didn't ask questions. They entrusted my sisters to Christian friends, and decided to place me in the monastery. Father took me there. The yellow star was affixed to our coats. When we got to the gate in the outer wall, he took my coat, removed his own, and folded them both over his arm with only the lining showing. Then he hugged me close and kissed me on the head. He didn't say a word; neither did I. We already knew everything we needed to know. Neither of us cried; he just held me close. After a minute he straightened up and rang the bell. I held on to his hand. Tight. The abbot appeared. Father told him he had brought a child. The abbot asked no questions. He probably didn't want to hear any lies. He knew. Father freed his hand and said good-bye. I felt the tears coming but knew I mustn't cry. The abbot led me in and closed the gate behind me. I was eight years old.

My world had vanished. I was on a different planet. There were dozens of children. I didn't play or make friends with any one of them. I knew I couldn't let them find out I was a Jew. On Sunday I was told to go to the chapel for mass. I hadn't the vaguest notion what I was supposed to do there or how people pray in a church, and I was afraid my ignorance would give me away immediately. I told them I was Protestant, not Catholic, so I didn't go to mass. I didn't know how to lie and I was terrified they would take me to some Protestant place of worship and then discover I was Jewish. I lived with that fear every day. My entire life, to this very day, I have never felt such terror again. I withdrew into myself.

Finally salvation came. The Allies starting to bombard Budapest, the bombs falling in every part of the city, including the vicinity of the monastery. It didn't worry me in the slightest; I probably didn't comprehend the danger. But my parents, and especially Mother, were frightened and felt that if there was a risk of being hurt in the bombing, at least we should all be together. Two weeks after they had left me at the monastery, deliverance from my anxieties and fears arrived in the form of my father, who came to take me away and bring me back to the family. My joy was uncontainable, even though we went home in the coats with the yellow stars.

A few days later an SS man accompanied by two Luftwaffe officers showed up at our door. We were told to evacuate our home within twenty-four hours and move to the ghetto, leaving behind all the items they indicated — our finest furnishings. The ghetto was a section of tall buildings in the city center. We lived there for about a month, the five of us in one room like hundreds of other Jewish families. Since our return to Hungary, Father had resumed his involvement with the Zionist movement. One day he arrived home with the news that he and his family had been included on a list of people the Germans had agreed to send to Palestine as part of an exchange package. The following day we would be going to a staging camp.

The concierge of the building we lived in, a virulently anti-Semitic woman, must have noticed the excitement in our room and thought we were trying to flee the ghetto. She summoned two Hungarian policemen. The moment my father and I came downstairs, each of us carrying a suitcase, the policemen pounced on Father and beat him brutally in the stomach and face. Father didn't resist. I stood there in silence. I saw how much it hurt, how much agony he was in. Even after he was on the ground, they kept on kicking him. He must have known that if he put up any resistance they would murder him on the spot. A few minutes after ten, three Wehrmacht soldiers arrived. Father had hired them in advance, offering them a substantial bribe to get us safely to the camp. They rescued him from the police, declaring that they had orders to transfer us out of the ghetto. Except for Father's bruises, we all made it in one piece to the camp on Columbus Street

In an attempt to save at least some of the Hungarian Jews still alive, the Zionist leadership in Hungary, headed by Yoel Brand, his wife Hansi, and Dr. Rudolf Kasztner, had struck a bargain with the Germans. In exchange for ten thousand trucks, a hundred thousand Jews would be transferred from Hungary to Palestine through some neutral country. This followed a series of several other deals made with the devil, such as the transport of 230 prisoners from Bergen-Belsen to Palestine in 1943 in exchange for the release of Templers held prisoner. The Rescue Committee began to arrange transports for implementation of the present transaction. Representatives of all the Jewish factions and all the categories of activists were included in the first group.

There were a lot of rabbis, both reform and orthodox, including the head of the ultra-orthodox Neturei Karta, Rabbi Yaylish, journalists, doctors, scientists, artists, and so on, all accompanied by their families. Professor Yehuda Blum, later to be the Israeli ambassador to the United Nations, was there too, at that time only a young boy but already considered a prodigy. My father was included because of his Zionist activities. The first group consisted of some nineteen hundred people, and the next groups were of similar size. Grandmother and Grandfather Ladany were in the third and fourth groups, together with Father's sister Lily and her family. The Germans allowed Yoel Brand to travel to Turkey in order to inform the Allies of the provisions of the agreement via the heads of the Jewish community in Palestine. He was arrested by the British. Neither they nor the Americans were willing to supply the Germans with vehicles and thereby abet in the rehabilitation of their crippled logistic capability, not even if it meant saving the lives of a hundred thousand Jews. But no negative reply was conveyed to the Germans, and the Zionist leaders continued to assure them that consent for the transaction was imminent.

In view of these circumstances, instead of sending the first group to a neutral country, we were sent to Bergen-Belsen, a concentration camp used mainly for foreign nationals from countries not occupied by the Nazis. Two months after the Zionist Federation deposited large sums of money in German accounts in Swiss banks, the Germans agreed to transfer three hundred members of the group to Switzerland. Since the original bargain was not implemented, no further group ever left the camp on Columbus Street. After further delays and promises, and the deposit of additional sums in the Swiss banks, the Germans transported most of the remainder of the first group to Switzerland. We had been in Bergen-Belsen for six months. Group number one is known today collectively as the "Kasztner Train."

On July 2, 1944, before we left the Columbus Street camp, we said good-bye to Grandmother and Grandfather Ladany who would wait there for their group to follow us, and to Lily's family, whose arrival had been little short of miraculous. One of their Christian friends in Monor warned them the day before all the Jews were to be rounded up and deported. Somehow they managed to flee under cover of darkness, and made their way to Columbus Street. After several weeks, when it became clear that there was an unnatural delay in the departure of the other groups supposedly being transferred to Palestine, they left the camp together with my grandparents.

With no papers, they moved around among the homes of friends in Buda-pest, constantly at risk of being seized and executed by the Arrow Cross guards. Later they hid for six months, until the Russians came, in an attic on a remote farm belonging to a former client of Imre's whom he had represented without asking a fee. The Columbus Street affair was engraved so deeply on their memory that when Lily opened a travel agency in Toronto in 1957, she called it Columbus Travel Services. Eugen, Marica, and Evi also survived the war. After hiding in Budapest, in the winter of 1944 they walked all the way to the Russian front, trudging through the snow, together with my Aunt Ila, her husband Laci Lampel, and his fatherless nephew Tomi.

The train to "Palestine" stopped at Magyarovár on the Hungarian border. The station master refused to believe the destination indicated on the travel documents — Auschpitz. He was convinced it was a mistake and should read "Auschwitz." We waited there for two days until he received instructions that persuaded him that the papers were in order. Thank God for the difference between "pitz" and "witz"! During those two days we were the target of an Allied aerial attack, and in the ensuing commotion, dozens of Jews on a train bound for Auschwitz managed to make their escape and join our group. Finally, we reached Linz in Austria, where we were taken to a public shower. There, at the age of eight, I first heard the word "gas." Father, who must have heard the incredible stories brought by Polish survivors, found some sort of metal box outside, held it up to his nose, and sputtered "gas." It was with considerable apprehension that he agreed to enter the showers. Fortunately, it was a false alarm. They were real showers. I was totally unconcerned; what did I know?

Two days later we arrived at Bergen-Belsen. I remember every day of those six months — the hunger, the rain, the cold, the endless roll-calls, the barbed wire fences beside the high voltage fence, the watch towers, the SS officers always shrieking at us, especially one with a harelip, and the Dutch prisoners in their striped clothes in the adjacent camps. These sights viewed by an eight-year-old boy are etched so clearly on my memory that fifty years later, on a visit to the memorial site, I pointed to a relief map of the camp and informed the director that the fence was indicated in the wrong place. Unwilling to rely on my childhood recollection, he checked a British aerial map and found, to his astonishment, that I was right.

I will never forget the latrine and the stench that rose from it, or the tomato plant that grew outside the high voltage fence, but so close that the tomatoes started growing on it. I've had an insatiable passion for tomatoes ever since. My mother and sister disappeared for six weeks into another latrine, converted into a quarantine unit, when Marta got scarlet fever and the leaders of our group decided to isolate them. They also took the decision to ready themselves for worse times, in case we didn't get even the meager rations we were now living on. They hid about a tenth of the bread we were allotted, thus building up a growing store of emergency supplies and constantly rotating them so they would remain fresh.

One day in October or November 1944, we were ordered to report our nationality to the Germans. Never will I forget the frantic debates and deliberations as everyone tried to decide what nationality to declare. The truth had nothing to do with it; the question was what to say, what was "good for the Jews." A lot of people had several feasible options. We, for instance, could claim to be Hungarian, Yugoslavian (Serbian), or Croatian. The decision might determine our fate. My parents declared Hungarian citizenship. Distant relatives of my mother, Hungarian-speakers from Transylvania, decided after lengthy consideration to declare themselves Romanian since the king of that country had not permitted his German allies to deport his Jewish citizens to the extermination camps. When, after we had been in Bergen-Belsen for six months, the Germans finally agreed to send us on to

Switzerland, they left behind all those who had claimed Romanian citizenship. It was their way of repaying Romania for withdrawing from the Axis and joining forces with the Allies. One of our relatives, Bandy Kassovitz, died soon afterwards from the starvation and disease rampant in the camp.

We reached Switzerland on December 22, 1944. I couldn't tell when we crossed the border. The journey took four days, with several stops on the way. We were halted once for two whole days, during which rumors flew that we were being sent back to Bergen-Belsen. So when we stopped at the border it didn't make any big impression on me. At one stop we were boarded by a number of officers in grayish-blue uniforms who greeted us in German. That was a surprise to me. It was the first time I had ever heard men in uniform speaking German pleasantly and politely, not shrieking or barking out orders. They handed out cocoa to everyone, and a square of chocolate to each of the children. I still remembered what it was, although I hadn't tasted any for over half a year. Suddenly I could sense a change in the mood; the tension was gone. We had arrived in paradise.

After showers in St. Gallen, we were transferred to Caux, a true heaven on earth. We were put up in a huge turn-of-the-century hotel on the slope of a mountain about 3000 feet above the city of Montreux and Lake Geneva, which before the war had catered to a wealthy international clientele. The spectacular façade boasted dozens of round towers topped with red roofs. The building was so impressive that it inspired Walt Disney, serving as a model for the Magic Castle at the entrance to Disneyland. The hotel was deserted during the war, save for a short period when it housed Allied pilots who had been shot down over Europe and succeeded somehow in making their way to Switzerland. The authorities turned the building into a refugee camp for us. Although a large number of people had to share each of the grand rooms, where we slept on army cots, we were overjoyed. The children romped and played in the snow in high spirits. To this day Switzerland is the land of happiness, mirth, and peace for me, and I go back again and again.

Father wanted to resume a normal life and work in his profession. While the authorities were willing to maintain us as long as we were in a refugee camp, they would not permit us to leave for fear we would take jobs away from the Swiss. Exceptions were only made for people who could prove they could properly support themselves. Father fell into this category, since we had smuggled money out of Yugoslavia in the thirties and deposited it in a Swiss bank. We were allowed to leave the camp, however, only after paying in full the bill they presented him with, detailing all the expenses they had incurred by accommodating us from the moment we arrived in Switzerland as refugees. Charges included the train fare from the border, the cocoa, and the square of chocolate.

Father was permitted to move to Basel when a Jewish professor at the university there, Tadeus Reichstein, agreed to let him participate in his research work without remuneration. Life in Basel could have been risky, even though it was in Switzerland. The city, on the border with France and Germany, was home to the Hispano-Suissa Co., a manufacturer of high quality anti-aircraft guns. The same 20 mm guns were later purchased by the Israeli army as well. The neutral Swiss had pledged to the Allies not to sell arms to Germany. Nevertheless, both out of fear of the Germans and for economic reasons, they surreptitiously supplied them with Hispano-Suissa weapons. The Americans cautioned the Swiss, who issued a denial. But when the sale of arms continued, one of the American raids on Germany "missed" the target and the shells fell on the Hispano-Suissa plant in Basel, totally destroying parts of the complex. Fortunately, the Swiss took the hint and the city suffered no further bombardments.

Father, Mother, and Marta moved into a rented apartment in Basel, and my sister and I were sent to a Jewish boarding school in Heiden run by the Jewish community of Switzerland. In normal times, it served as a summer camp, but during the war it became a boarding school for Jewish refugee children. There were around two hundred children of all ages there. Except for our group of Hungarians, the others were from France and Poland. I later found out that a classmate of mine at the Geula High School in Tel Aviv, Shlomo Goodewitz, was also there for a short time. As the forward observation officer during the reprisal attack on Kalkilya in 1956, he drew the artillery fire on himself, an act of bravery that won him the Chief of Staff's Medal of Honor.

We had a wonderful time in Heiden, where I celebrated my ninth birthday. They split us up by age and language and tried to teach us what we had missed. My lessons were taught in Hungarian and German. I got to Heiden in mid-February 1945, after not being in school for eleven months, and I was very glad to be back in class. The older children were given small plots on which to grow vegetables. When I begged for one too, I was granted a tiny piece of earth, one yard by two, for a trial period. Diligently I hoed, fertilized, planted, and watered, growing lettuce, onions, carrots, beans, tomatoes, and cucumbers. When I had proven my zeal and industriousness, the conditions on my "ownership" were lifted. In the summer we went to the public swimming pool in town where we were forced to walk barefoot over a gravel path on the grounds that it was good for our feet. I hated it, but that was the only thing I didn't like about Heiden.

One day they took all the children they thought needed to have their eyes checked, including me, to St. Gallen. When we'd all been examined, they asked us who wanted to go back to school on foot, about a twenty-mile walk. When I raised my hand, they refused to let me go, claiming I was too young. It would be too hard for me, they explained, and I wouldn't be able to make it. But I insisted, and they finally gave in. I kept up with all the others, the fourteen-, fifteen-, and sixteen-year-olds, not falling behind and not needing any help. Admittedly, toward the end I was exhausted and my whole body ached, but when one of the older boys offered to carry me, I refused. Finally I agreed to let two boys walk beside me and hold my hands as they pulled me along with them. The counselors never scolded me; they saw the genuine effort I was making not to succumb to exhaustion. I got back to Heiden on my own two feet.

I didn't miss my parents especially. They came to visit us once, and once my sister Shosh and I went to Basel to see them. Before we left, they hung large cardboard signs around our necks that reached almost to our bellies. In large letters they indicated where and when we had to change trains. At Rorschach we transferred from a cogwheel railway to an ordinary train, and had to change twice more, but we made it safely to Basel on time. There, in the space of two days, Mother taught me to swim in a pool in the River Rhine.

Father was very enthusiastic about his research. He had devised a cheap, efficient process for the production of a drug called calcium-gluconate. Although he was working under the aegis of Reichstein, the professor allowed him to take out a patent under his own name, probably as compensation for the fact that Father was not getting paid. After the war, Father's patent was used to produce calcium-gluconate in Czechoslovakia, Bulgaria, Yugoslavia, and Israel. However, his greatest pride in having had the chance to work with Reichstein came when the Jewish professor won the Nobel Prize

for Medicine in 1951. To his final day, Father cherished the thank-you letter
he received from Reichstein after congratulating him on receiving the prize.

With the surrender of Germany and the end of the war in Europe, a young
Yugoslavian refugee in Switzerland, Michael Etgar — later the chief medical
officer of the Israeli army — began to organize repatriation to Yugoslavia.
Father wished to return to that country to recover the property he had left
there. An entire train was arranged, and set out in September 1945. Shosh
and I went straight from Heiden to the place where we were to meet the train.
At first, Mother was very scornful of the fact that my luggage consisted
mainly of long cucumbers and tomatoes I had grown on my tiny plot and
which I had proudly brought with me. But when the journey lasted for two
weeks, and there was no food available, she was very glad of the unexpected
supply of vegetables. The route, taking advantage of the only functioning
tracks left in Europe, ran through Germany and Austria. In every town we
passed we saw destruction everywhere, signs of the war. But it caused us no
pain whatsoever; perhaps even the opposite.

When we arrived in Belgrade we went straight to our house. Grandmother's apartment on the first floor was still in ruins. The door to our quarters on the second floor was locked. Father rang the bell as the five of us stood
there waiting with all our belongings. The door opened and a man stepped
out. Father introduced himself: "I am Engineer Ladany, the owner of this
house. I've come home." The man's face went pale, as if he'd seen a ghost or
some creature from another world. He must have known the house belonged
to a Jew, and probably hoped we had been exterminated like most of the
seventy thousand Jews of Yugoslavia. He undoubtedly knew our name as
well, and probably recognized Father from our old photographs. Mother later
found our family pictures in the ruins of the cellar where someone had
thrown them after removing them from their pretty albums. Those torn
crumpled photographs are the only mementos we have of our family before
the war.

The man was stunned. Even I could tell how shocked he was. Without
thinking, in the panic occasioned by guilt (we soon discovered he had
"preempted" not only the apartment, but a good bit of our furniture, books,
and other possessions, too), he let us in. He lived in half of our original home;
the other half lay in ruins. He opened one of the inhabitable rooms for us and
we settled in there. If he hadn't been taken so much off guard, any attempt on

our part to reestablish ownership of the house or take up residence in one of its rooms by means of legal action would have been virtually impossible, and the case would have dragged on interminably.

We stayed there. Within two weeks, we had renovated another room and a bathroom, and in another four months had fixed up the first floor apartment and moved in. As soon as we got back to Yugoslavia, I was forbidden to speak German. The slogan that appeared everywhere and was stamped on every letter or document read: "Death to fascism — liberty to the people," and Germans and their language were universally despised. Unfortunately, I had completely forgotten Serbian. Mother worked hard to teach me the language and the Cyrillic alphabet. I was enrolled in the fourth grade of a large nearby school, although I had never really been in the third grade. I had also missed a few weeks at the beginning of the year, and I didn't yet speak Serbian.

Things got even harder for me when they started to teach us another language — Russian. For me, unlike the other children, written Russian was nothing like any other writing I knew. Once again I was the only Jew in the class, and along with my sister Shosh and the two Goldstein children — whose family had also returned from Switzerland — one of only four Jews in the whole school. Nonetheless, I didn't suffer anti-Semitism. By the end of the year, my grades had improved, or more precisely, the gap had closed some-what. By the time I finished the fifth grade, I won a certificate of honor and a prize, and was even an honor student in Serbian. I had two gentile friends at school, one of whom is a doctor today and the other a lawyer.

My parents found the grand piano they had received as a wedding present in one of the cultural clubs in the neighborhood. By order of the court it was returned to us. To this day it stands proudly in my mother's living room and is a source of pleasure for all her grandchildren. At the time, however, it caused me considerable distress; I was forced to learn to play it. I hated every minute. I dodged the pressure of being compelled to practice for hours by sitting down at the piano at the very moment that my parents were leaving the house. Then I'd occupy myself with something else until I heard them coming back, when I would play a few chords and close the piano, announcing: "I just finished practicing." Even more than the piano lessons, I hated the solfeggio I had to learn at the same time. In order to sweeten the pill, I invented a game that might be what turned me into a race walker. The solfeggio lessons were held in the center of Belgrade. I could get there faster if I got off the tram a few stops early and walked up the long boulevard past the government offices. As I climbed the steep street, I would pit myself against the adults walking ahead of me, trying to pass one after the other. I always won; nobody told my competitors they were in a race.

Father's factory had been operated by the Germans during the war, and was partly destroyed, especially the large smelting oven. He took out a mortgage and renovated the plant. About a month after it was back in operation, it was nationalized as a matter of course by the Communist regime without any compensation. Father was even required to repay the mortgage out of his own pocket. He fought the authorities in court for a long time. He was as obstinate as I am when he was convinced he was right. In the end, he won and was exempted from the mortgage payments. From mid-1946 he was employed as a senior scientist at the National Food Institute, and despite the Communist regime was sent abroad several times.

In late 1947, we had a guest from Palestine staying with us. I was eleven, but I listened eagerly to his stories, told in German, of the life there, the British Mandatory government, and the chances of gaining a Jewish state. Enviously I examined his Palestinian passport. We were all fascinated by his tales; even six-year-old Marta listened in silence. With the declaration of the State of Israel, the ruler of Yugoslavia, Tito, decided to allow the Jews to imigrate to the new country. He made only one condition: anyone who left had to sign a waiver turning over all his property (except what he could take with him) to the state. My parents signed, even though they still owned some property and land that had not yet been appropriated. They had no trouble convincing me to leave. They promised that in Israel I wouldn't have to study the hated piano any more.

In early December 1948, we boarded a ship at a small, remote port south of Rijeka (Fiume). Our departure was delayed for a week, even after all four thousand Jews had boarded. Much later I learned that the choice of port and the delay had not been a matter of chance. They were waiting for a shipment of weapons that had to be smuggled into Israel during the arms embargo against the newly declared country fighting for its life. The fourteen-thousand-ton ship flying a Panamanian flag of convenience had been converted from a freighter. The hold had been divided into three levels by means of lattices, and rows of triple-decker wooden beds had been installed on each level. The tightly packed beds and ladders for climbing onto them were a familiar sight: just like Bergen-Belsen, although the mood was very different. Up on deck they had installed dozens of shower heads to which sea water was pumped. Thus we became a floating camp.

Although it usually took three, at most four, days to reach Israel, we were at sea for two weeks. The ship, the *Kefalos*, which means "skull" in Greek, lived up to its name. It shook our bones. The total weight of the passengers and their luggage (crates were sent by another ship) was so light that the stripe along the side of the ship marking how deep it should lie in the water was at least twelve feet above the water line. Consequently, the ship rolled sharply from side to side, and even tossed from stem to stern more than it should have. Nearly all the passengers were seasick for most of the trip. I was violently sick and felt awful. Down below, vomit would spill from the upper level, through the lattices, onto the floor at the bottom. Somewhere off the coast of Greece we ran into a heavy storm, the engines broke down, and the ship began to drift. Despite the SOS signals transmitted, no help arrived. Two days later they managed to fix the engines and we resumed our journey.

Tour du Var race, 1974;
I am leading on the first day

■ Chapter Three | Adjusting to a New Country

As we neared the coast of Israel toward evening, the sight of Mount Carmel and the bright lights of Haifa filled us with joy and we forgot the ordeals of the journey. It was only the next day, December 20, 1948, that we stepped off the ship at Haifa. The War of Independence was still raging. Although Be'er Sheba had been taken two months earlier, the fighting was still going on, and Eilat was only secured four months later.

We were taken to an immigrant hostel at Be'er Ya'akov for two weeks, and then allocated two rooms with no bath or kitchen in an abandoned house in Lod. There was no electricity. Marta and I brought water in buckets from one of the two faucets in town, over half a mile away, but there wasn't always water there either. Shosh went to live on Kibbutz Hazorea as part of a group of city kids there. I lied about my age and got a few jobs from the labor exchange, working in the Nes Ziona orchards. I gave the money to my parents. Father decided to open a pharmacy in Lod.

In early spring, a school was set up in town for the local children. There were two classes. The kids in my class were between ten and sixteen years old, and spoke any number of languages, except Hebrew. The teachers didn't do a lot for me, but I learned a little Yiddish and Bulgarian from my schoolmates. I read incessantly in Hungarian, finishing a book practically every day. After a year and a half, I knew a little Hebrew. I was fourteen, and eligible for a sixth-grade diploma, although in Yugoslavia I had already done three months in the seventh grade. Meanwhile, Shosh had come back from the kibbutz and completed her first year at the Geula High School in Tel Aviv, a private school.

In the summer of 1950, Father took me to Geula and tried to enroll me in the ninth grade. I had no proof I had completed primary school, and chose not to show them the sixth-grade diploma I had gotten in Lod. They tested me orally. I barely spoke Hebrew but I already knew algebra from the sixth grade in Yugoslavia, although the kids my age in Israel hadn't studied it yet. I was accepted. Public transportation between Lod and Tel Aviv was arduous and unreliable. It took me two hours each way every day, but I was usually the first one there. I was the only new immigrant in the class and that wasn't easy. I had a hard time not only with literature, Bible studies, and just understanding what was being said in all the other classes taught in Hebrew, but with English as well. It was a new language for me, whereas my classmates had already been studying it for a few years. Nevertheless, I got the second highest mark in my class on the matriculation examination in Hebrew grammar at the end of the ninth grade. But I was really in my element in the sciences. It was those subjects that got me promoted year after year, despite my poor grades in Hebrew and English.

The school's gym teacher was Joshua Rozin, who coached the Maccabi Tel Aviv basketball team and was already known as Mr. Basketball in Israel. He encouraged the boys who were tall and quick, telling me, a strong stocky type who, without any training, did the yearly 3-kilometer race pretty well but didn't finish among the fastest, "We'll never make an athlete of you." For four straight years he gave me a C. When I ran into him after I competed in the Mexico Olympics, I asked him if he remembered where he knew me from. "You're Dr. Ladany," he said, "the Israeli race-walking champion. I've seen your picture in the papers." I reminded him I had been a student of his at Geula. I saw him again after I came back from the Munich Olympics and asked him the same question. This time he answered: "You're Dr. Ladany, the Israeli race-walking champion. I used to teach you at Geula. Even then I always said you'd be an outstanding athlete…"

Although I lived at quite a distance from my classmates, I made friends thanks to my intense involvement in the Gadna, pre-army training groups organized by the Israel Defense Forces. I was induced to join by my militaristic instructors, boys two years older than us who marched us around in parade drills as part of our Gadna classes, conducted on the beach from seven to eight in the morning, before school. I had to leave my house in Lod at five a.m. in order to get there on time. At the end of the ninth grade, I did a six-week company commander's course at Rosh Ha-Nikra, where they put me on the 10-kilometer running team. I then went on immediately to the continuation course for platoon commanders.

In the tenth grade, from the very beginning of the school year, I was in a Gadna gunnery group during the week, and an army scout group on the weekends. During the summer vacation of 1952, I took an artillery team commanders course, during which a sixteen-year-old pip-squeak like me commanded and fired a 75 mm Krupp field cannon. In the eleventh and twelfth grades I took technical assistant and signal operator courses, and I loved every minute. I was very military minded and wanted to be an officer in the army, but at the same time I dreamed of becoming an engineer.

In the twelfth grade I applied to the academic reserves, an option that would enable me to fulfill both my dreams by deferring military service until after I had gotten my degree. Then I won grand prize in a local newspaper contest, drawn by lot from among all those who sent in the correct solutions to a series of giant crossword puzzles. The prize was round-trip passage by ship to Marseilles. I decided to withdraw my application to the academic reserves and take advantage of the opportunity that had fallen into my lap. Unfortunately, my subsequent request to defer my call-up date to allow time for the six-week trip to Europe was denied, so I lost out on both counts.

Thus, one day in August 1954, my father drove me in his Skoda to the recruiting center. His parting words were: "You have been granted the great privilege of serving as a soldier for your country — the Jewish state." I knew precisely what he meant. His words are engraved on my memory, and even more so, on my consciousness. When my wife and I took our daughter Danit to the recruiting center in Be'er Sheba thirty-five years later, I parted from her in exactly the same way, repeating my father's declaration word for word.

But my father had something of a letdown, or at least a surprise, in store. After he left, they read out a list of names, the draftees filled the bus, and it drove off. Then they read out another list of names, including mine. We filled up a second bus. The driver had already put it in gear when a woman soldier appeared and called my name. She told me to get my things and come with her, saying they had gotten a communication from the Ministry of Defense to delay my recruitment and put me in touch with the office of the director general. We called his office, and his secretary informed me that he had seen that my request to defer my call-up had been denied and he wanted to see if the decision could be reversed.

The next day I presented myself at his office in Tel Aviv and received formal approval for the trip abroad. Later it occurred to me that I might have been one of the few people who benefited from the bickering and intrigues between the minister of defense at the time, Pinchas Lavon, and his director general, Shimon Peres (later prime minister and then president), occasioned by the scandal known as the Lavon Affair.

I was recruited, at my request naturally, to the artillery corps. Basic training was a snap for me. I was, however, punished once, ordered to report hourly to the regimental policeman throughout the night in full battle gear and with my bed made up because on my way to the mess hall on Saturday, a rifle in my left hand and mess kit in the right, I saluted my company commander while still holding the utensils. Nevertheless, at the end of basic training I was awarded the honor of outstanding trainee. I also breezed through the team commanders course given at the same base immediately afterward. I already knew the material from the Gadna gunnery group.

But the four months of combat duty on the border with the Gaza Strip were tough and much less pleasant. Once every two weeks we were taken to a kibbutz for a shower. We got no leave whatsoever, not even a few hours, for those whole four months. A friend of mine named Gideon wasn't even allowed leave for his father's *shloshim*, the traditional day of mourning thirty days after a death in the family. It was our job to provide cover for the border patrols. From time to time we were shelled, or we shelled the other side so a patrol cut off by fire could get out. And we often changed positions, digging ourselves in (with our hands!) all over again.

Once when we had taken up a new position in a wadi behind Kibbutz Nirim, but hadn't yet fired from it, we got to see the UN in all its glory in action. A UN jeep drove by, and the officer stopped, got out, took out his field glasses, and began to survey the area. Suddenly he caught sight of our battery in the wadi, despite the camouflage netting. He took out a compass and a map, marked something on the map, got back in the jeep and drove off. Our lookout saw him and reported to the command post. We were ordered to reposition ourselves immediately. Even before we had finished pulling up stakes, Egyptian shells began falling on our original position. We no longer needed to be told why we were forbidden to hitch a ride in a UN vehicle.

From combat duty I was transferred directly to the corps' pre-officers' training course. It was a real joy after the long months in the field, not least because I was also free of the tyranny of First Sergeant Linzer, whose atypical conduct for an NCO stemmed either from innate malice or sadism. At the

same time, I reapplied to the academic reserves, this time requesting defer-
ment of the rest of my service after completion of a year in the army. Thus,
unexpectedly, when we returned from a short leave at the end of the course
and all my friends went on to the officers' training course, I was ordered to
report to the induction center for demobilization as a member of the
academic reserves.

I lazed around for three weeks, getting myself ready for the start of my
first year in the mechanical engineering department of the Technion. In
November 1955, three weeks into the school year, all of us in the academic
reserves were ordered to attend a meeting with the general in charge of military personnel where we were informed — to our astonishment — that we
were immediately being mobilized back into active duty. The explanation we
were given cited "the army's long-term needs." A year later we learned the real
reason: the need to train additional tank and artillery officers in anticipation
of the Sinai Campaign.

My request to rejoin my friends now in the officers' training course was
denied. But the head of the training command, a general by the name of
Yitzhak Rabin (later twice prime minister of Israel), did approve my second
request, to join the next class of officer cadets without having to sign on for
any further years in the army. Until the start of the course, I would serve as an
instructor in the artillery corps pre-officers' training course, to which half of
the academic reserve soldiers were posted.

For the first time since I'd entered the army, I had free time I could use any
way I pleased. So for my own amusement, I started running. At the camp at
Sarafend, which was still more or less the way the British had left it, I trained
on the triangle of main roads that ran through the base. It was a little less than
two miles altogether, and it got so I could eventually make eight straight laps.
During one weekend leave I decided to try to run the marathon distance
(forty-two kilometers or twenty-six miles) along the roads circling my home.
I had no experience or training, and I ran in the hot midday hours. After
twenty miles, my strength was thoroughly exhausted and I was dehydrated.
Luckily, I had some money on me, so I hailed a cab to take me home. The next
weekend I tried it again. This time, however, having learned my lesson, I
didn't take any money with me so as not to be tempted to give up and take a
cab. After twenty-three miles, there I was again, exhausted and dehydrated.

Despite my precautions, I found a way around my problem: I hailed a taxi and told him he'd get his money when I got home.

The following Thursday that summer of 1956, a friend of mine showed me a modest three-line item in the paper about a marathon race in Hadera the next Saturday at six a.m. It was the first marathon to be run in Israel since Walter Frankel had done it during the Second Maccabiah Games in 1935. It was the accepted wisdom of the local athletic establishment that the Israeli climate was unsuited to the marathon, as if the summers weren't just as hot in Australia, Southern California, Tunisia, or Kenya. As a result, the longest competitive races run in the country were about ten kilometers. Even today there is no marathon in the Maccabiah Games.

My knowledge of the marathon didn't come only from history lessons, where we learned of the Athenian soldier who lost his life running the thirty-nine kilometers from the city of Marathon to Athens to bring word of the victory over the Persians. I had also read that at the London Olympics in 1908, the original route for the marathon was altered so as to pass in front of Buckingham Palace, and ever since the resulting length of 42.195 kilometers had become the accepted standard for the race. In the autumn of 1952 I'd taken advantage of a free hour to visit an exhibition of photographs not far from school. They were pictures of the Olympic Games at Helsinki, and the photographer had given pride of place to Emil Zatopek, winner of the gold medal in the 5-kilometer, 10-kilometer, and marathon races.

I was very impressed by the "Czechoslovakian locomotive." The photographs were superb, showing the expressions on his face — the face of a martyr — as he pushed himself to the very end of each race, showing himself no mercy and overcoming the enormous pain and discomfort. Zatopek achieved the impossible, winning all three of the longest Olympic distances, something nobody before or after was ever able to duplicate. He became a hero for me, virtually an idol. Even forty years later, when I met him, now a much older man, during his visit to Israel, my admiration for him remained undiminished. It was this admiration, combined with my great respect for anyone who could actually run a marathon, that had probably inspired me to spend my spare time attempting long distances.

And now there was going to be a marathon in Israel. I made all the necessary arrangements to take part. The timing wasn't very good for me. I was still suffering the effects of dehydration from the previous Saturday and my muscles still ached. In fact, from all points of view I was unready for this big test. But I was burning with the desire to prove to myself and everyone else that I could go the distance. And there was the fear that if I missed this opportunity, I would have to wait another twenty years for the next one. I found someone to switch duty hours with me so I'd be free on Saturday, and on Friday I hitched a ride to Hadera. After traipsing all over town in search of someone who knew something about the race, I finally found the hotel where the event's headquarters had been set up. It turned out it had been organized by the local Hapoel sports club in a bid to convince the athletic establishment to send their runner, Shalom Kahalani, to the Melbourne Olympics at the end of the year. Kahalani was the sole competitor in shape for the race.

The only other person there with any marathon experience was Yossi Loewenheim, a gym teacher from Tivon, who had run long-distance races before coming to Israel. Two of the other participants, Israel Assoulin and Eli Kommay, were leading 10,000-meter runners. Both had won the Mt. Tabor race, at that time the only field event in Israel. Kommay also held the Israeli title for 10,000 meters. Another familiar face was Uzi Cohen, known as the "workhorse," a former member of the Palmach from Kibbutz Gadot, who had been invited to participate. The last two entrants showed up like me, unknowns who had read the item in the paper and wanted to test themselves.

We took off early in the morning from a traffic circle at the entrance to Hadera on the old Haifa road, starting out in the direction of Haifa for half the distance and then turning around and going back the way we had come. Kahalani was the only one with an escort. He finished with a fine time of 2:41 (two hours forty-one minutes). Loewenheim and Uzi Cohen also finished the race. All the others dropped out. Even Kommay's strength didn't hold up. Who could have predicted that thirty years later, at the age of fifty plus, he would run a marathon in a faster time than the reigning champion. After twenty-two miles, with Assoulin, Kommay, and another runner already out of the race, my strength gave out. Obviously, the exertion didn't improve the cramps in my muscles, only made them worse. The lack of glucose and electrolytic drinks, whose importance I was still unaware of, left me in a state of total prostration. I couldn't go on. I just stopped. I was disappointed that I hadn't been up to the challenge, but I never said: "That's it. This is the last time I run a marathon." On the contrary. I tried to figure out what I had to do so I could finish future races.

I kept up my "triangular" training at Sarafend. In the spring of 1956 I was
sent to officers' training school together with the soldiers I had instructed in
the artillery officers' preparatory course. I was in excellent condition, and
wanted to take advantage of it competitively, but I wasn't given the chance.
This is how it happened. In response to an invitation to take part in an international march at Nijmegen, Holland, the army decided to send a platoon
that would walk as a group, along with three officers chosen separately. As a
result, in 1956 they organized the first all-army competition to select the
soldiers who would be sent to Holland, the sole criterion being time. The
four-day event consisted of a forty-kilometer walk each day. NCOs from the
rank of first sergeant and up were eligible to compete in the officers' category.
I applied as an officer cadet. My application was approved by the event HQ,
but my commanding officers refused to allow me to be absent from the
course. Thus I never got to pit myself against the man who eventually won,
Amos Medroni, later the commander of the elite Golani Brigade.

Even when we didn't get weekend leave, I was permitted to leave the camp
to train. I would run home and back, a distance of about twelve miles each
way. On one of our exercises, I caught the attention of the training school
commander, Israel Tal (later known as the inventor of the Merkava tank)
without sensing that I had done anything out of the ordinary. The officer in
charge of cultural activities, Captain Yair Burla, was taking the course with us.
The son of the writer Yehuda Burla, he had never actually had an officers'
training course, and he couldn't rise in rank unless he did it, even though he
was a good bit older than us. During that exercise, conducted some distance
from camp with no means of communication or transportation, he had an
attack of some sort that looked to us like a heart attack, and he needed immediate medical attention. I volunteered to run and get help, and considering
the urgency of the situation, I was even permitted to entrust my rifle to
another cadet. I flew back to camp and got help to him in time.

But my fitness also worked against me, and on another occasion almost
got me kicked out of the course. For each exercise, a different cadet was put in
charge. This acting officer always had "ants in his pants." Even if he wasn't in
the best of shape, the adrenaline would start flowing and he would advance at
a run at the head of his platoon. When my turn came, our mission was to
"conquer" a steep hill. I charged full speed ahead up the slope and overran the
target single-handedly, the rest of my platoon still far behind. When I

completed the course, my certificate included honors for exceptional physical fitness. But I alone knew that I was probably the only cadet whose conditioning had suffered adversely from the experience because of insufficient training. Nonetheless, I was very eager to earn my company commander's pin, and very proud when I did.

We returned to Sarafend for the artillery officers' training course, which wasn't very physically demanding for any of us. Most of the time was spent in the classroom or in exercises that required little physical exertion, but on the other hand, there was no free time for sports. Our athletic instructor, Nahum Stelmach, was often away playing for the national soccer team either in Israel or abroad. He recommended to my platoon commander, Lieutenant Arieh Levy (who was to rise to the rank of general and later become general manager of the Paz Petroleum Co.) that I be allowed to train on my own instead of taking part in the morning calisthenics and the weekly physical education lesson. As a result, most mornings I managed to run two or three "triangles," and every now and then got in a few hours more training.

In the summer of 1956, I heard that the military magazine *Bamachane* was organizing a championship meet the next day at the old Maccabiah Games stadium in north Tel Aviv, and that one of the events would be a 3-kilometer walk. I had never competed in a race-walking competition before. But I was convinced that I was in good shape for running — an assessment that hadn't been tested competitively yet, either — and could do long distances, so I expected it to be a piece of cake for me to finish among the leaders. I may even have harbored a secret hope of actually winning, but wouldn't admit that even to myself.

The starting gun went off. There were about twenty of us. We had to do seven and a half laps. The first and second didn't present much of a problem, although I was already panting. I barely finished the next two laps, but I was still among the ten in the lead. My strength ran out in the middle of the fifth lap. I dropped out. I couldn't keep up the pace. Even today I am embarrassed to admit that I withdrew — for the first and last time in my life — not because I couldn't have finished the race if I'd slowed my pace, even if it meant coming in last, but because I realized I would not be able to fulfill my own expectations of myself.

I was still in the officers' training course when I read in the paper, once again at the last minute, that Olympic trials were being held for the marathon in Melbourne. It was the autumn of 1956. The minimum time required was 2:40 (two hours forty minutes). I didn't delude myself. I knew I couldn't meet that time. "But what difference does it make?" I thought. Even beginning distance runners know that what drives them more than anything else is the challenge to go the distance and finish the race. The rest is icing on the cake. There can only be one winner. The others compete mainly against themselves, and only if they're in good enough shape do they even try to finish among the leaders. Because of the officers' training course, I was less fit than I had been for the marathon in Hadera, but I thought I could do it and I was eager to try. Having learned how essential an assistant could be, I asked a friend of mine in the course, Michael Marton, to follow me on a bicycle and keep me supplied with water. Neither of us imagined — not in our wildest dreams — that twelve years later we would both be competing in the Olympic Games.

The race began in the northern outskirts of Tel Aviv. As usual, the organizers had only told a few of their pet athletes about the event, and hadn't even bothered to notify all of us who had participated in the Hadera marathon. Once again there were only about ten runners.

The route ran along the Haifa highway as far as the Wingate Institute outside Netanya and back again. Shalom Kahalani, who led from the start, came in first. Yossi Loewenheim and Uzi Cohen again took the second and third places. Assoulin and Kommay didn't compete this time. It was a scorching hot day. I got to the turnaround point in about one hour forty, but my pace dropped off on the way back. Michael held a canteen out to me periodically, but the water didn't prevent me from losing ground. My pace got slower and slower. All of a sudden a car pulled up in front of me. Yariv Oren, in charge of athletics for the Hapoel sports club and one of the organizers of the event, held out two lemon halves, told me they would revive me, and took off. I squeezed the lemon into my mouth and swallowed the juice. I knew that people were sometimes given a lemon to smell or lick when they fainted. But I didn't know what every experienced athlete does, that during prolonged exertion, lemon juice increases the acidity of the stomach and causes vomiting. I was to find out.

Before long I started to get an odd feeling in my stomach that spread upward into my chest, along with discomfort and pressure on my brow. Without warning, a violent stream of tiny bits of partly digested food in a foul yellow fluid shot out of my mouth. I stopped, bent down, and vomited on the road. I felt a little better. I resumed the race, even picking up my pace a little. Then I vomited again. And ran again. When I threw up the third time, there was bile in the vomit. I felt awful. I slowed to a walk; your stomach bothers you less walking than running. I'd already covered about twenty-four miles. I didn't want to give up. I had to go the distance. I kept pushing myself, alternately walking and running.

Yariv Oren pulled up beside me again and told me to get in the car; I wouldn't be able to finish in the three and a half hours they had allotted for the race. I didn't care. I was going to make it to the finish line no matter what. It made no difference to me whether I did it in three hours or not. I kept going at a slow run for another half mile, but I still had around two more miles to go. It had been about three hours and twenty-five minutes since the start. Yariv, who had followed me in his car for the last mile, came up on my right and said: "Everyone else has completed the race or dropped out. We're leaving. There won't be anyone waiting for you at the finish line. Get in the car!" It was obvious he had no understanding of what drives a long-distance runner, had no interest in my finishing the race, and only wanted to get it over with so he could get out of there. "I don't give a damn if I'm wasting your time," I thought to myself. "I'm going to see this through." "Get in the car! There won't be anyone waiting for you at the finish line," Yariv repeated. I was exhausted, and suddenly realized that even if I kept pushing myself to the end, there would be no official recognition that I had ever crossed the finish line. I gave in. Got in the car. I could have come in fifth.

Even though Kahalani won with a time of 2:40, they didn't send him to the Olympics. I don't know why; maybe because he made such an unimpressive appearance. Whatever the reason, the fact remains that this talented athlete was so infuriated that he left the country and stopped competing, and his presence was sorely missed, resulting in a neglect of the whole sport of long-distance running in Israel.

The artillery corps officers' training course dragged on. It wasn't much of a challenge, either physically or intellectually. But there was one instructor who tried to make my life miserable, Lieutenant Yigal Gur. He was a year older than me, from Haifa, and we had been in the Gadna gunnery group together. One day I ran into his sister at the Technion in Haifa, and in answer to her question told her I thought her brother was pretentious. Now he was getting back at me. During one exercise he found some pretext or senseless excuse to discipline me by ordering me to dig a trench, foot by foot, as if I were back in basic training. Being stubborn and unwilling to lick up to him, I dug the trench. When I was finished, I had to fill it up again. Yigal Gur's eccentricities eventually became apparent to his superior officers as well. In the Six-Day War, when he was in command of a regiment of towed guns, he angrily fired on his own soldiers because he thought they were moving too slowly. They filed a complaint, and he was court-martialed and demoted from major to private.

I still wanted to be an officer, an aspiration that remained as strong as ever, but I wasn't as militaristic as I had been before I joined the army. I knew that a mighty military force was vital to the survival of Israel, and that we couldn't do without the draft, but the military lifestyle and the possibility of suffering the tyranny of a commander had made the image of a career soldier less attractive. So I decided that as soon as I won my second lieutenant's stripes, I would try to achieve my second aspiration, to become an engineer. Having made this decision, I applied for early release upon completion of the course so that I could return to the Technion.

October 1956. Our course, along with the rest of the army, was on full alert. The Sinai Campaign was launched. We were informed we had been instated as the corps' officer reserves, and would be assigned to units as required if and when their officers were wounded or killed. We returned all the gear we had been issued, including our weapons, and were left with only our blankets. While we awaited our postings, our instructors hastily attempted to complete the course material with us.

As a matter of policy, charges were brought against the cadets for the slightest infraction. Military trials were routinely conducted on Thursday or Friday just before weekend leave. Otherwise, punishing us by confinement to base would be meaningless. Since we were on alert, there had been no leave for quite a while, so they had held off on the trials. Now they had to "clear their desks" so that our transfers could be effected immediately. The typical sentence became "two-hour confinement to base" — in the middle of the war. Ludicrous.

The war ended and the Sinai Campaign ribbon was conferred on all of us, even though we didn't actually take part in the fighting. I regretted not sharing in that experience — if not like my friend Jacob Eisenbaum who stormed enemy outposts at Rafiah through a minefield, or Jacky Toledo, a gun-position officer in a paratroop mortar battery who, without jumping from a plane, reached the Parker monument and got to see the Mitla Pass — then at least like another friend who enjoyed a "pleasure trip" with the Ninth Regiment along the Bay of Eilat to Sharm al-Sheikh. We finally finished the course, but still didn't get our stripes. It was only basic instruction for the corps. Now we had to take a specialization course: field, anti-tank, or anti-aircraft artillery. Field artillery requires the most theoretical knowledge and mathematical ability. That's where I was posted.

About two weeks after the fighting ceased, I got my first weekend leave in a long time. I decided to use it to see the Sinai. There were very few cars on the road, either because of the shortage of gas or because the government, pressured by its coalition partners, had mandated that every automobile owner declare two days a week when their car could not be used. As anticipated, most people chose the Israeli weekend, Friday and Saturday, and were issued stickers accordingly. I managed to thumb rides as far as Be'er Sheba on Friday. Early the next day, I hitched a ride to Abu Ageila, where the battle for one of its military outposts became famous when the inept battalion commander was replaced on the battlefield by the chief of staff, Moshe Dayan. These were not pleasant sights.

I thumbed another ride, but wound up waiting for hours, all alone, near the airfield at El Arish. With my cap identifying me as an artillery corps cadet, I was picked up by a corps jeep which took me through the Gaza Strip straight back "home" to Sarafend. For the first time I realized just how close Gaza is to Tel Aviv. The driver was First Sergeant Nati Sharoni, whom I knew as the commander of a small unit of French SS-10 anti-aircraft guns whose sights were aimed by wires. Napoleon must have been talking about men like him when he said that every soldier carried a marshal's baton in his knapsack. Sharoni would go on to become the head of the artillery corps and later director general of the Ministry of Industry and Science.

We completed the specialization course in early December. In a morning ceremony, we received our stripes. I was now a second lieutenant. That afternoon I reported as ordered to the induction center for early release. I was the only one at the party that night in civvies: a soldier in the morning, a civilian by nightfall. Several of my course-mates remained in the career army, and some were later sent to the Technion to study. One or two reached the rank of colonel, and the only one who ever made brigadier general was the guy we used to call "terrorist." I tutored him after he failed the entrance exam for the officers' training course and wasn't overly impressed by his abilities, to say the least. Neither was anyone else. Apparently, the secret of success in the military is beyond my ken.

Training at the Columbia University gym, 1966

■ Chapter Four | The Technion and Four-Day Marches

When I got to the Technion, the Israel Institute of Technology, in mid-December 1956, the semester was well underway. Even the extra courses the university had organized for those forced to miss classes because of the Sinai Campaign were already over. I had missed about two months, a little more than half a semester. I didn't imagine I had a very good chance of catching up while at the same time trying to keep pace with what was going on in class — where the professors obviously assumed we knew the material taught before. I felt even more depressed after I spoke to some students who hadn't missed a single class, but had decided the course was too hard and had dropped out after two months. That bit of unwanted information did nothing to raise my spirits. But I refused to give up without a fight. I threw myself into the project, devoting every minute of my time to my books. I even took advantage of a technical loophole that entitled me to an exemption from the physical education requirements. I got no exercise whatsoever, save for morning calisthenics. All I did was study.

There were no electives; everything was a required course. Still, four or five of them were considered major subjects, and the rest minor. We were given a mark for each course on the basis of exams, quizzes, exercises, lab reports, and special projects. If you got an A or B in one of the minor courses, you didn't have to take the final exam. So most of us concentrated on these, hoping to get a high enough mark so that we wouldn't have to take the final, leaving us more time to study for the exams in the major courses. I adopted the same strategy. The effort was excruciating, but I managed by the end of the first semester to get a B in all the minor subjects; I was barely passing in one or two of the major ones.

This took some of the pressure off and gave me time for sports in the second semester. I had no interest in the required physical education hours — which were basically just calisthenics. I wanted to run again. If you were on a team you didn't have to attend PE class, so I decided to join the track team. I went to the track coach, Kurt Marx, and he agreed to take me, the exemption I had finagled notwithstanding. The team trained twice a week at the Kiryat Eliezer stadium. Although Kurt Marx was an experienced coach, he didn't see in me the potential for speed demanded of short- and middle-distance runners, so he left me pretty much alone, just telling me to run six miles each time. Thus by virtue of two undemanding training sessions a week, morning calisthenics, and weekend training during the academic year, I managed to complete four years of college without going entirely to the dogs.

Even after the tremendous effort of the first semester, the Technion was no picnic. University legend related that the old Yemenite who showed up on campus every day with his donkey selling sesame and peanut candies between classes once tied the donkey outside the building and forgot him there, only to come back four years later and find that the animal had been awarded a diploma. In reality, however, the situation was very different. We had more than forty classroom hours a week, including lectures, seminars, and labs. None of us could hold down even a part-time job during the year. We were at it every night until late, studying, doing homework, and writing papers. Naturally we needed a break every now and then, so we'd go the movies and then come back and hit the books again. I saw maybe four or five movies a week during that time. It must have been my lifetime quota, because now I only go to the movies once every ten years or so. In any case, my efforts paid off. I finished the first year pretty well. From my sophomore year on, my grades were high enough to earn me a university scholarship.

The students in my class in the department, our "course" as we called it, numbered one hundred. We were a diverse group. There was the paratrooper Uzi Trachtenberg, from Kibbutz Tel Yosef, awarded the Chief of Staff's Medal of Honor for holding off the enemy in the Gaza Campaign in 1955. He later changed his German last name to the Hebrew "Eilam" and became the head of the Atomic Energy Commission.

The oldest one among us was Yitzhak Ben-Efraim, a very modest intro-verted type. After he got his degree he became the head of the engineers' union, leading it through its tumultuous professional battles in the sixties, and later established the Holon Institute of Technology. He got his PhD in mid-life, and I recruited him when I was chairman of the industrial engineering department at Ben-Gurion University. Despite our close connections, it was only quite a while after we had become colleagues, after I had known him for more than twenty-five years, that I discovered who he really was. At his son's wedding he introduced one of the guests to me, saying casually: "This is Phyllis Palgi. I was in the war with her late husband." I realized that Yitzhak was one of the small group of volunteers from Palestine dropped behind German lines in World War II together with Hannah Senesh. He operated in Transylvania and lived to tell about it.

There were only men in the course, not a single woman. Classes were held in the old Technion building, an imposing, historic stone structure on a beautiful site in the center of Haifa. It gave off an aura of dignity and scholarship, but we had no contact with the students in the architecture department, who had already moved to the first building completed on the new campus in a different part of town. After a while, the chemical engineering department also moved to the new campus, known as Kiryat Ha-Technion. We were left without two departments that could boast a respectable proportion of women students. As a result, and despite the continued presence of Dina Hoffman, a "real looker" in electrical engineering, it was accepted wisdom that Israeli women could be classed into one of three categories on a descending scale: pretty, ugly, and Technion students.

A few weeks after I started the Technion, my parents moved into a small house they built in Ramat Chen near the Maccabiah Village. Since I didn't want to stay in Haifa on the weekends, Ramat Chen became my new home as well. Thus my friends consisted mainly of girls from Ramat Chen and the local boys who were also at the Technion. They have remained my closest friends to this day.

In early spring 1957 I decided to take part in the Mount Tabor Race (Hakafat Ha-Tavor) that circles the mountain. In view of the effort required, the entrance form had to be accompanied by a doctor's certificate testifying to the applicant's fitness. No certificate, no race. The option of having the entrant sign a waiver — accepted practice today — was not then available. To complicate matters, a lot of doctors, especially those in the public health system, refused to issue a certificate of health for fear they would be charged with malpractice should anything go wrong. I finished a training run and presented myself before the private doctor who treated the Technion students. He refused to sign on the grounds that my pulse was too fast. He wasn't swayed by the explanation that I had just run six miles. When I showed up again the next day, this time not running first, he was amazed by how slow my pulse was. He issued the certificate, but continued to insist that he could-n't understand how someone could have such a fast pulse one day and such a slow one the next. He obviously knew nothing about sports medicine, and apparently not much about basic physiology either.

The race was held on a Saturday morning. We started on the southern side of the mountain, ran eastward, crossed the main road, and followed it down to the lowest point. Then we turned sharply north and ran along a foot-path (today a road) toward the Bedouin village of Arab-a-Shibli. The path started out at a gentle slope, but the farther we got from the road the steeper it became, making it increasingly hard to run. The real test began when we got closer to the sparse houses in the village. The path turned west, getting steeper and steeper as it wound among prickly pear hedges, and the ground became studded with bumps and holes with one or more ruts cut in the center of the path by the winter rains. The end of the climb was not yet in sight. It was at this point that a lot of us blurted out "ball-breaker," the others keeping their opinion to themselves for the sake of propriety.

Most of the runners slowed to a walk when they reached the spiky hedges. A few kept up the effort, panting and running slowly as they periodically leapt to one side or the other of the twisting ruts in search of smoother ground. We climbed for about two and a half miles. Around half a mile from the top, we finally reached a stone-paved section where the slope angled less sharply. Some continued at a walk, at least for a little way longer, while others immediately accelerated to a run again. After another five hundred yards we could see the light at the end of the tunnel: we had made it to the northern slope of the mountain. Ahead of us the range stretched out to the north. Beyond that, there was only sky. As soon as we reached the spur, we were on a paved road. It continued to twist up the mountain to the monastery at the summit. Then it turned right, now going downhill.

The organizers set up a stand with glasses of water for the athletes. There were no glasses and no water left for the runners in the rear. The view was magnificent. We could see the picturesque village just below us, and the flat valley between the mountains. But none of us had time to enjoy the view. We kept our eyes on what was directly in front of us, what we could glimpse without turning our heads. As we started the descent, we all took off like a shot, even the weakest runners. It irked me that a small number of frauds tried to gain an illegal advantage by cutting straight across the bends in the road. What was especially annoying was not only the unsporting mentality of these cheaters, but the fact that the organizers hadn't plotted the route along those shorter paths in order to prevent such a possibility. At the very least, they could have stationed officials at the appropriate spots.

After about a mile and half down the hill, the course turned sharply to the left; and we were on a horizontal road that ran straight to the Afula-Mount Tabor road. At this stage we were all running, but a few of the weaker participants who hadn't trained enough beforehand soon slowed to a walk. Around a mile later, we turned off to the left onto a dirt road. There was still more than a mile to go. Anyone with enough strength left picked up the pace. Every now and then we'd leap across the center ditch, especially if some other runner seemed to be having an easier go of it on the other side. After all, the grass is always greener on the other side. The road wasn't flat, but rose and fell in waves. There was only about half a mile left. We all stepped on the gas. We could feel our muscles, especially our lungs. We couldn't go any faster or we wouldn't make it to the end.

We passed the "500 yards to finish" sign and could already see the finish line. Faster now, time to sprint. We gave it all we had left. It no longer matters how much the muscles are hurting from overexertion; it will all be over in less than ninety seconds. The only thing that matters now is to get ahead of the guy in front of you, not to let the guy behind pass you, or to improve your time. We're there, straight between the ropes that funnel you to the finish line. We slow to a walk, panting. Walk around a few dozen yards more as the sweat slows to a drip. The body is still hot. The senses become sharper again and you start to suffer all the aches and pains that were bothering you during the race but that you didn't let yourself feel before. It's such a wonderful sensation to have finished; what does it matter how much effort it took? We had run about seven miles. And we wanted to do it again next year.

I ran in the Mount Tabor Race each of the four years I spent at the Technion. I usually finished around twentieth out of the hundreds of entrants. In November 1957 I heard a new race was being organized — the Sinai Race. Despite its name, it was held in Tivon in memory of a soldier who fell in the Sinai Campaign. Although the official distance read ten kilometers, as in the Mt. Tabor Race, the route was actually over eleven kilometers and included a formidable climb. I entered this race every year as well. On one occasion, when I missed the start for the competitive group and took off with the casual entrants, I recorded the same time as the "professional" runner who placed second.

During those years there were only two other road races held in Israel, and I took part in both. One was the Magnes Race in Jerusalem that ended at the Hebrew University, and the other the Carmel Race whose route followed the top of the mountain range and began and ended at the Taverna near what is today the Haifa Cultural Hall. Both were 5-kilometer runs. It was at the Carmel Race that I first saw a serious walking competition with a large number of entrants, including the Israel Police race-walking team. I had no idea I would be a walker myself one day. It was running that appealed to me, and even in that sport I didn't do more than two short ineffectual training sessions during the week and one on Saturday, more as a break from studying than anything else. The radical change in my attitude came slowly, and started with the Four-Day Marches.

The Israeli Defense Forces decided to open their traditional Four-Day March to civilians. It was scheduled for the spring of 1957 and began at Sarafend. Male soldiers marched for four days, and women soldiers and civilians for two. The speed and individual competitions were eliminated, and the team competition was judged on the basis of how few members dropped out, appearance, and morale. The distance remained forty kilometers a day. The Technion Student Union organized a group and I signed up. We were issued yellow T-shirts with our name — ASA (Academic Sports Association) Technion. We wore our own khaki shorts and army boots. Spirits were high and it was a congenial group, although to our great disappointment there were no women on the team. We sang the whole time, and even I opened my mouth and moved my lips occasionally, making sure no sound escaped so as not to alarm my marching companions. The high leather boots were uncomfortable and caused blisters, but it wasn't too bad.

When it was over, we were each awarded a medal, which pleased us all, including me, because at that time only the three athletes who placed first in sporting events got any sort of medal, unlike today. As a rule, everyone else had to make do with happy memories as their only memento of the occasion. All in all, it was fun. Enough fun, in fact, that when the IDF organized the next Four-Day March in the spring of 1958, I again signed up for the ASA Technion team. Again the male soldiers marched for four days, starting in Be'er Sheba, but this time the women soldiers and civilians marched for three. We set out from Ashkelon, went through Beit Guvrin, and ended in Jerusalem. At the ceremony in Ashkelon before we set out, the head of the Southern Command, Avraham Yoffe — a stout man who joked that he was in favor of diets, "as long as it was a lot of diet" — announced that the IDF had acceded to the popular demand for equality and that starting the following year everyone would march for four days.

Having learned from the previous march, I wore the track shoes I customarily ran in and which never bothered me or caused any blistering during my training runs. I was the only "rebel" to do so, not only in my group, but among all the entrants in the march. People stared as if I'd lost my mind. Each time I passed the army doctors — there were plenty of them brought from military infirmaries to treat the marchers' feet (which primarily meant binding blisters), they would come up to me to tell me how bad, even dangerous, it was to march in track shoes. They claimed that without the high boots for support, I could twist or sprain my ankle.

I wondered how these doctors, most of whom didn't march themselves, could possibly know what was good for my feet or comfortable, or what did or did not cause blistering. In all the newsreels or movies I'd watched, I'd never seen athletes competing in hiking boots. Was there some fundamental difference between marching and running which made it necessary to give the ankle more support on a march? After all, we weren't walking on rocky ground at night where there might be a good chance of twisting your ankle. And besides, in the low-top track shoes I was strengthening my ankle muscles, which would be immobilized by high boots. I don't know who was right, but I do know that I still walk and march in track shoes, and I very seldom see anyone else with an ounce of sense in his head, and the freedom to choose, wearing hiking boots.

Our group marched fairly well, and no one dropped out. But since with my training and not having any blisters I was in much better condition than my teammates, I found their slow pace very irritating, almost as hypnotic as walking through a museum. On day two I arranged to leave the group after each judges' position, walk ahead at my own pace, and wait for them before the next judging point. I left them behind several times on the third day as well, but it didn't prevent us from taking second place. We were each presented with another medal, and for those of us who were taking part for the second year, it was silver. Without the blisters, I enjoyed myself much more this time. Nevertheless, I decided that there was no point in marching with a group again.

As General Yoffe had promised, in the spring of 1959, everyone marched for four days, this time starting out from the outskirts of Haifa. Participating as an individual entrant, I walked on day one with my friends from the electrical engineering department, Uri Bleiberg and Shraga Gorney, as well as Yossi Levine, a year ahead of me in mechanical engineering. He lived across the street from me in Haifa, and we had earned some pocket money together several times as armed escorts for school trips in the area of Nahal Zin. At that time, "trip" still meant "hike." Yossi was to go on to become assistant director of Rafael, the weapons development authority, and was awarded the prestigious Israel Security Prize.

The four of us marched together, chatting, eyeing the "chicks," and enjoying the walk. Every now and then we turned on the Army Radio, which was broadcasting extensive and continuous coverage of the march. That's how I heard that the first to finish day one was Uzi Cohen of Kibbutz Gadot. About an hour later, when we were still a few miles from the finish line, I saw Uzi running leisurely toward us. "Just cooling off," he shouted as he went by. Then he turned around and ran back to the finish line. Naturally, he made a big impression on all of us, particularly me. The glory he earned himself also goaded me on. "I can do that too," I thought. I decided to test myself the next day.

On day two I showed up early at the starting point. Nonetheless, a few people had already taken off ahead of me. Before you set out, they had to punch a hole in your entrance ticket. The rules didn't permit running. I knew that. I also knew you went faster if you ran, but I decided to uphold the spirit of good sportsmanship and not break the rules — a policy I follow to this day. So I had to walk as quickly as I could. I remembered the race walkers I had seen at the Carmel Race and the way they moved their arms back and forth and brought their straight legs forward while twisting the pelvis. I tried to mimic them.

There were dozens of people around me, some walking — including Uzi Cohen — and others running. It annoyed me to see them doing that in defiance of the rules. It takes less effort to run slowly than to walk at the same pace, so by exerting the same effort a runner can go faster than a walker. It isn't fair to pit a walker against a runner — even in an informal competition. It would be like pitting a runner against a cyclist. Still, I didn't give in to the temptation. I hate deceit. I didn't want anyone to think I could walk fast if I had cheated by running.

My foot hit the ground on the heel, the leg stretched straight out, and the knee locked. Then I rolled my foot forward on the ground and rose onto my toes, using them to push myself onward. At the same time, I twisted my pelvis in the opposite direction, moving the other foot forward, heel first. When the heel strikes the ground, the front part of the foot is slightly raised, and the process — rolling the foot, twisting the pelvis, and bringing the other foot forward — repeats itself continuously. At the same time, the arms, bent in a right angle from the elbows, move back and forth, synchronized with the feet: left arm and right leg forward, and then left arm back and left leg forward.

I wasn't then able to analyze all the elements of the race-walking technique, and it didn't particularly concern me at the time. I walked however I walked, like anyone else strolling down the street, only faster. The quicker pace was the result of the faster movements and the speed of the arms. I bent my arms at the elbows in order to increase the frequency of the movement and decrease its amplitude. It was the swing of the arms that pushed my body forward and dictated the pace of the pelvis twist and the speed of the steps. I did it all instinctively, without giving it any real thought. And I realized I was indeed going very fast. I passed Uzi Cohen. "He must be tired out from yesterday's effort," I thought to myself, keeping up the same style of walking and the same pace as I left him behind.

In the first thirty minutes I overtook all the other walkers, including those who had started out with me and those who had taken off earlier. But I could still see people running ahead of me. They weren't exceptional runners, or even fair runners who trained regularly. That was obvious from their speed and style, as well as from the fact that they had to slow to a walk every now and then even though the route was flat. Little by little, I started to overtake some of them as well. A few had tired themselves out, had stopped running, and were now walking rather slowly. Others were already running at a slower pace than I was walking. As I passed one of them, I couldn't keep myself from asking why he was running when it was against the rules. "It's easier," he answered, "and faster too," as if being among the first to reach the finish line justified the use of any means, legitimate or otherwise. In response to the same question, with the added comment that only walking was allowed, another runner replied: "I don't know how to walk as fast as you." By this time, I could only see two more people running ahead of me. I had already passed all the others. At Beit Lid we turned south. It took me about two more miles to catch the last two, when they had to slow to a walk.

I thought I was in front, but I was still afraid someone behind me might pick up the pace and pass me. So I couldn't afford to slow down. I wasn't feeling particularly tired, my muscles didn't ache, and my current pace didn't demand heavy breathing. On the contrary, my breathing was light and regular, and I felt I could even go faster, but I didn't try it for fear my muscles wouldn't hold out to the end at a higher level of exertion. All of a sudden, quite a way ahead of me, I saw another walker. He must have run too, presumably faster than the others, but by now his strength was exhausted and he was walking. I overtook him as well. I was still concerned there might be other surprises ahead, but I was very happy to discover I had nothing to worry about. I came in first!

Reporters were waiting at the finish line to interview me. Immediately, the Army Radio broadcast my name as the man who finished first on day two. I was thrilled by what I had achieved, as well as by the glory it brought me. In the spirit of Uzi Cohen flaunting his victory the day before, I decided to show him and everyone else not simply that I was first, but that I hadn't even exhausted my energy and was still in fine feather. So I went back the way I had come — walking, not running — in the direction of the entrants approaching the finish. When I passed the first group — no one running any more — I showed off for them. They knew I had overtaken them earlier, and most of them had already heard my name on the radio. About two miles from the finish line I found Uzi Cohen. That was enough for me; I had shown him I could do it too. I turned around again and went back to the finish at a moderate pace. I waited there for my friends, and was gratified to learn they already knew what I had done. I felt exhilarated, both physically and mentally. So I decided to try to repeat my triumph the next day.

The route on day three took us through Lod to Hulda. As far as the airport at Lod, things went pretty much the same as the day before. Immediately after the start I passed the large packs of walkers, and little by little overtook the runners as well. As I reached the airport, I passed the last of the runners, already walking, and was in the lead. At that point, however, I started to feel a twinge in the muscle in the back of my lower leg. It began as a bit of minor discomfort, and then grew into a slight pinch. As I walked, the pinch got worse until it developed into increasingly severe pain. It was getting very hard to bear. I stopped and examined my leg. It was red, swollen, and rigid. It even hurt to the touch. I had no experience of injury, but I had heard the term "strain" used to explain an athlete's incapacitation. So I figured I must have strained something. I continued to walk, but with the leg so painful I had to move slowly. After we passed the town of Lod, the walkers I had left behind started to catch up to me. I tried to increase my speed to prevent them from getting ahead of me, but the pain was too severe to ignore. As I made my way slowly onward, more and more people passed me. To each of them I explained that I couldn't walk any faster because "I got a strain," and pointed to my leg. I didn't want to drop out, despite the agony I was in. I kept up my slow pace. I got to the finish line in the Hulda Forest on day three behind ten or fifteen other marchers.

The IDF had set up a base camp with services in the forest. I was given a pup tent and I didn't budge from it from the moment I arrived. The pain was getting worse and I didn't want to move. I hoped it would improve by the next morning. When I awoke at five in the morning I could barely stand. The pain was excruciating. I hobbled to the starting point, convinced the average tortoise or snail could move faster than I could at that moment. On the way I ran into several limping entrants who reported that they had dropped out due to injury. I was in no doubt that my injury was at least as serious as theirs. The idea of dropping out was very tempting and their example made it seem legitimate, but I didn't want to give up. I was determined to finish the march. I continued to hobble in the direction of Jerusalem. After a short while, as my muscles warmed up, the pain eased a bit, but it was still horrific. Within an hour, I had been overtaken by all the groups of soldiers, as well as the individual marchers who had taken off late. I trailed after them, mortified to find myself among the injured weaklings and other "extra baggage."

Among the last of the soldiers, I ran into my neighbor from Ramat Chen, Nitzhia. The previous summer she had joined me on my six-mile runs a few times as she prepared for her army recruitment date. When she saw me she exclaimed: "Shaul, what's going on? I was sure you'd finished already. I heard on the radio that you finished first on day two." I felt miserable not to be first again, but I was determined to complete the march no matter what, even if I came in last. I got to the finish line in the late afternoon. If I wasn't the very last, I was certainly among the last few stragglers. Still, I was overjoyed that I had managed to surmount the pain and the obstacles and had successfully completed the task I had set myself. I was awarded a gold medal in honor of having participated in three marches. Years later, when I was much more experienced in both the techniques of race walking and injuries, I realized it was no "strain." I had given myself a very serious inflammation by overexerting the shin muscles. These muscles aren't very well developed in most people and are hardly needed for conventional walking or running, but they are used intensively in race walking.

In the summer of 1957, between my freshman and sophomore years at the Technion, I worked at the Kav tin can factory in Ramat Gan. The owner, Shimon Klagsbald, who knew my father from the Jewish Students Union when they had both been at university in Karlsruhe (and who later became the head of the Israel Industrialists Association), gave me a job as something between a production worker and an apprentice technician. It was very hard work, but it offered me the chance to earn enough by the sweat of my brow to pay my tuition for the following year. The next summer I got a job as a technician at the Bedek Airplane factory in Lod, later to become the Israel Aircraft Industries. Since the plant was in the process of expanding, and I wanted to earn as much as I could, I put in a lot of overtime. For the four months of that summer vacation I was on the job nearly every weekend and holiday, and during the week until nine, and sometimes eleven, at night. I didn't particularly like the work, but my employers were apparently pleased with me. When I graduated two years later, they offered me a position as engineer, although I hadn't even applied for the job. But I had different plans, so I turned them down. Nevertheless, the money I earned that summer paid the tuition for my junior year and left me with enough to buy a motor scooter.

On weekends and holidays during my sophomore year, I occasionally went hiking, even though I had to hitch a ride to get wherever I wanted to go. All alone I hiked the long distance from Sde Boker to Oron in the Negev desert, making my way along the dry river bed of Nahal Zin with the help of a 1:100,000 topographical map that was so old that neither the start nor finish of my route was marked. I had to use every ounce of the orienteering skills I had learned in the army. As I hiked through the desert terrain, I got to see hidden springs and water holes, came across a Bedouin goatherd expressing his joy of life by singing at the top of his lungs, his voice echoing through the stillness of the desert, and surprised a caravan of camels — an encounter that, fortunately, did not end in tragedy. Some time later I went back to the same region with two friends from Ramat Chen, Tzuri Kirschbaum, in my class at the Technion, and Uri Raudenitz, a year ahead of us.

Uri was an unassuming baby-faced boy whose appearance worked against him. Just before completing the infantry officers' training course, he was thrown out for lacking leadership qualities. Proof of his commanders' "perceptive" assessment emerged only later. Uri was serving as platoon sergeant when his division took part in the Nitzana Operation in 1955. They were ordered to take a hilltop Egyptian outpost. As they charged their target, they were sprayed by machine-gun fire from above. The company commander and platoon commander were killed, and the latter's second-in-commander injured. The rest of the platoon flattened themselves to the ground. The wounded officer ordered them to continue their attack, but nobody moved a muscle or dared to raise his head. Except for one soldier. Uri, whose position as platoon sergeant was in the rear, rose and charged the outpost, taking out the machine gun and gaining control of the hill single-handed. He was awarded the Medal of Honor by the Head of Command. He still has a baby face.

With the motor scooter I bought at the age of twenty-two, I finally had a means of transportation. Every Saturday the year round, especially in winter, we would go to the Sharon Hotel beach in Herzliya. There were about twenty of us, students from every department of the Technion. Eldad Kutner and I would run about six miles along the beach, and I would sometimes do a little more on my own. Finally, in an unchanging ritual, Shraga Gorney would check the temperature of the water, the band of "winter bathers" would dive in, and then Yossi Levine would stamp the personalized club membership cards he had made up for us, using a stamp he fashioned out of an ordinary eraser. I remained a faithful member of the club whenever I could get to Tel

Aviv on a Saturday — even after I had moved to Jerusalem — until I left for the United States.

My newfound mobility also had its drawbacks. My friends from Ramat Chen and I formed a motorcycle convoy to Eilat to help celebrate the tenth anniversary of the city at the southern tip of the country. When we got to Mitzpe Ramon on the way back, Naomi Zisman (today Dr. Naomi Merhav), who had been sitting behind me on my scooter, transferred to the sidecar of Shimale's (today Dr. Shimon Peled) three-wheeler. Drowsy from the heat and with no one to talk to, I tried the impossible. Just outside Yerucham, I decided to see if I could doze off while driving. I could.

I was awakened either by the bumps I was getting or the racket the engine was making as the scooter sped along the ditch beyond the shoulder on the left-hand side of the road, first upright and then horizontally, dragging me with it through the brush and stones. When it finally stopped and my head cleared as I lay there on the ground, I didn't panic. Instinctively I tried to turn off the noisy machine. As I stuck my hand out, I accidentally hit the horn, but then I got it right and switched off the engine. Luckily, both the scooter and I, each separately, were still in one piece. When I had gotten my breath back, checked the damage, licked my wounds, plucked the thorns out of my body, and straightened a few bits of twisted metal, I made my way to my companions who had noted my absence and were waiting for me in Yerucham. We continued on to Tel Aviv with one of the girls seated determinedly behind me to make sure I didn't fall asleep again. The next day I was black-and-blue all over. It was two weeks before I could run again.

In the summer of 1959, at the end of my junior year, I was accepted by an exchange program for engineering students called IESTA. I was to spend the summer working in the Van Gelder paper plant in Apeldoorn, Holland. To save money, I bought a deck ticket on a ship to Greece and then took the "student train" to Austria. There I met Uri Raudenitz, who was going to a plant in Rotterdam on the same program, and we hitched our way to Holland, stopping at a number of interesting sites on the way. As soon as I arrived at Van Gelder, I was issued a bicycle. No one asked if I knew how to ride it; the Dutch took that for granted. I rode the bicycle every day back and forth between the home of my host family and work. My first weekend in Holland, I decided to take advantage of my new means of transportation to tour the country. I mapped out a scenic route of about sixty miles, and had a great time. I had no trouble with my leg muscles, which were in shape from running. But for a week afterwards I couldn't sit down, not even on a simple chair.

At the end of work every day, I rode to the athletic field where I ran my usual six miles. After not training for several weeks because of the finals at the Technion and my trip to Holland, I had to get back in condition. I enjoyed that summer immensely. The Dutch are hardworking, cheerful people and I became very fond of them. I still like to go back there when I can and take part in their marches, especially the international Four-Day March at Nijmegen. And I still exchange New Year's cards with the lady who opened her home to me for those two months. When I'd been in Holland for four weeks, Dania, my neighbor from Ramat Chen, arrived, and I traveled around the country with her for a week, thumbing rides. When my time in Apeldoorn was up, I met up with Uri again and we hitched our way through Belgium and France to England, forking out money only for the ferry that took us across the Channel. From London, the three of us, Dania, Uri and I, went on to Scotland and then back to Paris, where we left Dania, still hitch-hiking all the way. Uri and I continued through Switzerland to Naples. Throughout those four months in Europe, for two of which I earned a token wage as a student, my budget allowed me about a dollar a day. True, a dollar then bought more than it does today, but it was still a pittance. I managed somehow to stay within that budget, notwithstanding the round-trip fare for the ferry.

While in Apeldoorn I grew a small beard around my chin that reached as high as my nose on the sides. I kept it very well trimmed. Thanks to that beard, when agents of the famous Italian director-producer Dino De Laurentis showed up at the youth hostel in Rome looking for extras, they offered me the role of a sailor in a film he was about to make in Sicily. They were even willing to give me a contract, but I had to commit myself to at least three months on the set. The money, to say nothing of the distinction of appearing in a De Laurentis film, was very tempting. But I knew that even without that delay I would be getting back to the Technion a week late. Obviously, to do the movie I would have to drop out of college for a year. Not only that, but I had already accepted the position of research assistant to Dr. Micha Bentwich. The salary that went with it, along with the scholarship I'd been promised, would cover most of my college expenses and I wouldn't have to ask my parents for money. So with a heavy heart, but with no second thoughts, I decided to forgo my chance to become a movie star.

In mid-December 1959, about a month after I got back to Israel and started my senior year, I signed up for a free Saturday hike from Kfar Vitkin to Caesarea organized by the Society for the Protection of Nature, then only a tiny anonymous group that had not been in existence very long. I got to the youth hostel in Kfar Vitkin early in the morning, parked my scooter, and joined the large group that set out on foot with a guide, hiking along the coast toward Caesarea. Three girls caught my eye and I struck up a conversation with them. I was particularly attracted to one, a sweet, intelligent, unpretentious type, maybe a little shy, with a good figure. I was especially impressed by the fact that she was not weighted down with jewelry, her fingernails were unpainted, and she wore no lipstick or makeup of any kind to make her look like an Indian brave off to do battle.

We kept up an animated conversation about any number of subjects, including science, but not sports. I discovered she had also gone to Geula High School in Tel Aviv, graduating two years ahead of me in the same class as my older sister Shosh. Her name was Shoshana too. I also found out that she had been an exchange student in Finland after getting her degree in biochemistry from the Hebrew University, that she still lived in Jerusalem, and that she had started studying for a PhD in endocrinology. Since I didn't know what that meant, she explained it in such clear and simple terms that even an ignoramus like me, who knew nothing whatsoever about the life sciences, could understand.

We walked side by side, talking the whole way. We ate the sandwiches we had packed on a hill to the south of the Crusader wall around Caesarea, a hill that isn't there any more. It was excavated, and deep below the archeologists found the exquisite Roman amphitheater which they suspected was buried there and which is used today for concerts and other performances as it was in the days of its ancient glory. As we sat there, and then resumed our hike to the old Haifa road near the present entrance to Or Akiva, I began to feel an attraction I had never before felt for any woman. But, being rather shy with women, I didn't dare reveal my feelings. Nevertheless, when we reached the

Haifa road and were all standing at the bus stop waiting for a ride or the first
local bus to Tel Aviv after sundown, I plucked up my courage.

I invited her to the movies. Without turning me down, she explained that
she had planned to go to the opera if she wasn't too tired. Ever since I was
forced to take piano lessons, music has been an alien world for me. Even at
Geula, where I had to study music history for two years, I wasn't ashamed to
inform my teachers of my dislike for music. That's why I invariably got a C,
even though I knew the material well enough. But if that's what it took to go
out with this woman I found myself so attracted to, I would gladly go to the
opera. "Anyway," I thought to myself, "the opera's not so bad. It's not like a
concert where the only thing that matters is if the seats are comfortable
enough to sleep on." So without hesitation I told her I was quite willing to go
to the opera instead. I offered her a ride to Tel Aviv on my scooter, and asked
her to wait for me there at the bus stop for an hour and a half, explaining that
it would take me that long to run the eight miles back to Kfar Vitkin and
come back for her on the scooter. She mumbled something I took as a yes,
and I set out at a run, still dressed in my hiking clothes with my knapsack on
my shoulder bouncing from side to side.

When I got back over an hour later, there was no one at the bus stop. Not
even Shosh. It was a real letdown. I didn't even know her last name, not to
mention her address, but I was determined to find her. The obvious place to
look was at the opera in Tel Aviv that night. I changed my clothes at my
parents' house in Ramat Chen and drove to the opera house in Herbert
Samuel Square. She wasn't there, and hadn't shown up even half an hour after
the performance began. I left in despair and went off to where my Ramat
Chen friends generally gathered. Excitedly, I told them about the girl I had
met on the hike and had been so taken with for the first time in my life, and
how I had really fallen hard for her. They may have been laughing inside —
they had certainly never heard such a confession from me before — but they
kept it to themselves. Just smiled. But I was resolved not to give up my search
for Shosh.

The only clue I had was that she had graduated from Geula two years
ahead of me. The next day, Sunday, instead of getting up early for the trip
back to the Technion, I waited until eight o'clock and presented myself at the
high school office. Obviously, I was ashamed to tell them the truth. So I said
that my sister, who was in Switzerland (which was true; her husband was

working on his PhD in Geneva), had asked me to look at the graduation picture and find out the last name of the other Shoshana in her class. It sounded authentic enough, although the school secretary could have asked me why my sister didn't just look in her own yearbook. Instead, she led me into the teachers' room and there, in the enlarged class picture on the wall, I immediately recognized the face of the Shosh I was looking for. Her name appeared below: Shoshana Ahlfeld. The secretary also gave me her address from when she was at school.

The thin Tel Aviv phone book — at that time there were few telephones in Israel — confirmed that her parents still lived there. I knew she was in Jerusalem during the week and only came to Tel Aviv on the weekend. So I called, identified myself to her mother, and asked for her address in Jerusalem. Then I wrote and informed her I would be coming to see her at her parents' house the following Friday afternoon. I got back from Haifa that Friday and showed up at the appointed hour. I rang the bell. She opened the door and it was obvious I had taken her by surprise. She hadn't gotten my letter, only heard from her mother that someone was looking for her. We were married eleven months later. Today, after forty-seven years of marriage, I love her just as much as I did then, if not more. She still doesn't wear makeup, and I still don't go to concerts. The only exceptions have been our daughter Danit's appearances in several operettas.

Our marriage created only one problem: the name. Shoshana Ladany was my sister. Admittedly, when she married she became Cohen. When they moved to Belgium they changed their name to Konen, supposedly so as not to be immediately recognized as Jews, but she was still Shosh. And now my wife was Shoshana Ladany too. Whenever the family got together, there was constant confusion as to which "Shosh" you were talking to. Every now and then we'd hear: "Not you, you," the speaker's head bobbing in the appropriate direction, sometimes with the addition of a pointed finger. We haven't yet solved the problem, but we've learned to live with it.

Even before the wedding, I realized I had made my father very happy. It turned out he knew Shosh's father from his college days in Karlsruhe. They had both belonged to the Zionist Jewish Students Union, and soon discovered they shared memories and mutual friends. My father was now in a funny situation, as was I, although not because of my impending marriage. I was about to graduate from the Technion, and suddenly I had a student for a

father. A shortage of trained pharmacists and a new law requiring the presence of a certified pharmacist in every pharmacy — even if it was owned by a
chemist who developed drugs himself, had worked in the pharmaceutical
industry, and knew as much, if not more, than the average pharmacist — had
convinced my father that he would have to get a diploma.

 Thus in 1958, at the age of fifty-five, thirty-three years after he had earned
his degree as a chemical engineer, he went back to school. He enrolled in the
pharmacology department of the Hebrew University. In recognition of his
earlier training, he was exempted from the first two years of study. The
family's students gathered in my parents' home on the weekends, my father
back from the third year in Jerusalem and me from the third year in Haifa. It
wasn't easy for him. He complained that the professors demanded rote learning, not real understanding, that the exam questions focused on matters of
little consequence rather than the main subjects, and that his memory —
which was all the system required — wasn't as good as that of his younger
classmates. But he did enjoy his thesis project on extracting pyrethrins from
chrysanthemums. Since his command of Hebrew was significantly less than
perfect, he wrote the thesis in German and it was translated by his assistant
Eli Fischer (today the celebrated owner of Dr. Fischer Pharmaceutical Labo-
ratories), who, it turned out, had studied with my wife Shosh.

 In the summer of 1960, I graduated from the Technion and Father graduated from the Hebrew University with the degree of Master of Pharmacy.
Three years later, at the age of sixty, he died of cancer. I nursed him devotedly
during the last six months of his life when he was confined to Hadassah
Hospital in Jerusalem. I loved and admired him deeply, but I didn't cry at his
funeral. Despite the pain and grief, since childhood I have trained, or perhaps
forced, myself not to exhibit signs of weakness and never to cry, no matter
how much I may want to.

In preparation for the Four-Day March in the spring of 1960, when I was still
at the Technion, I tried to learn the lessons of the previous year. The option of
not participating never crossed my mind. I remembered which exercises had
been most painful when my leg was inflamed, and started doing those same
exercises so as to strengthen the problematic muscles. Since my courses were

so demanding, I didn't have enough time to train, but I did get in a few twelve-mile runs. The march was to have a new format this year. The IDF set up a tent camp in the Hulda Forest, a real camp, not just an overnight bivouac. For the first three days, the march would follow a circular route — a different course each day — that would start and end at the forest. The route on day four would take us from Hulda to Jerusalem. The camp became a city of marchers and the march itself more like one big carnival. Anyone who wasn't there missed the opportunity to witness merriment. The holiday spirit was high.

The towns and villages we passed through were decked out in flags, and we were greeted everywhere by bands from the army, the police, the fire department, and Lord only knows what other voluntary organizations. They all kept up a medley of marching tunes that were broadcast by loudspeakers along the course. As befitting such a festive occasion, the route took us through the main streets and traffic was halted. The local residents were lined up along the pavement, standing or seated behind the ropes separating them from the road, and they followed our progress enthusiastically, clapping, waving, cheering us on, and even raining flowers down on us. In some towns medallions specially minted for the occasion were pinned on our shirts, some sporting blue and white ribbons as well. In other towns volunteers handed out free drinks and cake to all the marchers.

Commercial enterprises seized the opportunity as well. Billboards sprouted up everywhere. Food companies dished out hot soup, and no matter how bad it might have tasted ordinarily, it was absolutely delicious in the cold early morning hours or at the end of the day when we were tired and thirsty. The so-called "fruit juice," a bitter bright yellow or orange liquid containing no more than 3 percent real fruit, also tasted like ambrosia when we were hot and sweaty. The media joined in the celebrations. Dozens of journalists from all the local papers covered every day of the march. The evening papers published special supplements in honor of the march. Israel had not yet been introduced to television, but live coverage was provided by the radio stations, especially the Army Radio, which positioned numerous mobile units along the route and unceasingly interviewed marchers who sent greetings home on the air.

The tent camp emptied out each morning, and then filled up again in the afternoon. It was divided into four sections: male soldiers, women soldiers, individual civilians in pup tents, and civilian groups in larger tents. Floodlit "streets" were mapped out, and were invariably crowded with thousands of marchers strolling or scampering back and forth. The army canteen, where civilians were also welcome during the event, vied for popularity with the infirmaries divided into separate sections for blisters or muscle cramps. There were also crowds around the field toilets and the faucets scattered throughout the camp. Those participants who weren't thoroughly exhausted at the end of the day sauntered here and there proudly showing off the medals from previous marches pinned to their shirts. There were only two people who had also taken part in the four-day Nahal corps march in 1955 and the all-army march in 1956, making this their sixth consecutive event. They were local heroes and the envy of everyone there, including myself.

Once we had appeased our hunger and had our feet and leg muscles taken care of, the main attraction was invariably the civilian group section. Their tents were festooned in bright colors in a genuine carnival atmosphere. Public institutions and commercial companies had sent teams, supplying them with uniforms, catering services, and other logistical aids. In an effort to advertise their products or services and compete for the prize for the most enthusiastic group, they set up special tents and invited anyone they thought might further their cause. This time the teams were also being judged for morale and tent decorations.

On the eve of day one, a show was mounted on a stage set up at the bottom of a sloping field outside the camp. For several hours we enjoyed the performances of an army entertainment troupe and a number of well-known entertainers — called up for reserve duty for the occasion to save the cost of paying them for their appearance. It was great fun. The next night there was another impressive show with a different troupe and stars. In the morning, the individual entrants started out from narrow parallel lanes separated by metal bars, somewhat like the line at a bus station. Thousands of marchers crowded around the starting point. At the signal, soldiers armed with hole punches punched the entrance cards and we set off.

I finished first both on day one and day two. I got blisters on my feet this time around, but although they bothered me, I managed to ignore the pain and discomfort. But I still had competition from a few people who weren't completely exhausted yet. Some had kept up a fairly slow pace for the first two days, and the announcement of my name on the radio and in the papers as the first to finish for two days in a row whetted their appetite to share the spotlight. They did their utmost — which sometimes included running — to gain the glory that went with that distinction. By now the effort had already started to tire me out, so that on days three and four, although I was among the five leaders at the end of the day, I wasn't the first.

While still in the last year of the Technion, I decided to continue straight on to a master's degree in mechanical engineering. That decision later turned out to fit nicely with the plans of my future wife, about to get her doctorate. Micha Bentwich, for whom I was working as a research assistant, offered to serve as my thesis advisor for a project on the subject of air bearings, something like ball bearings except that they revolve on air pockets rather than balls, similar to the principle of the hovercraft. The idea excited me, so in the second semester of my senior year I took several of the courses I would need for my master's. In the summer of 1960, at the age of twenty-four, I received my Bachelor of Science in Mechanical Engineering.

Just after graduation, I was ordered to appear for army reserve duty culminating in a full-scale regiment exercise. My wedding date had been set and the invitations had already been printed. It fell right in the middle of the exercise. I asked for a deferral. "Cactus," the regiment commander, had the nerve to try to pressure me to defer the wedding instead. Naturally, I refused. Nevertheless, he would not change my orders but, in defiance of explicit military regulations, arranged for me to be released just two days before the wedding. I drew the appropriate conclusion and wangled a transfer to a different artillery regiment. We were married on the designated day and spent our honeymoon hiking through the Upper Galilee.

■ Chapter Five | The Engineer from Jerusalem

After our marriage in November 1960 we moved to Jerusalem. Our small apartment in the Cooperative Project bore the address 73 Ha-Palmach Street, but by some strange Jerusalem logic it was not on the odd-numbered side of the street, nor was it anywhere near other addresses in the 70s. The buildings adjacent to ours bore numbers in the 40s, and we weren't even on Ha-Palmach Street but about a hundred yards off it. It was the perfect address if we wanted to hide out from our friends, or anyone else. Living in Jerusalem meant that every Sunday morning I would go to Haifa, and would only return on Thursday night.

I started my master's degree at the Technion, but not as I had planned. Dean Frank informed me that the position of research assistant would only be available to me if I did my thesis project under Professor Ernreich. Since that was meant to be my sole source of income, I had no choice but to agree. Shosh, who earned a bit more than I did as an instructor, suggested I stay with Bentwich and we could live on her salary, but that was not really economically feasible. In my new circumstances, I became acquainted with the elderly Professor Kurrein, who had an impressive office done up in antiques in the Technion basement, a hideaway he referred to with typical German humor as his "seat." Professor Kurrein, a distinguished scientist even before he fled Germany and the only full professor in the mechanical engineering department, was already retired, but was frequently heard to remark that as long as he was alive, no one else in the department would ever be granted a full professorship. He was right. Professor Ernreich, whose office was also in the basement, didn't get a promotion even when he was elected dean.

In the spring of 1961 I was again looking forward to the Four-Day March. Because of my classes and my job, however, I had not trained enough, only running six miles twice in the middle of the week and doing my exercises each morning. On the weekends I would go out for longer sessions every day. On Fridays I ran about twelve miles and on Saturdays Shosh and I would take a long hike through the Jerusalem hills. As the date of the march drew nearer, I lengthened my Friday training runs. The march didn't fall during a school break, and I didn't want to ask Ernreich for the few days off for fear he would refuse, and then I wouldn't be able to go. Instead, I said nothing about it, just made sure I had fulfilled all my assignments as a research assistant and a student for the duration of the march. So I was positive I would not even be missed.

The march was organized along the same format as the previous year, the camp at Hulda already becoming an established institution. For three straight days I managed to come in first. The reporters knew me by now, and the news of my accomplishment merited a line or two in all the papers as well as an item on the radio. The journalists dubbed me "the engineer from Jerusalem." In addition to the participant's medal handed out at the end of the event, I received a special gold-plated medal in honor of having taken part in five marches. When I returned to the Technion, I was summoned to Ernreich's office. He had heard I had been absent for the march. He bawled me out and accused me of shirking my responsibilities. I explained that I had completed all my assignments in advance, and my only offense was neglecting to inform him that I was taking a few days off, but it made no impression on him. He was furious. His parting comment was: "I can understand your taking time off, but to do it in order to take part in a march? That's just stupid!" What can you do? Some people simply don't understand what it means to love sports and don't know how to enjoy them. Two weeks after that incident Professor Ernreich suffered a heart attack, and died several weeks later.

When I started on my master's degree, I decided to try to finish it in a year, rather than the two years it generally required. I was sick and tired of being away from home and spending the week in Haifa. By June 1961 I had completed all the required courses and passed the examinations, and had finished my research, written it up, and submitted my thesis, which Shosh helped me type. It was on "Cross-Chord Longitudinal Turning." As part of my research project, I devised a cutting tool that could be used for considerably longer than conventional turning tools without the need for resharpening. I took out a US patent on my invention. I had completed all the requirements

for my degree except for the oral exam. Because of the death of my advisor —
although Ernreich had never understood what I was doing even when he was
alive — the orals were postponed and I was only awarded my MSc in
Mechanical Engineering some time later. Nevertheless, in the summer of
1961 I returned to Jerusalem to take up full-time residence in the city. I didn't
go to the graduation ceremony in 1962; the ritual itself didn't interest me. My
father, who was still in fine health, was very glad of the opportunity to represent me and have his son's diploma placed in his hands.

At that time there were very few industrial plants in Jerusalem, so I felt
extremely fortunate when I was offered the job of head of the general
mechanical workshop of the Hebrew University. I got the position, so I was
told, because I had an MSc, still very rare among mechanical engineers. The
workshop was responsible for maintaining the university's mechanical equipment, manufacturing tools, and designing and producing apparatus for
scientific experiments. I had the luck of being presented with a particularly
challenging project when I was still a novice in my profession. For his
doctoral thesis in meteorology, a student named Gagin needed to examine
the features of clouds to see if they were suitable for iodide seeding, used to
artificially generate rain. He wanted to pass a series of thin glass rods coated
in different chemicals through the clouds and then examine the chemicals to
see what changes had taken place. I designed a periscopic device to be
installed on top of a light plane. By pressing a trigger at the end inside the
plane, glass rods were shot out of a magazine at the opposite end outside, flew
through the cloud, and were caught by a second magazine. Of course, on
paper things look good even when they don't work. But once this device was
produced in the workshop according to my design, it proved itself in the field.

As a full-time resident of Jerusalem, I took my leave from the Academic
Sports Association, ASA Technion, after five years and joined ASA Jerusalem. The moving spirit behind ASA Jerusalem was Hillel Ruskin, whom I
knew from Geula, where he had been in the same class with Shosh. He was
also in charge of sports at the university. He put me on the track team. I
started running about six miles every day after work, making laps around the
university stadium at a moderate pace, without the benefit of a coach. I took
part in several 3000-meter races, recording only fair times in each of them.
My highest achievement was third place in something known as the "Gulliver
Race." In preparation for the Four-Day March in the spring of 1962, I stepped

up and lengthened my Saturday training sessions as well. I would run from our house to Sha'ar Ha-Gai and then quick march back up the steep climb to Jerusalem, a distance of over twenty-five miles all told. For the last three weeks before the march, I walked the whole distance. It paid off: I came in first on each of the four days of the march.

When I set out on day one, hundreds of "marchers" took off at a mad run. They each wanted the fame and glory that went with being the first to reach the finish line. I'd seen it all before. Experience had taught me how long those runners could keep it up. I started at a quick walk, but at a pace I knew I could maintain for the whole course. Little by little I overtook each of the runners. Whenever I saw a runner up ahead turn around to see how close I was getting, I knew it was a sign that he was weakening and that sooner or later I would pass him. In the first six miles I overtook the weakest runners. By the time I had walked twelve miles, I had passed most of the others as well, and I found myself all alone somewhere between miles fifteen and twenty. When I got to a straight stretch where I could see pretty far down the road and couldn't spot anyone up ahead, I would ask one of the policemen or soldiers directing traffic or securing the course if anybody had already passed them and how far ahead they were. I knew I would have to confirm whatever they said the next opportunity I got, particularly in regard to their estimation of the distance between us. Their "100 meters" could actually be anywhere from a thousand to fifty.

I also took advantage of my experience and my familiarity with the course. If I was on the right side of the road and knew I'd have to make a sharp left a few hundred yards ahead, I would steer a diagonal course tangential to the turn. I did the same thing every time the road bent. Those who didn't know how to apply the axiom they'd learned to recite in primary school — that the shortest distance between two points is a straight line — had to walk unnecessary yards at each turn or bend in the road. This could add up to a few hundred extra yards a day. I knew that the combination of information and brains always gives you an edge, whether it's in science, business, or sports.

On day two, about an hour after the start, when I had already walked my way past a large number of weaker runners, a blond guy came running up behind me and asked "Where's the engineer?" Of course I knew who he meant, but still I asked, "What engineer?" "The engineer from Jerusalem!" he explained, running alongside me at the same pace as I was walking. I told him I was the man he was looking for. Incredulously, he turned to gape at me: "You?" he repeated, the doubt obvious in his tone. He had expected "the engineer from Jerusalem," who always seemed to finish first, to be a tall brawny jock with long legs that tripped gracefully over the ground. But what did he see? A solid type of medium height in glasses, who was losing his hair (I kept my hat shoved between my shorts and my shirt until the sun started beating down on my head). Despite my unimpressive appearance, he was convinced I was who I said I was by the speed of my walk — something he'd probably never seen before — and the fact that I could talk freely even at that pace and was barely breaking a sweat.

He told me that when he heard that the man who finished first was some engineer guy, he figured that, as an ex-army man and currently a farmer who worked out in the open all day, he had to be faster and in better shape than someone "who only sat on his ass." I was twenty-six to his twenty-two. He kept pace with me. Every now and then he slowed to a walk for a short way, but most of the time he ran, keeping right alongside me. Little by little we passed the other runners until we were alone at the head of the pack. For the rest of the march, we stayed together and finished together. When the reporters at the finish line asked which of us had come in first, he pointed to me and said: "I ran alongside him." That was the start of my lasting friendship with Yoram Cohen from Kfar Yedidya.

On day three Yoram took off with me and stuck by my side. Again we slowly passed everyone else and finished together, with him running for most of the way as I walked. Since each day the start was around 4:30 in the morning, I had already completed the course by about 8:30. Throughout the morning, the Army Radio reported the time at which I passed certain landmarks and exactly when I crossed the finish line. A lot of people told me they used this information as a benchmark to gauge whether their own pace was faster or slower than their normal rate. In other words, I became a "rabbit" for the other marchers.

Since I finished early and still felt pretty fit, I decided it was a shame to waste a good working day, so as soon as I completed my daily walk, I got on my scooter and went straight to the workshop. Naturally, this odd behavior of mine tickled the fancy of the journalists, who never failed to mention in their newspaper or radio reports that the engineer from Jerusalem had come in first and gone to work on his scooter. Needless to say, I enjoyed being the celebrity! And there was the added gratification of getting to work — albeit a bit late — and being told that my subordinates had already heard that I was on my way.

At the end of day three I left my scooter at home and took the bus back to Hulda in the evening. The next day Yoram took off with me again. The mass of "marchers" was larger on this, the last day, than ever before. With the repeated announcement that "the engineer from Jerusalem came in first today" flaming their desire to bask in the same sort of glory, anyone with an ounce of strength left in his body now set out like a man possessed. Nevertheless, things proceeded much as they had on the previous days. The only difference was the route. There was a long incline near Kibbutz Harel which most of the runners managed to make, even if they had to take it at a walk. It was followed by a descent, an easy section to run, until the road turned left. Then there was a straight leg, actually a gentle climb, and then another steep incline to Eshtaol followed by another long descent to the Har-Tuv junction. But here, where the road turned right at the gas station, the real ascent began, the one that separates the boys from the men.

Yoram himself couldn't keep pace with my walking speed at this point, not even by running, which is not an easy thing to do, and he couldn't walk as fast as I could on such a steep hill. This is where I very quickly took the lead, pushing myself to make the climb at a rapid pace. I actually passed several heavily loaded command cars that were having trouble making it up the hill even in first gear. Here I could get a real jump on the others, enough so that when we got to the downhill leg, not even those who could run faster than I could walk would be able to catch me. I realized I was now reaping the benefits of my persistent training runs to Sha'ar Ha-Gai and back, and that was what had given me an edge. I also knew that even if someone threatened to overtake me on the descent, there was still one more long steep climb left: from Ein Kerem to Mt. Herzl. I was getting blisters again, but I was determined to ignore the pain and discomfort they were causing me. I kept up a quick pace the whole way and was the first to cross the finish line in Jerusalem. I had completed my sixth march, and felt very proud when one of the onlookers at the end proclaimed: "Way to go! You're king of the march!"

One of the people who had run alongside me in the early stages of the course was an agriculture student from Rehovot. He was astounded by my speed, and declared I was much faster than the Israeli race-walking champion. He had no doubt I could win the Israeli title for the 3000-meter walk.

I had no idea there was such a thing as an Israeli race-walking championship. I had almost managed to repress the memory of my dismal showing in the race-walking event six years before. For me the walking technique was just a way to excel in the marches. But this fellow's comment persuaded me to test myself in competitive race walking again. When the march was over, I asked Hillel Ruskin to organize a competition for me. And he did. The ASA track and field championships were soon to be held in Jerusalem. Hillel approached the national headquarters with the proposal that they include a new event: a 3-kilometer walk. Since the former police officer Zalman Philip, the Israeli race-walking champion at that distance (the only distance for race-walking events at that time in Israel) was a student at the Tel Aviv branch of the Hebrew University, and since the members of ASA Tel Aviv had never heard of me, they seconded the motion and it was passed. They were in no doubt that this event was an opportunity for their team to earn extra points.

The meet was held at the university stadium at Givat Ram, my home court. As I was warming up for the race, an athlete dressed in a white shirt with blue trim came up and introduced himself as Zalman Philip. I knew he held the Israeli title, but I had never met him before. For his part, he knew I was a greenhorn in walking competitions, and he treated me accordingly. Instructing me that I shouldn't try to start fast because I'd have to slow down too much toward the end, he suggested I begin at a pace considerably below his. It was good advice if you believed, as he did, that I was in nowhere as good shape as he was. Nevertheless, the pace I took off at was one I knew from the marches I could maintain.

We started at the 200-meter marker at the northeastern end of the stadium, the side closest to the government office buildings. I overtook him right at the start. We had to do seven and a half laps. When I crossed the finish line, Philip still had almost a whole lap to go. I've never seen him again; he disappeared from the sports scene. For me, however, that was a turning point, the event that hurled me into the world of competitive race walking.

Hillel Ruskin signed me up for the Israeli track and field championships scheduled for early summer 1962. It was to include a 3000-meter walk. He also presented me with the excellent race-walking handbook written by Harold Witlock, the British winner of the 50-kilometer walk at the Berlin

Olympic Games. I devoured the book and adopted his suggestions. Grad-ually, over the years, as I increased my training time and learned — through trial and error — how my body responds to different types of training, exer-cise, and exertion, my performance improved. Hillel noticed that I wore ordi-nary athletic shoes for both training and competitions, and promised to order special walking shoes from the United States. Since he didn't know much about my sport, the sneakers he ordered weren't of much use to anyone but teenagers who might wear them for hanging out at the mall. Presumably, he took the catalogue description "walking shoes" to mean race walking. As soon as I put them on, I could feel the damage they did to the soles of my feet and my Achilles heel. But I still won the Israeli race-walking championship, a kid of twenty-six.

Spurred by the popularity of the Four-Day March among the Israeli public, local groups began to organize one-day marches: the Negev March, the Sea of Galilee March, and the midnight ascent to Mount Meron. The route for the first Negev March followed the main road from Dimona to Be'er Sheba. Shosh came with me for this one, so naturally we walked together. It was rough. She claimed I was "running," meaning I was walking too fast, although I tried to go as slow as I could. I kept complaining she was "crawl-ing," that is, walking slower than she was able to. We finished together, but the experience came to be known in our family as the "two-time march": the first and last time we would ever walk side by side. We still take part in the same events (although she doesn't come to all of them), but we each go at our own pace.

The first Sea of Galilee March followed a downhill route along the Tiberias–Rosh Pina road to Zemach. Yoram Cohen took off with me, staying beside me by alternately running and walking. After passing the Russian monastery on the lakeshore about two miles north of Tiberias, we left the road and made a sharp turn west. As expected, by this point we were out in front, a couple of miles ahead of all the rest. We climbed a winding path up a steep hill toward Upper Tiberias. The path twisted back and forth as it rose, with cows grazing contentedly on both sides. Because of the steep incline, Yoram began to fall behind.

All of a sudden one of the cows, or maybe it was a bull — I didn't actually take the time to examine its sexual orientation — came running at me with its head down. I wasn't wearing red, didn't look much like a toreador, and hadn't provoked it in any way. It came up quickly from behind. I heard a noise, and turned my head around slightly as I continued the climb and there it was, the cow/bull almost on top of me about to thrust its horns into me. Instinctively I leapt up and stuck a hand out behind me in a vain attempt to shield my behind. Luckily, the top of its head collided with me while I was still on my way into the air from my frantic leap. My left hand struck its left horn as I found myself encircled, one horn on each side of my body. Consequently, I escaped without any additional holes in my flesh save for those I was endowed with by nature. My vault and my hand had blunted the blow, so that except for a small scratch, a medium bump, and an extra-large scare, I wasn't hurt. The creature stopped short — as if it had successfully completed its mission — and I leapt up again, sprinting forward and making a wild run for my life. When I was a safe enough distance up the path, I turned and saw Yoram moving up on the cows. I shouted a warning and he slowed his pace. The cow/bull must have recognized him for the experienced farmer he was; it showed no interest in him whatsoever.

The midnight ascent of Mount Meron was just that. It was held on the anniversary of the death of Theodor Herzl. We took off at midnight in order to reach the summit in time to enjoy the spectacular sunrise. We started at the Meron Spring near the sharp bend in the Akko-Safed road at the mouth of the Limon River. Two weeks earlier, two terrorists had been spotted on the mountain, but hadn't been caught. Not very encouraging. Nevertheless, thousands of people showed up. It didn't put me off either; after all, you only die once. It was July, but it was very cold at the starting line and would be even colder at the top. We climbed a narrow winding path that had been paved by relief workers during the time of the British Mandate. It was pitch black, but the moon shed a bit of light in certain sections. The trail also forked periodically, with no signs to direct us.

Yoram and I started out together and took the lead pretty soon. There were no runners on such a steep slope, but Yoram was a bit behind me, switching from a walk to a run and back again every few steps. We were already way ahead of everyone else. Despite the stillness of the night, through which voices carry for some distance, our ears didn't pick up any sounds from the other marchers. At one point we took the wrong fork, or more precisely, I did. I chose the left-hand path, but after a few hundred yards I realized it was going in the wrong direction and heading downhill. We decided to go back the way we had come and try taking the right. That turned out to be a wise decision.

About fifteen minutes later, with Yoram some twenty yards behind me, I suddenly heard a loud commotion: branches were being broken and moved, and twigs cracked noisily as they split under the weight of heavy feet. It was coming from the wooded slope to our left leading up toward us, and the noise was getting closer very fast. Whatever it was, it had almost reached the clearing some two or three yards ahead of me on the left. By the light of the moon I could just make out a huge boar thundering across the path and disappearing into the heavy undergrowth on the right. It was a frightening sight. Then I heard another noise coming from the left. I tried to warn Yoram, to shout: "Yoram, look out! A pig!" but in the confusion all that came out was "Yoram! Pig!" He got the message though and didn't take it the wrong way. The second boar crossed the path between us. If one of the lumbering creatures had plummeted into us at the speed they were going it would have been the end for us. With our hearts pumping furiously, we kept going, taking quite a while to calm down. We reached the summit first, but that wasn't the only story we had to tell when we got home.

Shosh and I lived in Jerusalem but we weren't typical Jerusalemites; we knew how to swim. Twice a week in the hot summer months we would go to Moshav Shoresh, where there was a swimming pool that kept convenient hours and that was much nicer than the YMCA pool or the "abominators" pool in the German Colony. We were practicing for the popular swim across the Sea of Galilee. The event was organized in the same fashion as the Mt. Tabor Race. Armed with a doctor's certificate, we had to present ourselves at Zemach on Friday afternoon where we stood in long lines to register and then waited ages to be transported to one of the kibbutzim in the vicinity. We were put up, at our own expense, at Kibbutz Degania B.

That night at dinner we found ourselves at the same table with Eli Kommay, a fellow member of ASA Jerusalem. Eli was brought up on the communist kibbutz Yad Hannah and was studying physics in Jerusalem. We often trained in the university stadium at the same time. He was an outstanding runner. On one occasion he asked me to come with him to a talk given by the Member of Knesset Mikunis, one of the heads of the Israeli Communist Party. I told him it wasn't my cup of tea. He didn't say anything, but we never talked politics again and we are still friends. He turned out to be a perfect example of the old adage that goes approximately: If you're young and not a communist — you have no heart, and if you're older and still a communist — you have no head.

Eli was always very smart. After the Six-Day War he saw the light, politically speaking. There over dinner at Degania I discovered that he was a health nut, even more fanatical than me. I have been a vegetarian since childhood, I don't smoke, I don't drink alcohol, not even beer, and I only have coffee or tea on the rare occasions when I need some to keep me awake when I'm driving. Eli went to even greater lengths. He made an effort not to eat off of plastic dishes because of the low vapor pressure of most plastics, which are basically poisonous materials. Moreover, he didn't have the passion for ice cream that I do.

The swim across the lake began early in the morning at Kibbutz Ha-On and ended at Beit Yerach, not at Zemach as it does today. It is a galvanizing sight to see the swimmers, decked out in the colorful bathing caps provided by the organizers, covering a broad band of the lake that stretches far out across the water. Officially, we would be swimming between two and a half and three miles. It was our first time at the event, and we weren't exactly sure what direction we were supposed to go in. When your eyes are only a few inches above the water, you can't see the finish on the opposite shore. Consequently, Shosh and I swam side by side, following our noses and trying to go in the general direction of the other swimmers. Moving like this, it's hard to swim in a straight line from start to finish. You generally progress by alternating diagonal segments, first right and then left, or in the best case in one wide arc, which is obvious to anyone standing at a height on the shore. As a result, the distance we actually swam was longer in practice than in theory. Only later did I learn that before you go into the water, you have to take up some high position on the shore, locate the finish across the lake, and then find some tall enough objects nearby to keep your sights on. Over the years I discovered the yellow blot on the landscape — typical of a stone quarry — on the hill above Degania, and I used it to steer myself in the water.

Swimming is a monotonous activity; you can't carry on a conversation at the same time. The lake crossing starts out easily enough, but about halfway across you begin to feel the muscles used only for swimming. They don't come into play when you run or walk. Towards the end, all you want to do is get it over with. You're sick and tired of the whole thing! Finally, you reach the shallow water at the opposite shore. Obviously, you want to stand up and walk. But there's a surprise in store for you: you've lost your sense of equilibrium. Using your hands so as not to fall, you make it to the even shallower water, and very slowly you learn to stand up straight without falling over. You climb to the shore stepping gingerly on the sharp stones and gravel with the soles of your feet now softened by the water. Finally your feet touch ground that you can walk on comfortably. Thirstily you drink milk out of a plastic bag and wolf down the sandwiches supplied by the organizers. Then there is the pleasure of receiving the participant's medal and certificate.

By now you have forgotten the boredom and the effort it took to cross the last few yards and you declare: "That was great fun!" The memory loss is not only temporary. Every year since, providing I am in Israel at the time of the event and even if I haven't been swimming once in the past year or two, I cross the Sea of Galilee. Shosh has also repeated the experience more than twenty times.

Since Shosh worked in the medical school and I worked in the university workshop, I was entitled to free tuition. I decided to take advantage of the opportunity to get my doctorate. Because there is no school of engineering at the Hebrew University, the obvious solution seemed to be to do it in physics. But when I looked into the possibility, I discovered I would not only have to take all the master's courses in physics, I would have to do most of the Bachelor of Science courses as well. That put a damper on my idea of a PhD in physics.

While I was trying to figure out what to do, someone mentioned a new university program in a field new to Israel: business administration. I hadn't the vaguest notion what they were talking about. I found out it referred to a new two-year MA course designed for economists and engineers. The first class, some twenty students, had begun the course in 1961–62, and they were now registering students for the second class. I already had a master's degree, but I knew nothing about administration. So I applied and was accepted. Most of the classes were held in the afternoon or evening, and that suited my working hours. There were about thirty of us, but only two engineers and one lawyer; the rest had degrees in economics.

I had hardly ever cracked a book at the Technion, not even for my MSc. This was the first time I had to study from books, not just from the notes I took in lectures. The course opened a new world to me that I, as a technocrat, knew nothing about: economic processes and calculations. It required a lot of studying. I was up until midnight, and pored over my books all weekend as well. I wasn't particularly pleased by having to devote so much of my time to schoolwork, but I gained an appreciation of what I was learning and I enjoyed it. The economists among us claimed that the program taught them little they didn't already know, but I felt it gave me a great deal. Toward the end of the second year, Avi Meshulach, one of my favorite lecturers who was still working on his doctoral thesis for Harvard, asked me nonchalantly if I might be interested in doing a PhD in production management abroad. Without giving it any real thought, I said "Sure, why not?" I didn't do anything more about it, and that was the last I heard of it from him.

Two of the students in the class in particular stood out. One was Yudke Tager, who was older than the rest of us, and obviously enjoyed every minute of the course. He had been a company commander with the rank of captain in the War of Independence. After the war he was sent undercover to Iraq to organize the illegal emigration of its Jewish citizens to Israel. He was caught, tried, and sentenced to death. With the help of a bribe offered through a third party, they held off on executing his sentence. Instead, he rotted in prison for eight years. In return for another hefty bribe, he was released during the Kassem regime. As soon as he got back to Israel, he enrolled in university — paid for by the Ministry of Defense — and went straight on for a master's degree after his BA.

The other memorable student was Amiram Sivan, the head of the Labor Party faction of the student union. During the breaks between lessons, he would regale us with tales of his political intrigues, how he'd muzzled some opponent or other, ensured that his resolutions were passed, and formed expedient coalitions and alliances. His animated accounts were punctuated by vivid mimicry and gestures with his fist, the thumb alternately up or down, like a religious scholar grappling with a convoluted passage from the Gemara.

In late 1962, the university decided to reorganize its facilities and close down the mechanical workshop. Shortly before it was shut down for good, I found a job with the Knesset Building Construction Commission headed by the Speaker of the Knesset, Kadish Luz. I was to be the supervising engineer of electro-mechanical installations in the new home of the Israeli parliament, then under construction. The building site where I was now working was quite near the university, so that during my lunch hour I could continue my training walks along the Givat Ram roads and the valleys below. After work, I drove the short distance to the university stadium and ran six miles before class. Work on the Knesset building was not at all challenging, but the pay was good. In retrospect, I realized it had taught me a great deal about the construction industry, and I put that knowledge to good use when we built our own home.

Unfortunately, it also taught me a lot about the ugly side of human nature, made giddy by greed, arrogance, and a lust for fame. The competition for the design of the Knesset building was won by the Jerusalem architect Klarwein. When Baron de Rothschild donated a generous sum for its construction, the architects who had not bothered to submit designs suddenly realized that the prestigious and potentially lucrative project was really going to get off the ground. They raised an outcry, and in an attempt to secure themselves a piece of the pie, voiced scathing criticism against Klarwein's design. Thus, bowing to pressure, the powers-that-be decided to shift the building 180 degrees — after the foundations had already been dug into the earth and the rock below. This meant filling in the pit on one side, and cutting deeper into the stone on the other.

The blueprint for the building was constantly being altered in the course of construction, as changes were ordered. For example, after the vaulted ceiling of the plenary hall — exposed concrete with deep grooves for both aesthetic and acoustic reasons — had already been poured, at a much higher cost than any other type of ceiling, a team of architects — Deborah Gad and her partner Noy — was called in. They recommended that the finished ceiling be hidden by a second one constructed beneath it. When I spoke to the design office of the Knesset Building Construction Commission about it, although I was going outside my authority, they told me it was no big deal and precedents existed. A massive carved natural wood gate had once been installed at the entrance to a Ministry of Defense building, but in response to the objection that it looked too gaudy, it was painted over to hide the lovely wood and the artistic carvings.

The electrical subcontractor won the tender issued by the electrical designer because he had submitted the lowest bid. He offered a minimal price for Type A lighting fixtures, several hundred of which were to be installed, and a very high price for Type B fixtures, only a small number of which were required. After the subcontractor had already been awarded the tender, the designer changed the plans, so that most of the fixtures were now of Type B. The whole affair reeked of corruption and "collaboration" between the two men. I reported it to my superiors. They replied that they were aware of the situation, but couldn't do anything about it since the electrical consultant had persuaded them of the need for the change and it had been approved.

If a bad odor still rises from the Knesset building, it might be good for the legislators to remember where it all started. The fees for the subcontractors were supposed to be calculated by multiplying an item price per unit of measure (length, area, etc.) by the number of units. As a rule, any number of tricks were employed to inflate the number of units installed. I never understood why Menachem Begin, at that time the vociferous leader of the opposition (and later prime minister), who fought normalization of relations with Germany, didn't protest when he saw that some of the plumbing fixtures in the Knesset toilets were conspicuously stamped "Made in Germany." Since the items imported for the building were exempt from customs, levies, and taxes, they were cheaper than equivalent products manufactured locally, which did not enjoy this advantage. The members of the Knesset Building Construction Commission not only chose to pay mere lip service to the slogan "Buy Israel," but they also didn't seem to realize that if you deducted the taxes that went back into the state coffers, local products cost the same, if not less, than foreign imports.

I recalled this period of my life years later when Reuven Barkat (then Speaker of the Knesset), whose daughter Ariella was a good friend of Shosh, visited us in the United States. This politician remarked jokingly of the fellow members of his calling: "When God created man, he wanted to make him perfect. He searched for the highest virtues on earth and found three: man must be wise, honest, and a politician. When Satan heard what God was planning, he hurried to him and tried to persuade him not to make man perfect so that Satan could perform the role God had intended him for. God was convinced and agreed to compromise. He gave each man only two of the highest qualities. Ever since, if a person is honest and a politician, he isn't wise; if he is wise and a politician, he isn't honest, and if he is both honest and wise, he isn't a politician."

During the time I was working on the Knesset building, I had some unexpected encounters with wild animals in the center of Jerusalem without ever having to go to the zoo. One night as I drove down Ruppin Street I spotted a fox running across the road. It came from the direction of the field above the stadium (where the Science Museum stands today) and ran toward the complex of government buildings. It had the straight profile typical of foxes. I told a friend of mine, who said he had also seen the fox the day before. Two days later, during a noontime training walk, I saw its body lying by the side of the road. It had been run over by a car.

On some of those noontime walks I'd take the trail between Givat Ram and the Neve Shanan section of town and then south toward the Rasco quarter. At the entrance to the Rasco quarter, near the edge of what is today the Botanical Gardens, there were large groves of fruit trees. One day I saw a big deer that had apparently gotten it into its head to forage for food in the center of Jerusalem. It was only about eight yards away. All of a sudden it caught sight of me and took off.

Not every chance encounter was quite so pleasant. During one lunch break, a friend of mine from ASA Jerusalem suggested we run together. We took the path circling Givat Ram. On the western slope of the hill some thirty yards below the road and the fence around the campus, we suddenly heard a tremendous roar. We couldn't believe our eyes! In the very center of Jerusalem, some four yards to our left at the entrance to a natural hollow, was a hyena. It was startled by the sound of our running feet, a noise which had apparently awakened this creature of the night. As it stood there roaring, we were so frightened we nearly wet ourselves. We froze for a split second and then leapt onto a lower path to the right and ran for our lives. The hyena held its ground, screeching for a while longer — it certainly didn't sound like a laugh — undoubtedly pleased to have driven out these creatures who had invaded its territory. We were just as pleased to get out of there.

Twice I was surprised by the sight of vipers in the wooden hut that served as the supervisors' office, the site of the Knesset guard building today. I didn't like the company. We killed one of them with a metal pipe. The other hid under the wooden floorboards and we couldn't get at it. I hope its offspring don't still pay nostalgic visits to their paternal home.

Although I was studying and working at the Knesset, I took part in every athletic event I could. The Jerusalem school system organized a competitive relay race in memory of thirty-five Palmach reinforcements under the command of Danny Mass who tried to walk out to get supplies for the besieged kibbutzim in Gush Etzion in 1948 and were slaughtered in the attempt. It was called the "Race of the Lamed-Heh" (the number 35 in Hebrew letters), and true to its name it began at Kibbutz Ha-Lamed-Heh and ended in Jerusalem. The route was divided into thirty-five one-kilometer segments, each to be covered by a different runner. I decided to run the whole distance, with a fellow member of my athletic club, Uri Goldburt, riding alongside on his motor scooter to keep me supplied with water along the way.

I took off about ten minutes before the relay runners, but I was only overtaken quite some time after I had managed to make the steep climb to Mevo Beitar and the long descent toward the foot of Hadassah Hospital. The total distance clearly gave the impression of being thirty-five kilometers, with each kilometer carefully marked by the organizers. But following the example of George Orwell in *Animal Farm*, where everyone is equal but some are more equal than others, the route contained short kilometers and long kilometers. My body held up better than the scooter. For the last ten kilometers, including the steep incline at Ein Kerem, there was no sign of Uri and no water. I finished the race without feeling any pain or becoming dehydrated. Uri showed up much later. His clutch was in pieces.

In the spring of 1963 Shosh and I again took part in the Negev March. This time the route went from Arad to Be'er Sheba, and for some strange reason it was held at night. Arad was a new town, its construction begun only a year before, so that except for a few huts and a completed building or two it was still empty. Around that time, filled with the pioneering spirit and the desire to settle in the Negev and be part of the birth of a new town, we had looked into the possibility of moving there. I was probably still under the influence of the personal example set by Ben-Gurion and the talk he had given to high school seniors ten years earlier, at the amphitheater at Sheik Munis on what is today the southern slope of Museum Ha'aretz. Since there was no work for people in our professions, we abandoned the idea of settling in Arad. We couldn't have known that twelve years later we would indeed live in the Negev between Be'er Sheba and Arad. We set out at midnight. Before the start, there was a boisterous air of celebration. We built campfires to keep warm and sang and danced around the flames. Once the march began, it was back to the same old routine of overtaking the runners one by one.

Within two hours I was in the lead. Suddenly I heard a barking, joined by a chorus of other dogs coming from different directions and various distances. The barking got louder and louder. It was a moonlit night, and I kept myself on course by focusing on the different coloration of the asphalt road and the shoulders. As the barking grew nearer, I realized that some-where not too far from the road was a Bedouin encampment. Their dogs had gotten my scent and they were about to attack. I was gripped by terror. I stopped, quickly picked up a few large stones from the side of the road, and shoved them between my shorts and my shirt, held in place by the elastic around my waist. I kept four stones in my left hand and two in my right.

A few seconds later I was surrounded by a pack of about ten large vicious dogs. They kept leaping up and down as if they were about to jump on me as they periodically bared their claws. Showing their sharp teeth, they kept up the barking that sent shivers down my spine. I was sure it was the end for me. I might be a vegetarian, but they obviously weren't. The dogs encircled me at a distance of some two yards and were closing in. Their terrifying heads were only a yard or two from my feet. By the light of the moon I could clearly see their whole bodies. I raised my right hand and hurled the stone I held between my thumb and my first finger at one of the dogs. It found its target and the dog let out a thin squeal of pain. As I raised my hand again to throw the second stone, I saw the dogs retreating a few steps. I figured they must realize I was dangerous and were being cautious.

Swinging my arm as if to throw another stone — but not actually hurling it — I took a small step in the direction I had been walking. The dogs moved back another yard, but the atrocious barking didn't let up. In order to demon-strate my power, I threw the second stone at the nearest dog and quickly took a third from my shorts. It's easier to aim when you're only holding one stone, and you can throw it harder too. Very slowly, I continued moving, taking small, careful steps, and simultaneously threatening the dogs with the stone in my hand. I twisted my body around in every direction, tossing a stone from time to time. Now and again I raised my left hand, still holding four stones, in a threatening gesture. The dogs were still barking, but they were keeping a safer distance and starting to gather on the side of the road leading to Arad. I assumed the Bedouin encampment was in that direction. When I had put about eight yards between myself and the dogs, I bent down to rearm.

After a little more of this slow-motion pantomime — not unlike an evasive action to cover an army retreat — the dogs stopped following me. I was safe! Those few minutes felt like an eternity. I could still hear barking, but I understood I had left their territory. I resumed my customary walking technique, turning my head every now and then to size up the situation. I didn't get rid of the rest of the stones until the dogs had been out of sight for several minutes and I couldn't hear their barking any more. Knowing how intelligent dogs are, I didn't want them to sense I was no longer "armed," so I slipped the stones silently into the sand at the side of the road.

About an hour later I felt my strength draining away. There was just no vitality left. It wasn't that any muscles were aching, I was simply lumbering, barely able to keep going. I knew well enough that it was not the sort of feeling you get when you are becoming dehydrated. Although I hadn't had anything to drink, I also hadn't lost much fluid on this cool nighttime walk. I couldn't understand why I was feeling so weak, when it never happened to me in morning events or when I trained in the heat of the day. I remembered I had only eaten a light supper, concerned that any undigested food might cause me discomfort during the march, so I decided the problem must be low blood sugar level. I saw a campfire at the side of the road where the organizers were making tea for the marchers. I drank some down and kept going. The sugar helped: within a few minutes I felt my strength returning and I could resume my customary walking pace.

About forty minutes later, it happened again. I knew I needed more sugar. A police jeep on security detail drove by. I waved it down and asked the driver if he had anything sweet I could have. He didn't. Instead, he gave me two slices of white bread. I had never tried eating bread in the midst of intense physical exertion, but there wasn't much choice. I chewed it in small bites, letting them dissolve in my mouth. It worked. My strength was fully restored within a few minutes.

I reached the Tel Shoket junction at nearly five a.m. I'd walked about twenty-five miles. According to the program, at this point we were supposed to be transferred to the entrance to Be'er Sheba by bus, and from there we would march into the stadium. The junction was deserted. I didn't feel like waiting there in the cold for hours until the first bus filled up; and besides, that would mean denying myself the glory of coming in first. So without hesitation I kept going for the last seven miles to Be'er Sheba. I had no idea that fifteen years later this "extra" stretch of road would become the route I regularly trained on. When I got to Be'er Sheba, I realized I didn't know the way to the stadium. I was unfamiliar with the city, there were no signs, and at this hour on a Saturday morning there was no one there to ask. So I traipsed from one part of town to the next until I found it. I had walked nearly thirty-seven miles, but I still came in first. It was superb training for the Four-Day March only a few weeks away.

The Four-Day March in 1963 followed the pattern set in the previous years, save for one difference: this time I had two new companions for the whole event. Like Yoram, they alternately ran and walked, but unlike him, whenever we passed reporters, judges, or officials, they immediately slowed to a walk to give the impression they wouldn't think of doing anything else. My new walking partners, Zvika Oz and Moshe Rotenberg, were bus drivers. The four of us finished first on all four days. The same thing happened in 1964 and 1965. Nevertheless, their names were hardly mentioned in the press — maybe the reporters had caught sight of them from a distance and could see them running. The star of the show was still "the engineer from Jerusalem."

Moshe in particular was upset by this state of affairs. He printed little notes reading: "Leaders: Moshe Rotenberg, Zvi Oz, Yoram Cohen, and Shaul Ladany." When we reached the official rest stops along the way, where the reporters and media vans were stationed, he would pass out his notes to the journalists. I recall one such occasion when a reporter holding Moshe's note in his hand came up to us where we were drinking water, stuck a microphone in my face and said: "Ladany, tell our listeners how you're feeling." He had barely gotten the words out his mouth before Moshe grabbed the mike and screamed: "My name is first on the list!" I thought he was going to punch the poor guy. The reporter, apparently used to people trying to hog the limelight, calmly retrieved his mike and motioned me aside where he continued our interview.

As soon as the 1963 Israeli race-walking championship was over, I stopped running and devoted myself exclusively to walking. The intense training, using the techniques suggested in Witlock's handbook, paid off. My times gradually improved. But that wasn't the only event where I saw an improvement.

The ASA Jerusalem coach signed up the runners on his track team for a 3000-meter event. He needed one more runner for them to be able to compete as a team, so he asked me. I agreed and recorded a faster time than my previous personal best. He couldn't understand how race walking had improved my running time. What he didn't seem to grasp was that if I had devoted as much time to running as I had to walking, and used the same training methods — rather than only running 10,000 meters at a moderate pace as I had habitually done — I could have produced even better results. At the Israeli track and field championships in 1964, the 10,000-meter run took place about two hours after I had won the 3000-meter walk. I decided to enter, just for the hell of it, and was astounded when I came in third!

Up to then I had never gotten any sort of cup or trophy, only a few small medals as mementos of races or marches I had won. In 1963 I finally won my first trophy. I was voted the Hebrew University's athlete of the year and awarded a small olivewood letter opener with the university symbol glued to it. No inscription, no engraving. Who would have thought that fifteen years later I would design my house so as to give pride of place to the four hundred cups and eight hundred medals I had won meantime.

The Four-Day Marches and a few one-day events were the only opportunities I had to take part in walking competitions. So when Uzi Cohen organized the Tel Hai Marathon in 1963 and again in 1964, I decided to take advantage of the distance event even though it meant running, and I no longer trained as a runner. As befitting its name, it was held on Tel Hai Day (which commemorates the settlement and defense of Tel Hai, at the northern tip of Israel, where Joseph Trumpeldor was said to have uttered his famous dying words, "It is good to die for one's country").

The route ran from the Israeli outpost to the west of the Bnot Ya'akov bridge across the Jordan River to the famous monument to the battle for Tel Hai — the statue of a roaring lion in the Ha-Shomer cemetery at Kfar Giladi, about half a mile above Tel Hai itself. We were around twenty runners in the marathon. After the initial climb up to the main Upper Galilee road, the course was fairly flat until the Rosh Pina-Kiryat Shemona road. At that point, after we had already run for twenty-three miles, a sharp ascent began and got progressively steeper. The final climb from Tel Hai to the monument was the hardest of the whole race. I came in fifth.

I finished my degree in June 1964. Only seven of us were awarded an MA in business administration at the graduation ceremony held in the small amphitheater at Givat Ram, to the east of the National Library (the others hadn't yet completed all the requirements). The professional prowess of Israel Arkin, a descendent of Bilu pioneers from Mazkeret Batya, would eventually carry him to the post of head of the finance ministry budget office and later general director of Agrexco; Amiram Sivan, equally talented, would become the general director of Israel's social security system (Bituach Leumi) — his political affiliation with Labor surely not standing in his way when that party was in power — and later general director of the finance ministry. He retained that post even when the Likud came to power. Apparently he knew which side his bread was buttered on. Today he is the general manager of Bank Ha-Poalim, one of the one hundred largest banks in the world.

Four of the other graduates went on to get their PhDs and entered the academic world. Yehudah Shenhav, who, incidentally, was the ASA triple jump champion, later left his ivory tower to become a key figure in the Israeli capital market. Micha Peri, a lawyer who specialized in marketing and in 1975 beat me out for the position of vice-president of Haifa University, stayed on at the university but only part time, devoting most of his energy to the business world. Moshe Frankfurter went to seek his fortune in the United States, where he is now a professor of finance.

Shortly after I received my degree, Shosh completed her dissertation and was awarded a PhD. Her research was thoroughly Greek to me, but I helped her type parts of her thesis. I was wont to explain facetiously to anyone who would listen that she took urine samples from women, separated out their components, performed a number of chemical reactions, and then analyzed them using paper chromatography. The results, I claimed, showed that one of the components was yellow. Her defense was held in the medical school at the Russian Compound, near City Hall.

Her thesis advisor was Professor Michael Finkelstein, but the head of the laboratory where she did her research was the legendary Professor Bernhard Zondek, who invented the first pregnancy test together with Aschheim. In fact, it's known as the Aschheim-Zondek test. He had been nominated for a Nobel Prize in the thirties, when he was still in Germany, and rumor had it that he would have won if he hadn't been a Jew. To his dying day, after fleeing that country he never again set foot in Germany, and even ignored any German requests for reprints of his scientific papers. Zondek was quite a celebrity. The first time I saw him, I was shocked. He was an ugly man, short and stout with a slight hump and eyes bulging far out of his head as if they sat on a truncated cone stuck onto his face. But as soon as he opened his mouth, he revealed his remarkable personality, intelligence, wisdom, and humor. The old saw "you can't judge a book by its cover" was never truer than in his case.

Armed with a degree in business administration, I was offered the job of manager of the Atzmon sewing machine company in Safed. I accepted their offer, and just as when I was at the Technion in Haifa, Shosh and I once again found ourselves in a long-distance marriage. She stayed in Jerusalem where she worked at the medical school, and I moved to Safed. We met on weekends in Jerusalem or at our parents' homes in Tel Aviv. Having traded in my motor scooter for a new Ford Cortina in the summer of 1963, at least I had no trouble getting around, even in bad weather.

One Friday shortly after I had begun my job in Safed, Shosh and I planned to meet in Tel Aviv. At that time, the coastal road between Hadera and Netanya had only two lanes, one in each direction. Just north of Netanya construction had begun to widen the road to four lanes, and on the right the ground had already been flattened but the asphalt hadn't been laid yet. I was in a hurry to get to Tel Aviv. Driving south, some three miles north of Netanya, I took advantage of a straight stretch of road to pass the car in front of me. Still in the left lane, I realized that the car coming toward me was moving faster than I had thought and was getting dangerously close. The car I had passed was already far enough behind me. I turned the wheel sharply to the right to get back into my lane. From the lateral pressure on the tubeless right front tire, the rubber lost its grip on the metal drum and there was a sudden blowout.

The car spun back to front around the injured wheel, at the same time turning over and over in the air, totally out of control. That was before the era of seat belts. I didn't panic. I grabbed the steering wheel as hard as I could and pressed my feet to the floor, stretching my legs out in front of me and pushing my back up against the seat. As the car spun wildly, my tensed muscles kept me virtually motionless in the center of the twirling metal frame. It came to a stop on its wheels, facing in the wrong direction in the ditch to the right of the unpaved strip parallel to the existing lane.

Eyewitnesses later told me the car had performed six somersaults before rolling across the road and landing in the ditch. All the glass was shattered. The gym clothes I had left on the back seat were scattered on the ground all along my "flight path," together with the glasses I had been wearing and the

wallet that had been in my back pocket. When the car finally ended its acro-
batic contortions, I managed to open the twisted door and get out under my
own power. The drivers who had stopped to extract the body from the car
were left with nothing to do but help me gather up my belongings and suggest
I say a prayer to whoever was looking out for me up there. I didn't, since I'm
not a religious man, but I did learn my lesson. Today I'm a very careful driver.
In the more than thirty years since then I have never again been involved in
an accident, not even the smallest fender-bender, although I must have
driven at least half a million miles in that time.

Fortunately, no other cars or people were hurt. I had a few scratches on
the end of my nose from my glasses and a couple on my hands. I was also
pretty banged up, but an examination by the emergency medical services an
hour later found no serious injury. The next day I discovered I had cracked
the last vertebra in my spine, the coccyx that reaches down into the buttocks,
and I was forbidden to sit for two weeks. That meant I couldn't take a bus or
car back and forth to Safed. I flew from Tel Aviv to Machanaim a few times,
half sitting and half lying on my side.

After those two weeks I resumed my regular training. Every day I would
walk from Safed to Rosh Pina or Meron and back. Although the distance to
Rosh Pina was shorter, the steep climb back up to Safed made up for the
difference. Since I went out after work, it was sometimes dark by the time I
got home. One such evening when I stopped by the side of the road, blinded
by an oncoming car, I saw a field mouse up on its hind legs right by my foot. It
was blinded by the same light. We stood there side by side, like a scene out of
a Walt Disney movie. Considering that I also walked the several miles to and
from work each day, my fitness continued to improve steadily after the 1964
Israeli championships. Every now and then Shosh came to Safed, and we
spent those weekends hiking in the area.

One day I got a call in Safed from my former teacher, Zvi Ophir, the dean
of the university's School of Business Administration, offering me the chance
to study in the United States for a PhD in business administration, specializing in production management. In exchange for my assurance that I would
return to teach at the university, they would be willing to grant me a full
scholarship, including tuition and living and travel expenses. But first I would
have to be accepted by one of the better American institutions. I took the
offer without the slightest hesitation. Despite the title and the good pay, I

didn't particularly like the job in Safed. The plant had been losing money even before I arrived, and after I left Atzmon continued to go downhill until four years later when they did what they should have done a long time before — shut it down.

When I had already been accepted as a doctoral candidate by Columbia University, Zvi Ophir called me again. He informed me that the university had decided to divest itself of its Tel Aviv branch (which then became Tel Aviv University), and as their plans had called for my placement there, they no longer had a need for my services. Some other person had already been sent abroad to study, and there was no opening for anyone else in Jerusalem. He was sorry to inform me that the university was unable to honor its commitment to me. I knew that oral agreements "aren't worth the paper they're written on," and in my case it hadn't even been a real agreement, only an "assurance." He did add, however, that if I still wanted to do my doctorate, he would try to get me some other scholarship by way of compensation.

Now that I was all hopped up about the idea, I obviously wanted to continue my academic training, even though it had never crossed my mind before he brought it up. I made all the necessary arrangements to be in New York in time for the start of the school year in September 1965. At Zvi Ophir's recommendation, the Ministry of Commerce and Industry awarded me a one-time study grant of fifteen hundred dollars, without my having to commit myself in any way. It was peanuts compared to the original scholarship I had been promised, but it was better than nothing.

In March 1965 I took part in the marathon organized by the Health Lovers' Society in Haifa. It ran along the shore from Haifa toward Caesarea. Although I no longer trained as a runner, I leapt at the chance of a long-distance event. I managed to finish among the leaders, recording a time of 2:57. It came as quite a surprise to me to learn that the very next Saturday another local marathon was to be run for the Israeli championship, starting at Kibbutz Einat. I didn't want to miss this second chance to compete in a long-distance race, even though it meant running, and even though my running muscles, not used in race walking, were still sore and aching. Nonetheless, I went, and I came in fifth with a time of over three and a half hours. The race was won by David Simchoni, and I was also beaten out by Reuven Peleg who later became a good friend and a fellow race-walking competitor.

Two days later I got a call from Hillel Ruskin telling me he had received a notice from the Greek Sport Federation inviting runners from all over the world to an international marathon to follow the ancient route from the town of Marathon to the long marble stadium in Athens. It was scheduled for the first of April, the birthday of the king (subsequently deposed).

I'd never competed abroad. The idea of running the historic course, which had also been used for the marathon in the first modern Olympic Games, was very appealing, although I would again have to run rather than walk. Hillel said I was free to go if I wanted to, and was willing to pay my own way. All I needed was confirmation of my amateur status from the Track and Field Committee of the Sports Federation. He suggested I get in touch with Yariv Oren, the committee chairman. Up until that time, I'd had no dealings with the Sports Federation or its Track and Field Committee. Israel Brickner, Hillel's assistant, had always taken care of the paperwork for the Israeli championships. There was no question that I was an amateur; I didn't get a penny either for training or for the competitions I was in. I wasn't even reimbursed for my travel expenses, although international rules allowed for this. So I wasn't expecting it to be a problem to get the credentials I needed, especially as Yariv Oren himself had presented me with my medal at the Einat Marathon only a few days before.

When I found out how cheap the airfare to Athens was, I bought myself a ticket. The next Saturday I drove to Oren's home in Hod Ha-Sharon, naively believing he could supply me with the necessary piece of paper on the spot. I had a disappointment in store. He explained politely that since I had only come in fifth at Einat, the committee might not be interested in my taking part in international competitions. I asked him what difference that made; all I wanted was confirmation of my amateur status, which surely wasn't in question. The Greek organizers couldn't care less what kind of time I had recorded in some event they'd never heard of. He didn't offer me an explanation, but promised to submit my request to the committee at its next meeting. I was positive that as a genuine amateur I would be issued the credentials. Since Hillel had told me that event organizers the world over don't generally ask to see the document anyway (in fact, for the rest of my athletic career — until the rules for amateurs were abolished — nobody ever asked me for proof of my status), and since the next Track and Field Committee meeting was on the very day of my flight, I decided to leave without it.

The Greek hosts were very hospitable. I simply told them I had come in fifth in the Israeli championships two weeks earlier, what my best time was, and that I wanted to compete in the event. They didn't ask for any proof that I was an amateur. All the entrants were lodged in a hotel at the organizers' expense, two to a room. Since I knew Hungarian, they put me in with the Hungarian runner Sàndor Sütö, who had placed fifth in the marathon at the Tokyo Olympics in 1964. Sütö described his training program to me, and told me how the goodwill of his employer made it possible for him to maintain it regularly. He completed his morning training at 9:30 and started work at 10:00 or 10:30. Then he trained for another hour and a half during the lunch break. He was permitted to leave work early, at three in the afternoon, so that he could train with the team under the direction of its coach. His salary was also paid in full when he was absent for training camp, even when the camp lasted nine months, as it had before the Olympic Games. And when he returned to work after that absence, he was given a raise.

When I asked him who this exemplary employer was, he answered simply, "The Hungarian government." He went on to explain how worth his while it was, in all respects, to keep up his training, give it his all, and compete whenever he could. As an outstanding athlete, his financial circumstances were considerably better than those of the average Hungarian citizen. He had a car, traveled abroad where he bought items unavailable in Hungary, and earned a higher salary than he would otherwise be able to. In addition, he said, "I'm a celebrity and I enjoy sports." In the early seventies, Sütö chose not to return to Hungary from one of his trips abroad. He was granted political asylum by Switzerland and settled in Geneva. At first he continued to compete, but he soon retired. My Swiss friends told me that Sütö quickly discovered how much harder it is for an athlete to excel in a capitalist country, without the cosseting provided by the communist regimes.

Two days after I arrived, David Simchoni showed up, accompanied by Mordechai Magali, the secretary of the Israeli Track and Field Committee. David, nicknamed Pahima, explained how he had gotten there. After he won the Mt. Tabor Race in early March, the Sports Federation sent him and Amitzur Shapira, his personal coach, to the international field race in Paris organized by the paper L'Humanité. He had just returned when the Track and Field Committee received notice of the classic marathon in Greece, so they hastily arranged the Einat marathon at the last minute. When he won that race too, finishing with a good time — although he hadn't trained for that

distance — the committee decided to send him abroad again for the Athens
event, despite the fact that the proximity of the two races didn't allow enough
time for his body to recover from the first. His muscles were still sore.

The committee wanted to send a coach along with him, but since Shapira
had already been abroad that year — at the Paris event — they chose the next
in line for a perk, Magali. Magali had never coached him and knew nothing
about how to run a marathon or even 10,000 meters. He specialized in sprints
and middle distances. When Magali saw me he could barely contain his fury.
He bawled me out for having the nerve to show up there when the Track and
Field Committee had decided not to approve my request to compete. I told
him I hadn't asked for their approval, merely for their confirmation of my
amateur status, so they could have no objection to my presence there. I failed
to convince him. He argued, among other things, that I had only produced
average results and that at the age of twenty-nine I was too old to ever become
a good athlete. I have no idea what he felt three years later when I was the only
Israeli track and field athlete to meet the Olympic team standard.

For the moment, however, he was able to prevent me from taking part in
the marathon. I had no choice but to help Simchoni, keeping him supplied
with drinks, wet sponges, and information, and cheering him on for the
second half of the race. The two marathons back to back and his lack of training for the distance took their toll. He went into this race before his body had
recovered from the previous one, a situation that couldn't be remedied
merely by the massage Magali gave him the night before. The time he
recorded was relatively slow considering his ability. Had I competed, I would-
n't have come in last either. The next day, to make it up to myself for not being
able to take part in the event, I rented a car and Simchoni and I went to see the
canal and the ancient fortress of Corinth.

When I got back home, I continued to prepare for my trip to the United
States in August, at the same time resuming my race-walking training. At the
Israeli championships in the summer of 1965, Moshe Rotenberg, Zvika Oz,
and I took the first three places in the 3000-meter walk, with my two competitors coming in far behind me. As a result, the three of us were included in the
Israeli delegation to the Maccabiah Games. As a young boy I had witnessed
the opening ceremony of the Third Maccabiah Games, and as a student had
attended the opening of the fifth in 1957. I was thrilled to be participating in

these Jewish Olympics, and delighted in the carnival atmosphere of the opening ceremony and the get-togethers with the athletes from abroad.

Having learned my lesson from the bitter experience of Athens in April,
and as part of my preparations for my trip abroad, I applied to Israel Brickner
as soon as I heard I would be competing in the Maccabiah Games. I asked
him to arrange a certificate of amateur status from the Sports Federation. He
reported back that he had spoken with the general secretary of the Federation, a man by the name of Lalkin, who had promised to deliver the credentials when the delegation gathered for the start of the games. Lalkin headed
the Israeli delegation, but he didn't bring the document to the opening ceremony. I had to nag him about it several times until, on the last day of the
games, he finally handed me that precious piece of paper.

Although the Israeli delegation wasn't allotted accommodation in the
Maccabiah village, I was close by at my parents' home in Ramat Chen. Thus I
was able to practice on my old training grounds in the National Park in
Ramat Chen, adjacent to the athletes' village. During these sessions I became
friendly with all four of the foreign walkers who had come for the games. I
formed the closest ties with the oldest and most celebrated of them, the
renowned American Henry Laskau. He had competed for the United States
in three Olympics starting in 1948, held the world indoor record for 1 mile,
had won forty-two American championships over the course of twenty years,
and had won three gold medals at the previous Maccabiah Games.

He hadn't taken part in the 1961 games, having already retired from
competition at the peak of his ability. Now, after several years of retirement,
he felt a renewed lust for competition. He had returned to the track six
months before the Seventh Maccabiah Games and was eager to add a fourth
gold medal to his collection. He did, too, setting a new Maccabiah record and
breaking his personal record at the same time. He made a tremendous
impression on me. He had an easy style, as if he weren't exerting himself in
the least. I was envious of his accomplishments. I didn't believe I would ever
be able to walk as fast as he could. I certainly never dreamed that four years
later I would break his record and earn the Maccabiah record for myself.

I came in only fourth at the Maccabiah Games, but I improved on my
personal best. I still lacked basic speed. The three leaders put a significant
distance between us right from the start, and it grew consistently longer. Over
the last two and a half laps I managed to shorten the gap between myself and

the Canadian, Kiwa Kadisewitz, who finished third, coming in only three yards behind him. If the race had been longer, I would have caught him within ten yards, since I could see him weakening whereas I felt strong enough to keep going at the same pace. I only managed to finish ahead of one foreign walker, and the other two Israelis, of course.

During the Maccabiah Games I shared a number of training sessions with Henry Laskau. He was a genuinely nice person, not at all condescending, and very friendly, even offering me some training hints. When I told him I was soon leaving for New York, he gave me his address and phone number and made me promise to call as soon as I got there. He would arrange for me to join the other walkers who trained with him on weekends. His offer made me determined not to discontinue my training even while I studied for my PhD.

End of a walking
campaign from Jerusalem
to Tel Aviv, 1966

Part II

America, America

■ Chapter Six | Breaking the American Record

As soon as our plane landed at Kennedy Airport, Shosh and I realized that the New York variety of English, particularly as spoken by the black airport redcaps, was unintelligible to us. We did know enough, however, not to take the numerous billboard advertisements for motels that we passed on our way into Manhattan to mean that a lot of the locals were named "Mordecai," affectionately known as "Motel." Those first few moments left a deep impression. As the taxi drove off the Triborough Bridge onto 125th Street, the cabby instructed us to close the windows and lock the doors. In response to our request for an explanation, he replied simply, "We're going through Harlem."

He left us in front of Woodbridge Hall, the Columbia University housing for married graduate students on the corner of West 115th Street and Riverside Drive, but he didn't drive away until we, and all our luggage, were inside the building with the gate closed behind us. This unusually responsible cabby was simply showing concern for our safety, but we didn't understand why. We got the keys from the super. Inside, a sheet of "safety instructions" was waiting on the desk. The advice it offered included: "After dark, it is wise to use 116th Street, which is safer than 115th Street. Moreover, the police have been instructed to patrol that area more closely." Friends and acquaintances also advised us to make sure we always had a small amount of cash on us and never to resist a mugger waving a knife or a gun. Fortunately, I never found myself in such a situation, maybe because I generally walked at a fast pace. Still, when friends explained they were reluctant to come to Israel because it was too dangerous, I would immediately quote the statistics indicating that the number of violent deaths per hundred thousand — whether from terrorism or run-of-the-mill crimes — was about ten times higher in the US than in

Israel. To this I added sarcastically that if they did decide to visit Israel, they should demand a refund from their insurance company for the time spent in that safer environment.

I was stunned by what I found at Columbia University. The first time I went to the library and was greeted by utter silence — none of the rustling or whispered conversations I was used to in the university libraries in Israel — I was convinced there was no one there but me. Then I saw that the desks in the reading room, arranged in the center of the half-circle of stacks, were occupied by hundreds of students intent on their books. They sat there reading and writing for hours, never getting up or moving around — just studying. After my first few lectures, I found myself doing the same. I had never studied so intensively or for so many hours before. Nonetheless, I usually preferred to work in our apartment.

When I arrived in New York I didn't know a soul except for Aunt Trude and Henry Laskau. I discovered five other Israeli doctoral candidates in the School of Business Administration who had all begun their degree anywhere from six months to a year earlier. I'd never met any of them before, except for Micha Peri, who had studied with me in Jerusalem. The other four were Yitzhak Adiges, who devised what is today known as the Adiges Theory of Management, and who, I learned, had come to Israel on the Kefalos together with me; Amos Sapir, whose father was the finance minister Pinchas Sapir; Ingele (Michael Angel), who was to become one of the managers of the Discount Investment Bank; and Michael Abramov, who put what he learned about the capital market to good use by staying in the States and making a fortune on the New York Stock Exchange.

I was lucky enough not to be financially strapped while studying for my doctorate. Columbia granted me a scholarship, renewed for each of the three years I was there, which covered tuition and rent and left enough for Shosh and me to live on modestly. And modestly is certainly how we lived; studies and sports left us no time for a social life. That didn't bother us in the least. Even before that, and afterwards as well, social life and recreation were a very low priority for us. Before we left for the States, Shosh had been offered a research fellowship at the Columbia University School of Medicine, a sort of postdoctorate, even though she'd already been doing research for about a year after receiving her degree. We were able to save practically all her salary.

The day after we arrived in New York, I went to check out the neighborhood and found that the park right outside our apartment offered the ideal place to train. All I had to do was cross Riverside Drive and I was in a very long narrow stretch of park that ran between the street and the Hudson River. That very morning I marked out a course from the tennis court near Grant's Tomb at 120th Street to 96th Street, about one and a quarter miles each way. Here, along the asphalt path surrounded by trees and grass, I walked three laps for a total of seven and a half miles. It was my first training session in nearly two weeks, the time it had taken us to get from Israel to America. We'd taken the cheapest route for any Israeli student traveling to New York in those days: a plane to Greece, a train through Yugoslavia to Luxembourg, and another flight over Iceland. It felt great to be training again that morning in the chilly air of early fall.

The same day I called Henry Laskau and said: "Hi! I'm here." I'd been told that when you call an American you barely know, he can be very congenial on the phone, but the conversation usually ends with "We'll have to get together sometime." We were warned not to take that literally, just like we don't expect people to tell us all their troubles when we greet them casually with "How are you?" The expression, we were told, was merely a polite way of brushing someone off. But Henry's response in no way followed this conventional pattern. He was exceptionally warm and friendly on the phone, and informed me that the walkers weren't getting together to train as usual that Sunday because the American Race-Walking Championships were being held in Atlantic City, and most of them would be taking part. Unfortunately, he wasn't planning to compete. The following week they would be training as usual. Since it was hard, he said, to get from Manhattan to the course in Kings Point by public transportation, he suggested I take the train to where he lived in Mineola on Long Island. He'd pick me up at the station and drive me to Kings Point. He explained what train I had to take and what time it left, and we arranged to meet.

That Saturday I was itching to enter the competition Henry had mentioned, but I didn't have any details except that it was being held the next morning somewhere in a place called Atlantic City. I didn't want to call him again in case he thought I was trying to wrangle a ride, on the order of "give him an inch and he'll take a mile." On Saturday night we went to visit Trude, whom I hadn't seen for several years. She couldn't find any item about the championship in the *New York Times*, but she told me how to get to Atlantic

City by bus and got the schedule for me. I could be there by about six in the morning. I didn't know exactly where or when the competition was being held and had no idea if they'd let me enter, but I decided to go anyway and find out when I got there.

I left the house in the small hours of the night and arrived at the bus station in Atlantic City on schedule. It was deserted. Luckily, I found a police station nearby and the cops located the item about the championship in a local paper and gave me directions to the starting point: an athletic club in the center of town. I found it. A few walkers in training suits were already there, warming up and stretching. I went over to one of them. I told him I was from abroad and asked if I could enter the competition. He said he didn't think there should be any problem, but I ought to check with Charlie Silcock. Charlie was the chairman of the race-walking committee of the Amateur Athletic Union, the AAU, a man who volunteered his time and energy to the sport. I introduced myself. Good-naturedly he said I was a welcome guest and I was free to enter this or any other competition I might like to participate in.

When he heard I would be in the States for quite a while until I finished at Columbia, he asked for my address and promised to send me notices of other race-walking events. And he did, too! He never asked if I was certified as an amateur, and certainly never asked to see the document I had brought with me from Israel. That was the last time I ever bothered to take it with me. Anyone involved in the sport took it for granted that all race walkers were amateurs; there was no money in it for anyone.

The locker room was full of athletes changing clothes and getting themselves ready for the competition. As I looked around I realized that, like Robinson Crusoe, I had taken the long way around, the arduous painful route of trial and error, to arrive at the same practical measures that other walkers adopted routinely. Like me, they rubbed Vaseline over any part of their body liable to become chafed, including between the toes, stuck tape over the particularly sensitive spots on the soles of their feet, and some on their nipples as well. They pulled their socks up carefully to make sure there were no wrinkles left that might cause blisters. After getting into their track shoes they checked several times over — taking a few steps back and forth — that the laces were pulled just right, not too loose and not too tight. When they were completely satisfied, after a number of trials and readjustments, they made a double knot so there'd be no chance of the laces coming undone during the race.

Most of them, dressed in training suits over gym shorts and shirts, left the locker room to warm up. They did that, too, exactly the same way I did: first a few exercises to stretch and relax the muscles, then a slow walk, and toward the end a combination of increasingly quick steps alternating with a slower pace. "Five minutes to start" was called. Every one of us, myself included, took off our training suits without undoing our shoes, left them in the locker room, took a few sips of water, and went to pee, trying to squeeze it out to the very last drop.

There are some eighty walkers crowded around the starting point. I don't know a single one. I take my place in one of the back rows; I don't want to get in the way. The signal is given and we all take off. I haven't the vaguest notion of how I compare to the other entrants. I keep up a fast pace requiring a certain effort and hope I can maintain it for the length of the course. After about a hundred yards, I estimate there are more or less thirty people up ahead and the gap between us is getting bigger, although from this stage on no one overtakes me. At around two miles, it seems like the gap between me and the group in front is pretty constant — at least it has been for the last mile. I'm in no distress, neither from my muscles nor my breathing.

My style also proves to be perfectly legal; the judges — out in large numbers — don't issue me any warnings. I try to pick up the pace a little so as to catch up with the walkers ahead of me, and don't find the effort overly taxing. In the third mile I pass five opponents. I keep up the same pace, every few hundred yards overtaking another competitor, one after the other. At the halfway mark we have to turn around and go back the way we came. Someone tells me I'm in fifteenth place, but I'm starting to tire. As I come up on the turning point, the ones in front are coming toward me. I count five. So despite the fatigue, I set myself the goal of overtaking them. That's easier said than done. It takes me a mile to pass the first one. Now I'm in fourteenth place. By now I'm very tired, but I keep up the effort. I see a tall athlete about twenty yards ahead progressing with long strides, moving his arms energetically, and taking deep breaths I can hear even at this distance.

Slowly I close the gap between us and try to use the same momentum to get past him. But he doesn't give up easily and won't let me get ahead. As soon as he sees me, he responds by picking up the pace. We move side by side, shoulder to shoulder, for a mile at least. There are a little over two miles left. I can feel the effort in my muscles, and especially in my lungs. Still, I try to go even faster. So does he. After about a hundred yards I sense him taking just a fraction off his pace. That means he's even more fatigued than I am and has conceded the contest. So as not to tempt him to make the extra effort and try to pass me again, I maintain the same speed even though I'm having trouble keeping it up. My rival falls behind and I can hear his breathing slow. I'm at the last mile. We have to make a sharp left turn. As I take it I catch sight of him out of the corner of my eye — not turning my head or giving him any other sign that I am weakening and still wary of him. He's about twenty yards behind. I'm totally drained, but I know I can't slow down. A short sprint and that twenty-yard advantage will be gone and he will have overtaken me.

I can feel the pressure in my arms and legs, as if the muscles and tendons are stretched to the limit, as well as in my chest, but I still keep up the same fast pace. I can see the finish line. I don't hear my rival's breathing any more. Ignoring the pain, I try to go even faster and catch the walker in front of me. There are ten yards between us when I cross the finish line. I'm in thirteenth place. I wind down to a slow walk and turn around. I finish some fifty yards ahead of that tall guy. A minute later, with both of us still panting, he comes over and shakes my hand. It's another minute before we're able to speak, and then we strike up a conversation. He is my age, a dentist from Long Island. That was the start of my friendship with John Shilling and his fellow race-walking brother George and their families, a friendship that has lasted to this day.

The championship was won by Ron Laird, a man who became a living legend. But at that time I had never met him before, knew nothing about him, and couldn't have dreamed that one day he would be a guest in my home in Israel. The only thing I cared about at that particular moment was getting a ride back to New York with one of the other athletes. I was offered a lift by a tall walker who finished ahead of me, John Kelly. During the ride back, and over the years since, during which we have maintained a close friendship, I learned the story of his life.

John, born in Ireland, looked and sounded like a typical Irishman. He was tall, angular, and sinewy. At an early age he left his father and stepmother behind and went to New Zealand where he worked as a logger. As only to be expected in societies where men are judged by their physical prowess, he took up boxing and did very well. His aim was to represent New Zealand as a heavyweight boxer at the Melbourne Olympics in 1956, but he didn't make the team. He went to Australia to watch the games and was intrigued by the hammer throw. He stayed on in Australia and took up that sport very seriously, hoping to make the next Olympics. His record was about sixty-five meters, an excellent result at that time, but not enough to take him to the Olympics in Rome in 1960.

Disappointed, he moved to America where he settled in New York and started training as a long-distance runner. His goal was now the marathon race at the Tokyo Olympics in 1964. He won one marathon in Berwick, Pennsylvania, but his greatest achievement was finishing thirty-third in the Boston Marathon. During a visit to his sister in Ireland, he told her proudly of his accomplishment. She misheard him and reproached him sharply: "You've been training so hard, devoting your whole life to sports, and you only come in third?" He didn't correct her mistake, but it made him realize that ordinary people don't understand athletes and what it takes for them to reach the top.

His race results didn't improve, and his dream of running the marathon in Tokyo was shattered. Discouraged, he decided to try his hand at race walking. He started in a 1-mile event, and when he saw he could do it, entered the American 40-kilometer championship scheduled for the following week. It was a scorching day, and most of the walkers dropped out or were forced to slow down considerably. This greenhorn, taking part in only his second race, had the determination and endurance to withstand the heat. To his amazement, and that of everyone else there, he came in second. That was reason enough for him to stick to this sport.

His third race-walking competition, a 100-mile event, took place two weeks later in England. Anyone who can do a hundred miles in less than twenty-four hours is considered a Centurion. The route was a circular ten-mile course. After fifty miles he was ready to give up, but spurred on by one of the officials, whose name he didn't know, he completed the sixth and seventh laps as well. At this point he stopped. The same official gave him an aspirin and convinced him to go on. To get him going for the last lap, they virtually had to shove him back on the road. He finished the one hundred miles a few seconds below the twenty-four hour barrier and was declared a Centurion. The muscles throughout his body were so constricted that he couldn't crawl into bed on his own. It took four men to pick him up and lay him out on the mattress.

With this achievement under his belt, he dreamed of being in the 50-kilometer walk at the Olympic Games in Mexico in 1968. This time his dream came true. Not only that, but one blazing hot summer in the early seventies he broke the record for walking unaided across Death Valley. This accomplishment earned him an appearance on the Johnny Carson Show and he became a celebrity.

The Sunday after the Atlantic City championship I met with Henry Laskau as we had arranged. John Shilling had already told him about my finishing in thirteenth place. He drove me to Kings Point. The group met at the Merchant Marine Academy where one of the walkers, Bill Omelchenko, was a professor in the foreign language department. There were about thirty athletes who met to train together, some showing up nearly every week and others only when they happened to be in the New York area. Henry introduced me. Except for him and John Shilling, I didn't know any of the others. It was only later that I found out that the finest American race walkers were there, Olympic athletes and the holders of US records and titles in the past, present and future.

Everyone started out together, but after some five or ten minutes each went their own way, walking at the pace most comfortable for him, with the faster ones usually pulling the slower ones along behind them. This created an atmosphere of competition without the tension of the real thing. Sometimes after five miles or so the group would reform when the leaders slowed down to wait for the others to catch up, and then the pattern would be repeated. We started in the empty parking lot by the entrance to the campus, took a quiet shaded road that passed the estates and wealthy homes of Kings Point, and then turned around and went back the same way, about five miles in each direction. Most of the walkers made two or three laps, and every now and then someone did four.

On really cold days in the winter, we trained inside the huge gym, walking back and forth across its flat, unmarked wooden floor. The quickest athletes took the route around the outer rim and the slower ones kept to an inner circle, shortening the distance by cutting across the corners. In this way, we moved around together, carried along by the group.

At the end of my first visit to Kings Point, when Henry was driving me back to the train station, I asked him if he thought I should join a local athletic club, and which he would recommend. He agreed that it was definitely a good idea, since most events also included a team competition, with medals for the winning teams. There was no question in his mind that the best organization was the New York Athletic Club, which sent a team of at least three walkers to each of the major competitions and championships, footing the bill for the travel expenses and entrance fees of their best athletes. Among the current members of the NYAC were five walkers in the Kings Point group: Ron Laird, who had already represented the United States in two Olympic Games and later added two more to his résumé; Ron Daniels; Ron Kulik; and Bruce MacDonald, who had also competed in three Olympics. However, Henry noted, "they won't take you," not because I wasn't good enough, but because I was Jewish. The club was closed to black or Jewish athletes of any kind. In order to guard against accusations of discrimination, they admitted a token Jew whom they could take out and show off in public in the event any such charges were voiced.

During the winter months, when I trained in the Columbia University gym underneath the School of Business Administration, I became friendly with a number of athletes using the same facilities. One of them was the weightlifter Gary Lillien, a classmate, and I discovered that his grandfather Efraim was the celebrated graphic artist who had sketched and painted the landscapes of the Holy Land in the early part of the century. Another was Don Spiro, studying for his doctorate in physics, who won the world title in the skiff rowing championship in Bled, Yugoslavia, in 1965. He was the token Jewish member of the NYAC at that time.

In light of this situation, Henry explained that the only institution I could consider was the New York Pioneer Club. In days gone by, most of the race walkers had belonged to this club, but those who were good enough and met the other criteria of the NYAC had gone over to that organization to enjoy the expense allowance it offered. In 1968, Ron Laird told me that in only a few years at the NYAC, he had saved close to twenty thousand dollars out of his travel allotment by staying with friends instead of in hotels. With this incentive, only the Jewish walkers remained in the New York Pioneer Club: the two Shilling brothers and Bill Omelchenko. Naturally, I joined too. Two years later, when I received my doctorate, we became a team of professionals, although we remained genuine amateur athletes; all the race walkers in the club had PhDs.

The two athletics coaches, Joe Yancey and Ed Levy, both black, were very friendly, encouraged us, and signed us up for the race-walking competitions at track and field events, but they only coached the other athletes and left the walkers to fend for themselves. As a result of their efforts, there were quite a few excellent athletes in the club, people such as Vincent Mathew from Jamaica who ran 400 meters in 44.0 seconds in the trials for the Mexico Olympics, and Don Carlos who was famed not only for winning the Olympic silver medal in the 200-meter race, but also, and especially, for raising a defiant black-gloved fist as he stood on the podium at the medals ceremony.

From mid-September to spring 1965, I took part in about a dozen events. Most of the winter competitions were indoor short distance races of one or two miles. The first few took place in the armories scattered throughout Manhattan, most of which had a flat track a tenth or eleventh of a mile long. After that I entered two events in Boston, one at the YMCA and the other in the old stadium at Boston Garden. In both cases the track sloped at the curves, so that the walker on the outer track was higher than those to his left. It's never a good idea to try to pass an opponent on a turn, because it means you have to walk a good number of extra feet. It adds much less distance to pass on a straight stretch. That's even truer when the track slopes. If you attempt to pass on a curve, you not only add distance, you also have to "scale" to the height of the right lane, and the extra effort required for the climb is not compensated for by the lesser effort needed for the subsequent "descent." That's why most of the attempts to pass take place on the straight sections of the track, with the somewhat slower athletes fighting hard not to let their opponents get ahead of them there, knowing there is less chance they will try to do so on the turns.

On the other hand, the faster competitors put all they have into the effort to overtake before the end of the straight. If they can't, they usually stay on the heels of the opponent in the inner lane during the turn so as not to waste undue energy in the attempt to pass on that part of the track. On occasion, when the faster walker does decide to pass on a turn, the slower one will pick up his pace, forcing his rival to remain in the longer lane, thus at the same time causing him to exert more effort and preventing him from passing.

I improved from one event to the next, building up a faster basic speed, but it was still way below that of some of my opponents. Shorter distances are easier in terms of endurance, but put greater pressure on the cardiovascular system. Within a hundred yards from the starting line, the muscles and lungs are working at full capacity, so that an athlete's top speed is determined by the rate at which he can take in and utilize oxygen. The last quarter mile at a fast walk is the hardest. I could feel the pressure in my chest and in every vein, and I would have to fight to keep going by psyching myself into ignoring the pain of insufficient oxygen and pushing myself despite the sense of heaviness in my limbs.

In indoor events there is an added obstacle to overcome. In the dry, cold air, especially when it reeks of cigarette smoke, your throat feels like it's being slit by a knife, so that the pain you have to overcome in the course of the competition is even sharper. For some reason, when it's over and your breathing becomes regular again, you don't feel that stinging in your throat anymore; it vanishes without leaving a trace.

After the series of armory events, it was the turn of the race-walking competitions at the track and field meets at the famous Madison Square Garden. I had heard its name before mainly in connection with the great boxing matches held there. It had a ?-mile-long track with sloping turns. One of these events was organized by the NYAC in honor of its centennial and included dozens of competitions to which outstanding athletes from all over the world had been invited. One competition in particular, other than my own, captured my interest: the 3-mile race. It was dedicated to Paavo Nurmi, who had broken the indoor world record for that distance forty years earlier.

Except for me, there had never been an athlete in my family, distant relatives included, and no one showed any interest in sports. My mother even went beyond a lack of interest, and throughout the decades of my athletic career constantly rebuked me for my involvement in sports and in race walking in particular. She claimed I was killing myself, and that it was ludicrous for anyone to walk or run in the twentieth century, the era of the motor vehicle.

She knew nothing about any athlete or record holder, with one exception: Paavo Nurmi, the renowned flying Finn who won more Olympic medals than any other person in history. He became a living legend, and after his death a statue was erected in his honor at the entrance to the Olympic Stadium in Helsinki. He was the greatest athlete who ever lived, and still holds that distinction. Naturally, he was a hero for me too. And now, they had dedicated this race to him and he himself had been invited to attend. He was to make an exhibition run of four laps before the start of the race that bore his name. Everyone there, the spectators as well as the hundreds of athletes warming up in the stadium, gave him a standing ovation that continued for the entire time he was on the track. Of course, no one timed him.

The invitation was an opportunity for the organizers to pay homage to this extraordinary athlete. Since the 1-mile walk was already over, I decided to take a stab at getting his autograph. After his run, I went back to the locker room where he had been taken and asked him to sign the special program printed in his honor. He consented, but still I was in for a great disappointment. As this venerated luminary, the symbol of physical prowess, signed his name, his hand shook — not from emotion, but apparently because he suffered from Parkinson's Disease. Obviously, no mortal is exempt from old age and the ravages it brings with it, not even Nurmi. He died about six months later, but his legacy lives on. When I was in Helsinki five years later to watch the European Track and Field Championships, I was thrilled to see his statue standing at the entrance to the stadium.

At one of our training sessions at Kings Point I struck up a conversation with Elliott Denman. He was a year older than me, and although I was faster both in training and in competitions, that was only the result of his lack of training. It turned out that at the age of twenty-one he had represented the United States in the 50-kilometer walk at the Melbourne Olympics in 1956, and in 1961 had won the American title for both one mile and 50 kilometers in the space of a single week. In other words, he had both speed and stamina. I also learned that he had won the 3000-meter race walking gold medal at the Maccabiah Games in 1961 — the year that Henry Laskau was in retirement and didn't attend.

Elliott was a sports writer for the popular New Jersey paper *The Asbury Park Evening News*, and often reported on races and race-walking competitions. His articles were invariably an interesting, unconventional read, and it was obvious he lived and breathed his subject. In addition to his journalistic work, he volunteered a lot of his time to arranging and organizing races and race-walking events and promoting the Shore Athletic Club, which he headed. He was extremely friendly and gave the impression that warm-heartedness and eagerness to help other athletes and to devote his time to promoting sports came naturally to him. In the course of the autumn and winter, he organized several 10-mile race-walking competitions along the wooden boardwalks of Atlantic City and Asbury Park.

After the closing ceremony of one of those events, he told me he had been stationed in England as a soldier and had taken part in a walking competition from London to Brighton, a distance of fifty-two and a half miles. His tales of that event, along with the announcement that, inspired by the words of President Kennedy, he was planning to organize a 50-mile race, fired me with the incentive to try to train for long distances.

As a result, I stepped up my training, going out every single day without fail. Each morning I walked a fast ten miles, and on Saturdays between twenty and thirty miles. Even when there was a one-mile event in the evening, I didn't skip the morning practice; I'd just take it a little slower. I knew that the combination of the short and long distances could only increase my stamina and speed in the long run. On Sundays I invariably walked at a fast pace, whether I was training at Kings Point or taking part in some competition. This new regimen produced results: both my speed and my endurance improved. I also found an easier way to get to Kings Point when I discovered that one of the members of the group, Noah Gurock, was a journalism student at Columbia, so most Sundays I got a ride back and forth with him.

Since Noah didn't compete, I generally rode to competitions with John Kelly. He'd arrange to pick me up either at 168th Street or Van Cortland Park, both stops on the subway line near my house, and that way I only had to take one train and he didn't have to go out of his way. Shosh came along to most of the events, and even to some of the training sessions at Kings Point, and joined the other wives who had come to watch their husbands. But she always used the travel time, and sometimes the competition time as well, to look through the studies in her field that appeared in *Current Contents*.

As it got colder and windier — with nothing separating our house and Riverside Drive from the Hudson River, the winds there were fierce — I began to take more frequent advantage of the one-tenth of a mile track in the Columbia gym. It was very convenient, since I could use it when I had free hours between lectures and I was able to work out for quite a while without having to contend with the inhospitable weather. Nevertheless, every now and then I still went out to do long-distance training in the open air.

On one such occasion I arranged to train together with John Kelly, lapping Yankee Stadium from outside for a total of thirty-one miles. It was a very harsh winter day. A broad path had been cleared along the sidewalk, but the snow was piled up on both sides. The temperature was about 14 degrees Fahrenheit, but with the wind blowing at around forty miles an hour, it felt more like -10. We dressed appropriately for this Siberian weather. As I suffer from the cold, I had layered on two pairs of socks, two pairs of sweatpants, a T-shirt, a long-sleeved shirt, a sweatshirt, and a windbreaker, all topped off with two ski caps, a warm scarf around my neck and over my mouth, and two pairs of gloves. The only thing left uncovered were my eyeglasses. So dressed more for the Arctic than for athletics, we circled the stadium for five and a half hours. In certain sections of each lap we also had to contend with a strong headwind. We must have looked like polar bears, although we were moving pretty quickly.

Toward the end of the session, the wind died down a bit. All of a sudden we saw a group of tall, brawny guys heading our way. They'd been hanging around for a while and had seen us go by several times. We must have made a very odd sight, so they decided to strut their stuff and show us who was boss around there. Snickering, they spread out across the sidewalk and linked arms, blocking our path. Without exchanging a word, John and I reacted instinctively in perfect harmony. We increased our speed to about nine miles an hour, pulled in closer to each other, made a fist, and tensed our muscles, still walking in the same style with our arms moving back and forth. They were big and strong and outnumbered us, but we weren't intimidated. We kept going straight ahead, on a collision course with these local lads.

We weren't overly concerned, convinced that at this speed, with our muscles tensed and hands in a fist, nothing could happen to us. It was a classic example of heightened aggression in response to a threat, a reaction familiar to athletes who get an adrenaline rush to the brain at the height of exertion. The boys didn't know who they were messing with. At the very last second they realized we weren't going to back off. Maybe they loosened their grip on each other, but their arms remained linked. We plowed into them at full speed. Bruised by the impact, they toppled into one another, while we went straight on, unhurt, as if we had only pushed aside a few young branches in our way. We kept going as if nothing had happened, and never looked back. They seemed to have learned their lesson; the next time around they were nowhere in sight.

In early March there was a local 50-kilometer event at Kings Point. I'd never competed at such a long distance before. I started out around the same speed as I used for a ten-mile walk, and was feeling quite comfortable. But my lack of experience took its toll. During the competition I guzzled large quantities of orange juice and pineapple juice, even though it wasn't really hot. It was the profuse perspiration and prolonged effort that were making me so thirsty. After about twenty miles I began to fade, but more juice supplied the sugars my body needed and I perked up. A little while later I started feeling a certain discomfort in my belly. I downed a banana, thinking that would solve the problem, but I was deluding myself. I vomited. Still, I kept going, unwilling to give up. I threw up twice more, and saw other competitors doing the same. I slowed my pace and kept walking until I crossed the finish line.

Henry Laskau and Elliott Denman advised me to try out different types of drinks until I found which one my stomach could best tolerate under exertion. Bruce MacDonald, who finished behind me, suggested I choose something that was readily available everywhere and that I drink it during training until my body was used to it. After considerable trial and error, experimenting in a number of competitions, I finally settled on Coca-Cola.

The next Four-Day March was scheduled for April 1966. It would be my tenth straight year, and I didn't want to miss it. I was even willing to bear the substantial expense so as not to blight my record. I sent off a letter from New York to make sure I had registered in time. Since I'd decided to make this trip to Israel, I wanted to take advantage of it to organize something special, and was able to arrange it by corresponding with the editor of the army magazine *Bamachane*: I would walk from Jerusalem to Tel Aviv before the Four-Day March.

When I landed in Israel — having come by the cheapest route, over Iceland again — a very pleasant surprise was awaiting me. Most of the papers carried an item, apparently put out by the march press office, announcing that "the engineer from Jerusalem" was making a special trip from the United States to take part in the Four-Day March. I was very glad of the publicity. I arranged the logistics for my one-man operation with the people from *Bamachane*. They were to pick me up at midnight from my mother's house in

Ramat Chen. At one a.m., as I waited there impatiently, a jeep showed up with three soldiers: the driver, an army reporter, and an army photographer. By around three a.m. we had reached Camp Schneller in Jerusalem. I wanted to get started as early as possible to avoid walking in the hot sun for any longer than necessary. But I was held up by military bureaucracy.

While I was waiting, I explained to the reporter that during the walk I needed to be given the water and juice I had brought with me, and that someone should hand me a paper cupful every two or three miles when I asked for it. I went on to explain that since it was still chilly, I would start out in a sweat suit that I would later peel off, and that I needed someone to take it from me. Finally, I asked to be handed my cap when the sun came out. I arranged for them to either stay behind me or park a mile or two ahead and wait for me to reach them so they'd always be close by to give me whatever I asked for.

I finally take off just before five a.m., maintaining the pace I trained at and had walked with John Kelly. It's the first time I'll be attempting such a long distance, close to forty miles, but I hope my training has put me in good enough shape to do it without too much difficulty. The downhill stretch from Jerusalem to Motza gives me time to warm up. I'm very familiar with the climb to the Castel and the subsequent descent from when I used to train in Jerusalem. The ascent is hard and the decline is too steep to really walk, but they don't pose too much of a problem. Then comes the climb through Abu Gosh to Neve Ilan and the downhill slope through Sha'ar Ha-Gai, which I also take pretty easily. At the gas station below Sha'ar Ha-Gai the road makes a left to the Har-Tuv junction and then goes straight through Eshtaol and Harel.

So far so good. I'm maintaining a speed of close to six miles an hour and the soldiers in the jeep are doing just as I asked. At the Nachshon junction the reporter hands me my prescription sunglasses and I give him my regular glasses in exchange. I keep walking in the direction of Ramle. After the long ascent, with the hills of ancient Gezer on my right, I want another drink. It's getting hot. For some reason, the jeep is nowhere to be seen. It's somewhere behind me. I keep going. I don't want to stop and wait, nor do I want to leave the road in search of water; it would waste time. I'd like to record the fastest time possible. I get to Ramle, but the jeep is still not there.

I'm furious with the reporter and the photographer. They don't seem to understand that it's their job to keep up with me and keep me supplied with liquids, and that they can't shirk this duty even if there's something wrong with the jeep. One or both of them should have taken the water bottle and thumbed a ride — anything to do the job they've been given, to look out for me. Apparently, they considered it their duty to look out for the jeep and the driver. It occurs to me that their function in the army has accustomed them to the luxury of a private vehicle wherever they go. I'm dying of thirst, but I don't want to lose time, so I keep going. The jeep shows up somewhere between Sarafend and Beit Dagan. Already on the verge of dehydration, I gulp down as much as I can. The reporter apologizes: the car broke down and it took a long time to fix it. I'm incensed, but I keep my mouth shut.

An ambulance passes me near Azor, honking out a beat. Suddenly the mustachioed face of a man called Nachtche appears in the window. He's a member of Kibbutz Nachshon and a veteran of the Four-Day Marches. He shouts out at me: "Shaul, I heard you'd come from the States for the march, but what are you doing out here?" Without stopping, I explain what it's all about and part from him with: "See you at the march."

By now it's very hot, but from here on I'm getting as much water as I need. A little while longer and I'm in Tel Aviv. "I made it!" I congratulate myself. Forty miles in 6:14. I get in the jeep. I'm exhausted. Not only did this long walk take a lot out of me, but I've also been awake all night. I can feel every muscle in my body. The salty sweat drying on my skin is very unpleasant. "I did my bit," I think. "Now they can take me home." But there's another surprise in store for me. The reporter and the photographer want the driver to take them to Tel Aviv first, and then drive me to my mother's. I insist they take me first, especially since Ramat Chen is closer. They put up an argument but finally give in. They let me off outside my mother's house.

After I shower, I realize I left my glasses with the reporter and he didn't put them in my bag. I call and he confirms that he still has them. I don't harbor the slightest illusion that he'll take the trouble to bring them to me, and say right off the bat that I'll come and get them. I find his house and ring the bell. His father answers. I explain why I've come. He raises a finger to his lips and whispers: "Shh…don't wake him up, he's very tired. He worked all night." Laughing to myself, I think, "If he's tired, what am I supposed to be?" I get my glasses and thank him without another word.

As expected, the next issue of *Bamachane* contained a long illustrated article about my one-man exhibition walk. It was very professionally written and highly complimentary.

A couple of days later I took part in the annual march. I finished first on each of the four days. This time I didn't have to hurry to work in Jerusalem when I was through, so on the first three days, when the marchers began and ended at Hulda, I had a chance to show off what I could do. As soon as I had completed the route for the day, I turned around and did it all over again in the opposite direction. All the people I passed going the other way greeted me by name; by now everyone knew me, although I knew only a few of them. As usual, the march was covered by the press and a great deal of space was devoted to me, so I earned a lot of publicity. At the end of the march I was awarded the special medal for ten straight years of participation. In retrospect, doing fifty miles for each of three days and twenty-five more on the fourth for the climb to Jerusalem, a total of 175 miles, was very good training.

When it was over, I went back to New York. The US Eastern Regional championship for the 50-mile walk took place in mid-April in Point Pleasant, New Jersey, on the Atlantic coast. Elliott Denman was in charge of organization. It was held on the ¼-mile track of the local high school, an all-weather track, which means it was made of a semi-rigid material, a compound of rubber and asphalt, rather than cinders. This sort of surface doesn't require constant upkeep and you only have to paint the lane lines in once. It can be used even in the rain, since it isn't affected by water; and the athletes' feet don't make depressions or holes in it, so it doesn't need to be hosed down and the lines repainted every few days, and it doesn't have to be renewed by replacing or adding crushed cinders every couple of years. Most importantly, when you come off the track you don't look like a chimney sweep with your body and clothes covered in black dust, as you do on a cinder track. In the long run, it comes out much cheaper, so it should be the obvious choice whenever a track is being laid out.

On Saturday, Shosh and I took the bus to Point Pleasant and got a room in a motel near the site of the event. Our luggage included Coca-Cola, glucose, plastic cups, a bucket, and large sponges. The competition was scheduled to begin the next day at six a.m. We were at the track more than half an hour before start time. Elliott Denman showed up with the keys, opened the gates and locker rooms, and set up the apparatus for registration and officiating. There were about thirty entrants, most of whom arrived with a whole support team. Elliott joined the competitors and his wife and three daughters took over the job of organization, aided by a large staff of volunteers to serve as officials: judges, time-keepers, and lap counters.

Right after the signal was given, a cluster of around eight walkers took the lead, and I was in there among them. I was feeling very good and the pace was comfortable, only a little bit faster than my speed on the march. The track was perfectly flat — no bumps to hit into, no sand to slip on, no holes to look out for — so it didn't slow us down. Above all, I could get a drink whenever I liked. The lap before I wanted one I'd signal to Shosh and the next time I came around she'd be holding a cup out to me. I taught her not to fill the cup more than half-full, to stand to my right at the edge of the track, and to hold the cup at the top with two fingers, her arm out at right angles perpendicular to the direction I was going in and more or less at my chest height. In this position, I could grab it as I passed by without having to twist my body or make any unnecessary movements with my hand. I snatched the cup, brought it up to my mouth, and poured the contents in. Then I threw it away, or rather let it fall virtually without the need to exert any force. Of course poor Shosh would have to pick it up, but this way I wasn't wasting energy. When I wanted glucose, she dissolved it in the Coke so it didn't leave any residue at the bottom.

When we had gone around ten miles, I found myself at the head of the pack together with Paul Schell. Paul, a member of the North Medford Club from Boston, was a nice, sociable guy I knew from previous competitions. He had also been stationed in England as a soldier, and had taken advantage of the opportunity to enter the London to Brighton event. I knew that, but I also knew that less than a week before I had walked fifty miles a day for three straight days without any particular difficulty. Admittedly, the march wasn't a competitive event and I hadn't maintained a competitive pace, but the knowledge that I had done it encouraged me to try for first place and gave me confidence. Paul attempted to pass me on the right several times by picking up his speed, but I responded each time by stepping on the gas myself. He couldn't do it. He stayed with me for another ten miles or so and then started to ease off. I was in the lead, having left all the others behind.

At the twenty-five mile mark, I was half a lap in front of the walker in second place, my friend John Kelly. We had to do two hundred laps. After the first hundred, the countdown begins. You stop counting how many laps you've done — one hundred one, one hundred two, etc. — and start counting how many you have left — ninety-nine, ninety-eight, and so on. It keeps you aware that the remaining distance is getting shorter and pumps up any athlete, myself included. The officials operate differently, however. As the walker passes the recording point, he's told his total time so far. His individual lap-counter — each of whom is responsible for several competitors — records his time and reads out how many laps he has completed. Thus the total distance a walker has completed can be measured precisely: there should be more or less two and a half minutes between the recorded times of any two successive laps.

Laymen often remark that such a long distance inside a stadium must make the athlete dizzy and be desperately boring. The opposite is true. At all times you can see every one of your opponents and are constantly aware of everything going on. The slower competitors are challenged to pick up their pace when a faster athlete is trying to pass, and the faster ones are driven to increase their speed in order to overtake the slower walkers ahead of them. This incentive keeps up lap after lap for the whole race. You know exactly how fast you are going and can adjust your speed to suit your strategy. You also know the precise distance you have already gone and what condition your opponents are in.

After twenty-five miles, each time I walked the straight leg down one side of the track, I looked across to the other side, without turning my head, to see where John Kelly was at that moment. On the next lap, when I got to the same point again, I checked his position once more: was the gap between us bigger or smaller. I was pleased to see that gap growing a few yards longer with each lap. I did the same with all the other walkers who gave me cause for concern. At the thirty-mile mark, I was leading by more than a full lap, with several of the others already a number of laps behind me.

At some point I came up on Paul Schell again; by now he was three laps behind. He kept up with me again, taking the lane to my right. I told him he shouldn't waste his energy walking in the longer lane, but his reply was: "It doesn't matter. It's only a few inches more." I didn't want to argue with him, but I was amazed that an educated person like him didn't realize that by using lane 2 instead of lane 1 he was doing 6.28 yards more each lap, which adds up to 1257 extra yards in a two-hundred-lap event. For my part, I was trying to save myself as much distance as possible: keeping as close to the innermost edge of the lane as I could, especially on the curves.

By forty miles I was two whole laps ahead of John Kelly, with all the others somewhere behind. A few had already used up all their strength and had dropped out. By now I was feeling very tired, my muscles ached, and I had very painful blisters on the soles of my feet. I wanted to win, but I couldn't keep up the pace I had maintained thus far. I asked Shosh for a cup of Coke with an extra-large dose of glucose. That perked me up for a few minutes, but afterwards I felt even more drained. Taking more glucose apparently wasn't the trick. It lowered my blood sugar level. I was also feeling immense pressure in my bladder and wanted desperately to relieve myself, but I didn't stop. If I took the time to go to the bathroom, I'd lose my whole advantage. I kept going.

My mind was constantly calculating how much faster John Kelly would have to go per lap in order to catch up with me. Even though I had slowed down, the gap between us was still growing. Nevertheless, I kept doing the mathematical calculations to make sure he had no chance of overtaking me. I only stopped calculating when there were just ten laps to go. John was about three laps behind. In order to catch me, he'd have to sprint and I'd have to slow down drastically. But I couldn't lay my fears to rest, so I tried to draw on all the strength I had left. I picked up my speed. On the last lap I used up the last ounce of energy I had in me. I knew it was over, that I didn't have to pace myself any more, that in a little over two minutes it would all be behind me. I don't know where I found the strength to do it, but, incredibly, I walked the last lap in two minutes two seconds. I crossed the thin rope stretched across the finish line and stopped short. I had come in first. John Kelly still had four more laps to go.

I was in a state of prostration. I could barely move, but I didn't feel the pressure in my bladder anymore. I leaned on two men, one on each side, and very slowly they got me back to the locker room. My clothes were soaking wet and brown, saturated with a mixture of sweat and the sticky Coca-Cola that had spilled on me during the race. I couldn't even take off my shirt and shoes by myself. They helped me get undressed and totter to the showers. The minute I turned on the faucet and the water hit me, I let out a shriek of pain.

Several of the blisters on my feet had burst, and the water on the raw flesh stung sharply. I managed to get a grip on myself despite the agonizing blisters and the excruciating pain of the water wherever my shirt or pants had chafed the skin raw.

After ten minutes or so under the shower had cleansed me of the salty perspiration all over my body, I began to feel a bit less miserable. Emotionally, I was high — I had won — but physically I was in sad shape. Shosh sent my bag of clean clothes into the locker room. Ten minutes more and I had gotten myself dressed and could come back out. As I was leaving, John Kelly came in. He had finished second. He was more or less in the same shape I had been in a little while earlier, maybe just a little better. I shook his hand. He said I had "the strength of a bulldog," and I answered, "You have the strength of a bull." As I emerged from the locker room I saw Elliott, who had finished third. Fourth place went to Bruce MacDonald. Paul Schell didn't finish the race; he had to drop out.

About an hour and a half later, Elliott arranged a modest ceremony right there on the track. I had finished in 8:35:35. Not only had I won the race, but I had set a new American record, breaking the oldest standing record on the books, set in 1878. The time-keepers and judges signed the record form and I was told it would be sent to the AAU for confirmation. Less than a month later I received in the mail the official certificate confirming the new American record I had set. John Kelly's time of 8:47 was also faster than the record set eighty-eight years before by G. B. Gillie, so he set the new record for an American citizen. We winners of the first three places were awarded great big trophies, but all the other competitors also got trophies, albeit smaller ones.

Bruce MacDonald, who had come alone by car, was planning to drive back home to Long Island after the ceremony and agreed to take John, Shosh and me back with him as far as New York City. After a two-hour drive, he dropped us about a hundred feet from a subway station in Queens. Both John and I were so sore all over that we couldn't even carry our own bags; we had to give them to Shosh. So like a comedy act, the two glorious record holders hobbled very slowly to the entrance to the station, looking more like invalids or the war wounded. We were ashamed to let anyone see us with the trophies, in case they thought it took no more than "cripples" like us to win championships and break records, so we asked Shosh to hide them in our bags.

With great effort, we managed to walk those hundred feet in several

minutes, but it took even greater effort and a longer time to reach the plat-
form. We left the Broadway train at 116th Street and said good-bye to John.
He went on to 242nd Street near his home, forced to carry his own bag, while I
staggered slowly beside Shosh from Broadway to our house on Riverside
Drive. After we'd taken care of the blisters, Shosh congratulated me on what
she believed to be the last major achievement of my athletic career, considering that I was already thirty years old. I agreed. I didn't for a second imagine
that this was only the first step on the road to fame and glory.

As a rule, it took me five minutes to get from our house to one of the
lecture halls at the university or to my small office on the third floor of the
Graduate School of Business, Uris Hall. Actually, it was a tiny cubicle with a
desk and chair separated by high partitions from identical cubicles reserved
for other doctoral candidates. On the day after the 50-mile championship, I
estimated it shouldn't take me more than half an hour to get there. Every
single muscle ached. I never knew there were so many muscles in my body,
and it never occurred to me that I would be using all of them for race walking.
I could understand that my back and shoulders hurt; that came from moving
my arms back and forth. But I couldn't comprehend why each finger was so
painful, and why moving one even a little bit added to the pain emanating
from other parts of my body.

I couldn't even dress myself; Shosh had to help me. The worst part was
putting on my jacket. I stretched my arms out very slowly behind me and
Shosh managed somehow to insert them into the sleeves and then pull it up
over my shoulders inch by inch. The thirty minutes I'd allotted myself to get
to class were not enough at the rate I was shuffling. I was five minutes late. I
needed help taking my jacket off. A classmate tugged at it gently while I stood
in place with my arms behind me. Little by little the pain subsided during the
next few days and within a week it was gone completely.

I received hundreds of congratulations on my triumph. The *New York
Times* of the following day contained a short item reporting that I had set a
new American record and broken the oldest one on the books. With the
added spice of breaking such a long-standing record, my achievement gained
widespread notice. The Columbia University student paper published a long
article about me. On its own initiative, and without my having any contact
whatsoever with the editors, the Israeli student paper reproduced the *New
York Times* item on its front page under the headline: "Israeli Breaks

American Race-Walking Record," alongside a cartoon of a bent old man walking from 1878 to 1966.

Since the news was also sent out over the wire by Reuters, it appeared in most of the papers in the States and throughout the world, including Israel. Elliott Denman wrote a very nice long piece about the championship — the way only someone who had himself experienced the effort could describe it — and it appeared in his paper and a few others in New Jersey, as well as in the sports magazine *Ohio Race Walker*. The *New York Times* sent a reporter and photographer to interview me and take pictures of me training in the Columbia gym and on the streets near the university. The next day a long illustrated article appeared in the paper. The following week *Sports Illustrated* had my picture and a short item in its column of special athletic achievements. They also sent me an inscribed silver-plated bowl as a gesture of appreciation.

Pat Summerall, the celebrated football player, who was then a famous sportscaster, called and invited me for a live television interview. I couldn't accept because I had a lecture at the time his program was on, and I didn't then understand how vital public relations could be. I regret that decision today, but it didn't concern me in the least at the time. As a result of the championship and other achievements, in autumn 1966 the New York Metropolitan AAU voted me the year's outstanding athlete in race walking. The prize — a plaque — was presented at a special dinner.

■ Chapter Seven | The AAU 50-Kilometer Championship

Within a few days after the 50-mile championship, I was back to my usual training routine. I checked which exercises particularly strained the sore muscles, and once the pain had faded I worked on them intensively. I now decided to try to ready myself for the AAU 50-kilometer championship scheduled for the coming summer in Chicago.

Starting in early May, I had quite a few race-walking competitions to choose from. In the metropolitan New York area alone, including Long Island, New Jersey, and Connecticut, evening track and field meets were held every week, and invariably included one- or two-mile race-walking events. On the weekends there were various races of between ten and twenty miles and occasionally, a marathon which generally also contained a walking category. From time to time events devoted solely to race walking were also organized. Thus, during the work week I was able to enjoy both daily training walks of ten to twelve and a half miles each morning and at least three short-distance competitions in the evenings. For me — as for most of the athletes taking part — these meets served as fast-paced training sessions in a competitive spirit.

For routine training, I much preferred long-distance walks at a comfortable pace to high-speed exercises that put extreme pressure on the body and are singularly unpleasant. Going slower, I could talk — if need be — and think. I would go over the lectures and see what I remembered or try to solve mathematical or statistical problems in operations research in my head, preparing for the exams.

I could concentrate on a problem, consider it, and decide on the approach to a solution, define variables and remember them, and then construct a mathematical model and manipulate it until I came up with a solution.

Without pencil and paper, I became accustomed to doing differentiations of equations to find the optimum conditions, holding parts of an equation in my memory until I needed to substitute them for variables in other equations, and calculating the results. If anything distracted me while I was immersed in a problem as I walked, and that tended to happen periodically, I'd have to go back to the beginning and start all over again. As a matter of course, I also used these training sessions to plan my day and consider and analyze any decisions I had to make. Over the years, these morning walks became a tool for organizing my thoughts, and they remain so today. That's probably why I enjoy training and have never quit.

But to win a race you also need speed. You get it both by speed training — which invariably produces results — and by endurance training at very long distances. When I was working on speed, I couldn't lose myself in thought, but had to concentrate on the effort and the pace, just like in competitions. As for long-distance training, it started out like an ordinary walk, but as the distance and the physical effort increased, my brain began to feel fatigued and my thinking became less cogent. By the end I could only concentrate on the actual physical exertion. So it was hard to convince myself to do the speed training I needed, and somewhat easier to find the incentive for long-distance walks. Consequently, I was very pleased when I had a competition or an opportunity to pit myself against other athletes, and therefore had to push myself to go faster.

The short races in the evening during the week supplied the necessary quota of speed training. Since they came as a supplement to my morning practice on the same day, they also helped to improve my endurance and shorten the time my body required to recover from exertion. Every weekend I tried to compete at least once at a distance of 10 kilometers or more and on the other day go out for long-distance training, which meant no less than fifty kilometers and sometimes even as much as fifty miles.

Although I was training for the 50-kilometer championship, I took my lead from the training program of the New Zealander Peter Snell, an 800-meter runner. His famed coach, Arthur Lidiard, made him do marathon training, so that during the immense exertion of running at top speed he would have an edge over his opponents in terms of endurance. When Snell was already the celebrated New Zealand titleholder, he was, as he stated, "humiliated" at his first marathon by coming in last, well behind the other runners. Nevertheless, this training gave him an advantage over his rivals in his event, and he won the gold medal for 800 meters at the Rome Olympics. So it was obvious to me that if I wanted to do well at 50 kilometers, I would have to be able to walk much further than that.

In early May 1966 John Kelly drove Shosh and me to the American 20-kilometer championship in the town of McKeesport, near Pittsburgh. After the pleasantly cool weather of New York in early spring, it was the first really hot day I would be competing on in a long time. The heat played a very conspicuous role in the race. Those who had come from the West Coast, where it was always hot, recorded their customary times, while those from the East Coast — whose bodies had not yet adjusted to the heat — performed below par. I was no exception. I came expecting to do well and achieved only average results, finishing in twelfth place.

To cheer ourselves up, the three of us, together with John Shilling who had driven over with his wife Wynne, decided to tour the Pennsylvania Dutch country on our way back to New York, visiting the Amish towns. The Amish resemble the Jewish Hassidim not only in their attire and long beards, but also in their adherence to the customs of past centuries. I would imagine that if a Hassid ran into an Amish gentleman, he would be likely to greet him in Yiddish, and he would probably even be understood, considering that both their languages are German-based.

Mid-May took us to Toronto where I could "kill two birds with one stone": enter the Canadian 50-kilometer championship and visit my cousins and grandmother at the same time. The competition was held in northern Toronto on a 1¼-mile course on the York University campus. My cousin Peti agreed to help keep me supplied with drinks during the race. The weather was good; the start of Indian summer. There were about fifty walkers, but I very soon found myself among the leaders. Unfortunately, however, after twenty-two miles I couldn't hold it in any longer and had to go to the bathroom. Still, I came in second after Alex Oakley. Oakley was an old warhorse who had already competed in three Olympics. In 1964 in Tokyo, he finished seventh in the 50-kilometer walk and eleventh in the 20-kilometer event.

I was very pleased with my accomplishment. Since medals and trophies are generally awarded in both the US and Canada, but no certificates, I asked the organizers for some sort of official document confirming my result, and they wrote one out for me. To make it clear that I could do better than the actual time I had recorded, they noted that I was forced to make a "rest stop" of three and a half minutes in the course of the race — a pit stop in motor racing terms — due to "the call of nature."

In early June 1966 I went to Chicago for the American 50-kilometer championship held at the city's famous Soldier Field. It was again a circular route, this time around the park's cement paths, about a mile each lap. Although it was flat, the course snaked around the park like most such paths. It was more or less in the shape of a figure eight, so that each lap took us twice past the central point where the drink stands were set up. About two weeks before the event, I had contacted the Israeli consulate in Chicago and asked them to try to find an Israeli student or local resident who would volunteer to assist me during the race. They put me in touch with a member of the Maccabi Chicago Athletic Club who agreed to help. Each time I came around, he held out my Coke, adding glucose or handing me a wet sponge when I asked him to.

Naturally, I took optimal advantage of the course. I walked the shortest distance on the curves, the straight line that cut across them. Thus, if at the end of a sharp bend to the right I was at the right-hand side of the path and the next curve arced to the left, I angled myself over to the left side to take it from there. My assistant noticed me moving from right to left and back again and, in a desire to help, told me I was wasting energy by crossing the path unnecessarily instead of staying on one side. I finished third, after Larry Young and the Canadian Alex Oakley, improving on my time in Toronto despite the heat. Larry Young went on to win two Olympic medals.

When it was over and I was beginning to recover from the exertion, I went over to the man who had voluntarily assisted me so faithfully and thanked him for his help. He repeated his advice, suggesting that in the future I try not to waste effort by moving back and forth across the path from one side to the other. I thanked him politely for his tip, not wanting to offend him by saying he didn't know what he was talking about. I was afraid that even if I explained the principle to him, he would think I was just being patronizing or trying to show off my erudition. But when he told me he used to be a competitive runner, his best time for ten kilometers being twenty-five minutes, I couldn't restrain myself. Cynically I remarked, couching my words in a very courteous tone of admiration, that it was a wonderful achievement and it was too bad he hadn't set that time in an official event since it was a full two and a half minutes faster than the current world record. Fortunately, he only heard the praise and missed the sarcasm.

During the summer there was a race-walking competition every Monday night at seven o'clock, an hour when it was still light out but not so hot any more. The course circled Lake Takanassee in Long Branch, on the New Jersey coast. This weekly event was also the brainchild of Elliott Denman. We took off near a white church with a red rafter roof beside the main road near the bridge across the lake, and we used its tiny basement to change clothes in. We had to make four laps around the lake, which included crossing the bridge. All in all, it was a little over five kilometers, around 5200 meters (three and a half miles), but its official name was the "Five-Kilometer Race." Dozens of athletes competed, using the event as a training session and a way of gauging their weekly improvement. It took me close to two hours to get there by bus from the Port Authority in Manhattan, but I hardly ever missed a week because I took such pleasure in the special atmosphere of this race. Sometimes John Kelly also competed, and then he would give me a lift. Shosh usually came too, enjoying the pastoral atmosphere of the lake and the landscape with its picturesque church.

By talking and competing repeatedly with athletes who had been in the Olympics, or aspired to be in the next games, I also caught the Olympic bug. I guess it was an infectious spirit, that yearning to reach the height of every athlete's dreams, to climb the highest mountain, so steep that only a few can make it to the summit. As my performance improved and I won more and more competitions, I also became hungry to take on the Olympic challenge. For American athletes, the terms for realizing that dream were simple and straightforward. They had to train hard and improve their times so as to finish in one of the first three places in the Olympic trials organized by the US Olympic Committee. Only those three, in both 20 and 50 kilometers — with no exceptions — would be on the American team.

For me, it wasn't quite so simple. I didn't for a second consider trying to get a green card — the first step on the road to American citizenship — and competing for a place on the American team. I was proud to be a citizen of Israel, and I still am. For someone like me, who lives with the memory of growing up in the Diaspora during the Holocaust, Israeli citizenship has very special significance, and I was unwilling to compromise it even by obtaining dual citizenship, like John Kelly, for instance, who was a citizen of both

Ireland and the USA. But it wasn't at all clear to me how I was supposed to get to the Olympics as an Israeli.

A friend suggested I join one of the more influential Israeli athletic clubs whose officials were willing to fight to promote their sportsmen. It wasn't hard to convince me. I recalled how lethargic ASA Jerusalem had been about getting me certification of amateur standing before I went to the classic marathon in Athens just over a year before. It may have been nice to be a member of that club where everyone treated me very well, but after five years, during which all I got from them was one pair of shoes, one T-shirt, a book, and a letter-opener, I didn't feel I owed them my fealty. Furthermore, ASA had never stood in the way of any athlete who wanted to change clubs, despite the existing regulations and prohibitions. And Hillel Ruskin had offered the same advice when I was in Israel for the march in April 1966. He heard me out and suggested I look into the possibility of transferring to Maccabi Tel Aviv. So after ten years in ASA, five at the Technion and five in Jerusalem, I moved to a different club. But I still consider ASA my breeding ground, my athletic alma mater.

Following Hillel's recommendation, I wrote to the man in charge of athletics at Maccabi Tel Aviv, Avraham Green, a well-known coach and a member of the track and field commission of the Israeli Sports Federation. He received consent for the transfer from ASA Jerusalem and officially registered me as a member of Maccabi Tel Aviv. In response to a second letter, in which I asked him what I would have to do in order to represent Israel at the Olympics, he replied that he would find out for me since Israel had never had a race walker of Olympic standard. He asked me to be patient, however, because he was presently at odds with the track and field commission over some demands he had made and had severed contact with them for tactical reasons. He assured me that I had nothing to worry about and it was only a temporary situation. As soon as his "tactical snit" worked, he would take care of it. I had never heard of a "tactical snit," and it was certainly not considered a behavioral norm among my friends and acquaintances, but I knew that Green was a wily, well-seasoned sports functionary-politician who planned his strategy carefully, knew what he was doing, and presumably got what he wanted.

At the end of August I competed in the American 40-kilometer championship in Long Branch, New Jersey, organized every year — as it is to this day, thirty years later — by Elliott Denman. I was one of the favorites to win. We took off at ten o'clock on a very hot day. Nonetheless, I started out at a fast pace. The course began with three laps around the town, about four and a half miles each. After the first lap I was in the lead and held it until almost the end of the third lap. Then the course turned south along the shore toward Asbury Park. At the dividing line between the two towns, we had to turn around and go back the way we had come as far as Lake Takanassee, and then circle the lake eight times. Because of the heat, I was drinking large quantities of both Coke and orange juice, with Shosh mixing in considerable amounts of glucose powder.

Toward the end of the third lap around town, I started having stomach discomfort. Then, on the stretch in the direction of Asbury Park, I began to throw up. Since it was still very hot, I went on taking drinks with added glucose, but instead of improving, I was weakening steadily. Not only was it hard for me to walk fast — I had already slowed my pace — but I couldn't even stand up straight. I had to stop and sit down on a bench. Meanwhile, a lot of the other walkers passed me, the same opponents I had overtaken long before and who had been a good distance behind me. I didn't want to throw in the towel. I sat there for a few minutes — the first and last time I ever sat down to rest during a race — and then started walking again, moving slowly. In place of what I had been drinking, I quenched my thirst with water and ate bananas. I began to feel a little better. I was able to go at a somewhat faster speed.

I got back to Lake Takanassee and now had about ten kilometers to go. Looking for an external source of energy, I took another drink of Coke and glucose and was able to pick up my pace even more and overtake several other competitors. But after two laps of the lake, the same pathetic scenario played itself out again. Vomiting, followed by total prostration and the need to rest. This time, with no bench in sight, I lay down on the grass. A few minutes later I got up, resumed walking, and slowly circled the lake lap after lap.

At the end of the sixth lap I came up alongside my friend Don Johnson. He was at least fourteen years older than me, but he had the body of a young athlete, as well as the soul of an angel. We'd competed together many times. I knew his wife and his son Greg who had volunteered to help officiate at the 50-mile race, and it was obvious that at his age he should be slower than me.

But here he was rushing on ahead, one by one overtaking other competitors who were feeling the fatigue brought on by the heat or the distance. He was aiming to pass a few more so as to finish in twenty-fifth place since, so he had informed me, the first twenty-five would get trophies. I was almost totally exhausted, but I stuck to him, urged on too by the thought of those twenty-five trophies. As we began the last lap, we overtook two more walkers. With half a lap left to go, one of the spectators shouted that we were in twenty-fifth and twenty-sixth place. Hungry for a trophy, I gave it everything I had and increased my speed despite my near prostration and extreme discomfort. I managed to finish twenty-fifth, a few yards in front of Don, and to this day I still feel bad about having snatched the trophy away from him. Nevertheless, we remained friends until he passed away.

Analyzing the reasons for my poor showing in the race — after all, everyone was expecting me to take one of the first places — I realized that the high acidity of the Coca-Cola and the juice, especially in the extremely large quantities I was drinking, had raised the acidity in my stomach and caused me to vomit. At the same time, and totally independently, the increased amounts of glucose had unwittingly caused hypoglycemia: a lowering of my blood sugar level resulting in prostration and a sense of incapacitation. Naturally, I applied this newfound knowledge. I took every precaution in future competitions to avoid a drastic rise in the acidity in my stomach. But it took me four more years of suffering until I learned how to control this factor. By trial and error I also learned how to prevent hypoglycemia by combining sugars absorbed rapidly into the bloodstream with others that are absorbed more slowly, and by not gulping down a large quantity of sugar all at once. I found that small amounts taken frequently invariably had a good effect on me.

When winter came, competitions became fewer and followed the same pattern as the previous winter. But there was a radical change in my own training program. I now had my heart set on competing in the Olympics. It seemed obvious that I would have to concentrate on the 50-kilometer walk, since my basic speed, although improved, was not fast enough for 20 kilometers. I was also determined to take part in the US Eastern Regional 50-Mile Championship. With these goals in mind, I intensified my distance training, or more precisely, lengthened it. I was able to walk as much as ten or fifteen miles in the open air, because the faster pace at that distance keeps your body warm despite the cold weather.

But I couldn't attempt longer, and thus naturally slower, practice walks outside in the freezing cold. I had to use the Columbia gym. Half of this indoor track with its two curves ran along a gallery above the basketball court. While I was training, I could look down past the inner railing on the ballplayers or peer over the outer railing at the weightlifters. The other half of the track followed a narrow corridor about two yards wide housing offices, exercise rooms, and a variety of courts. For long training sessions, this part of the track was very dull, but since I was accustomed to carrying on a conversation or losing myself in thought during training, this didn't constitute a serious psychological hardship for me.

The only problem was that the boiler room and the heating system for the whole campus were situated underneath the gym, so that the fumes and the stench of the diesel oil seeped into the closed section of the track. It was not particularly apparent if you were only there for a short time, but after several hours on a long training walk, I would get a headache and start feeling dizzy. Some of my training sessions lasted as long as seven hours, and by the end I almost felt like I'd been poisoned and it would take me a long time to recover once I'd left the gym. I don't know whether or not this was the reason, but after I left Columbia they built a modern new gym and dismantled the old one. Whatever its failings, that old gym served me very well, making it possible for me to hone my skills for long races despite the harsh winter.

In the spring of 1967, I wrote to Green to inform him I was planning to be in Israel for the Four-Day March. He wrote back saying he had arranged for a trial in Israel to give me the opportunity to demonstrate my readiness for the 50-kilometer walk. It was to be held at the old Maccabiah Games stadium in north Tel Aviv and would be organized by an attorney by the name of Yitzhak Braz. He assured me the event would get extensive coverage in the press because he had pitched it as a contest between myself and Moshe Rotenberg. He explained that Braz had already organized a 50-kilometer race near the Dead Sea and that it had been won by Rotenberg, recording an excellent time, which, so he believed, was due to the low altitude where the air is rich in oxygen. My friend Yoram Cohen told me much later that Rotenberg's time actually resulted from the combination of two other factors: first, part of the course was the steep descent from Arad to the Dead Sea, and secondly, Rotenberg took this downhill leg at a run when he thought no one was looking.

Green's letter arrived on a lovely spring day in New York when I had just returned from a twenty-five mile practice walk in the park. I was tired and contented with what I had done, feeling I had trained well and sufficiently for that day. When I got back to the apartment, I found the letter. I didn't then know what Yoram was to tell me several months later, after the race. To tell by the letter, Rotenberg was in very good shape. That was enough to get me going again. When I walked in the house I was quite satisfied with the training I had completed that day, but after reading the letter I went back to the park to do another twelve and a half miles.

The Israeli press touted the race between Moshe and myself as a "duel between the Israeli titleholder and the American titleholder," and kept interest high for nearly a month. I have no idea why they called it a "duel," why I was termed the "American," or how Moshe got to be "the Israeli titleholder." Be that as it may, it gave me the incentive to train intensively. As a result, when I competed in my second US Eastern Regional 50-Mile Championship in April 1967, again held on a stadium track, I won it for the second time in a row. I was thirty-one years old. The exertion was less than it had been the previous year, and left my muscles somewhat less sore. Not only did I win the championship, but I again broke the American record, and not by a few seconds either. Incredibly, I finished in 8:11, improving on my own record of 8:35 by a full twenty-four minutes! I couldn't take it in. The previous year I had pushed myself to the limit, and now, with less effort, I had shaved all that time off my old record. My accomplishment again earned me a great deal of publicity, and a very large dose of self-confidence.

Four days later I arrived in Israel for the Four-Day March of 1967, which I didn't want to miss. It would be the eleventh straight year for me. I even managed to get my travel expenses paid, although that hadn't been the intention of my benefactors. As a graduate of the Technion studying for a doctorate, I was awarded a scholarship by the Friends of the Technion Society because my courses at Columbia included industrial engineering as well as business administration. Both disciplines actually deal with the same sort of problems, but from different perspectives. At that time I had no idea that eight years later I would leave the School of Business Administration to

become a professor in the industrial engineering and management department. For the moment, however, I was able both to satisfy the demands and
expectations of the scholarship committee and cover the cost of my participation in the march.

Before I left the States, I arranged to meet the organizer of the trial event
at my mother's pharmacy in Lod. As soon as my plane landed on Friday
morning, I went straight there, arriving in advance of the appointed time.
Yitzhak Braz was an odd creature — a successful lawyer with the soul of an
athlete. For years all he wanted was to be first. But how could an attorney,
whose professional ethics forbid self-publicity, ever be first? He did it by
making sure that every year Case No. 1 in the magistrates' court in his home-
town of Petah Tikva and in Tel Aviv, as well as in the district court, all bore his
name, and he repeated this feat year after year, even after other attorneys
decided to vie for the same distinction. Everyone knew about this obsession
of his, even the press.

In 1965 he came up with a new project: organizing marches. He founded
the Popular Sport Division in the Maccabi Israel headquarters, a cover for his
one-man operation (with the active support and assistance of his wife Rina).
Then he started organizing "Seaside Marches" along the Mediterranean
coastline, ultimately being able to boast of hundreds of marches that were all
his doing. Some became established events, some had a political overtone,
and some served as a means of introducing march fanatics to parts of the
country they wouldn't otherwise get to see. He succeeded in flaming the
enthusiasm of thousands of marchers and attracting a group of loyal volunteers. With his natural flair for publicity, he challenged the Israeli athletic
establishment to "compete" with him in offering the public a wider and richer
repertoire of marches. He himself marched along with the other participants
in several of the events, and periodically incorporated races as well.

After carrying the torch, and the burden of organization, on his own for
ten years, he transferred the whole operation to a division of the Maccabi
headquarters, retaining for himself the status of overseer. He was eventually
appointed to the bench of the magistrate's court. The contacts with the press
and the instinct for publicity that he had gained during the years he was
actively involved in organizing the marches seemed to stand him in good
stead as a judge as well, when the juicier cases that came before him titillated
public interest.

Braz had no experience in organizing race-walking events, but since the competitors were familiar faces from the marches, so that the race could be used to obtain publicity for his projects, and since he wanted to help out Maccabi, he agreed to take the task on himself. Over the years, as I got to know him better, there were several occasions when I benefited from his willingness to voluntarily organize important events. But I didn't know him then; I had only heard about him from my sister Marta who had taken part in several of his seaside marches. However, he had heard of me, read about me, and maybe even seen me in other marches as I sped past him — whether by daylight or in the dark. I don't know how he pictured me. Most likely as a tall he-man type.

As I waited near the entrance to my mother's pharmacy, talking with Marta who had come to welcome me home, he came in and scanned the room for someone at least his height. Not finding anyone who fit the image, he turned to Marta, standing beside me, and asked: "Hasn't Shaul come yet?" Marta pointed to me and said: "Here he is!" I could easily read the astonishment on his face. He hadn't envisioned the American record holder as a compact, balding man standing only 5 feet 8½ inches tall. His expression showed his disappointment and the disbelief that I could actually have accomplished what I was supposed to have done. He didn't have to put it in words; his body language said enough. There and then we settled the logistics. At my request, the race would begin the next day, Saturday, at four a.m. so that we wouldn't have to be out in the hot sun any longer than necessary.

It's 3:30 in the morning and I'm standing outside the locked gate of the stadium. Yoram Cohen and Uri Priel are there to help me. So are Moshe Rotenberg, Braz, time-keepers and judges, other assistants, and spectators who read the hype in the papers and have come to see a duel of a sort never before witnessed in Israel. Everyone is on time, except for one person: the man who has the keys. What begins as a slight delay in start time extends into two hours. I know that means two hours of extreme heat instead of the two cooler hours we could have had. We are summoned to the starting line. The signal is given. Moshe rushes forward. It looks to me like he's running; sometimes both his feet are in the air at the same time and he doesn't straighten the supporting leg to a vertical position. But I'm not a judge, and to be absolutely certain you have to look on from the side, not from behind while you're moving. The judges don't comment or issue a warning. I start at an appropriate pace for a distance of 50 kilometers.

At first the gap between us grows steadily, but then it remains constant and within a short while begins to close. After the first five hundred yards, along the straight following the first curve, I pass Moshe and take the lead. By the end of the second lap he's far behind me. The distance between us is getting bigger. After twelve laps I'm a whole lap ahead of him. I'm maintaining the pace I started at. In fact, I keep the level of exertion steady for the whole distance: when it gets hotter and it takes more effort to progress, I slow my pace accordingly. The gap between us is still growing. I'm not in the least worried that he might overtake me. I can see he doesn't have the stamina for a prolonged effort at high speed. We're about a hundred yards from the sea. The high humidity and the heat, intensifying after eight in the morning, are getting to me. I'm drained and exhausted, but I keep up the same pace to the end.

For the last two hours, there's no contest. I'm already a few miles ahead of Moshe. I still want to record a good time and now that's the only thing driving me. I finish the race, totally exhausted, in 4:48. If it weren't for the heat and the humidity, I'm sure I could have taken at least fifteen minutes off that time. When I cross the finish line, Moshe still has around three miles to go. To his credit, he doesn't give up and walks the whole distance. But this was to be his last race. He retired from race walking and stopped attending the marches. The only connection he retained with sports was as the masseur for the Hapoel Tel Aviv basketball team.

I was drained but happy. I could see from Braz's face that he now regarded me in a new light. I had demonstrated what I could do and I was his hero again. Yoram and Uri took me back to my mother's house. She was on duty in the pharmacy, and I had left the key in my sweatpants and they had been forgotten at the stadium. Yoram went back to look for it while I sat on the stoop for nearly an hour, hardly able to move, with Uri keeping an eye on me to make sure I didn't pass out.

The next day, Sunday, I had to be at Hulda for the start of the Four-Day March. Thanks to my long-distance training, especially two days in a row, my body had learned to recover quickly and I got my strength back in time. It seemed like everyone knew me and had heard or read about the race. Hundreds of people greeted me by name and asked how I felt. I answered them all, even though I didn't know most of them. On each of the four days of the march I demonstrated my capabilities again, walking quickly — although obviously below competition speed — to the end of the route and back again on the first three days, and then up to Jerusalem on the fourth. As was to be expected by now, I finished first each day, with Yoram beside me, alternately walking and running. That year some twenty thousand people showed up for the march, which was again covered extensively by the media. My name was mentioned on the radio almost hourly, as the reporters announced the precise time when I passed one landmark or another. I'd become the marchers' benchmark for assessing their speed.

When it was over, I went back to the States immediately and resumed intense training for the American 50-kilometer championship scheduled for June 11, 1967, on the same course in Soldier Field in Chicago. In preparation for that competition, John Kelly and I drove to Montreal in early May for the Canadian 50-kilometer championship. It was held in the town of Ville d'Anjou outside Montreal. It's a good thing I knew a little French, however haltingly I spoke it. At least I could understand what people were saying and make myself understood.

I told my cousins in Toronto that I was coming, and Larry, my cousin Vera's sixteen-year-old son, drove over with a cousin on his father's side to assist me during the race. Although he volunteered for the job, when it was over he admitted he had been expecting to be thoroughly bored. But he found himself caught up in the excitement of watching positions change, competitors unexpectedly dropping out or collapsing, and the tension and interest created by the fact that most of the walkers were on a comparable level.

Larry eventually became a doctor and amateur race-car driver. Outside his office he built an enormous garage for his fleet of cars, including a Porsche and a car that once won the Indianapolis 500 and that he often drives in races. Whenever he has free time between appointments, he goes out to the garage, puts on his overalls, and gets down on the floor to work on one of the cars. I wonder if, along with his father who was an outstanding swimmer, I didn't play some role in encouraging his love of sports, and in his realization that money is no substitute for actually participating in some sport.

I came in second again in the Canadian championship. John Kelly came in behind me. This time Felix Capella was first, Oakley third, and Carl Merchenz dropped out. Who could have known that a year later all three of them would finish ahead of me at the Mexico Olympics.

A week later that same May, Shosh and I rented a car and drove to the American 20-kilometer championship in McKeesport. I improved on my time from the previous year, but still wasn't among the top athletes in this event. Despite the relatively short distance, I got huge blisters on my feet. Back in the locker room after the race, I used a needle dipped in alcohol to burst them and then drained them. I was finally able to walk comfortably. That night I got shooting pains in one foot and started running a temperature. Apparently, one of the blisters had become infected. The year before I had had the same problem and it went away in twenty-four hours with the help of a shot of penicillin. The doctor I went to accepted his patient's diagnosis and gave me the injection. By the time we got back to New York, I was fine.

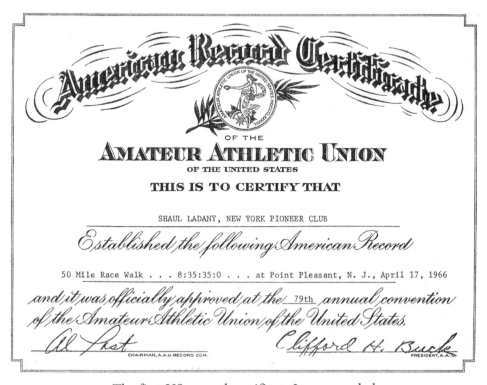

The first US-record certificate I was awarded

■ Chapter Eight | The Six-Day War

I finished the courses required for my doctorate at Columbia and passed the four exhaustive tests we all had to take. By May 1967 my orals were also behind me. The only thing left now was to do my dissertation and defend it, and then the PhD I was working so hard for would finally be conferred on me. The tests are generally used to screen out the last of the doctoral candidates; having passed that hurdle I could be fairly sure of getting my degree, if I could just find the right dissertation subject and put the necessary time and effort into getting it done. Even at this late stage degrees aren't granted automatically. A lot of people get this far and then find themselves at a loss because they don't have the classroom framework, the pressure, the self-discipline, or the ideas; they never even start a thesis, much less finish it.

I'd become friendly with a number of students in New York, among them our neighbors, David and Phyllis Weisberg. David was studying for an MBA, specializing in finance. He went on to put his studies to good use by establishing one of the soundest investment companies in Israel. When they left Columbia, their place in the Israeli contingent at Woodbridge Hall was taken by Hannah and Shmuel Horowitz. Shmuel was doing his master's in architecture. Some years later he came back to the States and got a doctorate in city planning, a field in which he worked in Israel until he lost his life in an attack on an Israeli tourist bus in Egypt.

Another friend was Colonel Chaim Domi, who had been sent by the IDF to get a master's degree in industrial engineering while he was being "kept on ice" until the army decided what to do with him. He was very bright and wanted to go straight on for his doctorate, but he was ordered back to Israel. He was promoted to brigadier general and put in command of the ordnance corps. After he retired from the army, he managed the oil refineries at Haifa until his untimely death.

While lifting weights in the gym — something I did infrequently for fear of injury — I met two Americans, both doctoral candidates in the chemistry department: John Malmin and Bob Reedy. They liked to run, but I talked them into giving race walking a try instead. Bob, a NASA scientist in New Mexico these many years, still takes part in marathons and race-walking competitions.

In mid-May Nasser booted the UN forces out of Sinai and closed off the Tiran Straits, effectively placing Eilat under naval blockade. The tension in Israel was high. Even then, before the age of CNN, the American press reported extensively on the situation. We also subscribed to the weekly review published by the Israeli daily *Ha'aretz* on newsprint as thin as cigarette papers. By international law, a naval blockade is a *casus belli*. Add to that Nasser's declarations that he meant to throw the Jews into the sea and destroy the State of Israel. While this might not have altered the legal status, it certainly made his intentions clear.

We heard that the Israeli military reserves were being mobilized. I called the embassy in Washington to ask if I was needed. They told me that if the army wanted me, my corps commander would submit a request and the embassy would get in touch with me. Not content with that reply, I wrote to the commander of the artillery corps, Colonel Israel Ben-Amitai, whom I had met during reserve duty. Ben-Amitai was an active member of the pre-State right-wing underground movement Etzel and was detained in Kenya during the British Mandate. Unlike most of his colleagues, who never rose to any significant rank in the army as long as the left-wing Mapai Party was in power, he was put in command of the corps and retained that position for longer than any other artillery corps commander before or since. He was gifted with extensive professional know-how, leadership qualities, integrity, and tact. I told him I was ready to leave the States and volunteer for reserve duty if they needed me.

Meanwhile, the media was reporting on the feverish diplomatic activity aimed at raising the blockade and thwarting the threat to Israel. The Israeli foreign minister, Abba Eban, featured prominently in the news in New York, presided over the diplomatic maneuvers. The Americans were very impressed by his brilliant oratory. As evidence of his powers of persuasion, it was said that when he was Israeli ambassador to the UN in the fifties, he returned to Israel to report to then Prime Minister Ben-Gurion on the debate over the Israeli retaliatory attack on the Jordanian villages of Budrus and Qibya, saying: "When we launched the attack, I thought we were right, but as I defended it at the UN, I became convinced we were wrong." Ben-Gurion replied: "When we launched the attack, I knew we were wrong, but when I heard you defend it, I became convinced we were right."

Nevertheless, as we listened to the reports of the mood in Israel, it appeared unlikely that Eban's diplomatic efforts to gather an armada of foreign ships to reopen the Tiran Straits would be successful. It seemed that while acknowledging Eban's talents as a superb diplomat, defined as someone who could "talk for hours without saying anything," the Israeli public did not believe that diplomacy would provide the solution.

The situation grew increasingly tense with each passing day. An appeal was issued for volunteers to guard the El Al planes on the ground in New York to avert any attempts at sabotage. I answered the call and was assigned to Kennedy airport, where we also guarded foreign cargo planes taking on supplies for Israel. On June 5, 1967, after I'd been doing this for three days, the war broke out. Nobody had submitted a request for my services, but I knew my duty. I checked out the possibilities for getting back to Israel. All the airlines, including El Al, had canceled their flights to the country. I learned that one of the cargo planes I had guarded at the airport, belonging to a company called Flying Tiger, was taking off in a few hours for some unknown destination in Europe, and was carrying supplies meant for Israel. I decided to try to get on it and reach Israel together with the cargo in its hold. I called Shosh and told her I was flying home for the war. She didn't put up a fuss, argue, or try to convince me not to go. She knew it was the right thing to do. I asked her to go out right away and buy me a duffel bag with a shoulder strap, underwear, socks, khaki shirts and pants, and canned food. Meanwhile, I hurried off to 42nd Street to get the other things I needed.

I know the IDF very well and how disorganized it can be when it comes to equipping a reserve unit. I was afraid I might get there and discover they didn't have any guns left. You need a license to buy a pistol or a sub-machine gun in New York, but I didn't have the time for the mandatory waiting period. In Herman's enormous sporting goods store I found a semi-automatic .22-caliber rifle. The trigger mechanism and magazine could be detached and stored in the plastic butt, so when the rifle was disassembled it was easy to carry, both lightweight and compact, and only took a couple of seconds to reassemble. It seemed to be designed with professional hit men in mind, but it was perfect for me. I could pack it in my duffel bag, and if they didn't issue me a gun when I got to my unit, I'd have my own personal weapon, even if it was only good for fifty to one hundred yards.

Without wasting any time, I bought the rifle, a spare magazine, and a thousand bullets, together with a commando knife housed in a leather sheaf. I remembered how the Egyptian forces had recently gassed the population in their war against the royalists in Yemen. The international convention against the use of gas didn't seem to carry much weight with them. The press was full of analysts debating whether or not they'd do the same thing against Israel as well. In fact, most of the cargo being loaded onto the planes I had been guarding consisted of gas masks and atropine. So I also purchased two gas masks with active charcoal filters, one for me and one to give to someone else who might need it, maybe my mother. They looked like the contraptions from World War II, but luckily I never had to find out whether the charcoal was really still active.

I went home and put on the khaki clothes, although I didn't change my sneakers, then packed the duffel bag, kissed Shosh good-bye, and went back to the airport. Two other Israelis were waiting near the Flying Tiger plane: one a captain in the paratroop reserves and the other the nephew of the chief of staff, Yitzhak Rabin. The crew agreed to take us along. We climbed aboard and took off. No passport control; we just left the States without any bureaucratic procedures whatsoever. Between the cockpit and the cargo tied on behind us, there were two long rows of narrow seats. Raising the arm rests, each of us stretched out along three or four seats and went to sleep, despite the noise of the propellers. It was quite comfortable. Strange though it may sound, on my way to the war I flew in considerably greater comfort than on most flights.

Since the plane wasn't a jet, the ocean crossing took a long time. After about half a day, we landed. It was dark outside. We discovered we were in Italy, at some military airfield not far from Rome. Disembarking together with the crew, we were greeted by a civilian, not an agent of the local government but an Israeli who spoke to us in Hebrew. He was very surprised to see the three of us, but when he heard why we'd come, he didn't see any problem in getting us to Israel. The cargo was going to be transferred to an Israeli Air Force freighter, and in just a few hours we could join it on its way to Israel.

Meanwhile, we collected our belongings and followed our host to his office in one of the stone buildings at the airfield. No name on the door, no indication whatsoever of any Israeli presence. As we waited there, listening to the instructions he delivered in Hebrew and Italian, it became obvious that this was a regular transit field for the Israeli army or Ministry of Defense, carefully disguised and concealed in the tradition of the pre-State days of the underground and illegal immigration. After he had dealt with the necessary administrative tasks, our host, who realized we must be very hungry by now, invited us to join him at a restaurant in town. As we passed through the gate, he made sure the guard would let us back in. So after a hearty meal of pasta, we went back to the airfield, boarded the Air Force cargo plane, and took off. At that time, Israelis needed a visa to enter Italy, and we obviously didn't have one. In fact, no one ever looked at our passports and they carry no indication that we were ever in Italy.

The plane was a large Stratocruiser normally used not only to fly cargo, but also to shuttle dignitaries to official events or secret meetings. The part we could see consisted of a long cabin the width of the plane with a sofa running down the two sides and joined in the middle to form a horseshoe that could be used by a large number of participants for conferences or strategy meetings. We each chose a section of sofa and stretched out using our duffel bags for pillows, continuing our journey to Israel in style. We landed at Lod, disembarked, and were about to leave the airport when I remembered that we hadn't gone through passport control again. At some later stage, someone might decide to charge us with illegal entry to the country.

The airport was very quiet without the usual sound of airplanes taking off and landing. We walked back toward the terminal and found a bored official at the passport control desk. He was dumbstruck to see us there. We explained how we had come and he stamped our passports. I took advantage of the opportunity to call the artillery corps headquarters at Sarafend. They put me through to the administration officer, Colonel Shdemati. I knew him. In the spring of 1955, when I was in command of a cannon crew deployed for months in a field opposite the Gaza Strip, he had interviewed me and recommended I be sent to the preliminary officers' training course. I introduced myself and told him I'd come back from the States for the war. He remembered me, maybe because of my athletic activities, and told me to come to Sarafend. So that's where I went.

When I walked into his office I found him conducting the war logistics of the artillery corps over the phone. Congenially, he informed me that my place in the battery was already filled, and if it were anyone else he would just send me away. But since I was an officer and he knew me personally, he could offer me the post of artillery specialist on a technical intelligence team that was being formed. That wasn't the sort of job I had been looking for, but with nothing else on offer, I obviously agreed.

A jeep was sent for immediately. But before I left Sarafend, I managed to get in a call to my mother. She was thrilled to hear my voice and discover I had come home for the war, until she came to her senses and realized I might get hurt. Then her maternal instincts took over and she balled me out: "What did you come back for? You should have stayed in the States until they sent for you!" I called Shosh's parents too. Her father answered. He was surprised to hear my voice and became very emotional when he learned that I had come home voluntarily. He urged me to take care of myself, but I could hear how proud he was of what I was doing and how pleased he was that we members of the younger generation were not abandoning our parents to suffer the trials of war on their own.

I reached El Arish on the third day of the war. The region had been over-run by the first wave of armored troops breaking through enemy lines and continuing full speed ahead toward the Suez Canal. The second wave had only started to arrive. Thousands of armed Egyptian soldiers whose units had disintegrated were everywhere, along with the serviceable weapons and armaments left behind. Some had started to reorganize themselves and were striking out at our forces.

The IDF set up technical intelligence teams, each consisting of an engineering officer, an artillery officer, an ordnance officer, and an armored corps officer. I was on one of those teams, equipped with a command car and responsible for the sector northeast of El Arish. It was our job to scan aerial photographs in order to locate weapons and armaments, neutralize them before the Egyptian soldiers could use them against us, and report to the booty crews behind us so they would know where to find and collect this materiel.

There was a large camp on the northern outskirts of El Arish, near the main road. A small sign at the entrance read "UN Base," but graffiti in huge black letters on the white wall of a long brick building facing the road screamed: "UN. DON'T SHOOT. WE ARE IN." Thanks to that message, the camp had remained intact. The few UN personnel still there had dug long trenches in the floor of the building and taken cover there. The UN forces stationed in the area after the Sinai Campaign in 1956 to prevent any Egyptian attack on Israel had clearly not done their job very well. The secretary general, U Thant, had given in to Nasser's demands and removed most of the UN units from the region. I was sorry I didn't have a camera. I wanted to take a picture of that message in outsized letters and make sure it got hung in the photo gallery at the UN building in New York. I was aching to show the visitors to that institution just how much they could trust the UN forces, and that was even long before Bosnia. I wonder if it's just a coincidence that in Hebrew the name of the UN rhymes with the word for "nothing."

Our unit was positioned between the forward troops occupying enemy territory and the rear units that had not yet arrived. The staff arrived more or less at the same time as we did on the morning of the third day of the war, and set up headquarters in the sections of the camp abandoned by the UN. There we received our first briefing. It's a good thing I had brought my own khaki outfit and rifle. As I had predicted, despite the assurances I had been given at artillery corps headquarters, there was no one there who could issue us any gear. We were ordered to leave our personal belongings in one of the buildings and go out and get to work. And so I left for the battlefield armed only with a .22-caliber rifle for my own protection. I don't know where I drew my confidence from, but I wasn't scared.

The first thing we did was to find ourselves an abandoned Egyptian jeep and truck with the keys still in the ignition. They gave us a means of transportation, as well as the ability to carry more equipment. As the artillery corps officer, I would pore over the aerial photos, looking for the signs typical of a cannon position, locate them in the field, and, basing my judgment on the conventional deployment of artillery, indicate where the rest of the battery or the regiment should be. I would remove either the striking pin or the entire firing mechanism from the breech lock, along with the optical sights, and load them onto the truck. From the way the guns were positioned and the topography, I would also try to locate the theodolites (surveying equipment used as part of the initial aiming system of the cannons) and take them with us too.

We found dozens of abandoned batteries of field guns and mortars, some so well camouflaged that they were invisible in the aerial photos. Each of the other members of the team did the same sort of thing in his own specialty, but we worked together, helping each other out. At one site we found a massive store of munitions for Russian 122 mm cannons that was so well hidden no one had any idea it was there. It later served to arm the regiment of Russian guns pressed into service by the IDF and put to good use for close to ten years. Every now and then we surprised Egyptian soldiers. They even fired on us ineffectually from a distance a few times, but none of us was ever hit. I never responded to any such attack. Not only was my rifle useless beyond a very short distance, but I was afraid that if I fired back, I would be giving away the nature of the only weapon I had.

When we got back to the UN camp at El Arish after nightfall, we discovered that some of the rear, non-combat troops had already arrived and settled in. They stood out conspicuously. As soon as we climbed down from the jeep, a few of the soldiers passing by noticed the commando knife I had bought in New York hanging from my belt, and asked, one after the other: "Who did you take that off of?" or "Where can I get hold of an Egyptian knife like that?" Unlike combat soldiers, these men were only interested in what they could plunder. I was surprised and dumfounded by their attitude. I'd never encountered it before. Perspectives were very different among my friends and acquaintances, and in every unit I had ever served in. I was especially taken aback by their remarks since I was filled with the spirit of self-sacrifice, the willingness to do whatever had to be done to defend my country, rather than the desire to take advantage of the war for my own benefit or to plunder the property of anyone else, even the enemy.

I soon found that my own duffel bag and everything in it had also become the spoils of one of those "brave warriors." I was left with nothing more than what I had on and what happened to be in my pockets. The next morning we discovered that most of the equipment we had removed from Egyptian weapons so as to render them unusable — equipment that was essential if the Israeli army was to employ those weapons in the future — had similarly vanished from the truck and was never seen again. From that moment on, we made sure our things were always under guard. The food I had brought from the States disappeared together with my duffel bag, so that first day on the battlefield I had next to nothing to eat. The next day, as we continued with our task of locating and neutralizing enemy weapons, several abandoned Egyptian vehicles yielded dried dates compressed into the shape of a small box and wrapped in paper. They served as very tasty, filling field rations until the army set up a regular mess kitchen for us.

The fighting ended on the sixth day, but the situation in the area we were responsible for remained unaltered. That same day, June 11, I was also musing over the American 50-kilometer race-walking championship taking place at that very moment in Chicago, a competition for which I had been preparing myself for almost a whole year. I was in top form, and now I had lost not only a year of training, but, more importantly, the chance to prove myself and achieve what I knew I could. My heart had been set on taking first place, or at least second.

When the battle died down, I tried several times to train by walking around the improvised parking lot, going out early in the morning before we had to leave the camp. The ground was very sandy, a difficulty I could deal with. The more serious deterrent, however, was the stench rising from the corpses lying around everywhere. It was bad enough to discourage me from training very often. Within two weeks we had completed our assignment. Our unit was dismantled, and I was given leave to return to the States.

I had been in the country for twelve days before I was again able to contact my mother and father-in-law, who called Shosh in New York and told her I was okay. It was the first sign of life she had gotten from me since I'd left. I had tried to write, getting hold of a UN aerogramme and an Egyptian military letter form which I addressed to her, but lacking stamps I could only write "On active duty" and my APO number on the outside and hope they'd get there. And they did, but only after I was back in the States. I was amazed when they were delivered despite the fact that there were still no stamps on them. The American postal authorities apparently honored the message "On active duty," even though it was written in Hebrew, and didn't demand any postage due.

With my duffel bag stolen I had no soap or shaving kit. The stubble on my chin was uncomfortable, not to say unattractive, but gradually a beard started to grow in. By the time I was released and made it to my mother's house, it was quite long and I had become used to it. Like a lot of other soldiers at that time, I decided to keep it. The very same day, Israel Helman, who had studied business administration with me, drove me to Jerusalem. I had heard that the city had been shelled by the Jordanians and I wanted to see if our apartment was still standing. I was very pleased to find it hadn't suffered any damage. I also went to the Western Wall, my heart filled with the odd sensation that we had recovered our roots.

On my return to Tel Aviv, I went to the Ministry of Defense. The army had told me that the ministry would make the effort to fly all the volunteers back to where they had come from. There weren't too many. I heard that only six soldiers had managed to reach the country during the six days of the war. Many more came after the fighting was over, when the airlines resumed their flights. So at their expense, the Ministry of Defense flew me to France on the same Stratocruiser that had brought me from Italy. From there I was on my own. I took a bus to Luxembourg and flew back to New York, again choosing the longer, but cheaper, route over Iceland.

Shosh hardly recognized me with my new beard, despite the advance warning she had gotten from her parents. Obviously, there are no words to describe the joy of our reunion. She kept her opinion of the beard to herself, although I have no doubt that she found it unattractive and annoying. She must have heard that beards were now a fad among the soldiers returning from the war.

A short while after I got back to New York, I got a letter from the artillery corps commander. It was a personal message confirming receipt of my letter from before the war and thanking me for my willingness to return to Israel at my own expense for army duty. However, it concluded, by now I certainly understood that there had been no need for my services as the artillery corps had successfully carried out its missions even without my help. It was signed by Israel Ben-Amitai. What could I do but laugh?

I did indeed know that the artillery corps had carried out its missions and received the approbation of the other corps it had supported and of the chief of staff himself. Still, I was glad that I had been able to do my part and that I had left the States without waiting for a reply to my letter. Years later, our paths crossed again. When I became a professor at Ben-Gurion University, he was the administrative director of that institution and was in the habit of calling me "gunny." Even after he retired, we continued to meet annually when he presented me year after year with the trophy for first place in the walking category in the Omer Race held in memory of his son, who had been a pilot.

On the first Saturday after my return to the States, Shosh and I went to Long Beach for a 10-mile race, which I won. The next day we went to Taunton, Massachusetts, for the annual 20-kilometer race organized by the North Medford club. I won again, recording my best time yet at that distance: 1:32. I couldn't understand how I was able to do it when I hadn't trained for about three weeks. Perhaps I had become accustomed to hotter weather, or perhaps after the war, everything seemed different. It's possible that after what I had seen there — charred corpses, tanks and cannons mangled and scorched, vehicles raked by bullet holes, and weapons twisted out of shape, as well as Beit Shahin where Israeli tanks were ambushed and destroyed by Egyptian forces — it's possible that after all that, ordinary life takes on a new meaning. Perhaps I now had a higher threshold of endurance, making it easier for me to cope with the strenuous effort of the competition and more able to take pleasure in a non-violent contest. Whatever the reason, I felt great and really enjoyed the races.

I also enjoyed the trophies I won. The one from Taunton is taller than any of the other four hundred odd cups I've won in my entire athletic career. The next day, a newspaper report of the race was headlined: "Desert Training Pays Off. Race-Walking Champion Returns from Sinai." I learned that on June 12, the day after the American 50-kilometer championship in Chicago, there had been a piece in one of the New York papers stating: "It should have been Ladany's championship," and explaining that I had been expected to win but that I had gone to war and there was no word of me. It was essentially a eulogy, not unlike another such tribute I received five years later when it was reported that I was among the athletes murdered at the Munich Olympics.

I wanted to start on my thesis, but for some reason I was too restless to apply myself to the scientific literature, the studying, and the work it demanded. The media was still reporting extensively on the war, the fate of the territories, and the political efforts to conclude a peace between Israel and its neighbors. I devoured all the items, devoting several hours a day to reading each and every one, unable to drag myself away from those overriding issues and concentrate on my thesis. I still didn't have a subject. But despite my preoccupation, I didn't let my training slide. Two months passed. In September I decided to take myself in hand. Within two weeks I had settled on an idea for the dissertation, formulated it into a polished proposal, and submitted it. It was approved without any delay.

When I had first come to Columbia, the Israeli doctoral candidates already there had briefed me on the university's do's and don'ts. I was cautioned not to show up at Richmond's lectures without a jacket and tie unless I wanted him to ask the class sarcastically, "Isn't the air conditioning working?" or request that the student sitting next to me lean a little to one side so that he wouldn't have to look at me. I hate ties. They're like a noose around my neck and I don't see any functional value in them — I use a handkerchief if my mouth or nose needs wiping. I also bathe and put on a fresh shirt every day, so I don't feel the need to hide a dirty collar or choke off a smelly neck. So I didn't wear a tie to Richmond's lectures either. If it was cold out, I put on a jacket or sweater, with my shirt collar folded over it. I still dress like that. Richmond saw me dozens of times and didn't say a word. And moreover, I was even his research assistant in the 1966-67 academic year. Now he was my thesis advisor.

At this point, the doctoral committee also burdened me with another responsibility, whether thanks to Richmond or to Marty Star, another professor of mine who was the editor-in-chief of the most prestigious scientific journal in my field, *Management Science,* and sometimes asked me to fill in for him when he was at a conference. As partial restitution for the scholarship I was receiving, I was asked to teach a course in Production Management to first-year students at Columbia College during the first semester of 1967-68. It was indeed a burden, but also an honor, albeit an honor I couldn't refuse. I tried to give it my best. Thus, from mid-September 1967 I was both teaching and working on my dissertation.

Several years later, Richmond was elected deputy dean of the school. When he failed to be reelected after two years in the post — he claimed it was because of politics — he left to become dean of the School of Business Administration at Vanderbilt University in Nashville, turning it into a model academic institution during his ten years there. But as a mere doctoral candidate, I was not yet aware of university politics. I had, however, heard the stories about the circumstances surrounding General Dwight D. Eisenhower's departure from the presidency of Columbia, but I thought it was just a joke. It was said that after several years at the university, Eisenhower had decided to run for president. When friends tried to deter him, citing the political battles he would have to fight both as a candidate and as president, in contrast to peaceful campus life, he replied: "I'm sick of the politics here."

The only political activity I knew of at Columbia, although I wasn't personally involved, were the student protests against the war in Vietnam. Large-lettered graffiti on the wall of the 116th Street subway station at the entrance to the campus, read: "Lee Harvey Oswald, where are you now when we really need you?" That year also saw the massive student demonstration, with the students taking over the administration offices for several days. Eventually, armed police were called in to put an end to the protest by force. My friend Ingele and I stopped to watch the excitement on our way back to our apartment from the college and almost became victims of the attempt to break it up. As we stood there among the other onlookers at some distance from the demonstrators, mounted police suddenly charged in our direction, their horses nearly stomping us underfoot. I managed to leap aside at the last minute, avoiding a head-on collision with iron horseshoes. The students occupying the administration offices were dragged out, some of them wounded. The police were charged with the use of excess force, while I, without ever meaning to, got a lesson in how demonstrations are put down.

In early August 1967 I took part in the American 40-kilometer race-walking championship at Long Branch. This time I finished among the leaders. The New Jersey 50-kilometer championship was scheduled for the day after Yom Kippur. I'm not a religious person; in fact, I'm not even a believer, and the moral guidelines for my behavior derive not from the fear of divine punishment, but from the natural values of justice and morality instilled in me by my upbringing and human society and enforced by the laws of the country in which I live. Nevertheless, I am proud to be a Jew, although the ultra-orthodox might consider me a heathen, and I customarily observe several of the traditions that have been part of Jewish life throughout the centuries. I only eat matzos during Passover — although I couldn't care less if the plate I eat them on has been properly prepared for the holiday or whether my food has received an official kosher stamp of approval from someone paid to sign off on it — and I fast on Yom Kippur. So I fasted on the day before the 50-kilometer championship, too.

Still, I was feeling very fit on the day of the competition. The route ran through the streets of the New Jersey towns along the coast. After twenty miles I was in the lead and steadily increasing the gap between myself and the walkers behind me. By twenty-five miles I already had over a six hundred-yard lead. Enjoying this advantage, I continued walking along the pavement or the edge of the asphalt road, when a car filled with teenagers suddenly pulled up alongside me. Laughing and having a gay old time, they called me all sorts of names. I didn't react. That seemed to get their goat. They threw an empty soda can at me, but it missed. I didn't want to stop to pick up the can and throw it back at them for fear of losing my lead and lengthening my final time, and anyway it hadn't actually hit me.

After a couple of minutes, they drove off. About a mile later they showed up again. A salvo of two more empty cans came flying toward me, similarly missing their mark. I continued to ignore them. All of a sudden a large ball hit me. I was coming up on a bridge over a wide river. I followed the rolling ball, scooped it up, and kept going, taking it with me. When I got to the middle of the bridge, I tossed it in the water. The boys were taken by surprise, especially since their previous efforts to provoke me hadn't been successful. I could see them sitting there with their mouths hanging open, not knowing what to do as I walked off with their ball. After I threw it in the river and it started out to sea, they left me alone. I came in first in 4:35.

Now that I was working intensely on my dissertation, I was training less. The first American 100-mile championship was scheduled for October 1967. Although I wasn't in shape for the competition, I didn't want to miss this rare opportunity for such a long-distance race. However, not only had I never trained for 100 miles, but I hadn't done distance training of any kind for several months, even competing in the New Jersey 50-mile championship without the proper preparation. Still, I was dying to go. The biggest problem was that it was being held in Columbia, Missouri, about a mile or two from the end of the world in my terms, some 125 miles west of Saint Louis. The trip cost a lot of money, and my budget had already been strained that year by the unexpected expense of getting back from Israel after the war. On the other hand, all things being equal, going by statistics and my results at fifty miles, I should be the favorite to win the race.

Joe Yancey gave me fifty dollars from the New York Pioneer Club budget to partially cover my expenses. No other race walker in the club had ever received any sort of expense allowance, and it was the first time for me, too. In retrospect, it turned out to be the last time as well. Fifty dollars was about half the price of a bus ticket, and plane fare was obviously a lot higher. I took the bus. The trip took twenty-six hours. I arrived exhausted, dried out from the air conditioning on the bus, and poisoned by the cigarette smoke I was forced to inhale. Moreover, my dietary regimen was thrown out of kilter, as was my digestion. The few hours I had to rest before the race weren't enough.

The championship was held on a regulation quarter-mile track. We had to do four hundred laps. Start time was noon. Anyone who could finish in under twenty-four hours would be dubbed a Centurion. I knew I wasn't ready and was too tired, but as I looked at the other competitors lined up at the start, none of whom had taken part in the 50-mile championship or had ever recorded respectable times at 50 kilometers, I thought I still had a chance of winning. Everyone else was convinced I would take first place, but they didn't know what kind of shape I was in.

We took off. It was hot. Deluding myself, I started out at a fast pace. After only ten miles I began to feel myself weakening. By twenty miles I decided that in my present condition it wasn't worth the excruciating effort to complete the whole 100 miles and ruin my feet in the process. I would drop out after fifty miles. There were trophies waiting for competitors who only did half the distance, too. Even the fifty miles were hard for me to complete. I don't know what bothered me more, the weakness or the blisters on my feet. At thirty-eight miles I stopped to treat the blisters. They were more plentiful and bigger than I had ever had before, despite the surgical tape I stuck over the vulnerable spots before the race in an effort to prevent them. I managed to drain some and bandage them, and then got back on the track. I finished the fifty miles at a slow pace.

More than thirty walkers started out, but only two went the whole distance. Ironically, the competition was won by Larry O'Neal, a young man who had just turned sixty and had never before taken part in any race-walking event of such length. He finished in twenty-three hours. As the favorite, I was put to shame, but Larry deserves every credit. It took me a long time to prove to myself and everyone else that I could excel at 100 miles too, recording a fast time and declared a Centurion in the very same championship at the same place on the same track six years later.

Throughout that winter I worked very hard on my dissertation. I finished writing up the first draft on an electric typewriter I rented. I didn't know blind-typing, and did it all with one finger of my right hand. It took me a week. My dissertation was officially submitted on February 1, 1968. All that remained was to defend it, but I wasn't anticipating any problems. Now I had all the time in the world. As a rule, doctoral students usually start university teaching while they're still working on their theses, or at the very latest by the time they've begun writing them up. This was equally true at the Hebrew University in Jerusalem. Of course, you have to start looking for a job in advance. And there's surely nothing to prevent you from teaching after you've already submitted your thesis, even if you haven't officially gotten your degree yet.

If I had looked, I'm positive I could have secured a job as a lecturer or instructor at some university starting in February. I could have made six to eight thousand dollars just for that one semester. That was a lot of money for us. But I wanted to devote all my time to training for the Olympics. The money was important, but to me, competing in the Olympic Games meant immeasurably more. I wrote to Green and told him what I had in mind. He wrote back warning me not to do anything that would jeopardize my income since it was very hard to make the Olympic team and it would be a shame if I wound up poorer as well as disappointed. Despite his cautionary remarks, I decided — without any hesitation whatsoever — to concentrate all my efforts on the Olympics. I set about looking for a job at an Israeli university, while making it clear I could only start after the end of the Olympic Games in Mexico.

Thus, from the first of February 1968, I became, or more precisely continued to be, a parasite, letting Shosh support me while I slacked off. "Slacking off" consisted of extremely aggressive protracted training sessions twice a day seven days a week. Within a short time, I was back in the form I had been the year before, and was starting to improve on it. In March I competed in a 50-kilometer event at a stadium on Long Island. It was a cool day, which was good, but it also rained for most of the race. With my clothes and shoes soaking wet, I was carrying more weight than usual. We were using an all-weather track, so at least it wasn't slippery despite the rain.

About twenty competitors started. Henry Laskau and his wife Hilda were among the judges. Each of the officials had an umbrella. After twenty miles, I had about a one-lap lead over the walker in second place, Ron Daniels. I could see him taking a bit off his pace and the gap growing slightly longer from one lap to the next. So I didn't feel especially motivated to push myself to go faster; after all, it's never fun to overexert yourself. I knew Ron was a miler and around half a minute faster than me at that distance, although I had already finished a mile in six minutes fifty-two seconds. He was also faster at ten miles, but invariably I was considerably better at longer distances, so I wasn't anticipating him to pose a serious threat. I could only pull farther and farther ahead.

By twenty-five miles, Ron is almost two whole laps behind. With no one on my heels, I slow my pace slightly. All of a sudden I realize that Ron is moving faster and closing the gap. I am now in front by only a single lap, and he is still picking up his pace. I step on the gas, having enough reserves of energy to do so without much of a problem. But my basic speed is still below his, and with each lap he's cutting into my lead. He can see that just as well as I can. We both pick up the pace, but his is still faster than mine, and he is steadily closing on me. With two laps left to go, I'm only a hundred yards in front. I start to sprint, and he does the same. I can't see him anymore, not even out of the corner of my eye as I complete the turn and start down the straight, and I'm certainly not going to waste time by turning my head. If I can't see him, it means he's very close. I go even faster. I can hear his footsteps behind me. There are only a hundred yards left. Now I'm moving as fast as I can.

About forty yards from the finish line, Ron overtakes me. His sprint is faster than mine. He comes in around three yards ahead of me. My time is 4:29:11; his is one second less. Since this race was held on a track, unlike most 50-kilometer events, the judging and timing were accurate, and as a result my time remains on the books as the Israeli and Asian record to this day. It was also my personal best at the time, although since then I have improved on it considerably many times over, and always in poorer conditions in terms of the heat.

My condition had improved so much that the very next day it was no trouble for me to do a fifty-mile practice walk. Admittedly, as I hadn't perspired in the rain, my body hadn't lost salts and could recover faster. The route I trained on took me to the bank of the Hudson River, along Hudson

Parkway to the northern tip of Manhattan at 225ᵗʰ Street, and then north along Broadway to Van Cortland Park. I kept on the parkway to Yonkers, where the road becomes Route 9, and on through Ossining, the home of Sing Sing Prison, to the long Tappanzee Bridge across the Hudson. It was twenty-five miles each way. North of Yonkers, past the small houses with their enormous lawns, was the leg of the route I liked best and where I often met Ted Corbitt, the legendary black runner who was the outstanding American athlete in all the ultra-long-distance races for many years.

John Kelly had moved to California at the end of 1967. My partner in weekend training was now Ron Kulik. Twice he joined me on the paths through Riverside Park, but more often I'd take the bus across the river to his home in Nutley, New Jersey, and we would do fifty kilometers around the huge reservoir nearby. Each lap was five kilometers, and we would go faster each time around, carrying on an animated conversation the whole way. Ron was faster than me, his basic speed comparable to that of his fellow club members Ron Daniels and Ron Laird, and it seemed strange to me that all three shared the same first name. On the other hand, I had more stamina — although he had won the American 40-kilometer championship — so that we both benefited from training together. He improved his endurance and I improved my speed.

In early April 1968 I went back to Israel for the Four-Day March. I had just celebrated my thirty-second birthday. Before I left, I made arrangements with *Bamachane* for another one-man exhibition a week before the march — this time walking from Jerusalem to Be'er Sheba through Hebron. I was totally unfamiliar with the region and the roads running through it, except for the last section from Tel-Shoket to Be'er Sheba. I thought it should be interesting. A *Bamachane* reporter and driver followed me in an army jeep and kept me supplied with drinks. I studied the map carefully in advance in order to familiarize myself with the route and plan how to pace myself.

I start out early in the morning from Jerusalem. It's chilly. Every now and then the jeep disappears for quite a long time. It's rare that we see a vehicle that isn't Arab. It's a disquieting feeling. Just a few days before, grenades and Molotov cocktails were hurled at Israeli cars along this very road near the refugee camp outside Hebron. Not far from Hebron it starts raining. When the jeep shows up, I ask them to get the white, lightweight rainproof parka I bought in Canada from my bag and give it to me. I feel cozier with it on. When the rain picks up, I pull the hood over my head and tighten the drawstrings, leaving only a small portion of my face exposed to the wind and rain. My beard also comes in handy, protecting my cheeks from the weather.

As I cross through Hebron, my escorts are nowhere in sight. From time to time I see Arab faces catching sight of me, staring and shouting "*majnun*," whether as a sign of respect or fear I can't tell. I don't speak Arabic, but that term for "maniac" is one of the few words I do know. What I don't know is what it implies or what its connotations are. Should I be pleased and relax or should I be doubly cautious? Nothing happens; these encounters pass uneventfully. Between Hebron and Dahariya I suddenly feel myself weakening. The road twists and turns, alternately rising and falling. It's the Mandatory road, or more correctly the old Turkish road, left virtually untouched by the Jordanians. Occasionally I spot a group of Arab laborers working on a short section of the road to eliminate a curve or level the surface. I take something sweet to drink and eat a banana, and within an hour or so the weakness passes. From Dahariya south I can pick up the pace again. Finally, I reach Be'er Sheba. I've done about fifty-five miles in nine hours. It's the longest distance I've ever walked. I'm tired, but not utterly exhausted. They take me back to my mother's house in Ramat Chen.

The reporter took pictures along the way and informed me he was preparing a lengthy article, suggesting I call him two days later to find out when it would appear. When I did so, I learned that not only would the coming edition carry the item, but my picture was going to appear on the cover as well. I thanked him profusely, grateful for the publicity. The day the magazine came out, I went in search of it at the local newsstand. I found it on the rack, the bottom half hidden by some other paper. I was sadly disappointed. The reporter had misled me: the top half of the cover, the only part I could see, bore a picture of Ibn Saud, the Saudi Arabian king, in his traditional robes. Dispirited, I walked off. Glancing at the display at another newsstand I passed, I caught sight of the full cover of *Bamachane*. I could now see that below the bearded face of Ibn Saud, he was wearing gym shorts, sneakers, and a white parka. In fact, it wasn't the sheik at all — It was me walking in the rain! The article inside was an ode to my athletic feat.

It was time for the Four-Day March of 1968, my twelfth straight year. This time the format had been changed and the idea of the camp at Hulda discarded. What a pity! The organizers had destroyed the special atmosphere and the very essence of the experience. Instead, the IDF had decided to introduce the marchers to the newly occupied territories. Each day's route was somewhere in the region of Jerusalem, at times following the Jerusalem-Hebron road I had walked only a few days before. There were now three new terms in Israeli marching lingo: "security," "access allowed," and "clearing the route." Army sappers checked every inch we were to pass for mines or traps, and only after they had finished "clearing the route," was "access allowed" to the marchers.

A small group of people, myself included, were permitted to go ahead before that process was completed. All of us were already accustomed to danger, and I trusted in my speed more than anything else. Looking back, that might have been a pretty stupid attitude, but that was the kind of person I was then, and actually still am. We crossed Arab residential areas in the dark, before the security forces had time to take up position. It wasn't always a comfortable feeling, but as long as we kept moving fast… In fact, the signposts were nothing to write home about either. Some were unreadable in the dark and others were missing altogether. My orienteering skills served me in good stead, keeping me on course and enabling me to avoid all sorts of trouble and natural obstacles. I finished first each day, and, as in previous years, was featured extensively in the media.

While I was in Israel, I wanted to find out from the athletic establishment what I would need to qualify for the Israeli Olympic team to the Mexico games the coming October. I hoped I had already done enough, considering the publicity from the Jerusalem-Be'er Sheba walk and the Four-Day March, along with my personal 50-kilometer record of 4:29 on a stadium track and my results from the preceding year. I was referred to the Hapoel official Emanuel Gil, who, I was told, also held some post on the Olympic committee. He was very courteous, not at all supercilious, and I knew he was a well-educated person who was considered an authority on sports.

The Olympic committee had decided that the minimum for athletes in individual events would be to match the sixth-place result at the previous Olympics, with a leeway of one or two percent. Emanuel Gil had been assigned the job of preparing the official tables. He took out his files and pointed to the line referring to the 50-kilometer race walk. His data was basically correct. Although the winner in Rome eight years earlier, Don Thompson of Great Britain, had finished in 4:25, four years later, at Tokyo in 1964, sixth-place time was 4:18 and some seconds. It didn't take more than a primary school education — maybe even third grade, which I had skipped — to figure out that allowing for 2 percent, the minimum should be 4:23 (and however many seconds as long as it was below 4:24). To my astonishment, I found the minimum on his table listed as 5:09. There was a similar mistake in the +1 percent column. The error was so blatant that I found it incredible that Gil didn't notice he had added 10 and 20 percent instead of 1 and 2.

I then met with the chairman of the Israeli Sports Federation's track and field committee, Brigadier General (Res.) Aharon Doron, or Erwin, as he was known. As a student at the Technion, I had heard from my friends that he was their superior officer, the commander of the Nahal corps. When I had urgently needed the army's permission to leave Israel for the marathon in Greece three years earlier, a form that required the signature of the head of personnel administration, the same Brigadier General Aharon Doron, I went to his office and he signed the form while I waited, without any delay or red tape. This time he was equally welcoming, straightforward and friendly, without any display of self-importance. His extraordinary personality shone through during our conversation.

He had heard of my results, including the 4:29 I had recorded on the track the month before. It had been reported in the Israeli papers, and the official certificate of the record, bearing all the necessary signatures, had been received by the track and field committee. Erwin informed me that I was the committee's first choice for the Olympic team and urged me to keep up my training so that I could meet the minimum. He assured me repeatedly that if I did, he would make sure that no obstacles were placed in my way. When I told him about the figures that Emanuel Gil had shown me, he laughed and said I was too good a person to take advantage of his mistake. He asked me to keep him posted as to my times and wished me luck.

That conversation boosted me up tremendously. He gave every impression of being reliable and trustworthy, and everyone I spoke to was of the same opinion. Moreover, I learned that as a member of Kibbutz Yagur serving in the Mandatory police, he had taken part in race-walking competitions organized by the British authorities in the early forties. So unlike most athletic functionaries, he was familiar with my sport. After talking with Doron, I now knew that an improvement of only six minutes stood between me and the Olympic team, and the ball was entirely in my court. I was convinced I could do it.

As soon as I returned to the States in a buoyant mood, the US Eastern Regional 50-Mile Championship was waiting for me. The manager of the Point Pleasant motel where I had stayed the two previous years read about the imminent date for the competition in the New Jersey papers and was expecting me. When I called to book a room, he said he had already reserved one for me. That was nice to hear. By now I was very familiar with the track, including the different angles at which the sun shone through the stands at various times of the day. Shosh had become expert at assisting me.

"*A la guerre comme à la guerre*," in a war you do what you have to do, and in a championship you make a championship effort, but this year it didn't exhaust me. Neither was I "rewarded" with blisters, the sort of reward I'm very happy to forgo. But I did win the race. And again I improved on my own American record. I finished in 8:05 — six minutes off my time from the previous year. In two years I had succeeded in shaving thirty minutes off my time. The next day, as only to be expected, my muscles ached, but I could manage some light training. It was hard for me to absorb the fact that I had improved so much and gotten so much stronger in only two years.

When I went to Columbia to arrange for a date to defend my dissertation, I ran into my favorite professor, Wayne Marshal. He was a sports fan and had already heard how I had broken my own record. As I watched, he plotted my times at fifty miles over the past three years and drew a line through them producing a hyperbola. He then issued his pronouncement based on this graph: "You can expect no significant improvement in the future." Looking at that graph, I came to the same conclusion. But there were still a lot of surprises in store for me.

At the end of April 1968 I successfully defended my dissertation. Finally, I was awarded the precious degree. I was now Dr. Shaul Ladany. The title began to appear next to my name in the press, and it still does, even though five and a half years later I became an associate professor and several years after that a full professor. But I realize it's only the force of habit, and not just among journalists. I still sign myself "Dr. Ladany" just to be sure there's no question about the authenticity of my identity or my signature. It took me about two and a half years to get my doctorate. It wasn't a contest, but the fact remains that all my Israeli friends who had started before me received their degrees anywhere from six to eighteen months later. Both the Hebrew University and Tel Aviv University offered me a position as lecturer. I accepted the latter offer and was now assured that a job awaited me in the Tel Aviv School of Business Administration starting in October 1968.

My beard was still growing. At one 10-mile competition along the boardwalk at Coney Island, Brooklyn's famous amusement park, we had to walk back and forth four times. The boardwalk was crowded with pleasure-seekers alternately gazing at the Atlantic Ocean and watching the race. Each time I neared certain sections of the boardwalk, I could hear people calling out, "The rabbi is coming, the rabbi is coming." My long beard must have reminded them of the many pictures of rabbis prominently displayed in Brooklyn.

In early May I competed in a 10-kilometer event on the track of the same Long Island stadium where I had recorded my best time for 50 kilometers. I was very happy with my result even though I only finished third. Training with Ron Kulik had paid off, and my basic speed was now faster. Ron Daniels was ahead of me for the whole race, and in the end he came in first. But Ron Kulik and I were neck and neck for the entire course, and he only beat me out by two seconds, thanks to his sprint at the very end. My time of 47:44 stood as the Israeli record for many years, as well as my fastest time on a track. I never imagined then that four years later I would do the first ten kilometers of a 50-kilometer race even faster than that.

In the little free time I had between training sessions, I developed an idea I had gotten for an extension cord that would be more compact, cheaper, and more efficient than anything available at the time. The necessary length of cord could be released from its holder and would then wrap itself back around a small drum in an orderly fashion without the need for a special winding mechanism. It was the extension and application of an idea that had occurred to me from the way sewing machines wind the thread around the spool. I submitted a patent application and was granted an American patent a year later.

■ Chapter Nine | Preparing for the Olympics

A round May 1968 I learned that the American 20-kilometer champion-ship was going to be held in Long Beach, California, in early June, and the 50-kilometer championship three weeks later in San Francisco. Mexico City, about 7500 feet above sea level, was to be the site of the Olympic Games. The air is thinner at that altitude, so that athletes function differently than they do closer to sea level. As a result, the Americans had decided to alter their usual procedure of automatically selecting for the Olympic team the winners of the first three places in the US championship in each sport. This time, the best contenders, in the championship competition and other events as well, would be invited to a training camp to be set up at an altitude compa-rable to that of Mexico City. Trials would be held at the end of the camp, and the three who took the first places under these Mexico City conditions would be selected to represent the United States at the games.

Hoping to meet the Israeli Olympic minimum, I wanted very much to compete in the American 50-kilometer championship. I figured that by taking part in the 20-kilometer championship race and then training intensely between the two events, I could improve my form and increase my chances of meeting the minimum at the later race in San Francisco. If I didn't make it then, I could certainly do it after working with the best American race walkers at their training camp. I wrote to Doron and asked him to inter-vene with the American athletic establishment so as to obtain permission for me to carry out this plan of action. Justifiably or not, I was convinced I could meet the Olympic requirements and finally fulfill my dream of competing at the games.

Shosh and I packed up everything we had amassed in our two and a half years in the States and shipped it back to Israel, arranging for it to reach the country around the same time we were scheduled to return, in November. Shosh stayed on in our apartment in New York until we were sure my plans were approved, while I flew to California in early June. The luggage I took with me, a small suitcase and a carry-on bag, was full of sports equipment and designed to suffice for the five months until we returned to Israel. Just before I left, I received a reply from the track and field committee. Doron informed me that the Israeli Sports Federation had decided to grant me a thousand dollars to cover my travel expenses and training in California. That was a pleasant surprise. The trip and the time on the West Coast would certainly cost a lot more than that, but money was no object when it came to realizing my dream.

The American 20-kilometer championship at Long Beach was organized by Don Denoon. I came in ninth, recording a mediocre time of 1:41, but I didn't take it to heart since I regarded the race — in terms of not having time to rest beforehand and my own motivation — as merely training for the real test of 50 kilometers. I was the only foreign entrant, but after competing repeatedly with the others for two and a half years, and even training with some of them, I was considered "one of the gang." I felt the same. I was on friendly terms with everyone. When they heard I was planning to remain in California for the 50-kilometer race, Bill Lopes — a member of the Golden Gate Walkers Club together with Goetz Klopfer, Tom Dooley, and Bill Ranney — invited me to stay with him in San Francisco. John Kelly also invited me to his house in Santa Monica. I decided to accept both invitations, staying with John Kelly for two weeks and then with Billy for the third.

As soon as the race at Long Beach was over, John drove me to his matchbox apartment in Santa Monica, and I joined him for his intense training routine. He had also stopped all other activity and was concentrating on the attempt to earn a ticket to the Olympics. Fortunately for him, he had two irons in the fire: he could represent either the US or Ireland. On arrival in California, John had joined the Santa Monica Athletic Club and trained there under their coach Michael Igloi. At five in the morning, when it was still pitch black outside, we showed up at the entrance to the stadium. Other athletes were already waiting. Igloi arrived on time, opened the gate, and started spelling out the training program for each athlete for the day.

Igloi was Hungarian and had been that country's national coach, working with the celebrated runners Iharos, Tábori, and Rózsavölgyi, the world middle-distance champions and the major rivals of Landy from Australia and Roger Banister from the UK before those two broke the four-minute barrier for one mile. In 1956 he coached the Hungarian team at the Melbourne Olympics. Like many of his athletes, he chose not to return to Hungary after the games in light of the Soviet repression of the Hungarian uprising. Instead, he moved to the States, but despite his skills and fame, he received no offer of any suitable senior position. Although he coached a few outstanding runners, along with the hammer thrower George Fren who represented the US twice at the Olympics, he had only the very modest title of athletic coach at a small club. In later years he was to become the Greek national and Olympic coach, a position he held for close to twenty years.

John introduced me to Igloi, who was very pleased to discover I spoke Hungarian, and he agreed that we could train together while I was in Santa Monica. We got to work immediately, carrying out his instructions. John was his only race walker. We started by doing a fast 880 yards around the track four times, with a one-minute rest in between. Then came four times 1100 yards, with two-minute rest periods, followed by four times 440 yards. Igloi didn't map it all out for us in advance. Instead, he simply said, "Do a fast 440 yards," and when we were finished, "Now do it again." We worked hard, walking as fast as we could and hoping that each time was the last. Holding a stopwatch, he would inform us of our time after each lap, and then order us to do another 2200 yards. He repeated this pattern, assigning us a distance and then surprising us by demanding another one. We gave each task all we had, as if it were the last one, while he kept his little surprises coming. John told me that he used the same system with his runners; none of his athletes ever knew in advance when the training session would be over or how long it would last.

It was nearly nine o'clock when we finally finished that first session, totally exhausted. We went back to John's apartment, had something to eat, and went to sleep. At four in the afternoon we were back on the track, and the morning's scenario played out again, with only the sequence of distances altered. The next days followed the same pattern. One day we were instructed to circle the outside of the stadium ten times, alternating it with shorter distances for speed. If Igloi checked our times and the expressions on our faces and concluded that we still had enough strength left, he would extend the training, even if all the other athletes had already gone home. With no thought to how much time he was devoting to us, he would stay on to issue instructions and urge us on to greater effort.

We hated the way Igloi constantly kept us in the dark, but we were very appreciative of his willingness to give us much more of his time than his measly salary warranted. Although we could sense our basic time improving steadily, I was concerned that this alone wouldn't be enough for us to do well at the 50-kilometer race; we also needed distance training. So, despite the fact that Igloi assured us he had used the same routine when he coached the Hungarian race walker Antal Roka, who took one of the first places at the Helsinki Olympics in 1952, I convinced John Kelly to join me in rebelling. Every few days we played hooky from afternoon training and went out on our own for a twenty- to thirty-mile practice walk through the Hollywood Hills. We felt that this combination of speed and distance training was really doing the trick.

On our second long-distance walk we were joined by a runner by the name of Bob Brunner who had just begun training with Igloi. Bob ran at the same pace as we walked, but the distance was too much for him. After the first ten kilometers he stopped, waited for us to turn around and come back, and then ran alongside us again for the last ten kilometers. He was a Canadian about to start his doctorate in political science at the University of Southern California and had decided to train for the marathon. Although he was a long way from being in condition to run the marathon, he had an impressive athletic record. Short and slim, he started out as a boxer, going so far as to win a gold medal at the Canadian championships, a silver medal at the Commonwealth Games, and a bronze medal at the Rome Olympics in 1960; and he even found time between these major events to win a gold medal at the Maccabiah Games. So you couldn't really call him a poor athlete.

After the Olympics he set his sights on becoming a professional boxer, but his first professional bout put an end to that ambition. Years later I learned that he had gotten his doctorate in physical education, moved to Australia, and become a renowned ultra-long-distance runner, winning 100-kilometer and 400-kilometer races against horses, and performing similar feats no other mortal could match. Later he became religious, changed his name to Reuven, grew a heavy beard, and settled in Jerusalem, where he tried to convince orthodox Jews to run. He could be seen at marathon races in Israel running back and forth among his protégés and urging them on.

Sunday was our "day of rest"; we only had one training session with Igloi. Naturally, John and I used the opportunity for another long-distance walk. This time we went out with Ron Laird, walking through huge Griffith Park. As we followed the watershed across the park hills, we were exposed to one of the risks faced by athletes training in Los Angeles at that time. All of a sudden, the three of us — all extremely fit athletes — were struck almost simultaneously by agonizing headaches. We were being poisoned by the gases in the notorious smog hanging over the city. Our body temperature began to rise and we were forced to quit. The next day, in the clean air of Santa Monica, we were pain-free again.

After training for about two weeks with John Kelly and his coach Igloi, I flew to San Francisco. I called Billy Lopes from the airport. Apologetically, he explained that it would be three hours before he could come to pick me up. As I glanced at the view from the terminal, I noticed a line of hills a few miles away. I decided to use the time until Billy arrived to get in some more training. I changed into my gym clothes in the rest room, left my bag and my traveling clothes in a locker, and stuck my wallet in my pocket. I walked over to a gas station, pointed to the hills, and asked the station attendant, "How do I get there?" Following his directions, I walked along the edge of the freeway and reached the hills. Once there, I walked up and down the slope, and even discovered an open athletic track which I used for speed training. On my way back to the airport, again keeping to the shoulder of the freeway, a police car suddenly pulled up alongside me.

It wasn't my first experience with law enforcement officers. One afternoon in early spring, Elliott Denman, Don Johnson, and I had gone out on a practice walk through the towns along the coast of New Jersey. There was no longer any snow on the ground, but it was still cold out. In place of sweatpants, Elliott was wearing his wife's tights. The sweatpants I was wearing had seen so much use and been washed so many times that they were full of holes. Add to that my long beard, and I don't think I looked much like your typical PhD. Not surprisingly, the three of us aroused the suspicion of a cop. He trailed after us in his car through several towns, and when it was obvious that we weren't going to go into any house, he decided we must be hoboes and was about to run us in. It took all our powers of persuasion to convince him not to haul us off to the station for questioning. Elliott kept his mouth shut and let Don and me do the talking. When I mentioned that Elliott was a sportswriter with a column in the *Asbury Park Evening News*, the cop took a closer look and found a certain resemblance to the photograph that regularly graced the column head. He eventually grasped the fact that there are some people who prefer walking to going everywhere by car, and let us get on with our training.

The California cop demanded, "What are you doing here?" and I replied simply, "I'm walking." Not satisfied with my answer, he kept at me, "Why are you walking?" "Because I like to walk. I'm training." My laconic answers did little to allay his suspicions and probably provoked him as well. I must have looked like a hippie with my long beard, and as he saw it, no one with an ounce of sense in his head would be out walking in the middle of the day. Roughly he proclaimed: "You're not allowed to walk on the freeway. I'm writing you a citation." I explained that I wasn't from around there, that I had asked at the gas station and was only following the directions I had been given, and that I was in town for the American 50-kilometer race-walking championship and was using the time I had to get in some training until a friend came to pick me up. He wouldn't be moved, insisting he had to give me a ticket and demanding to see some ID. Luckily, my Columbia University student card was still in my wallet and still valid. It convinced him that I wasn't a hippie and that I was indeed from New York. He must have realized that a person from out of state could easily avoid paying the fine, but rather than admit it, he recited, "Since you're not from California, I'm going to let you go this time." He wouldn't let me resume my walk along the freeway, but ordered me into the rear seat of his car and I sat there, separated from him by a metal grating, as he drove me back to the airport.

I took advantage of the few days I stayed with Billy at his parents' house in the quiet town of Mill Valley, across the bay from San Francisco near Paradise and Sausalito, both to train hard and to arrange for someone to assist me at the championship. Before leaving New York, I had written to the Israeli Student Association of San Francisco and asked them to try to find a volunteer to hold out my drinks as I attempted to meet the Olympic minimum. Their reply contained the phone number of a man who was willing to help out. I called and introduced myself. He said he was Uri, had been in track and field at the Olympics, and would be glad to help. I had never heard of any Uri representing Israel at the Olympics in any athletics event, so I assumed he meant he had once been a spectator at the games. He had never heard of me either, and had never seen a race-walking competition. Not wanting to frighten him off with detailed explanations of what he would have to do, I decided not to ask him to bring the ice, bucket, and sponges I would need in this hot climate. We arranged to meet at the starting line shortly before the race was scheduled to begin.

The championship was held in beautiful Golden Gate Park beside the spectacular Golden Gate Bridge. It was organized by Bill Ranney, who even made sure of television coverage, including one airborne crew in a helicopter overhead. The route was mapped out along the main road through the park, which was closed to traffic for the occasion. We had to do ten laps of five kilometers each, two and a half kilometers in each direction. Uri showed up on time. He did exactly what I asked and even tried to cheer me on during the race, but unfortunately I hadn't had time to explain the changes in the amount of glucose I would need as the competition progressed or that he had to stir it well into the Coke in order for it to dissolve properly. As a result, not only did he put too little glucose in to start with, but a lot of it was left at the bottom of the cup he handed me so it didn't get into my mouth.

As we walked back and forth along the route in each direction, we had to contend with four steep climbs and one small one. They placed an extra burden on all the competitors and lengthened everyone's time by several minutes. But while the others were only interested in their final placing, I had to record a time that met the Israeli Olympic minimum, and those ascents could make that an impossible task. The heat and humidity were also working against me. I had given myself a complete rest from training for three days before the race, the proper thing to do before a major event like this that is so long and exhausting it calls on all the body's reserves of energy. So I had come not only fresh, but determined to make every effort to achieve the result I needed. My final placing per se didn't matter, except insofar as it meant I'd win a bigger trophy or a prettier medal.

At long-distance events, like the 50-kilometer race walk or the marathon run, an athlete who does the first half fast often finds himself incapable of finishing or has to reduce his speed drastically in the second half. This is sometimes described colorfully as "hitting the wall." I wanted to avoid that risk, however small, because it could keep me from fulfilling my Olympic dream. I had to plan my strategy accordingly, even if it meant that my time would be slower than if I started out at a fast pace.

In retrospect, it turned out to be a wise decision. At the halfway mark I was tenth, and then gradually began overtaking my opponents, eventually finishing in fourth place with a time of 4:23. One thought immediately echoed through my brain: "I did it! I met the minimum!" Actually, judging by the way I felt and by the speed I was going at, I had been sure I would make it for the final five kilometers, assuming nothing unexpected happened. But in long-distance events you can never predict when something will go wrong. According to the unofficial times I was given two and a half kilometers before the finish and at the start of the final kilometer, I had calculated that I would meet the minimum without having to sprint. I was afraid that if I suddenly sped up, my style would change and I would be disqualified by the judges, who were watching the walkers like a hawk near the finish. It had never happened before — in fact I'd never been given a single warning, not even in short-distance races — but this race was too important for me to take any risks just to improve my time by a few seconds or even as much as a minute. Larry Young, Goetz Klopfer, and Dave Romansky came in ahead of me. John Kelly was fifth, a minute and a half behind me.

Bill Ranney shafted me at the medals ceremony. According to the rules, I deserved fourth place, but he wanted a nicer trophy than his final placing in the race warranted, so he presented me with a special award for outstanding foreign athlete, causing everybody else to move up one place and earning him the last of the more impressive trophies. I received an unsightly ceramic plate with a metal inscription glued on it. I was very annoyed, but I kept my feelings to myself. Bill was a nice guy, but not known as a model of integrity. I may have been irked by his sly tactics, but it couldn't overshadow my joy at having met the Israeli Olympic minimum. I sent the plate to Shosh in New York; it was shattered in the mail. So except for the small metal inscription, the official certificate of the time I recorded, and the pleasant memories I came away with, I had no real memento of the championship. Even the color photos Uri took came out too fuzzy for any of the figures to be recognizable.

It was at the awards ceremony that I discovered who Uri really was. His full name, which was actually familiar to me, was Orion Galin. He was a discus thrower who had indeed represented Israel at the Olympic Games in Helsinki in 1952. Being an amateur pilot as well, he was asked to fly over an official ceremony held at Kibbutz Ma'agan on the Sea of Galilee in 1954 in honor of the tenth anniversary of the Jewish volunteers from Palestine who had dropped behind enemy lines in Nazi-occupied Europe. He was to toss out a greeting to the invitees that was in a bag tied with a drawstring. When he threw the bag out the window, the string got entangled in some part of the plane. As he tried to free it, his plane, still flying low, dived into the crowd, hitting one of the stands reserved for distinguished guests. Several lost their lives, including a number of those who had survived their extraordinarily dangerous wartime missions.

The incident became known as "the Ma'agan disaster." The commission of inquiry that was set up to investigate determined that it was caused by a sudden air pocket rather than pilot error. Nevertheless, the tragedy made Uri so notorious that wherever he went people pointed and called him "the Ma'agan disaster pilot." Eventually, he left the country. When I met him, he was studying physiology at Berkeley, and he invited me to stay with him. Years later he returned to Israel and joined the faculty of the Wingate Institute of Physical Education.

Since I had passed the Olympic minimum, I decided to go to South Lake Tahoe the next day, the site of the high-altitude training camp for the top ten American contenders in each athletic event. I arrived by bus and went straight into the office of the camp director appointed by the US Olympic Committee, a man named Bowerman. I had written to him from New York, but, unusually for an American, he hadn't replied to my letter. I had heard that a good number of governments, as well as individual athletes, had requested permission to train with the Americans at the camp and that they had all been refused. Nonetheless, considering my involvement with American race walking, I decided to attempt the impossible. I introduced myself to Bowerman and presented him with my athletic achievements and my request. He didn't kick me out. Since it was early and not all the athletes had arrived yet, he allowed me to put up for a few days with the American race walkers in one of the small rooms where there was still an empty bed, until I could find accommodations outside the camp.

As soon as I arrived, I sent the track and field committee in Israel the official confirmation of my time at the American 50-kilometer championship in San Francisco. They soon wrote back that since I had made the minimum, I would be included on the Israeli Olympic team. I was thrilled to get official notice, although having recorded the required time I had no fear they would decide otherwise. I wrote back asking the committee how I would get the special Mexican visa for Olympic sportsmen, the thousand dollars I had been promised for expenses, and the team uniform. I included my size and noted that my measurements were on file with a certain tailor in Jerusalem who had custom fitted a suit for me before I left for the States. I also asked them to send me Israeli insignia so I could exchange them with the foreign athletes I met, as is accepted practice. I never got an answer to the letter, but I assumed that everything was being taken care of because Lalkin, the head of the Sports Federation, sent me the pins I had asked for, attaching a note saying that they were in response to my request.

The Olympic Committee had organized the camp with typical American efficiency. An area had been cleared at the top of the mountain and a tartan-surfaced track had been laid out among the trees. Nearby, dozens of comfortable trailers had been installed and hooked up to electricity to serve as living quarters, communal bathrooms, or gyms. The administration offices and dining hall were at the bottom of the steep mountain, about five or six miles away. I was assigned a place in a four-bed unit in one of the trailers where Ron Laird was staying. The next day the other two beds were taken by Jim Hanley, against whom I had competed twice in Chicago, and Martin Rudow. When they went off to the American dining hall, I bought myself something to eat at one of the lunch counters in the area.

The day after I arrived, I hung up several notices saying that an Israeli Olympic athlete was looking for a room to rent in the vicinity while he trained at high altitude with the Americans. I asked that replies be left at the camp office. I also noticed a lot of private cabins here and there in the woods near the camp, and started going from door to door looking for a place to rent.

Three days later Ron Laird came back from the dining hall with the news that "some babe in a white Corvette" was looking for me and was offering me free accommodation. He had a rather lascivious smile on his face the whole time he was telling me this. He sent me to ask at the office. She had left a note saying that she and her boyfriend would be delighted to help out by letting me stay at the cabin they shared near the camp. I went to see them. In the middle of the forest near the edge of a cliff offering a splendid view of the valley below, I met two genuinely nice people: Donna Pritchet and Warren Harding, the very same name as the American president during the Depression. They lived modestly, were sports lovers, and simply wanted to help an athlete in need. They had rented the cabin for the summer while Warren was working on the construction of an airfield nearby, and they were offering me one of the bedrooms.

As soon as I moved in I discovered why they had chosen this particular cabin. Warren was a rock climber, and Donna an enthusiastic partner in the preparations for his feats. There was a towering boulder close to twenty feet high in the yard, and whenever he had a free moment, Warren would practice on it. He would hang for a long time by the tips of his fingers from the tiniest cracks on the rock face, which to anyone else appeared totally smooth and virtually perpendicular. Then he would find nearly invisible knobs for his feet and use them to climb a bit higher, his goal being to hang by pure muscle tension for as long as he could in every possible position. I found out that he was well known, and was the first person to climb the face of El Capitan in the Yosemite Valley where the two walls of the 3300-foot mountain meet to form almost a straight vertical line. Since he had to drill support holes into the mountain and tie himself to them, it took him a whole month, during which time he slept hanging in the air.

While at Tahoe, they were planning out his next expedition, climbing the straight south face of the Yosemite Valley mountain known as Half Dome. Donna designed and sewed the hammock he would sleep in as he hung from the mountain — where he would have no cover from the rain or the cold — and made sure it was strong, well sealed, insulated, and as comfortable as possible. Warren was eventually to perform this feat, on his second attempt, attracting an enormous amount of media interest. They both must have thought I was crazy to waste all my time and energy on walking. But considering that they devoted so much time to climbing to the tops of mountains that could be reached by car, I guess we're all crazy in one way or another...

I trained regularly with John Kelly and a small number of other walkers, and a large group of us also went out together for long-distance road training. Occasionally I went north from my cabin along the narrow forest paths to Lake Echo and from there into Desolation Area. This is a huge nature reserve off limits not only to motor vehicles and horses, but even to planes overhead. It was a genuine paradise studded with clear rivers and small lakes. In the six or eight hours I walked through it, I didn't usually run into more than three or four hikers. I even found snow on one of the sheltered mountainsides, although it was only August. Sometimes I saw deer, but I was lucky enough never to have a run-in with anything more dangerous. I kept to the paths for fear of snakes, and after I caught sight, from a safe distance, of a large rattle-snake chasing a mouse, I became even more cautious.

A few times either John Kelly or Dave Romansky and Ron Laird joined me on the lower portion of these paths. Since they didn't have the experience of forest paths I had gotten from the marches, they didn't really enjoy training here despite the amazing view. They tended to trip over roots and stones, unaccustomed to avoiding such obstacles by skipping over them or altering the length of their steps. At the end of one such session, Dave dubbed me "mountain goat," and he wasn't referring to my beard. A few months later, Ron Laird sent me a picture he took at the end of one of my long-distance practice walks, writing on the back: "The amazing bearded walking man of South Lake Tahoe still going strong after eight hours."

I suffered from the lack of a support system. Studies in physiology have shown that athletes who come from sea level do not employ their muscles to the full at high altitudes, so they run the risk of losing muscle tone. It is thus considered wise to compete at some lower altitude every ten to fourteen days. As a result, several times during the course of the training camp, my American friends were taken down the mountain for a few days to compete in various events. Knowing the importance of working out at different altitudes, I went to Berkeley once for three days where I stayed with Uri Galin and, lacking competitions to enter, set myself long, strenuous training tasks.

The American Olympic Committee might have gone about setting up the training camp with enviable efficiency, but it turned out they did it in the wrong place. As soon as he arrived, Jim Hanley, a high school teacher, complained that although the altitude was comparable to Mexico City, the camp was in a region of high air pressure, meaning that the air was richer in oxygen. It was common knowledge that the thin air of Mexico City would play a role in any event lasting more than one hundred seconds, and particularly in the race-walking and marathon competitions. Even after the athletes had adjusted to the conditions, the lack of oxygen would slow speeds by an average of 8 percent. Yet the whole purpose of the high-altitude training camp was to give our bodies a chance to adapt to the conditions we would encounter in Mexico.

Although we were instructed in how to use our diaphragms so that the lungs could take maximal advantage of the available oxygen, practicing this technique was no substitute for actual acclimatization. When Jim Hanley's arguments began to sink in, about a month after the camp opened, the Olympic Committee transferred the race walkers and marathon runners to Boulder, Colorado, a more appropriate site in terms of both altitude and oxygen concentration. Not having the financial means or necessary arrangements to go with them, I remained in the less conducive conditions of South Lake Tahoe for another two and a half weeks until the camp was disbanded, and had no choice but to train on my own.

The Tahoe camp brought together the elite of American track and field. There were celebrated champions, medalists from previous Olympics, world record holders, and athletes with a good chance of winning Olympic glory, such as the famed miler Jim Ryan; Bill Toomey, who would soon win the decathlon at the coming Olympics; the broad jumper Bob Beamon, who would smash the world record, setting a new distance that would stand for twenty-four years; and a long line of other major figures in world athletics. In addition, the who's who of the American athletic establishment at the time was also in attendance.

Most of the athletes were just as good as those eventually chosen to represent the US at the Olympic Games, but were simply unlucky in the final trials. Such was the case with the blond miler Dave Patrick from Villanova University, whose lightning final sprint was unmatched by any of his opponents and brought him in first in most competitions, even though he usually stayed at the tail end of the pack until he jetted ahead toward the end. At the final trial he delayed his sprint for too long and didn't leave himself enough time to overtake the other runners. As a result, he wasn't one of the three in his event chosen for the team. A similar tragedy befell the world decathlon record holder, Russ Hodge, who, although built for the sport with amazing muscles and power, was also very fragile. He strained his hamstring in the hurdles, sending his Olympic dreams up in smoke in a split second.

From the very first day at the camp, the immense gap in the training loads required by the different categories of athletes was very conspicuous. While the distance runners and race walkers were accustomed to long hours of arduous training every day, and the middle-distance runners did only a little less, the training program for sprinters and athletes in the field events was much less demanding. This was most blatant in the case of the sprinters. By intensifying their training they were able to improve both their times and their ability to compete in successive races — preliminary heats, quarter-finals, etc. But even after they stepped up their training, they were considered idlers and aroused the envy of everyone else in camp.

Dr. Jack Daniels, the camp physiologist, himself an outstanding athlete in the modern pentathlon, outlined for the distance runners and walkers the conclusions of the latest Swedish study which showed how to temporarily raise the level of glycogen in the muscles by gorging on carbohydrates. According to his directions, during the last week before an important race we were to train very hard for three days while keeping to a diet high in protein and fats, and then rest for the next three days, maintaining a diet high in carbohydrates. I tried this. The first three days were awful, especially the second, and it got even worse on the third. I got progressively weaker and developed a constantly increasing appetite for anything sweet, even bread. The last three days were quite easy and I got my strength back. But I didn't see any improvement when I used this method. It was only five years later that I saw any real improvement in my competition times as a result of the diet, and that was only after I decided, in the wake of extensive trial and error, to eliminate the recommended eggs and walnuts (which have a high fat and protein content) and consume almost nothing but carbohydrates.

One day, doing speed training on the track in a T-shirt with the words "ASA Technion" in Hebrew on the front, I heard someone call out to me in Yiddish: "Hey, countryman, come over here!" I turned and saw Danny Kaye, a very familiar face from the many films of his I had seen. He was performing at one of the casinos in South Lake Tahoe and had decided to come and see how the American athletes were training for the Olympics. With the combination of my rabbinical beard and the Hebrew letters on my chest, he could not have had any doubt as to my identity, but then again, one of his hosts might have told him there was an Israeli there. He was very friendly and asked a few prosaic questions. A local photographer who happened by took our picture and gave me a blowup a few days later.

When the rest of the walkers departed for Boulder, Ron Laird left me his old Volkswagen Bug in return for my promise to drive it to Los Angeles and leave it with his girlfriend Violet when the camp shut down. I didn't have any need for a car in South Lake Tahoe until Shosh arrived. When I got definite word that I would be going to the Olympics, heading straight for Mexico from California, I arranged for Shosh to come to Tahoe a few days before my training there was over. When Donna and Warren heard she was coming and that I was looking for a place where we could both stay, they offered to take her in as well until we had to leave. Shosh was flying into Reno, so I drove over in Ron's car to pick her up. She missed one of her connections and wasn't on the flight. I assumed she'd be on the next plane, three hours later.

I decided to use my free time in Reno for the one thing that most interested me in that famous city: the largest automotive museum in the world just outside of town. It was home to about two thousand cars, including some that had won the trans-Asian rally at the start of the century or the Indianapolis 500, armored cars belonging to heads of state, experimental cars, the very first automobiles, and so on. The place was a joy for anyone who loved technology, history, and sports. The museum belonged to Harrah's, a chain of casinos located throughout Nevada's gaming cities, so for the price of a ticket I also got a coupon that could be exchanged for chips at Harrah's casino in the center of Reno. That might be incentive enough for most people to try their luck, but apparently it's not only in race walking that I'm not like most people. I don't gamble and I'm very good at calculating the odds of winning or losing. The promotion worked differently on me. I did go to the casino and exchange the coupon for chips. Then I went to another cashier and turned in the chips. They were worth more than I had paid for the museum ticket. That was the end of my career as a gambler and the first and last time I was ever in a casino. Some years later, the museum was closed down and the cars were auctioned off to collectors.

When the training camp was over, we took Ron's car to Los Angeles. Donna came along with us to visit her family in Fresno, and suggested we go through Yosemite Park where she worked and could act as our guide. She mapped out half-day and whole-day routes for me along the park trails, and while I went out to train, she and Shosh took the car and toured the sites. I met up with them when I was through, having walked some of the most fascinating trails that only a few visitors ever reach. In the course of four days of training, I got to see almost every interesting corner of that immense park. The first night after driving in through the east gate, we slept in sleeping bags at a campsite.

Donna had warned us to be on the lookout for the grizzlies that come to forage for food during the night. She directed us to sleep at some distance from the picnic tables and garbage cans and to make sure all the food was locked in the car. We awoke in the middle of the night to find we were almost under attack from a group of bears. It seems we forgot an unopened can of food on a nearby picnic table, and we could hear the animals tearing into the tin with their teeth and claws and then rummaging through the garbage. As they passed back and forth right beside us, we lay perfectly still and didn't make a sound so as not to attract their attention. When we got up in the morning we found garbage scattered everywhere, the can twisted, full of holes, and empty, and bear tracks in the wet ground right next to where we had been sleeping. We didn't stay at that campsite, and we didn't leave any more cans outside either. After touring Yosemite, we left Donna in Fresno and went on to Los Angeles. Donna was later to marry the decathlon champion of Taiwan, who represented his country at the Olympics.

A stop along the way at the Titanic Company garage in Be'er Sheba, en route to the Gadna camp at Ein Yahav, 1952

On leave from officers' training course with my sister Martha (left) and my cousin Evie, 1956

My wife Shosh and me in Ramat Chen, 1960

With my parents on the balcony of the house in Ramat Chen, 1957

At the ceremony awarding the rank of second lieutenant at the end of the artillery officers' course, 1956. I am second from the left.

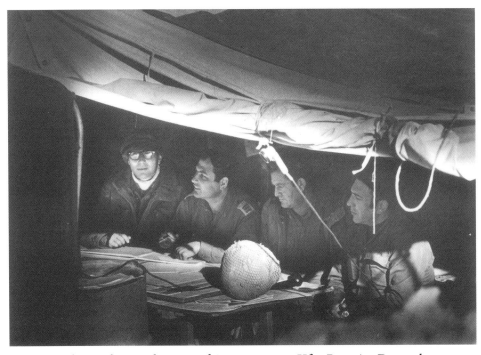

Command post during the War of Attrition near Kfar Ruppin, December 1969; to my left, Eitan Benderly, Avraham, and Shmuel Miller

Walking campaign from Jerusalem to Be'er Sheba, April 1968: fending off the rain

The 20-kilometer race in Manhattan's Central Park, 1968

Training in California at the Olympic camp of the US team, 1968

With the actor Danny Kaye at the Olympic training camp of the US team, 1968

Competing against Howie Jacobson in the 3000-meter race at the Maccabiah, 1969

With Reuven Peleg (no. 2) and Howie Jacobson (no. 3) on the winners' podium
after winning the 10-kilometer competition at the Maccabiah, 1969

Soldiers escorting me during the Maccabi torch relay, December 1968

The closing ceremony at the end of the 26th torch relay, 1970, at the President's House; from right to left: Menachem Savidor, me, and President Shazar

The effort is reflected in my face at the end of the Belgian 50-kilometer championship, Marcinelle, 1971

I'm leading in the Belgian 50-kilometer championship, Marcinelle-Beaumont, July 1971

Fatigue registers on my face when Paul Nihil (on the right) congratulates me at the end of the **London to Brighton Walk**, 1971

The program of the **London to Brighton Walk** 1971 noting that I am the holder of the winner's trophy

Eli Shahar handing me a sponge at the 100-kilometer world championship race, Lugano, October 1971

DR. SHAUL LADANY
50 Mile Race-Walk World Record Holder 7:23:50

sunday, april 16, 1972
ocean township, new jersey
U.S.A.

Crossing the finishing tape as I break the world record in the 50-mile race, 1972

The Mayoress of Bradford awarding me the winner's trophy, 1973

In the Munich Olympic stadium, 1972, one hundred meters before the finish line

Approaching the finish line as the winner of the second day portion of the Tour du Var, 1974

After the end of the Tour du Var: the effort still registering on my face, the chafing in my armpit bothering me

SHAUL LADANY HÉROS DU 39ème MARCINELLE – BEAUMONT – MARCINELLE

Déjà sur le chemin du retour, Shaul Ladany croise un petit groupe commandé par le remarquable vétéran Charles Dorckens qui, fort efficacement, salue du geste le grand champion israélien. Derrière Dorckens, on reconnaît (numéro 52) le gendarme E. Surinx.

LE PETIT PROFESSEUR DE TEL AVIV PULVÉRISE TOUS LES RECORDS !

LEON PEETERS A MUNICH ?

Report in the Belgian press on my winning the Belgian 50-kilometer championship, 1972

The first day of the cross-country walk from Metulla to Eilat, 1970

During the 100-mile championship in Columbia, Missouri, 1967

I continue to lead on the way back in the Belgian 50-kilometer championship, July 1971

1967 METROPOLITAN A.A.U. AWARD WINNERS

Meritorious Award Winner

THOMAS LARIS .... Track & Field - Men
New York Athletc Club

Outstanding Athletes

WILLIAM HANSON .... Basketball
Downtown Atheltic Club

FOREST WARD .... Boxing
Police Athletic League

ALICE BRUNNHOELZL .... Gymnastics - Women
Unattached

DAVID JACOBS .... Gymnastics - Men
Brooklyn Central YMCA

MARTIN J. POPPE .... Horeshoe Pitching
Unattached

SHIRO OISHI .... Judo
New York Athletic Club

EDWARD WINROW .... Long Distance Running
New York Athletic Club

ALEX KAZICKAS .... Swimming - Men
Unattached

DONALD F. COLOMBO .... Diving - Men
Levittown Swimming Association

KARLENE F. TREBESINER .... Swimming - Women
Jersey City Y.W.C.A.

JAN VERMILYE .... Diving - Women
Women's Swimming Association

BYRON DYCE .... Track & Field - Men
New York University

FRANCES BUSH .... Track & Field - Women
Unattached

SHAUL PAUL LADANY .... Race Walking
New York Pioneer Club

CHARLES H. HARRIS .... Water Polo
New York Athletic Club

EDWARD RODRIGUEZ .... Weightlifting
Unattached

MICHIO TOMINO .... Wrestling
New York Athletic Club

List of outstanding athletes of the Amateur Athletic Union (AAU) in the New York area for 1967; I am the winner of the prize for walking

Settimana internazionale della marcia

100 km.
Gran Premio Caffé La Chiassese
Olivone-Gambarogno - Lugano

1. Dr. Shaul Ladany, Israele,   9.38.56,4
2. Michel Vallotton, C.M. Ginevra   10.02.00
(campione svizzero di gran fondo)

VIII Settimana internazionale della marcia

100 Km. di marcia

III Criterium mondiale della I. A. A. F.

VIII Gran Premio Caffè La « Chiassese»

Campionato Svizzero di gran fondo

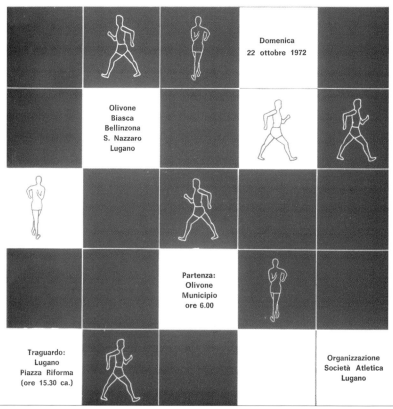

Domenica
22 ottobre 1972

Olivone
Biasca
Bellinzona
S. Nazzaro
Lugano

Partenza:
Olivone
Municipio
ore 6.00

Traguardo:
Lugano
Piazza Riforma
(ore 15.30 ca.)

Organizzazione
Società Atletica
Lugano

The program and the results sheet of the 100-kilometer world championship
race, Lugano, 1972

■ Chapter Ten | The Mexico City Olympics

I called Shmuel Horowitz, who was collecting our mail for us in New York, and then tried Tahoe. There was no letter from the Israeli Olympic Committee. I still hadn't gotten the special visa issued by the Mexican authorities for the Olympic team members and delivered to the national committees. Time was running out. As soon as I got to Los Angeles, I went straight to the Mexican consulate, armed with the letter from the Israeli Sports Federation confirming that I would be representing the country at the Olympics. I wanted to get to Mexico City as soon as possible to continue intensive training and give my body time to adjust to the altitude. The American athletes were already there, as was John Kelly. He hadn't made the American team, but his excellent results had convinced the Olympic committee of his native land to send him to the games as the lone race walker representing Ireland.

I showed up at the consulate early in the morning, filled out the application form, and was told to wait. So I waited — and waited — and the time passed and nothing happened. When I checked with the clerks, I was instructed to go on waiting: "The vice-consul is reviewing the applications." Finally, in the late afternoon my name was called. Some junior clerk informed me that they could not give me a visa because the foreign ministry had already issued special visas for the Olympic athletes and forwarded them to the national Olympic committees. I explained my situation and asked for a tourist visa that would get me into the country in the meantime. But a new application, so I was told, could only be filed the following morning.

I barely managed to get in a little training that evening; it took two hours to get from where I was staying to the Mexican consulate. The next morning I skipped training again and was at the consulate by eight a.m. I filled in the proper form and then went through the same routine as the day before.

Toward the end of the day, my name was called. The clerk informed me that the vice-consul had not approved my request for a tourist visa, since I was going to Mexico to compete in the Olympics and not as a tourist. I was furious.

The greatest irony was that two months earlier, when I received the letter from the Sports Federation confirming my place on the Olympic team, I tried to dissuade Shosh from using it to apply for a visa for herself. We knew the Mexicans were very stingy with their visas — as if theirs was the land of milk and honey and the whole world was standing in line to get in, and it was especially hard to obtain one for the duration of the Olympics. I tried to convince her that when my special visa came, she would automatically get hers for free as my wife. But Shosh never liked to trust in the future, and with typical prudence she preferred to pay the fee and know she had it in her hand. And now with that same letter I wasn't even able to get myself a visa.

Early the next morning I went to the Israeli consulate to ask for their help. I was given a letter addressed "To Whom It May Concern," confirming that I was indeed a member of the Israeli Olympic team and requesting that I be afforded any necessary assistance. From there I went straight back to the Mexican consulate, arriving before noon, and again filled out an application, attaching the letter from the Israeli consulate. It was a Friday. At the end of business I was informed that the vice-consul had not had time to review my request and that I should come back after the weekend.

On Monday I paid a second visit to the Israeli consulate and asked the consul to intercede. He explained that he couldn't just pick up the phone and ask the Mexican consul personally to approve my visa application because "there are no free lunches." He would have to do a favor in return for his Mexican counterpart, and it might turn out to be against Israeli interests. He did, however, give me an official letter addressed to the Mexican consul, who, he said, would understand that it wasn't a personal request but might still feel uncomfortable ignoring it. At noontime I was back at the Mexican consulate. I asked to add the Israeli consul's personal letter to my application and requested an interview with the consul. Before closing, I was told that my request was being reviewed and asked to come back the next day.

By now I knew the way to the consulate with my eyes closed. I sat there from early in the morning, but nothing happened. Finally, it dawned on me that the runaround I was getting was no more than a tactic to convince me to grease the palms of the Mexican clerks. I remembered someone once saying that "when a Mexican driver gets stopped by a cop, he gives him ten pesos if he didn't do anything illegal and twenty pesos if he did." Later I heard that "the verdict in a Mexican court depends on which side pays the judge more." But I had never given or received a bribe, and I didn't want to start now. I was determined to get the visa I was entitled to without compromising my integrity.

In the afternoon, after wasting seven days when I could have been training, my patience ran out. I started yelling at the clerk who had taken care of me, threatening him, at the top of my lungs, with diplomatic repercussions when I went to the press with the information that they were preventing an Olympic athlete from competing in the games. I demanded to see the consul and be issued a visa. The clerk tried to calm me down, assuring me that if I came back the next morning he would see what he could do.

Even before I flew off the handle, I had decided to go to Mexico City on Thursday, with or without the visa. Shosh had already bought two plane tickets and booked us a flight. It would be risky, since the Mexicans were known for arresting anyone entering the country without a visa, and the conditions in their prisons were notorious. In order to forestall the possibility of my enjoying the hospitality of the Mexican penal system, I had called the Israeli embassy in Mexico City and requested them to inform the ambassador that I would be arriving without a visa. I gave them the details of my flight and asked that someone from the embassy be at the airport to ensure that I wasn't arrested.

On my way to the Mexican consulate the next morning — by now a daily commute — I sent a telegram to the Israeli ambassador in Mexico to underline the seriousness of my phone message and make sure it wasn't ignored. At the Mexican consulate things moved at a snail's pace and, as usual, I had to wait. But I didn't care anymore. I knew I would be on the plane the next day, and I told the clerk as much, making a point of the fact that the Israeli ambassador would be there to greet me. An hour later I was summoned to the office of the vice-consul. He issued the tourist visa he had refused to grant me eight days earlier. I had finally gotten my visa, and I had also gotten some valuable experience. But it had cost me precious training time.

As we deplaned at Mexico City, I was paged even before we got to passport control. Chaim Globinsky, the honorary chairman of the Israeli Olympic

Committee, was waiting for me with a Mexican liaison. As soon as I introduced myself, he jumped down my throat: "Do you know what kind of trouble you've caused me, calling the ambassador, sending telegrams? All because of you I have to waste my time here!" That really infuriated me. It was his fault that I hadn't gotten my athlete's visa, that I had lost nearly eight whole days of training, and now he had the nerve to accuse me of wasting a few hours of his time. Beside the fact that he was to blame for the whole mess, someone should have told him that his title didn't only entail honor and perks, but also required that he do his job. And I told him so to his face. He didn't like it one bit; apparently he was only used to people licking his boots. His response was to refuse to take Shosh to her hotel, agreeing only to drive me directly to the Olympic Village.

I eventually learned that Globinsky's enormous power in the Israeli sports establishment came from his tight hold on the money. Not only did he occupy an important position on the Lottery, Pool, and Gambling Commission that afforded him significant influence in the allocation of funds from those sources to the athletic associations, but he was also very close with Hezkiel Cohen and his buddies, the heads of the American Committee for Sports in Israel who channeled their contributions through him. Atypical for an Israeli, he liked to drink and, although he seemed able to hold his liquor, he was disorganized and inefficient. An oft-repeated joke claimed that when he found himself at the airport in Lod he would strike his forehead and ask himself: "Am I coming or going?"

When I finally got to the Olympic Village, I resumed training with my old friends the Americans, the Canadians, and John Kelly. Four days later the rest of the Israeli team arrived. I was thrilled to find my former classmate from the officers' training course, Michael Marton, who had assisted me in the marathon race in 1956 and was at the Olympics because of his excellent results in pistol shooting.

When I met the delegation manager, Shmuel Lalkin, I discovered to my surprise that they hadn't brought a uniform along for me. Nor did he have the thousand dollars I had been promised. He gave me a hat and a sweat suit that I couldn't wear because the thick seams caused chafing. He asked me if I had black walking shoes and socks and a white shirt, and when I said I did he announced that I wouldn't be getting them from him. He was very annoyed by my demand for an explanation, considering that every other member of the delegation, including the escorts, had been issued those items. He merely repeated his pronouncement, justifying it on the grounds that I already had what I needed. It wasn't important enough to argue over, but what was important was that I didn't have a shirt with the name "Israel" on it to compete in.

I was very upset about not having a uniform. It had been my dream to march into the stadium for the opening ceremony wearing the uniform of my delegation, a dream shared by every athlete in the world. The day after the others arrived, they all took part in the official raising of the Israeli flag, but lacking the proper outfit, I wasn't able to enjoy that privilege. It was particularly irksome because I had specifically raised the issue and even sent the committee my measurements way in advance. John Kelly, who had also joined up with the rest of his team at the Olympic village, proudly showed off his Irish uniform and the rest of the gear they had brought him. I was green with envy.

When I met the head of the delegation, Joseph Inbar (Izo), who, like the other escorts, was not staying at the Olympic Village, I immediately complained. He was very nice and tried to console me, saying: "It's not so terrible. When Gideon Ariel came straight from the States to the Tokyo Olympics in 1964, he didn't have a uniform either. And he carried the Israeli flag dressed in a sweat suit!" I got the picture: if you don't come with the rest of the delegation, they not only save on the flight, but they don't have to worry about outfitting you either. It had never occurred to either the manager or the head of the delegation to look out for me. I don't know whether they were just trying to save money or whether some other person, who wasn't entitled to it, got my gear.

I refused to let it go, and Inbar promised to bring my grievance up at the next committee meeting. I was invited to attend. They tried to explain that there was nothing they could do to amend the situation and that it wasn't such a tragedy — so what if I couldn't take part in the opening ceremony. Not one member of the committee offered to lend me his uniform and forgo the honor of marching into the stadium behind the Israeli flag. I argued that there must be some similar material in Mexico and they could have a suit sewn for me, and they finally gave in, but I got the feeling that they only agreed because they were sure it would never happen. I borrowed Michael's uniform and went looking for the right shade of blue, accompanied by Shosh and a Mexican liaison.

I found what I needed and ordered a suit identical to the one I had brought with me. It was ready in two days. The Mexican liaison made sure the bill was sent to the delegation. They raised a stink, claiming that I should have gotten their approval before buying the material and ordering the suit. It just proved I was right, and they had only been paying lip service to my protests when they agreed in the first place. Whoever had designed the uniform didn't know what he was doing, outfitting us in Nehru jackets buttoned up to the chin. Not only were they ugly, but they were also uncomfortable. I never wore mine again after the official Olympic events, except for masquerade parties.

Nevertheless, it was an unforgettable experience to march in the opening ceremony in the Israeli uniform. I had dreamed of that moment for years. Everyone was in high spirits, obvious from the broad smiles on their faces and their exuberant gestures. Although we had to stand there for ages while the speeches — some of them in Spanish — went on and on, the ceremony made a deep impression on both the athletes and the spectators.

There was one little incident that none of us will ever forget. Each delegation marched into the stadium and circled the track behind a flag bearer before taking its place on the field. The flag bearers were equipped with a small conical holder strapped on around the waist and across the chest. The metal flagpole went into this holder, and the flag bearer held it with two hands a little above the bottom of the pole. The weight of the flag was transferred to the body through the straps, so that all they had to do was to hold it steady and make sure it didn't fall. When the large Soviet delegation marched in — both they and the Americans had three entrants in each of the individual events — it was led by the weightlifter Jabotinsky. He was a monster of a man, what Goliath must have looked like. With one hand stretched out in front of him, he held the flag straight up in the air as if it were a matchstick, slowly circling the stadium with all eyes fixed on him in amazement.

The Israeli team consisted of eleven athletes: five swimmers, four marksmen, the runner Hannah Shezifi, and myself. We were escorted by a swim coach and a shooting coach, Lalkin, Inbar, Globinsky, and a few other functionaries to whom I was never introduced before, during, or after the Olympics. We were also joined by the Israeli national soccer team — which had made it through the preliminaries to the games — together with its own officials, but except for a short period around the time of the opening ceremony, they weren't housed in the Olympic Village. Instead, they stayed in the small city nearby where the soccer competition was held, and when they didn't make it to the round of sixteen, they left Mexico. The soccer team was a "world unto itself," and didn't consider themselves an integral part of the Israeli delegation, nor were they treated as such by the Olympic committee.

Before and after the opening ceremony, with all the teams ensconced in the Olympic Village, the mood was very relaxed. Although everyone was training hard, within the confines of the Village we regularly ran into athletes from other countries. During training sessions I met most of the other walkers, as well as many of the marathon runners with whom we shared similar training sites and routines. At the end of one session, I met the Ethiopian marathon runners Abebe Bikila and Mamo Wolde. Bikila was already a living legend, the first African athlete to race to glory when he shocked the world by winning the marathon at the Rome Olympics in 1960, running barefoot. He repeated his triumph four years later at the Olympics in Tokyo and proved that he was really the best. In Tokyo, Adidas apparently paid him a considerable sum to run in their shoes, and they took him to gold. But as soon as he crossed the finish line, he kicked them off with a scowl and threw them aside, running his victory lap barefoot. It was rumored that they had given him blisters.

Abebe's reputation preceded him, and I admired him greatly. But when I met him and tried to carry on a conversation with him, using my hands to make myself understood, I discovered something I later heard described by General Shlomo Gazit when he was president of Ben-Gurion University. Shlomo had been the head of army intelligence and had conducted talks with the Egyptians after the Yom Kippur War, discussions known as the 101st kilometer talks (or the Kilometer 101 Agreement) for their site on the road to Cairo. Speaking from personal experience, he remarked: "Do you know the difference between a mountain and a government minister? The closer you get to the mountain, the taller and more impressive it looks..." That was how I felt after meeting Abebe Bikila. From up close he gave the impression of being a boor. He completely lost his halo, leaving me with the sense that behind this well-oiled running machine was a very drab personality.

Other athletes often sat down at my table in the dining hall. This was how I met the fine Tunisian runner Mohamed Gammoudi, the winner of several Olympic medals in the course of his career. A lot of the athletes gathered in the evenings at a central spot in the Village, looking to meet new people and swap mementos. Whenever I went there, I felt I was really in my element. Using what I had learned watching the athletes at the Maccabiah Games swapping buttons and patches, I soon collected over a hundred different Olympic insignia. It didn't hurt that I spoke eight languages (and that my knowledge of Serbian and Croatian made it possible for me to carry on a halting conversation with the Bulgarians and the Russians as well), and so could translate for a lot of people who didn't know any foreign language.

My services were highly in demand, and periodically someone would go looking for "the Israeli with the beard" to translate for athletes in the same event who had no other way of communicating. Two Hungarian women came up to me once and the first burst out laughing when I answered her in her native tongue. It turned out that her friend hadn't believed there was a Hungarian-speaking athlete in the Israeli delegation and was willing to bet on it. It was a triumphant laugh I was hearing.

The Olympic Games offered a unique opportunity to meet and talk with people from all over the world, bridging gaps that under ordinary circumstances would be impossible to ignore. Thus, at the very height of the Cold War we were able to converse almost freely — if we avoided political subjects — with athletes from behind the Iron Curtain whose countries had been hostile to Israel since the Six-Day War. I was especially excited by the chance to talk with Jewish athletes from Communist countries who came up to me, an Israeli in the Israeli uniform, and introduced themselves as Jews. It was obvious from their faces how thrilled they were to be able to speak with a proud Jew and Israeli. Such encounters were, however, rare, and invariably took place when there were no other members of the Eastern European delegations in sight.

To my regret, in contrast to my warm relations with most of the athletes, I had no contact with any Arab sportsmen save for Gammoudi. I made a few attempts to talk to them and swap mementos, but as soon as they heard I was from Israel they turned away demonstrably and cut off any further contact. More than being offended, I was disgusted by their unsportsmanlike behavior in public.

The choice of Mexico to host the Olympic Games was a controversial decision. Avery Brundage, the overbearing president of the International Olympic Committee, had been severely criticized in the past for vetoing a boycott of the games in Berlin in 1936, organized by the Germans with strict adherence to their racial statutes. This time, the critics aimed their barbs primarily at the rarefied air of Mexico City, which would put athletes from lower altitudes at a distinct disadvantage compared to those used to higher locations.

Ron Clark, the legendary Australian runner, was particularly outspoken against Brundage's decision. For a long time, Clark had been the world's best runner at almost all distances between 3000 meters and 20 miles. He held a considerable number of world records, a distinction that worked against him in major competitions where the goal of all his rivals was to beat the best runner in the world. They turned the races into tactical battles that forced him to adopt a less-than-optimal strategy in terms of pacing himself. Thus the world record holder had never managed to win Olympic gold. Clark, the first athlete whose training routine included three daily sessions, was in excellent form for Mexico. But knowing that in the thin air he would not be able to win the medal that could otherwise be his, he lashed out furiously at Brundage. He was right. In the 5000-meter final, he started out faster than he should have in those conditions and collapsed in the middle of the race. He had to be carried out of the stadium on a stretcher.

There were also problems stemming from the level of hygiene, organizational skills, and efficiency of the Mexicans. "Montezuma's revenge" is a familiar term throughout the world to describe the diarrhea and dysentery suffered by many Western visitors to Mexico who drink the water and eat the local food. The human feces in the fertilizer, open untreated sewers, and poor sanitation result in intestinal disorders for almost anyone whose body has not developed an immunity by being accustomed to such conditions. All the athletes were warned to drink only bottled beverages and eat only at the Olympic Village where the food was specially treated, and under no circumstances to eat anything raw. These restrictions were particularly confining for the race walkers and marathon runners. Not daring to drink the local water when we went out of the Village for long-distance training, we either had to cut these practices short or arrange for assistants to bring bottled beverages with them.

As a matter of course, I trained twice a day. The first practice lasted from six to ten in the morning, after which I'd eat a large breakfast and go back to my room to rest. At three I'd go out again until six or seven in the evening. After supper — my second meal of the day — I'd go to sleep. This routine didn't leave any time for recreation or touring the city. I was glad that at least when I trained along the roads outside the Olympic Village I got a chance to see something of what the city and the surrounding area had to offer.

I generally trained with John Kelly; the Canadians Alex Oakley, Carl Merchenz, and Felix Capella; and sometimes with the Americans Larry Young, Goetz Klopfer, Dave Romansky, Ron Laird, and Rudy Haluza. We'd all known one another for a long time by now and enjoyed the closeness of fellow athletes, although there was no question that each of us hoped to beat out the others on the day. We trained as a group almost every day in the afternoon, walking the twisting mountain road out of the Village. We believed that by training at altitudes a few hundred yards above Mexico City, where the air was even thinner, our bodies would be better acclimatized to the conditions of the race and, this would give us an edge over the athletes who didn't practice at these heights.

Whenever we went out, one of the American or Canadian officials would drive out to meet us with drinks. Nobody ever suggested that John Kelly or I wasn't entitled to this assistance, or that members of our delegations ought to take their turn providing the service to all of us. But we knew our duty without having to be told. At John Kelly's request, an Irish official accompanied us once a week. I also addressed a similar request to Lalkin, but he replied that he couldn't help me. It was hard for me to accept his refusal as an objective evaluation of the situation. The Mexican organizers had provided a car and driver for each delegation, Lalkin had exclusive control of the car, and none of the other Israeli athletes had a need for it for purposes of training.

I was ashamed to seem to be taking advantage of my friends when my own team refused assistance even once. So one day, in order not to appear a complete parasite, I told them I wouldn't be going out with them but had decided to practice on the stadium track instead. I trained alone that day, but with no one to provide me with drinks and afraid that if I put anything in my mouth without knowing where it came from I might be stricken by diarrhea, I didn't have a drop to drink the entire time. By the end I was almost completely dehydrated. It's a well-known fact that after strenuous exercise an athlete's resistance is temporarily weakened. Not surprisingly, then, the next day I was sick. The Village doctor examined me, wrote out a prescription, and told me to rest.

I didn't need him to tell me; I felt lousy and barely had the strength to move. I gave Lalkin the prescription and asked him to have it filled. It took three days of nagging before he finally sent his driver to get the medications. Had I had any contact with Shosh, I could have asked her to do it, but she didn't want to interfere with my training regimen and only very seldom snuck into the Olympic Village to see me. Two days after getting the medicine, I felt better, but in the meantime I had again lost five precious days without training. Fortunately, I had arrived in Mexico City about five weeks before the day of my event.

The Mexicans were as friendly as they were inefficient. On the whole, they were very agreeable people, but signs of their incompetence were everywhere, both in and out of the Olympic Village. Without the help of the foreign professional committees, I doubt they would have been able to organize the games. Even with this assistance, foul-ups were the rule rather than the exception. Still, the entrances to the Village were always crowded with fans cheering any athlete who passed. The rhythmic chants of "Mexico, Mexico, tah, tah, tah" echo in my brain to this day. Not only did they "pounce on" the athletes with requests for autographs — usually without the benefit of any writing utensil, paper, or hard surface to lean on — but they often showered us with free souvenirs. It was truly heartwarming to see their enthusiasm, affection, and joy in being given this opportunity to host the Olympics.

One comical symptom of the Mexicans' inefficiency and the fact that a large portion of the uneducated populace was idle was obvious in each of the residences in the Olympic Village. Meant to serve as apartment complexes after the games, the buildings were equipped with an automatic elevator that could carry three people. The organizers stationed a congenial uniformed elevator operator in each one, and he would man the doors, riding up and down and pressing the buttons for the appropriate floors. When a group of us entered the building — and we usually arrived in groups — only two could go up in the elevator since the operator made three. So the rest had to wait or take the stairs. And since the Mexican spoke only Spanish, it was hard for us to make ourselves understood, so as a rule we just pressed the buttons ourselves. Thus the operator did little more than to take up space that could have been used to speed up the process of getting the athletes upstairs.

Shosh had booked an expensive hotel for a few days and went looking for someplace more suited to our means for the rest of her stay. It turned out that at the small hotels she found listed in the popular tourist guide *Mexico on $5 a*

Day, they were incapable of taking a booking for a future date in any organized fashion, either by room or by date, so she couldn't be sure that the room
she reserved would actually be waiting for her when the time came. When
she tried to explain how it was done, they told her it was too complicated and
didn't matter anyway; the worst that could happen was that someone would-
n't have a room or that they would be left with a few that were unoccupied.

Entrance to the Olympic Village was restricted to national team members
and officials. The masses of Mexican locals were indeed kept out, but anyone
else could pass himself off as an athlete and get in without any trouble. Shosh
bluffed her way in regularly by wearing my sweat suit jacket, and she was just
one of many foreigners who did the same.

About ten days before my race, the whole delegation took the afternoon
off to be guests of the Mexican Jewish sports club. Before we left, I asked
Lalkin when we would be getting back since my rigorous training program
demanded that I be in bed by nine. He promised we'd be back by then. It took
over an hour to get to the club. The function was attended not only by us
Israelis and a great many Mexican Jews, but also by Jewish athletes and
coaches from other countries. It was a very convivial evening. At nine I
reminded Lalkin that I had to get to bed if I wanted to train properly the next
day. He assured me we'd be leaving right away. I spoke to him again at ten. He
reiterated his previous response and told me not to nag him.

A British coach standing next to me remarked that it was a crime to keep
the athletes there so late, even if they were enjoying themselves, because "the
first thing on the minds of the Israeli officials should be the well-being of
their athletes and their success in the games, and not social contacts with the
Jewish community." The officials could have stayed and sent the rest of us
back, or at least the swimmers and the track and field athletes. At 10:30 I
spoke to Asahel Ben-David, the head of the Sports Authority who had also
been invited, and asked him to tell Lalkin to arrange for us to get back to the
Village. At the same opportunity, I asked for his help in getting me a shirt with
the name "Israel" printed on it for the race. A few minutes later I ran into
Shaya Porat, a sportswriter for the Israeli daily *Ma'ariv*, and asked him to put
pressure on Lalkin as well.

Soon afterward, Lalkin approached me with a sour look on his face and
said he wanted a private word with me. Following him into an empty room, I
tried to ask him again to send me back to the Village, but he cut me off

angrily, exploding, "If you ever complain to a journalist again, or even speak to one, I'm going to send you straight back to Israel!" He probably used the same tone when he wanted to intimidate young athletes, but I was in no need of his good auspices and I could never stand pompous fools. I shot right back at him: "I know my rights and your legal responsibilities too. I'm not here because of you! I'll talk to anyone I want to!" He was stunned by my audacity and only muttered under his breath, not saying a word in reply. But he flaunted his power and his contempt for me by keeping me there until the party ended around midnight.

The next morning I couldn't train properly; I was too tired and groggy. I kept up regular strenuous practice until three days before the race. Then finally I gave myself a respite to raise the level of glycogen in my muscles before the big test. The 20-kilometer walk was held on my first day off. I went to the stadium to watch the start. It was my first experience of the actual competitions. A huge electronic board bore the names of all the starters, and I was startled to see my own name there among them. I figured it must be some mistake. But when it happened again four years later in Munich, it occurred to me that the Israeli officials did it on purpose. By inflating the number of athletes in the competitions, they could get more free tickets for themselves and their associates.

After lapping the track twice, the walkers left the stadium to continue the race on the road, following a circular route just outside the stadium. I followed them out to watch the race. It was tense and exciting, with the order of the walkers changing with each lap. This time I was only a spectator, and I could cheer my friends on. In addition to the Americans and Canadians I knew from before, I had met a lot of the other race walkers in the Village.

At the start of the last lap outside the stadium, I went back in to watch the finish. The Russian Goloubnitchyi, whose exquisite style left no doubt as to its legality, was leading. His teammate Smaga was about thirty yards behind, followed about ten yards later by my friend Rudy Haluza. An airline pilot, Rudy used his time between flights to train at whatever airport he happened to be. Although Ron Laird beat him out in most competitions, his job seemed to have prepared him well for high altitudes and now he was showing the whole world what he was capable of. Just another two hundred yards and the bronze medal would be his.

A few seconds behind Rudy, the Mexican "walker" José Pedraza entered the stadium. It was a race-walking event, but he was obviously running. When the Mexican spectators caught sight of him, they all rose and started roaring, chanting "Pedraza, Pedraza, viva Mexico." Pedraza raced ahead, ran past Rudy, quickly closed the gap with Smaga, and passed him as well. Driven on by the frenzy of the race and the roar of the crowd, he kept going and nearly passed Goloubnitchyi, when he suddenly seemed to hold back, as if he was afraid to overtake him at a run, and made do with crossing the finish line second, just steps behind the winner. Ron Laird felt ill during the race, but he refused to drop out and finished among the last competitors. The crowd showed its appreciation by cheering him noisily as he entered the stadium.

The next day I ran into General Doron near the entrance to the Olympic Village. We were chatting when Pale Lassen passed by. He was the Danish head of the Race-Walking Committee of the International Track and Field Association and the chief judge of the walking competition. He recognized me and joined us, and I introduced him to Doron. Lassen told me that three judges from three different countries had disqualified Pedraza in the 20-kilometer race even before he entered the stadium for the finish. When Lassen was handed the third red warning card — and it takes three to actually disqualify a walker — he had run after Pedraza to take him out of the race, but the Mexican was already in the stadium. He could still have been disqualified even after crossing the finish line, but Lassen was afraid he'd be lynched by the spectators if he did that to the first Mexican ever to win an Olympic medal in track and field. So Pedraza got his silver medal because Lassen feared for his life — and who can judge a person under such pressure — and Rudy was unjustly denied his bronze.

I took the opportunity to ask Doron when I would get the thousand dollars I had been promised. He was surprised to hear I hadn't received it yet, and said that Lalkin had brought it with him and was supposed to give it to me. When I told him that Lalkin had claimed he didn't know what I was talking about and hadn't brought me any money, Doron stated unequivocally, "Lalkin's lying." It was over six months more before I ever saw the money. Although I had been promised a thousand dollars for expenses, and I was also entitled to a return of the fare from California to Mexico for a total of thirteen hundred dollars, after that long delay I was eventually handed only six hundred dollars on the grounds that I hadn't submitted receipts. Nobody had ever told me I needed to save them; during the hundred days or so I had spent in California I hadn't eaten in restaurants and so I didn't have receipts, and the other athletes were reimbursed at a per diem rate.

I was the only walker who appeared at the briefing before the 50-kilometer competition; all the others were represented by coaches or officials appointed by the team managers to assist them. I tried asking Lalkin, Inbar, and other officials to second me during the race, but was answered with a litany of excuses. It was obvious that the whole band of functionaries sent to the Olympics at the expense of the taxpayers — whether as officials or under some other guise — considered their presence there an occasion for fun and games and had no sense of any duty to perform their jobs and help the athletes. The other people at the briefing were very surprised to see an athlete there himself, but I couldn't do anything to alter the situation. The briefing provided a great deal of contradictory information, necessitating the scheduling of a second briefing. I attended that one as well.

I was given thermos bottles, and since I wanted a specific beverage during the race and not just water, I had to turn them in to the officials on the morning of the competition. I delivered eight cold boxes with four thermos bottles in each — two filled with orange juice and two with Coke. Glucose had been added to one of each pair. I labeled each cold box and each thermos bottle with my name, the word "Israel," my number, and the contents, and numbered each box according to the watering stations along the way. I hoped that way I'd be able to drink whatever I needed at each station, depending on how I was feeling. Officially, the Mexican organizers were supposed to fill the cups themselves and arrange them on the table so that each athlete could pick up the one with his number on it or take it from the hand of the person in charge. Nevertheless, it was obvious to everyone at the briefing that each competitor would need a representative at each station to ensure that the proper beverage was poured out when the walker was approaching and to hold it out himself or instruct the Mexican as to how the athlete wanted it done.

Lacking any assistance from the Israeli delegation, I tried to organize some minimal help on my own. Shosh wrote up notices in Hebrew asking for volunteers to help out during the race or just to cheer me on along the way. She stuck dozens of them up in hotels around the city and at the main entrance to the Olympic Village. I wasn't inundated by offers as a result, but two young tourists from Eilat, Maya and Yossi Ramon, got in touch with

Shosh and offered to help. She also heard from a journalist who wanted to film the competition for the fledgling Israeli television station. He had a rental car. Shosh made arrangements with all three of them.

The race was to start at some distance from the Olympic Village, follow the main roads through Mexico City, and end inside the Olympic stadium. The eight watering stations were set up five kilometers apart from the tenth to the forty-fifth kilometer. Before the competition, I cut my long beard short so it wouldn't get in my way and wrote ISRAEL on the front and back of my white shirt with a blue ballpoint pen. Since I'm a good draftsman, the hand-drawn letters looked pretty good from a distance, although they made a sad sight from up close. Unfortunately, I hadn't anticipated that the sweat, juice, and water that would pour down my shirt during the race would make the ink run until the shirt was covered with a mess of stains and splotches, something of an embarrassment to the State of Israel.

The race started at two in the afternoon, in the worst heat. I spoke to John Kelly while I was warming up and stretching before the start. He was in sad shape. He had started to feel lousy the day before, developing the symptoms of flu. That morning he had awakened with a high fever. Not wanting to forgo his dream of competing in the Olympics, he had taken aspirin and reported to the starting line. The Irish officials in his delegation had tried to dissuade him, but with the obstinacy of a true sportsman he had refused to give in. I had no escorts, no one there even to wish me luck, but I didn't care. I knew I was in fine form, and despite the days I had lost in Los Angeles and while I was sick in the Olympic village, I was sure my present condition should enable me to finish somewhere between tenth and fifteenth. I also knew everything now depended on getting my drinks and glucose at the right time and in the right amounts.

We took off. About forty walkers. I reached the first watering station at the tenth kilometer in the second group, around fifteenth place. I knew my strength was endurance, but the pace wasn't too fast anyway. I'd lost a lot of fluids so I was already thirsty. I bypassed the first table with its cups of water so that I could drink as much of the Coke and glucose I had prepared as possible. It was supposed to be on the next table. When I got there, I picked up the only cup with something brown in it beside the card with my number. Keeping up a quick pace as I left the table behind, I brought the cup to my lips and drank it down. Suddenly I felt the bitter taste of black coffee in my throat.

I don't like the taste of coffee so I don't drink it. Without thinking, I immediately spat it out. "Those clumsy organizers got my Coke mixed up with someone else's coffee," was my instant reaction. "Now that I didn't take any water and didn't drink the coffee, I'm going to get dehydrated." If I had had an assistant at the watering station, that would never have happened. I wasn't going to get anything else to drink until kilometer 15, so I hoped that at the sponge table coming up soon, there would be enough water in the sponge that I could drink some instead of trickling it over my body.

The sponge I got was squeezed almost dry. The people in charge apparently didn't know, weren't told, or weren't clever enough to realize that the sponge wasn't there to wipe off the sweat but to splash water over the body, so it ought to be sopping wet. The few drops of water I managed to squeeze into my mouth tasted awful, most likely still containing the residue of the perspiration of some previous competitor combined with the dust left on it after he had finished with it and tossed it on the ground.

I didn't slow down even though I'd had nothing to drink and was sweating profusely in the heat. I was still in the second pack when I reached the watering station at kilometer 15, although I was almost totally dehydrated by then. Having gotten burned once, I didn't want to take any chances this time, so I took the glass of orange juice from the table next to my number. As soon as I poured it down, I could taste the bitterness. Someone must have taken it out of the cold box early in the morning, filled the cups, and left it to stand out in the sun for hours. It had all gone sour. Not wanting to make the same mistake again and suffer dehydration, I drank it down despite the acidity.

As we had arranged, Shosh was waiting for me at the watering station at kilometer 20. That was the first time I got what I needed, Coke with added glucose. I was still more or less fifteenth. Shosh, the Ramons, and the reporter tried to get to the station at kilometer 25 in his car. If they'd been in the official delegation car, they wouldn't have had any trouble. But without a sticker permitting them free movement, they were held up at the police barriers and couldn't make it. So they decided to try for kilometer 30 instead. At kilometer 25 I got to drink rancid juice again, and I paid the price. Around kilometer 30 I started to vomit and felt awful, which naturally forced me to slow down. Several other walkers overtook me one after the other. About kilometer 35 I began to feel pressure in my bowels; the rancid juice had given me the runs. As we passed an empty lot beside the route, I stepped off the road, squatted down behind a bush, and answered the call of nature. While I was still bent over, one of the Mexican spectators came over and in a humane gesture handed me a newspaper. It was obvious to both of us that he didn't expect me to read it...

In those precious moments I lost, I was passed by a few more rivals. I got back on the road, keeping up a fast pace. Around the forty-third kilometer I closed the gap between myself and the Mexican Pablo Collin ahead of me. I could feel my strength coming back and thought I could go even faster. I tried to overtake Pablo, but I wasn't allowed to — literally. A motorcycle drove onto the road and kept up position behind him. The police didn't do a thing about it. I was being choked by the clouds of black fumes spewing from the motorcycle's exhaust pipe. When I tried to pass Pablo on the left, the motorcycle moved to the left, staying right in front of me and choking me off. I tried moving to the right and it did the same, blocking my path and poisoning me with its exhaust fumes.

Crowds were lined up on both sides of the route chanting "Pablo, Pablo," and "Mexico, Mexico," and every time I made an attempt to pass him, the chanting got louder and the motorcycle cut me off. I felt strong enough to pick up the pace, but the cyclist was in my way. Things went on like that until we were about eight hundred yards from the entrance to the stadium, when the motorcycle was stopped by the police. I took immediate advantage of the opportunity, overtaking Pablo, entering the stadium, and completing the half lap to the finish line at a fast pace. I came in around 150 yards ahead of him. He would go on to win Olympic gold in the future.

I finished in twenty-fourth place in 5:01. Elliott Denman, covering the event for his paper, was standing not far from the finish line. I hadn't yet caught my breath when he informed me: "Shaul, you missed your chance to take tenth place. In your condition you could have done it." It hurt to know that the lack of an assistant at the first watering station had stolen my chance to finish between tenth and fifteenth.

My result was the second-best achievement of the Israeli Olympic team, after the swimmer Abraham Melamed's eleventh-place showing in the butterfly stroke. My race was won by the East German Christophe Höhne in 4:20, a full ten minutes ahead of the Hungarian Antal Kis in second place and my American friend Larry Young, only a few seconds back in third. Höhne's time was astounding, comparable to Bob Beamon's legendary long jump. He managed to finish no less than two kilometers in front of his strongest competitor! Most of the journalists knew absolutely nothing about race walking and had no experience of the sport. So unlike Beamon, Höhne never got the wide-eyed appreciation of the press that he deserved. Perhaps it was to compensate him for that omission that the East German team, one of the strongest at the games, gave him the honor of carrying their flag at the opening ceremony of the next Olympics four years later.

In that rarefied air, most of the competitors in the 50-kilometer walk recorded times some thirty to forty minutes slower than at sea level. John Kelly, competing with a fever, collapsed after about ten kilometers and had to be carried off on a stretcher. The Canadian Carl Merchenz got his revenge on the West German Horst Magnor. During training, Horst had taunted Carl, who was German by birth, saying that he wasn't good enough for the West German team and wouldn't even be there if he hadn't emigrated to Canada. Carl showed him. He finished sixth, ahead of the German braggart. Horst avoided Carl after that, having been put to shame. Goetz Klopfer, in comparable form to my own, came in tenth. Dave Romansky didn't feel well during the race, but he refused to drop out and finished last in six hours, earning a sustained standing ovation from the crowd for his tenacity, effort, and spirit.

I never got to see the film shot by the reporter who followed me with Shosh during the competition. He sent it back to Israel that same night and it was consumed in the fire that raged through Lod airport, destroying whole sections of the terminal, all because someone had been careless with a blow-torch.

As I had promised Shosh, I shaved off my beard the day after the race. I must admit I felt better without it. Now I was all skin and bone — and muscles. I had weighed 154 pounds when I graduated high school, but fourteen years later, my normal weight had gone down to 138 pounds, and I would temporarily drop another eight to eleven pounds after every training session or competition, mainly from loss of fluids. I was dying to rest, not only from the race but from the intense training leading up to it as well. While working out in Mexico, John Kelly and I had confided our deepest desires to one another. We were both tired of putting in so much effort, and it was only our Olympic aspirations that had driven us to keep up the constant exhausting training despite the supreme physical discomfort involved.

But at the same time, we were well aware of how much we loved sports

and how much we yearned to compete in the next Olympics too. We tried to
come up with other fields we could excel in but that wouldn't be as physically
demanding. The 50-kilometer race walk is the hardest Olympic event there
is. The exertion required throughout the race is enormous — similar to the
marathon or the 100-kilometer bicycle race — but you have to keep it up for
over four hours, not the two and a quarter or two and a half hours it takes to
finish the other two long-distance events. We considered the possibility of
trying our hands at the modern pentathlon once the games were over. The
pentathlon included a middle-distance run and a swim, both of which
required strenuous training, although nothing like that demanded by the 50-
kilometer walk, and we had both proven ourselves in those two events. As for
the other three, they were a walk in the park: target shooting and fencing were
technical sports with no physical requirement, and in horseback riding it's
the horse that does all the hard work.

From talking with other athletes, I discovered that they all shared our
craving for some time off after the Olympics. But cravings are relative. The
day after my race, I went out eagerly for my morning practice. It was pleasant
and refreshing, although admittedly I cut it short and didn't push myself too
hard. I found most of my fellow race walkers doing the same. And the marathon runners as well. No one forced us to do it. We simply enjoyed physical
activity, and may even have formed a physiological addiction to it. Whatever
the case, the phenomenon was especially conspicuous among the long-
distance athletes, and in utter contrast to the behavior of the majority of
swimmers. In 1975, Mayer Feldberg, then the dean of the Faculty of Business
Administration at Cape Town University and today in the same post at
Columbia, told me that although he had been the South African butterfly
champion, he had never once been in a pool or swum a single yard since he
competed at the Rome Olympics in 1960.

The day after the race, I went on a shopping spree. I'd been told that
Adidas, Puma, and Tiger gave shoes out free to Olympic athletes as a promo-
tional gimmick. I visited each of their stores in the Olympic Village and came
away with five pairs of race-walking shoes. That was barely enough to get me
through one year, but I felt I'd done a good day's work. I guess I didn't put
enough effort into it, or was too modest, or didn't have a big enough appetite
for handouts. My friend Jack Mortland, the writer, editor, and publisher of
the race walkers' "bible," the *Ohio Race Walker*, who competed for the US in

the 20-kilometer walk at the Olympics in Rome, reported in the mid-eighties that he had finally used up the supply of free shoes he'd gotten in 1960!

The closing ceremony was still over a week away. Shosh and I decided to use the time to visit Mexico's famous antiquities. Since we went by bus, using the public transportation employed by the Mexicans themselves, we got a taste of their way of life. We weren't taken aback by the chickens carried onto the crammed bus by some of the passengers, but we were stupefied when we rode through the jungle and the bus stopped in the middle of nowhere to pick up a peasant who waved it down. The driver pulled up at the side of the road, the peasant disappeared into the jungle, and then reappeared dragging something behind him by a rope. When the other end of the rope emerged from the underbrush, there was a huge boar attached to it. The man loaded it into the luggage compartment, shoving it inside so he could get the door closed, and then calmly boarded the bus. We were the only passengers who seemed to think we had witnessed anything out of the ordinary.

The Mayan ruins of Chichen Itza and Uxmal in Yucatan were indeed magnificent. As we toured one of the sites, we happened to pass the same two men several times. I was wearing the Olympic sweat suit with the word "Israel" on the back. Walking by them again, I heard one of them spit out to the other, "*Schwein.*" Not only did I recognize it as the German word for "pig," but I also remembered how the anti-Semites in my childhood had used it as an epithet for Jews. In an instant I had turned to the speaker, a corpulent man whose puffy red cheeks were a clear indication that he was no teetotaler. I gripped his arm and he was obviously shocked by my reaction. Increasing the pressure, I asked him in English, "Did you say something?" That put a fright into him. He must have realized that I was a strong Olympic athlete who wasn't afraid of him. He replied haltingly in bad English in a thick German accent, "I say nothing." I felt like punching him, but I let him go, making do with embarrassing him in front of his friend.

From Merida, the capital of Yucatan, we returned to Mexico City in a pint-size airplane that flew low over the jungle. There were several times along the way when we were flung about by the wind and were sure we were about to crash. We got back in time to take part in the closing ceremony. It was very impressive. The athletes were all in high spirits, glad that the burden of readying themselves for the games was behind them and they could ease off on their training. The thousands of white doves suddenly released into the air to fly over the stadium made for a thrilling sight. Some of them decided to leave us with a small memento, and one such trinket landed on my head.

Along with the exultation, there was a note of sadness in the ceremony. The athletes were sorry to see this chapter in their lives come to an end, especially now that they felt the relief that comes after the competition. For their part, the Mexican spectators were sad that this tremendous joyful national festival that had focused the eyes of the whole world on them was about to end. In the final portion of the ceremony the sign "Mexico 1968" was lowered, replaced by the greeting "See you in 1972 in Munich." That phrase was stamped deeply on my consciousness, as it was for many of the other competitors there.

The next day, the Israeli Olympic Committee organized a short vacation in Acapulco for the whole delegation. After two very pleasant days and a long bus ride back to Mexico City, we flew to New York. Shosh suddenly encountered a problem at the Mexico City airport. Her tourist visa had expired two days earlier. When she went to the government office that handles such matters, she was told she had to go to Guatemala to extend her visa! When the official at passport control at the airport discovered that her visa was expired, he informed her that she had to pay a fine of four hundred pesos. Shosh claimed she only had a hundred. He took it and let her through. A stickler for details as usual, Shosh demanded a receipt and got the answer "You don't get a receipt for a hundred pesos, only for four hundred."

We spent four days in New York. There didn't appear to be any good reason for this stopover, except that it gave the functionaries on the delegation a free trip, all expenses paid and a daily allowance to boot. Since we could do what we pleased with our time, we were given a lump sum in advance to cover our meals and other expenses, something the officials didn't see fit to do when it came to reimbursing me for the time I spent training in California. During that weekend in New York, I took part in the Long Island 35-mile competition. It had been almost two weeks since I'd last trained, but I was still in good form. Dave Romansky, fired with a lust for glory, beat me out by a few seconds, leaving me to finish in second place. John Knifton, a former member of the Belgrave Harriers Club in London who joined the NYAC when he moved to New York, came in third, far behind me.

Henry Laskau, one of the organizers of the event, rightfully considered himself my patron for having introduced me to the American race-walking scene. Wanting to do something to demonstrate the special relationship we had now that my stay in the States was coming to an end, he offered to drive me all the way back to my hotel in Manhattan in a typical display of his warmth and friendship.

Treating my feet after fifty miles of the 100-mile championship in Columbia, Missouri, 1967

Part III

In Israel

Chapter Eleven | The Unrecorded World Record

When I returned to Israel in November 1968, I entered a different world, that of academia. I was now a lecturer at the Tel Aviv University Graduate School of Business Administration. Starting out as a branch of the Hebrew University in Jerusalem, it had become an independent institution two years before. I nearly collapsed under the pressure of work, being assigned to teach six different courses, each of which I had to prepare from scratch since I didn't yet have a pool of material I could draw on. I was kept busy from early in the morning until late at night, preparing and delivering lectures. I barely had time to breathe. We rented one of the few detached houses in Givat Shmuel, about a ten-minute drive from the campus in Ramat Aviv.

I no longer had any incentive to train so I didn't push myself. Nevertheless, since I enjoy physical activity, whenever I happened to get a free moment, I took advantage of it to work out a little. Unfortunately, such moments became increasingly rare, so that I often went for several straight days — and once even for a whole week — without being able to train. After a day with no physical activity, my legs and back started to hurt, I felt generally lousy and fatigued, and at the same time I had a hard time falling asleep at night. Shosh claimed that I was also irritable and insufferable to be around. When I finally managed to get in a practice session, it was like someone had waved a magic wand over me. All the pains and malaise disappeared, I fell asleep as usual as soon as my head hit the pillow, and Shosh said I was back to being my old nice self again. There were no race-walking competitions in Israel, no trophies to win, and no incentive to train, except for the pleasure I got from being out in natural surroundings on my own with all the everyday pressures behind me.

The marching season began in the spring of 1969. I started training more seriously again. My customary route took me from Givat Shmuel along the Geha Road to the National Park in Ramat Gan. I enjoyed training in the park where I could do two and a half-mile laps through the orchards. It was quiet, the perfume of the citrus blossoms was intoxicating, and the route kept my interest high by being studded with sections that rose and fell. The water fountains near the lake along the way made this an ideal course. The same features apparently brought the chief of staff, Chaim Bar-Lev, to the park, where he went horseback riding regularly with the British military attaché and exchanged a few words in Serbian with me whenever he passed.

I took part in all the marches, both long and short. There were a few new ones on the calendar, introduced since I had left for the States in 1965. Best of all was the Mount Gilboa March, with a magnificent view not only from the summit, but during the climb and the descent as well. As usual, I was the first to finish each march. They were excellent training sessions for me, presenting me with the challenge of overtaking all the others who had started ahead of me and preventing those who chose to run from finishing first. Yoram Cohen kept alongside me again, but now I regularly also had a new companion: Moshe Arieli, a natural born race walker from Bat Yam. Unlike Yoram, he walked more than he ran, and he had a good style. If he had been willing to devote the necessary time to serious training, he could have improved enough to take part in walking competitions, but unfortunately the idea didn't appeal to him.

The march schedule was tight. The Galilee March, Mt. Tabor Race, and Yehiam March all took place on the same day. I decided I wanted to do all three of them. For that to be possible, I had to begin the Galilee March on the Golan Heights very early, and finish it quite a few hours before the official start. I managed to convince Yoram and Moshe to join me in this wacky scheme, and together we set out in my car for the Golan Heights just after midnight. In the wee hours of the morning, still dark out, we tried to locate the starting point for the march somewhere at the head of the road parallel to the Iraqi oil pipeline. When we got to an army camp nearby, we decided to ask the sentry at the gate where the road was. We had to wake him up! He was startled, but when he realized that the three unarmed figures in sweat suits spoke fluent Hebrew and were only sports nuts, and not terrorists or the duty officer making a spot check, he pointed us in the right direction to the east of the camp.

Yoram stayed with my car at the starting line, while Moshe and I took off along a route we had never walked before. The moon shed enough light to prevent us from stepping off the asphalt surface into the Syrian mine fields on both sides. At about the halfway mark, Yoram drove up to see how we were doing. Moshe got in the car while I kept going until the finish at the Banyas. The sun was just coming up and we could see the march organizers arriving. We made it to Mt. Tabor in time for the start and circled the mountain. By the time we got to Yehiam, most of the marchers had already taken off long before. Still, I finished the route in time to get my third participant's medal of the day. It was a good feeling to know we had done something that had been considered undoable.

Braz organized the Sea to Sea March, from Kibbutz Ramat Yohanan in the Zevulun Valley (where supposedly you can catch a glimpse of the Mediterranean if you climb to the top of the water tower) to Migdal on the shore of the Sea of Galilee. He announced that in addition to the non-competitive march, the event would also be a race-walking competition, with trophies for the three finalists. We stayed at the Ramat Yohanan youth hostel. It rained all night. Starting time was around five a.m., when it was still dark out. The rain had stopped. There weren't too many people there for the competition, maybe only about a hundred. I started out fast and took the lead. I was all on my own this time, no one even running alongside me. Everyone else was far behind.

As I was walking down one of the side roads outside Shfaram — a road that was obviously in serious disrepair with lots of potholes of all sizes — my foot suddenly hit mud and started to sink in. All of a sudden I was going down with both feet. I tried to free myself, but I just kept sinking deeper. Although I was on a road, it felt like I was in the middle of a marsh. I tried to grab hold of the edge of the asphalt, but it broke apart into lumps that bobbed on the surface of the thick mud. Despite my feverish attempts to climb out, I was sinking deeper, already up to my hips in the mud. Although initially I had considered this merely an unpleasant mishap, by now I was getting very scared, thinking "if I keep sinking like this, it won't be long before I'm over my head in mud."

I bent over at the waist, lying flat on the bobbing lumps of asphalt with my arms stretched out in order to spread my body weight over as large a surface as possible. My fingers searched out some solid section of the road that wouldn't give way. It all felt pretty flimsy, but some parts less so than others. I was also afraid that some car might come by and take my head off. I had to get out of there fast, but whenever I tried to move quickly the lumps holding me up slipped away and I sank more rapidly. So very slowly I inched the top half of my body across the lumps of asphalt, clinging with my fingertips to the more solid sections of the road and pulling my lower body out of the mud. I was free! I broke out in a cold sweat. Brushing the mud from the lower half of my body, I waited for the first marchers behind me to show up so I could warn them of the danger.

This experience gave me a new understanding of the story I had heard about the change in the customs of the Bedouins in North Africa. Before World War II, the man would ride at the head and the women would walk behind him. After the war, the women walked in front and the man followed. It seems there were still mines buried in the field after the war. But despite what I had been through, I didn't alter my customary practice; I continued to speed on ahead of everyone else. The mud sticking to me slowed me down, but I finished first, still feeling fresh when I reached the finish across from the entrance to Villa Melchett, coming in nearly two hours ahead of my closest competitors.

The Four-Day March had now become a Three-Day March. It would be my thirteenth in a row. This year it would be based at Beit El, between Ramallah and Shechem, and the routes would all be in the West Bank. A tent camp for the marchers was set up at Beit El, outside an army camp, but there wasn't the same spirit and excitement here as there had been at Hulda. Still, I enjoyed getting to know new places and landscapes I'd never seen before, especially considering the historical significance for Jews of Beit El and the other sites along the routes. I finished first each day. By now I was a familiar face. The thief who set his sights on my new sleeping bag and stole it from the tent I was assigned to was probably the only one who didn't know who I was.

Soon after the march, Braz organized the Benjaminite Marathon, named for the member of the Tribe of Benjamin who ran the exceptionally long distance to Shilo to bring the news that the Ark of the Covenant had fallen into the hands of the Philistines. It was very hot. I walked the route, although everyone else ran. A long-distance competitive event like this helped me stay in condition for long-distance race walking. There were very few participants, either because there are hardly any long-distance runners in Israel or because of the political overtones of this event through the West Bank. First place was taken by Zvika Segal, a member of the police force. I came in second.

I was very pleased to hear that Braz had decided to turn his attention to ultra-long-distance events as well, organizing a 100-kilometer march. The first one was held in May 1969. We took off on a Friday at two p.m. — after posing for a group portrait — from the Karei Deshe Youth Hostel on the Sea of Galilee. About twenty endurance freaks turned up, but I was the only one who had any experience walking for such a distance. The route was demanding. We had to climb the twisting mountain road to Rosh Pina and on to Vered Hagalil, and from there take a narrow road through Kurazin that descended back down to the lake. Then we turned north along a dirt road parallel to the Jordan River, hacked out in an effort to divert the water to the national water carrier before it flowed into the Sea of Galilee. We crossed the Bnot Ya'akov Bridge and climbed to the Golan Heights. That ascent took us to a road on the Eastern bank of the Jordan River that again dropped back down to the lake. After that we circled the lake clockwise, reaching Ein Gev with twenty-five miles still to go.

Yitzhak Braz and his wife Rina drove back and forth constantly to keep the marchers supplied with water. We were spread out over a good number of kilometers, and as the march progressed, the distance between the leader — me — and the marcher in the rear kept getting bigger. As a result, they got the water to me less and less often. It fell dark, but there was a full moon. The straight stretch of road running south from Ha'on seemed to go on forever. I was afraid of stepping on a snake warming itself on the asphalt road. Snakes are hard to make out in the dark, especially from far enough away to leave time to give it a wide berth. Luckily, I didn't run into a single one. There were more cars on the road between Ma'agan and Zemach and on to Tiberias.

The restaurant at the Kinneret Junction was open so I bought myself a Coke. The man at the counter was amazed when I asked for salt and added it to the soda. The salted drink refreshed me. When I got to Tiberias I could buy myself another bottle. By now there had been no sign of Braz for several hours. There were under twenty kilometers to go. I had to follow the road twisting around the lake to Migdal. The roadside lunch counter was closed. I was exhausted and thirsty. But I kept going. The road was now straight, boring and stretching endlessly ahead. I could hear the rhythmic sound of the pump outside Migdal at the left-hand side of the road. It echoed for miles around. Then the sound faded into the distance. I reached the gas station at the entrance to Kibbutz Ginosar. It was closed, but I took a drink from the water hose to quench my thirst. My whole body was exhausted and my feet hurt. Onward.

I felt like the straight road would never end. By the headlights of a passing car, I could see an upcoming bend to the left. I knew that it was only about a mile from there to the start of the climb up the hills above the site of the national water carrier pumps. I picked up the pace. I passed the turnoff to Hukok and was soon at the base of the incline. It was a very steep climb, but I took it like a horse who could already smell the stable. It was only around half a mile, and from there it should be a snap: one last descent for about a mile and a quarter. The decline may be easy, but that's when you start feeling the pressure on your feet. Every now and then I had to move onto the shoulder to let a car by, and it hurt whenever I stepped on the gravel. I realized I must have blisters. At the bottom, near the junction, I made a sharp right and then right again. From there I sped the half mile down the straight road back to the entrance to the youth hostel.

In the light beside the sentry box, I glanced at my watch: I had completed the distance in about eleven hours. The guard wouldn't let me in. To the left of the gate there was a water tap outside the fence. I washed myself off and went to "bed" in my car, parked nearby. After some three hours or so, the rest of the marchers showed up. All in one group. In order to deal with the logistical problems of supplying everyone with water, and at the same time avoid waiting long hours for the stragglers, Braz had "bunched them up" by "advancing" some of them in his car. These two new terms came to enter the lexicon of Israeli marches. Each of us got the same medal, even those who had not actually walked for more than half the distance at best.

I tried in vain to convince the organizers of the Maccabiah Games to include race-walking competitions for the Olympic distances of 20 and 50 kilometers. For lack of experience, or reluctance to devote the necessary time to the project, the Maccabiah functionaries were leery of long-distance events, running and walking alike. The fact that the man in charge of organization, Dr. Robert Atlas, was an old friend of Shosh's father and a fellow member of B'nai B'rith, persuaded him to include a 10-kilometer race walk in addition to the 3-kilometer race already in place. I started training for the games. General Doron made sure that 3- and 10-kilometer walking competitions were included in the meets organized by the Track and Field Committee of the Sports Federation. I managed to have them made part of the events organized by Maccabi Israel as well. So almost weekly I found myself breaking my Israeli records for these distances.

My major rival was my friend Reuven Peleg from Kibbutz Ein Hahoresh, also of Yugoslavian extraction. But he invariably finished behind me. A lot of athletes, whether jokingly or out of envy, accused me of not giving my all to the races so that I could break the record again the next week and make the headlines on the sports page. That was far from the truth. I always pushed myself to the limit, but since the bulk of my training was devoted to short distances, my form in these events was improving rapidly. Once more I was the subject of numerous flattering items in the press. I can't deny that it was gratifying to get this acknowledgement, to hear my name recognized when I identified myself on the phone to the clerk at some office, or to be told that my students had seen me working out somewhere or read about my latest achievement in the paper.

It was the height of the War of Attrition, the localized fighting along the new borders after the Six-Day War. The army asked for volunteers from the faculty of Tel Aviv University to give talks to the soldiers posted along the Bar-Lev defense line opposite the Suez Canal. I signed up. I was instructed to choose a subject in my specialty, and decided on "The Use of Quantitative Tools in Management." In June 1969 I was flown to the airport at Refidim in central Sinai, where I was assigned a bunk. At dawn I went out for my morning training. As I walked past one group of soldiers, someone called out: "You haven't got a prayer. Ladany's better." A soldier in another group tried to cheer me on, assuring me that "some day you may even beat Ladany." Although my name was becoming a household word — in fact it had even appeared in crossword puzzles and quiz games — and although the phrase "to walk like Ladany" had become a popular synonym for walking fast, my face was not yet familiar and I could still enjoy anonymity.

I was driven to the Bar-Lev Line. It was rather discomfiting to pass the crossroads near Ismalyiah where a large sign warned: "This sector is in Egyptian sights. During shelling, cross quickly." We reached the first outpost. I was led into an underground bunker packed with reserve soldiers. My escort, the culture officer, introduced me and read out the name of my talk. I saw the faces of my audience fall and heard one solider whisper, "We're in for another boring lecture." All of a sudden one of them called out, "Are you Dr. Ladany the walker?" When I admitted I was, the whole bunker chorused, "Tell us about the Olympics." My talk was a hit. The news was passed from one outpost to the next by field telephone: I was talking about the Olympics in Mexico City and it was really interesting. The culture officer was inundated with requests for my appearance at posts I was not scheduled to visit. Thus in the space of two days, I spoke in almost all the outposts along the line. Luckily for me, those were two days when there wasn't a single incident of Egyptian shelling.

In the evening I was put up at a mobile camp some fifteen miles east of the Suez Canal. The "camp" served as an overnight stopover for tanks in the desert and was moved daily to make it hard for the enemy to plan any action against it. Lying outside the range of the Egyptian guns, it was used as a rear base not far from the outposts along the line of defense. As soon as I arrived, even before supper, I went out to train. When I got to the nearby road, I turned east. I was in the middle of the wilderness. The sun had set, leaving the gray light of dusk, and the only sound was that of the gentle breeze. After about twenty minutes, when I was at least two and a half miles from camp, the regiment adjutant suddenly sped up in a jeep. He spotted me, braked, and ordered me to get in. I could see the relief on his face. He bawled me out, saying that I was not only a lunatic for putting myself at such risk by walking alone in a sector often visited by Egyptian commandos, but I had also disobeyed the order, issued because of that very danger, requiring that vehicles move only in pairs. I assured him that I was not guilty of any infringement; the directives referred only to vehicular movement and I was walking.

The Eighth Maccabiah Games took place in July 1969. Naturally, Reuven Peleg and I represented Israel. I was in good form. I judged that my primary rival would be Howie Jacobson, an American friend of mine. I had trained with Howie for three years at Kings Point and had been to his house on Long Island. His wife was a former Israeli. Oddly enough, they had divorced and subsequently remarried, and had two sons from their first marriage and two daughters from their second. The opening ceremony was as splendid as it had been the last time.

I took part in the two race-walking events, 3 kilometers and 10 kilometers, and won gold in both. Howie came in second in the 10-kilometer race, and Reuven took silver in the 3 kilometers. Both of them finished far behind me. For the closing ceremony I hung the two gold medals around my neck, as did the other medallists, and it felt very good. In recognition of my double victory, I was given the honor of lowering the Maccabiah flag at the end of the ceremony. The honor guard beside me, representing the five continents, included the famous swimmer Mark Spitz from North America. It was the period between his failed attempts at the Mexican Olympics, despite his bravado before the games, and his stunning future success.

The pressure was off after the Maccabiah Games, and so I cut back on my training again. In November 1969 I was called up for reserve army duty. It wasn't the first time and wouldn't be the last. In the space of twelve months spanning two fiscal years during the War of Attrition, I was in reserve duty for close to one hundred days. I was assigned to a field cannon regiment equipped with Russian 122 mm towed guns taken in the Six-Day War. Given the accuracy of these cannons, and the fact that a great deal of ammunition had also been seized, it was worth the army's while to press them into service, so we had not yet been converted into a mobile unit. We were stationed in the Beit She'an Valley. I was battery position officer for one of the three batteries in the regiment, deployed over a considerable area throughout the valley.

In effect, I was in command of the battery, since the commander on paper was also the officer who coordinated operations at headquarters with the forces requiring our support and therefore was not in the field. His subordinates, including myself, hardly ever saw him. That had been the traditional arrangement in the Israeli artillery since the establishment of the State, an absurd situation that was eventually corrected. We were on active duty, interspersed with periods of relative quiet. Periodically we supplied artillery cover for operations against infiltration attempts, or aimed our guns at sites where the intelligence had discovered terrorists grouping or hiding. I earned the respect of the soldiers, and the regiment commander, mainly because I was "the famous walker."

I did my best to train within the confines of the battery. After I was assigned a second-in-command, I went beyond the perimeter of the battery for a longer practice when things were quiet and I could get the regiment commander's approval. I had to file my route in advance so they could send a car to bring me back if need be. On one such occasion, I went out for a long training walk, starting from the battery, somewhere to the east of Kibbutz Hamadiya, and then on to Beit She'an. From there I circled around the Shata prison and Beit Alpha back to Beit She'an, finally returning to my starting point, around twenty-five miles all told. A few days later at an officers' briefing at the regiment headquarters near the abandoned Turkish train station to the southwest of Beit She'an, the transportation officer, a tour guide in civilian life, informed me with a smile on his face that one of his drivers had reported seeing me near the prison. Although he recognized me and had seen me training in Tel Aviv several times, the driver was unaware that I was an officer in the regiment. In utter stupefaction, he had marveled, "I never knew that Ladany's training walks take him this far from Tel Aviv!"

One day, deployed in trenches behind a hillock among the fish ponds east of Kibbutz Hamadiya, we were ordered to shell a certain target. The barrage lasted for two or three minutes. Experience had taught us that it took the Jordanians about five minutes to calculate our position and aim their guns at us. Well drilled in carrying out standing orders, as soon as our cannons fell silent, I ordered all the soldiers in my battery, along with my second-in-command, into the nearby fortified bunkers which provided protection even from a direct hit.

Three of us remained at the artillery command post, a trench about forty to sixty inches deep, shaded by a tarp: the red-headed technical assistant, Sergeant Major Shmuel Miller, and myself. Shmuel, an excellent soldier, was a former classmate of mine at the Technion who had come to Israel from Shanghai, to which his family, originally from Russia, had migrated. Although he was older than me, we had a lot in common. Not only could I trust him implicitly with anything, including professional problems, but he was very well liked as well.

After three minutes or so, I was ordered by telephone to send the technical assistant to the bunker. There was no need for words, merely a nod in his direction and he took off at a run, heading eagerly for the safety of the bunker. Shmuel and I were ordered to remain where we were by the field telephone since the bunker could only be reached by trunk line. The enemy barrage began. We could hear the shells falling quite close by. Finally, I received a call giving permission for the two of us to enter the bunker. Shmuel was standing near the entrance to the command post, staring at me hopefully. I nodded and blurted out "run." He did, with me on his heels. Shells were falling and bursting all around us. Some exploded even before landing, apparently equipped with proximity or time fuses.

I ran as fast as I could. Within a few yards I had caught up with Shmuel, passed him, and left him behind. I've never run so fast in my whole life, but I didn't even feel the effort. The thunderous explosions were frightening enough to put anything else out of my mind. I could see the sloping entrance to the bunker straight ahead. Another few yards and I'd be safe. I slid in horizontally, half leaping, half stumbling inside. A few seconds later Shmuel — a good bit heavier than I was — landed on top of me at the same angle, giving me a good wallop. But it didn't matter — we were both safe! "I wish someone had been timing me," I thought. "I'm sure that was faster than the world record for 100 meters." When my tour of duty was over, I brought home a souvenir, a particularly large shell fragment I had found inside the battery perimeter after the enemy barrage. With a mischievous smile I announced to Shosh, "This one missed me."

During the shelling, the battery medic — who'd been safely in the bunker the whole time — went into shock. He didn't recover until long after it was all over. He was utterly hysterical — although some of the soldiers just called him chicken — and I was worried that his behavior might be generally demoralizing. When my request to have him transferred was refused, I decided to reassign him to regiment headquarters, even though that meant we were left without a medic, claiming it was better to get wet than to lug around an umbrella that wouldn't open when it rained. The regiment commander took my point.

About two miles in front of us, along the border that followed the bends and cliffs of the bank of the Jordan River, there were a number of outposts manned by infantry soldiers. Spread out miles apart, they were incapable of sealing off the border hermetically. After a number of terrorist attacks on the outposts were repulsed, it was discovered that the enemy sometimes left behind rockets aimed at the Israeli positions and set to go off several days later. The ground around them was studded with traps and mines. As a result, all units were ordered to patrol their perimeters at frequent intervals. The order applied to us as well.

It would have been easier for me to put Shmuel or my second-in-command in charge of the patrol, but I knew that leadership meant not only issuing orders, but actually taking the lead. I asked Shmuel to organize a team, left him and my aide in command of the battery, and went out at the head of the patrol squad. We spread out for fifty yards, more or less in a straight line. No one uttered a word, but I could see the fear on their faces. Step on a mine and in the best case you are killed instantly; in the worst case you are left a cripple for the rest of your life, totally dependent on other people and unable to enjoy the simple pleasures of life. I was just as scared as they were. I could see them moving very slowly, trying to keep as far to the rear as possible. As commanding officer, I had the military authority to stay back in relative safety and order some member of the squad to take point position, but I didn't feel I had the moral authority to do so. Instead, I moved out in front, with the rest of them following far behind. We patrolled the entire perimeter. We didn't find anything and no one stepped on a trap or a mine, but I did win the respect of my soldiers.

■ Chapter Twelve | Winning the London to Brighton Walk

By early spring of 1970 I was back in pretty good form. With the help of the army magazine *Bamachane*, I tried to organize something really special: a cross-country walk from Metulla in the north to Eilat in the south, and maybe even as far as Sharm al-Sheikh at the southern tip of the Sinai. The idea appealed strongly to the editors of *Bamachane*, but they didn't have the financial or logistical resources to organize such a big project. A few days after I approached them, they told me they had found a solution: they had interested the physiological research unit of the medical corps in the idea. In practical terms, this meant the army would use me as the subject of a study — I was going to be their guinea pig.

The cross-country walk was scheduled for February 1970 during semester break. I planned to cover some one hundred kilometers a day, fifty early in the morning when it was still chilly, and fifty in the cool hours of the afternoon and evening. I would be accompanied by a reporter and photographer from *Bamachane*, a truck, several jeeps, and a large team from the army medical corps under the command of Dr. Yair Shapiro. I wanted to start out from Metulla at four a.m. It didn't happen. We were held up until nearly eight o'clock. The War of Attrition was still raging and there was danger of mines on the road. The army sappers couldn't clear the route and allow access any earlier.

It's an unseasonably warm day and by the time I get started it's very hot. I begin at a fast pace, maybe too fast. When I want something to drink, I signal to the escort car. It takes them a while to convey my request to the person authorized to decide which member of the physiological team will check the volume of the beverage in a graduated cylinder and who will hand it to me. Sometimes I have to wait for nearly fifteen minutes. I'm thirsty and starting to get dehydrated. When I feel pressure in my bladder and want to relieve myself, I have to signal the car again. Then I have to hold it in until the two honorable gentlemen in charge of collecting my urine and taking my temperature get their act together and extricate themselves from the jeep with all the tools of their trade. Finally they're ready.

While I pee into the beaker one of them proffers, the other sticks a thermometer in my ass, and I'm instructed not to move so as not to break it. It's hard to squeeze the last drops out under these conditions. Instead of a few seconds, the whole business takes several minutes. It's aggravating and uncomfortable, but I know I agreed to do it, even if I didn't realize what it would actually entail. Luckily, before we ever got underway I told them I wouldn't let them take blood. That's all I needed, having needles stuck in me all the time.

As usual, I drink while I'm walking. Since I'm moving quickly, some of the beverage spills out of the cup onto the ground or my shirt. My escorts complain that I'm lousing up their data and I have to stop walking when I take a drink. I don't agree to that, but I do promise to be more careful. Instead of completing the morning stretch around nine o'clock as planned, I finish close to one in the afternoon. It's blazing hot, I'm sweating profusely, and I'm exhausted. I'm taken to a room on Kibbutz Ayelet Ha-Shahar to rest. I don't have any appetite. All I can get down is a banana and two moist dates.

I start to feel hungry about half an hour later and ask the medical corps guys for something to eat. They refuse on the grounds that they have already completed their measurements and calculations and have no intention of doing it all over again. I insist on being fed. In the face of such adamancy, they announce that they are unwilling to conduct their study under these conditions and are removing themselves from the project. I bid them good-bye and they leave the room. The representatives of *Bamachane* are at a loss. Informing them I'm going to finish what I started, and I'll do it on my own if I have to, I stretch out on the bed. Fifteen minutes later the physiologists are back, ordered to continue the study even if I insist on eating when I'm hungry.

I had planned to start the second fifty kilometers of the day around five or six and finish at ten or eleven at night. But it turns out we're not allowed to be on the road late at night for fear of terrorists. I have to start out at three, in the worst heat, without enough time to rest and get my strength back. I complete the day's route, as planned, beside the 100-kilometer marker. It's eight o'clock.

I'm exhausted and dehydrated, and my feet are covered in blisters from walking in the heat.

The next two days followed the same pattern. I walked in the hottest hours of the day with almost no break between the two halves of the route. On the second day I was given a room to rest in at an army camp near the Damya Bridge in the Jordan Valley, and I spent the night at the Jericho police station. I crossed the city of Jericho all alone, my escort vehicles somewhere far behind me, and the Arab residents staring in wonderment at the strange sight of a man walking at a speed close to ten kilometers (six miles) an hour (about twice the average person's walking speed).

The second half of the route on the third day ran along the shore of the Dead Sea. I was supposed to get to Kibbutz Ein Gedi where I would sleep that night. The road ended south of Ein Fashkha and there was no way a car could get through, certainly not one without front-wheel drive. I knew the area well. The year before I had taken part in the Dead Sea March organized by Braz, and I had been on my own then, too, spearheading the rest of the marchers along the footpath that led to Ein Gedi. Road works had begun meanwhile, and were going strong at the northern end of the route.

The medical corps attempted to keep up with me, but at a certain point they were blocked off completely. No one had checked the route beforehand. I told them I was going on without them, and they could circle around through Jerusalem and Arad, a detour of some 150 miles, and wait for me near Ein Gedi. I wasn't afraid to be alone out there, and I was happy to be rid of their annoying tests for a while. I got to Ein Gedi before them.

Thanks to the sponsorship of *Bamachane* and the hype they gave it, my feat was covered widely in the media, with daily reports of my progress. The radio joined in the fun, particularly the army station, sometimes broadcasting my precise location several times a day. Nevertheless, on the fourth day I decided to quit. I knew I would have to make it the rest of the way to Eilat through the desert-like Arava when the road was open, which meant walking in the hottest hours of the day in the blazing heat on a nearly deserted highway with very little traffic through a monotonous landscape. I was tired, my muscles were constricted, my feet were covered in blisters, and the physiological tests were getting on my nerves. And unlike any other event I'd ever been in, this time I wasn't getting any encouragement. I didn't talk to anyone except my unsympathetic escorts. I no longer had the desire to make the supreme effort to cope with all the problems.

So at the end of the first half of the fourth day, when I arrived at the Sodom Potash Plant south of the Dead Sea, having walked nearly 220 miles since I started out in Metulla, I announced that I was calling it quits. "I've had enough," I declared. Yair Shapiro examined me and pronounced in amazement, both to me and the reporters, that I was perfectly healthy, my body temperature and blood pressure were normal, and he couldn't understand why I didn't want to go on. Everything he said was true, but he was unaware of the most important factor, well known to every athlete and every coach: it's all in the head — in the athlete's motivation to make the effort. I was sorry not to meet the challenge I had set myself, but I had nothing to be ashamed of and didn't feel I had to make any excuses.

In the spring of 1970 I was back in top form. I was training hard and also working hard at the same time. I was a familiar face: "Dr. Ladany the walker" had become a celebrity, and I'm sure that didn't get in my way when it came to job offers. I didn't go looking for outside work, but it wasn't easy for me to say no when I was given the chance to earn some extra money. Every additional bit of cash was put aside to buy our house. So in addition to my full-time job at the university, I was teaching courses in production management, quantitative methods in management, and quality control at other colleges as well. I also got research grants from the Bank of Israel and the Ministry of Commerce and Industry. And if that wasn't enough, I was serving as a consultant for the transport ministry and overseeing projects for the large Koor concern. I didn't have a single free minute.

When I left the house in the morning, I took along a large bowl of food to get me through the whole day. I ate while I was driving from one institution to another, spreading a napkin over my clothes and sticking a corner of it into my shirt collar as I picked bits of food out of the bowl on my lap. Any free hour during the day was devoted to practice. I always kept my gym clothes in the car. The car also served as my locker room, so there wasn't a minute lost.

It's a good thing there are weekends. There was a march scheduled for almost every one of them, and I took part in them all, usually covering the route twice, once in each direction. By now the tent camp at Beit El had become an established tradition for the Three-Day March. This would be my fourteenth straight year. The army, still in charge of organization, distributed a detailed map of the route to all the participants, with each kilometer clearly marked so that the marchers would know exactly how far they had come and how far they still had left to go. I finished first on each of the three days. As soon as I got to the end of the day's route, I turned around and went back in the opposite direction.

Before I started back, the march commander would call out to me: "Shaul, how far was it today?" He knew that the official distance of 40 kilometers was inaccurate, and that the kilometer markings on the map were mere guess-work at best. I would look at my watch, and with the experience of racing on precisely measured tracks could gauge the effort I had made and convert it into a fairly accurate estimate of the speed I had been going. I would multiply that speed by the time it had taken me to complete the route and deliver my verdict: "thirty-six kilometers." If I was off, the figure could only be too high, that is, I could only have been walking at a slower pace than I thought, so that the route could only be shorter. That's why when I hear that soldiers have marched a certain distance in training or for some special occasion, I always assume that it has been inflated by 10 or 20 percent at least. I tend to refer to the reported figures as "army distances."

I was determined to compete in the Olympics again. Actually, I had come to that decision immediately after Mexico City, but now that I was back in good condition, I knew that was the goal I had to work for. The Track and Field Committee also considered me a candidate for the Israeli team at Munich, and was therefore willing to cover the expenses of my participation in European competitions during the spring break in April 1970. I had over three weeks off. I also wanted to compete in the Eastern US Regional 50-Mile Championship, which had been won the year before, in my absence, by the Englishman Steve King.

The Sports Federation would not consent to pay for a trip to the States, but they agreed for me to work it into my stay in Europe and pay the additional cost myself. I would even have to cover my own living expenses for the short time I would be in the States. Luckily, the vice president of El Al in charge of marketing was a student of mine in the executive training program at the university, and he helped me get a ticket to the States that allowed me to stop over in Europe, so the amount I had to pay out of my own pocket wasn't astronomical.

Already a veteran of competitions, I took with me an oversized sponge and a one and a quarter-gallon insulated jug with a drinking spout and a mouth big enough to get ice cubes through. My luggage consisted entirely of this jug and a small bag, both of which I carried on the plane with me. This was the period of the first skyjackings of Israeli planes, so the strange container in my hand immediately aroused the suspicion of the security guards. It also aroused interest at customs. However, the indifference of the sniffer dogs, its light weight, and the invitation to the championship I showed to my interrogators got me off the hook.

I stayed with Don Johnson at his home in Red Bank on the New Jersey shore. Don took me to a supermarket that stayed open late, and I bought myself a large cooler, bags of ice cubes, and gallons of various beverages. Early the next morning we arrived at the championship stadium with all our gear. Greg, Don's son, assisted me faithfully during the race. I won it again, breaking my own American record for the fourth time, shaving thirteen more minutes off it by completing the course in 7:52. I couldn't believe how much I had improved, finishing a full forty-three minutes faster than my first record. And I wasn't as exhausted at the end of it, either.

The next day I was back on a plane over the ocean, now moving in the opposite direction toward Switzerland for the 25-kilometer race-walking competition in Lausanne. Although I was still a little tired from the 50-mile championship five days earlier, I put in a good time. I also met a race-walking coach from Frankfurt who told me that several of his athletes, including Nermerich, who was then one of West Germany's top walkers at every distance between 10 and 50 kilometers, would be taking part in a famous international competition in "Mailand" that week. I asked him in German where Mailand was. He was stunned by my ignorance, unable to comprehend how I had never heard of that famous Italian city. It took me a while to grasp that the Germans refer to Milan as Mailand. That race wasn't on my schedule, but I decided to add it to the program and took a train to Milan.

The competition was virtually a replay of the Olympics. It was held on May 1 in an independent hamlet in northern Milan called Sesto San Giovani. The event had been organized by the township, which had invited walkers from all over the world at its own expense, allowing for three representatives from each country. The Italian Communist Party was in control of the town council, accounting for the selection of May Day for the race; thus the competitors included athletes from Russia, East Germany, Poland, Czechoslovakia, Hungary, Romania, and Bulgaria, in addition to the Western Europeans. The three Americans and myself, there only by chance, were the sole walkers from outside Europe. It was very nice to run into people I had met for the first time in Mexico City, and once again I served as interpreter for athletes from many different countries.

I arrived at eleven a.m. and the start was scheduled for two o'clock. Officially, it was a 30-kilometer race, but in effect the route was 32 kilometers. We took off from the local stadium, walked through the center of town, and then did four laps of four and a half miles each before returning to the stadium. The local residents were out in force on both sides of the route, standing five or six deep and shouting encouragement to all the competitors, Italian or otherwise. It was my first encounter with the sports-loving Italians, and I had never before seen such massive enthusiasm and support. Fortunately, the day was overcast and it started to rain in the middle of the race. For us the rain was refreshing, but I assumed that it would chase most of the spectators indoors. Apparently, I had underestimated their devotion to sports. People opened umbrellas or held plastic sheets over their heads, but stayed put, even when it came down hard, their thunderous support unabated.

I finished in thirteenth place and was very pleased with myself. Thirty kilometers wasn't my best distance, and if I had come in thirteenth among the finest race walkers in the world, it meant that my speed at shorter distances had also improved. At the medals ceremony I realized that the interpretation of the rules governing amateur status, which were upheld much more strictly then than they are now, at least formally — and in the field of race walking nothing was ever "informal" — was a matter of geography. As noted in the program, which I hadn't seen beforehand, the first twenty finalists were awarded prize money. As thirteenth, I received peanuts compared to those who took the first places, but it was still a few thousand. Unfortunately, it was a few thousand Italian lire, worth less than a hundred dollars.

The Prague-Podebrady race is not only the Czechoslovakian 50-kilometer championship, but also one of the oldest and most prestigious of the European race-walking events for that distance, introduced even before World War II. In recent years, most of the top European athletes at 50 kilometers

have competed. I had read about the competition and yearned to take part in
it in order to test and demonstrate my ability against the walkers who would
subsequently be my rivals at the Munich Olympics. The medals ceremony at
Sesto San Giovani presented a golden opportunity to investigate the possibility of competing in Czechoslovakia.

Here I had free access to all the athletes, even those from behind the Iron
Curtain. It appeared quite obvious that the man in charge of the Czechoslovakian walkers wasn't a political lackey. He was tall, around my age, and had an
athletic build. When I spoke to him I discovered that, like most Czechoslova-
kians, he was also well educated and was an active race walker himself. He
knew who I was and was familiar with my results. I asked him about the
Prague-Podebrady event and, specifically, if I could wangle an official invitation, which would enable me to get a visa. He gave me all the details, but
added that considering the break in diplomatic relations between the Soviet
bloc and Israel in the wake of the Six-Day War, he didn't believe I had a
chance of being invited or even allowed to enter the country to take part in
the race.

He seemed credible, was open and friendly, and didn't hide his regret at
the incursion of politics into sports. But many years of experience have
shaped my character such that I never rely on a single source of information. I
usually like to get a second opinion. So when I returned to Israel I wrote to the
Czechoslovakian Sports Federation, introducing myself and my athletic
achievements and asking for an invitation to the Prague-Podebrady competition. In order to remove any doubt, I made it quite clear that I wasn't asking
for money, but merely for an invitation so that I could apply for a visa. The
Czechs are very conscientious, and the reply wasn't long in coming. Although
worded very courteously, it was a swift kick in the butt: "Unfortunately, we
are unable to invite you because the event is restricted to world-class race
walkers." After the race, I learned that 80–90 percent of the European invitees
had recorded times considerably slower than mine. It was obvious to me that
I was paying the price for the Cold War.

After the ceremony in Italy, the West German national race-walking
coach, Jurgen Kramer, offered me a ride as far as Lugano in Switzerland.
From there I took a train to Zurich, arriving the night before the international
20-kilometer race I was planning to compete in. The organizers put me up in
a tiny hotel on the outskirts of the city, where I shared a room with the British

walker Paul Nihil. Although he had been the British champion at various distances a good number of times, his primary claim to fame was winning the silver medal for 50 kilometers at the Tokyo Olympics. The race began and ended at Zurich's famous soccer stadium, Letzigrund. Knowing I wasn't at my best at 20 kilometers, I was again very pleased to finish fifth in what was for me a very good time. This event, coming on the heels of the previous ones in Milan and Lugano, gave me a chance to familiarize myself with the European race-walking world and establish myself in that arena.

During the summer vacation of 1970 I was invited to Rutgers University in New Jersey. Closing up the house in Ramat Efal that we had just moved into, Shosh and I went to New York for three months. There we rented a furnished apartment near Columbia, about fifty yards from Riverside Drive, and once again I was back on my old training grounds in Riverside Park. Now that George Shilling had switched to running and Bill Omelchenko had retired from the sport, I decided not to return to the New York Pioneer Club. Howie Jacobson had founded a new club and invited me to join. Thus I became a member of the Long Island Athletic Club, whose ranks included Gary Westerfield, Steve Hayden, and John Markon. We trained together on Long Island nearly every week.

There was a double advantage to being in New York: the weather in the summer is immeasurably better for training than in the blazing heat of Israel, and the large number of race-walking competitions held in and around the city made it a walker's paradise. Every week I took part in two or three races, most of them for short distances. When they were held in the evening, I'd train the same morning in Riverside Park for anywhere from 20 kilometers to 20 miles, usually together with John Markon. Since John was slower than me, I would start out a few dozen yards behind him, catch up to him and pass him by a similar distance, and then turn around and go back until I was again a good bit behind him. Each time I repeated the process, I had the challenge of closing the gap between us as fast as I could, while he tried to keep ahead of me for as long as possible, so the system worked well for both of us, helping to improve our basic speed.

There were usually two or three days each week when there was no competition in the evening and I had nothing special to do in the morning either. On those occasions I would go out for long-distance training. John joined me at least once a week. These long-distance walks from my apartment to Tarrytown, Ossining, or even as far as Sleepy Hollow or Irvington, and back — at least fifty miles all told — improved my endurance tremendously. The time always passed quickly when I went out with John, who was a shop teacher at the Bronx High School of Science — considered the best of its kind in America. We would carry on heated arguments about the Middle East, arms and munitions, politics and politicians, Vietnam, South America, the French, the English, the Americans, and the Israelis. I told him some of my more amusing experiences from the war, training sessions, and marches, the same stories that appear here. John called them "Ladany tales" and repeated them to other walkers as well.

Whenever we passed a mulberry tree, I gave in to my passion for the ripe fruit. He would wait, a puzzled expression on his face as he watched me eat something that might be poisonous — otherwise why had nobody else picked the berries off a tree that was right on the road? When we got back near my apartment, exhausted and drained, I would add another ten miles to the day's workout along my customary route through the park, convincing myself that I had to make that extra effort if I wanted to be in good enough form to emerge victorious when the real test of my ability came.

Elliott Denman had put the idea of that test in my head. I don't quite know how he did it, except that every now and then he would talk about the London to Brighton event he had competed in many years before, always referring to it as "the blue-ribbon race-walking competition of Great Britain." Since Britain is the birthplace of race walking, I pictured it as the most famous race-walking event in the world. It turned out I was right. Paul Schell and John Kelly also told me about it. Little by little, I was infected by Elliott's fervor. After hearing from him repeatedly that my abilities at 50 kilometers put me in the first rank of world walkers for that distance, and that it was a shame I didn't take advantage of my superb condition to participate in The Competition with a capital "C," I found myself fired with the desire to do it. I decided I would fit it in on my way back to Israel. Most of my training during that summer in New York was aimed at preparing for the big event. John Markon caught the bug from me, and decided that he too would test his abilities at the London to Brighton race in early September.

In New York, I conducted one of my most significant studies, later published in the prestigious journal *Management Science*. Commitments related to this project kept me from getting to London early enough to rest up sufficiently from the flight. I couldn't leave Rutgers until late Thursday night. From there I took a cab, stopping to pick up Shosh who was waiting with our luggage, and we made it to the airport for the red-eye to London. The event organizers had reserved a room for each competitor — at their expense — at the YMCA in the South London district of Stockwell. We arrived on Friday afternoon, tired out from the flight, my arms aching from carrying the heavy suitcases stuffed with all the things we had needed for our three-month stay abroad.

John Markon was waiting for us. He urged us to come with him then and there to get ice cubes for the next day's race. It took two hours each way to reach the only place in London where, according to John, we could buy ice cubes. It never occurred to him that the barman at any five-star hotel would have supplied them in exchange for a small tip. When we got back to the YMCA, I barely had time to make the phone call to finalize arrangements for the assistance I had lined up for myself.

Before leaving New York, I had gotten in touch with Maccabi England and asked them to find me a volunteer to assist me during the race. The man they came up with was Shmuel Benkler, an Israeli who knew me from the Four-Day March and who had been sent to London as a representative of the Jewish Agency. At 4:30 the next morning, he and his son showed up at the YMCA to drive me to the starting line. Shmuel was a tall, bearded man who made a very imposing figure, an impression borne out by his personality and manners as well. We took off from Westminster Road near the tiny park in front of the Houses of Parliament. From there, the fifty-two and three-quarter-mile distance to Brighton followed the very same route used for the event since 1901.

Never before had I had such a grand starting signal. On the stroke of six, Big Ben sounded and the mass of nearly two hundred competitors took off. I didn't immediately grasp that the signal had been given. It came without any warning. I was standing at the far end of the first row and suddenly realized that everyone else was about a yard or two in front of me.

I start out at a fast pace. After a few dozen yards I'm in the lead. By the middle of Westminster Bridge, I'm a couple of yards ahead. I keep up the same pace and can't see anybody alongside me. Shosh hands me my drink just the way I like it. She arranged with Shmuel that every time my escort car stops, he should stand about fifty yards in front of her and shout out to her what it is I want so that she has time to get it ready. Shmuel's son stands around thirty yards behind her, holding a bucket in one hand and a sponge dipped in ice water in the other, so after I have something to drink I'm handed a sponge with water that not only cools me down, but also washes away the remnants of sticky soda. By ten miles, I already have a lead of some seventy yards, which grows to 120 after twenty miles.

When it was all over, I was told that the organizers were convinced I was moving too fast and laid bets that I wouldn't make it past thirty miles. Although they knew I was an Israeli, they were unaware of my results in the Eastern US Regional 50-Mile Championship. It turned out I had done the first twenty miles in a time equal to the winning time for the British 20-mile championship several years before. When they realized this, they raised their bets.

At the twenty-five-mile mark, my lead has grown to nearly 140 yards. At that point, near a large traffic circle, Shosh and Shmuel direct me to the road leading off the right. I'm rushing forward when I suddenly hear them shouting. Turning my head, I see them waving their arms and pointing to the left, where I can see the walker behind me moving ahead. I'm furious that I've lost my lead for such a stupid reason. I cut across the grass between the two roads. My rival is already about ten yards in front. I pick up my pace and within a minute or so I catch up to him. I found out his name later — Ray Middleton. The moment I come up on him, he steps on the gas and tries to shake me off. I respond by going even faster, not letting him get ahead. This duel, with the two of us keeping shoulder to shoulder, goes on for almost eighteen miles. Every muscle in my body aches, but I am determined not to concede the battle. I'm dying to pee, but I know that if I stop I'll lose a few precious seconds that will be very hard to make up. So I grit my teeth, ignoring the pressure in my bladder, and refusing to make a stop. It seems Ray is suffering from the same problem, but he eventually gives in and stops to pee for two seconds, enough for me to take a ten-yard lead.

Still holding on to that lead, I reach Dale Hill, the highest point on the way to Brighton. There are still about seven miles to go. I decide this is the critical moment to ensure my victory. I have to leave my rival behind and extend my lead enough to discourage him from trying to overtake me again. I pick up the pace even more, virtually sprinting up the hill. It seems to go on forever. The steep climb lasts for close to a mile. But my sprint produces the desired effect. Although I don't turn to look, at the top of the hill Shmuel reports that Ray is over five hundred yards back. I know I've won a psychological victory and that first place is mine for the taking, but I can't take anything for granted. I fight to keep up my speed in case he should overtake me on the gentle down slope or on the straight to follow. I ask Shosh and Shmuel to estimate my lead every time they give me something to drink — and I now need fluids at increasingly shorter intervals. I'm very gratified to hear from them that my lead is growing even longer, but I still don't ease off.

It's hot, very hot. There isn't a cloud in the sky, so unlike typical English weather. I keep pushing myself forward. I've already reached the city and can see the bobbies directing the traffic to the right-hand side of the road. Finally, I get to the end of the straight that has stretched for over five miles and can see that it ends in a pier over the water. I'm pointed to the left. As I make the turn, I look back to make sure I'm in no danger from any competitor who might have managed to draw close, and am very pleased to find there's no one in sight. I can already see the funnel to the finish line. One last exertion. It's over. I'm panting and sweating like a horse after a gallop. Every single muscle aches. I take a few steps back and forth as I get my breath back. The mayor, in full parade dress with a long gold chain and massive medallion lying on his chest, shakes my hand. He has his picture taken with me and congratulates me officially on behalf of the City of Brighton.

Tradition calls for the winners to enjoy a warm bath in the local spa. Bath number 1 is reserved for whoever takes first place. It was absolute bliss to lie there in the warm water. Shosh complained that I went in first and came out last, to which I replied: "The race is over, I don't have to move fast any more." My whole body ached, my muscles were sore, and my feet were covered in blisters. Still, at the medals ceremony I gritted my teeth and pretended to be as fresh as I was at the start. I don't know if I managed to hide my limp entirely, but I do know I was applauded loud and long as the "little Israeli."

Over the years, eight Olympic champions had won the London to Brighton Walk and only eight had finished in less than eight hours. My result was the third fastest time ever recorded in the long history of the competition. It had only been beaten by Don Thompson, the British gold medalist at the

Rome Olympics, and Abdon Pamich, the Italian who won gold in the 50-kilo-meter race walk at the Tokyo Olympics. As the Israeli reporters had requested, I called them after the race and informed them of my result. It didn't make the slightest impression on them. On the other hand, the British sports magazine *Athletic Weekly* printed my picture a few days later over an article by Colin Young, the race-walking editor who had himself taken part in the competition, declaring: "Shaul Ladany, the globe-trotting Israeli who competed in 50 kilometers at the Olympics in Mexico City, demonstrated the best form of his athletic career, winning the London to Brighton Walk in the very fast time of 7:46:37. The way in which he did it was unique. Taking off like the wind from Westminster Bridge, he left all his rivals behind, including Ray Middleton and Don Thompson...." At the end of that year, when the readers voted for the outstanding athletes of 1970, I won second place! In sharp contrast, I wasn't even nominated for any type of special recognition in Israel, and I must admit it hurt.

Ray Middleton recorded his personal best in the competition, but he still came in ten minutes behind me. Don Thompson, who had won several times in previous years, was even farther back. John Markon put in a respectable time. Like all the other foreign competitors, he too was assigned an assistant who followed him the whole way on his bike and supplied him with the drinks John had given him before the start. With a wry smile on his face, John told me that early in the race his escort had thrown away the bag of ice cubes he had made such an effort to obtain so as to keep his drinks cool. Apparently, the Englishman didn't think it was worth the trouble to lug it on the back of his bike just to indulge the whim of some American athlete. Had I been in John's shoes, I would have been livid.

Shmuel Benkler's son, who had never seen a race-walking competition before and who was keenly caught up in the tension and exertion throughout the event, declared that it had been even more exciting than an English soccer match. I don't know if that's true or not, but it was gratifying to get such a vote of confidence from a kid who had no reason to lie or butter me up.

As it was every year, the competition had been organized by the Surrey Walking Club. The man in charge, who also liaised with the foreign athletes and introduced me to the black South African walker Eddy Michael, was a genuine English gentleman by the name of Maurice Horton. He himself was a race walker who came from a whole family of walkers; his brother had won

London to Brighton several times. He told us he had been stationed as a soldier in Palestine in World War II and that explained how he knew a few words of Hebrew. As we chatted with him, he provided the solution to another riddle that had stumped us for some time. He was the one who had given John Kelly aspirin and shoved him back onto the road to complete the 100-mile competition so many years before.

In addition to a medal and a small plaque, I was also entrusted with a giant silver trophy passed from each year's winner to the next, and bearing the names of all past winners. I was kindly requested not to take it out of England — they must have been afraid they'd never see it again — and I promised to leave it at the Israeli embassy for safekeeping. But I still wanted the pleasure of gazing at it, so I scoured London for a similar antique cup and had the prodigious engraving copied onto it.

When I went to the embassy to entrust it to their care, I first had to submit it to a scrupulous security check to ensure there was no bomb inside. Then I was referred to one of the attachés. To my surprise, he turned out to be Yudke Thager, a classmate from Jerusalem who was taking advantage of his tour of duty at the embassy to complete his PhD thesis. Yudke introduced me to the ambassador, who was very impressed by the trophy and asked me if the British customarily gave such imposing cups for second place. It was hard for him to grasp that, unlike most Israeli athletes, I had actually come in first. Not only that, but I had won the most famous English race-walking competition there is.

Before I left for the States in the early summer, the army had called me up for a long stretch of reserve duty. Finally, they agreed to defer my call-up on condition that I be back in the country by September 8, when I would be seconded to a different unit. Now that my form was improving, I wanted very much to spend an extra month and a half in Europe so I could train there and take part in the 100-kilometer world championship in Lugano in mid-October. Before leaving the States, I checked with the army again to see whether they might have had a change of heart and would allow me to extend my stay abroad. The answer came back unequivocally — No! So on September 7 we returned to Israel and the next day I was back in uniform. Without warning, the army was put on red alert. The Syrians had deployed their forces in offensive formation and were moving toward the border.

I was stationed at headquarters. My original regiment was mobilized on emergency orders and I was sent to join it. The full alert was cancelled as suddenly as it had been declared. I was assigned as gun position officer to one of the batteries deployed in the Jordan Valley. The soldiers there all knew me, and the regiment commander was an ex-student of mine. We were positioned in a ravine very close to the southeastern slope of Sartaba — the hill commanding the area, where a bonfire had been lit in ancient times to announce the beginning of each month in the lunar calendar.

I was notified that the commander of the Jordan Valley Brigade, Colonel Eilam, would be inspecting the troops with the regiment commander. When they reached our battery, my commander was about to introduce me to the colonel when we informed him simultaneously that there was no need for introductions. He had been a classmate of mine at the Technion, Uzi Trachtenberg, before he changed it to a Hebrew name. He had been in command of the paratroop regiment that took the Western Wall in the Six-Day War, after which he reenlisted in the regular army. The inspection revealed no faults in my battery, and wouldn't have even if I had not been personally acquainted with the two officers.

The border was quiet. The War of Attrition had ended and a cease-fire had just been reinstated. I tried to get in as much training as I could. It was broiling hot during the day, but the nights were pleasant, except that at night any moving object was fired on, so I had no choice but to go out in the heat of the day. I trained on a section of road about two hundred yards long that crossed the battery. As a rule, I had to cut these sessions short, but on three occasions, during the holidays, I managed a long-distance training of some sixty miles each time. I placed bottles of water and Coke along the side of the road and walked back and forth again and again from early in the morning until late in the evening. The soldiers — off-duty for the holiday except for the guards and those on the duty roster — watched me from their tents, whining that their necks were starting to hurt from having to move their heads constantly from right to left to follow my progress. These practices helped keep me in reasonable condition, although there are certainly better ways to prepare for a world championship.

All quiet in the sector! I hear of an imminent operation to check the

Jordan River crossings. I volunteer to serve as the forward observation officer, accompanying the patrol and directing artillery fire if necessary. The regiment commander agrees, and for one day I am assigned to a navy commando unit, together with a signals operator and several infantry soldiers as escort. We are taken to the staging area, some distance from the border, in broad daylight. There is constant movement in the region, and our arrival shouldn't attract any special attention. The briefing goes on for hours. Should we be discovered in the course of the operation or encounter any danger, it will be my job to call out the artillery units put on alert to effect a rescue. It's pitch black, the night of a new moon chosen for the mission.

We set out in the middle of the night, first blackening our faces and hands. Jumping up and down, we make sure there is nothing on our bodies or in our pockets that jingles or makes any sort of noise. We move quickly. The pace is too fast for my signals operator, so I take the heavy walkie-talkie from him and carry it myself. The terrain is hard to cross, mud alternating with wet swamp ground and studded with roots and reeds that trip us up. Total silence. We get to the river, right under the noses of a manned Jordanian outpost towering above us on the opposite bank. The commandos slip into the water to check whether the river is passable for vehicular traffic, and we stay on the bank to provide cover. Fifteen minutes later they reappear. We start back in the same silence we maintained on the way there. Mission accomplished, and the Jordanians remained oblivious to our presence. It feels good.

I still wanted to compete in the 100-kilometer world championship in Lugano. My situation reminded me of the joke about George Bernard Shaw, whose eye was caught by the star of one of his plays. He offered her a thousand pounds to spend the night with him and she consented. Shaw then lowered his offer to fifty pounds, at which the prima donna burst out: "Mr. Shaw, what do you think I am?" Shaw answered: "What you are I established from your answer to my first question; now we're just negotiating the fee!"

The Israeli Sports Federation never functioned according to any plan; everything was always a last-minute decision. I had to decide way in advance if I was going to take part in the race, because it takes months to prepare and train for such a competition. Having made my decision, I had directed all my training since early summer to long-distance events. So now, as with Shaw, it was only a question of money: would I have to cover my own expenses again, or would the Federation pay for the trip? Of course I never told them I was going no matter what. Had I done that, I wouldn't have been able to expect any help from them at all. I was very happy to learn, eventually, that Doron had managed to persuade them to cover my travel expenses. At the same time, the army agreed to release me three days early.

The week before I finished reserve duty, I got a weekend pass. I hadn't been home in two weeks. The officer sent to take over for me showed up rather late on Friday. As soon as I made it home, I took off for the north so as to get there in time to take part once more in Braz's 100-kilometer march. Naturally, I was late and finally started three hours after the official start time. The new Arik Bridge had been built across the Jordan, just above where the river flows into the Sea of Galilee, so this year we went straight from Karei Deshe through Capernaum and the Arik Bridge to the road north of the lake, rather than taking the road from Kurazin, over the Bnot Ya'akov Bridge and through the Golan Heights as we had the year before. But then when we got to Zemach, we had to do Zemach-Kibbutz Gesher-Zemach to make up the difference.

Only a very few of the participants walked the whole route. Most of them never even started the Zemach-Gesher loop, saving themselves the "extra" twenty-two miles needed to complete a full circle of the Sea of Galilee. One of the somewhat older participants not only "saved" himself those twenty-two miles, but also hitched rides for fairly long sections of the route and ran — rather than walking — the rest of the way. From one year to the next, he shortened the distance he actually did on foot, until eventually he only ran a few miles at the start and the finish, deceiving only himself in the process. It took me close to 11 hours to walk the whole way. It wasn't the most agreeable feeling in the world to be out there all alone on foot where it wasn't entirely safe, especially around Kibbutz Gesher.

Lugano in Switzerland has earned itself a special place in the race-walking world for organizing biannual federation cup competitions for the Olympic distances of 20 and 50 kilometers. Held the years preceding and following the Olympics, they move from country to country, but are still always known as the Lugano Cup. Over the years, these events have become the world championships, but they continue to follow the same format as they always have.

Every year, Lugano is home to an International Race-Walking Week in a festive atmosphere. It begins with a relay race — seven walkers per team — from Oriole to Chiasso on the border with Italy. Dozens of countries send teams, and some international teams form themselves as well. A 10-kilometer race takes place in mid-week in the evening. The climax comes on the weekend: the Cento — the 100-kilometer race.

Race-Walking Week had followed the same pattern for years, but that year the IAAF (International Amateur Athletic Federation) decided to afford certain competitions world championship status — "*criterium mondial*." The first track and field event, and the only one in race walking, to be recognized as a world championship race was the Cento in Lugano. The entire week was organized by the SAL (Societa Atletica Lugano), headed by a very nice man by the name of Armando Libote.

The academic year hadn't started yet. So the day after I was released from the army, in the middle of October 1970, I was on a plane bound for a long weekend in Switzerland where I would compete in the 100-kilometer world championship. When we landed at Kloten airport near Zurich, I ran into an Israeli studying in the city and working part-time as a security guard for El Al. The plastic foam jug I was carrying aroused his curiosity, and when he asked to see my passport he recognized my name as that of "Dr. Ladany the walker." He displayed considerable interest in my athletic career, and since I didn't have anyone to assist me during the competition, I asked him if he would be willing to help. I offered to pay for his train ticket from Zurich to Lugano and back and to get him a place to stay the night before the race. Happily, he agreed. We arranged to meet the next day at my hotel in Lugano.

Championship headquarters were housed in a modest hotel with a gay Italian spirit. Competitors had come from all over the world. I knew some of them from the Olympics and the London to Brighton Walk, and was particularly concerned about the East Germans. Kurt Sakowski had won the previous year, but he wasn't competing this year. I couldn't take any comfort from that fact, however, since East Germany was now represented by Christophe Höhne, the gold medalist in Mexico City; Peter Selzer, who came in fourth in those games, and Luschke. But the rival who inspired the greatest fear was the Japanese walker Saito, holder of the Asian record for 50 kilometers until I stole it from him at a Long Island stadium in 1968.

I sat down at the East Germans' table in the hotel coffee shop. They were accompanied by an official watchdog who hadn't the slightest idea about sports. They recognized me from Mexico City and introduced me to their bodyguard. I had brought some dates with me from Israel, a highly nutritious fruit that's easy on the digestion. I offered some to the East Germans, but they declined politely. Either they were afraid it was some sort of plot to eliminate the competition or they just didn't want to try anything unfamiliar before the race. When I offered them the few pieces I had left after the race, they agreed to taste them and remarked on how good they were, tacitly acknowledging the fact that they knew I was only being sociable the day before and not trying to poison them. Chatting in German, I asked them the East German athletes' secret of success. As their watchdog pricked up his ears, they recited, "The government." I could barely keep myself from wondering out loud: if that's the case, how come all the lame and the corpulent in the country aren't outstanding athletes too.

The race starts out early in the morning from Olivone at the northern tip of the Swiss-Italian canton of Ticino. I begin at a fast pace and hold the lead until kilometer 35. My assistant arrived in Lugano as planned, but since he doesn't have a car he has to ride in one of the official vehicles and can't get my drinks to me as often as I would like. My main goal is to prevent Saito from getting past me. At kilometer 35, near the town of Biasca, the three East Germans catch up to me. They're walking as a group, one beside the other, and I keep pace with them. Now we are four, lined up shoulder to shoulder.

As we pass kilometer 40, their assistant hands them something to eat. I've never seen anything like that consumed during a race. The assistant holds out a cup of hot water with what looks like a boiled sausage inside. With two fingers, Höhne grabs the top of the sausage sticking up out of the cup and sticks it in his mouth. The other two do the same. I don't know what it's made of, but if it's meat, it doesn't seem like a very good idea to me. But it doesn't appear to have any ill effects on any of them.

At the halfway point between Biasca and Bellinzona, Libote checks our time: 4:23. Incredible! It's the same time I recorded at the American 50-kilometer championship in San Francisco when I made the Olympic minimum, but this time, not only am I not moving at my top speed, but I'm actually conserving my energy for the second fifty kilometers. About three kilometers later, I realize that the pace is too fast. The three East Germans also ease off, but I have to slow down more than they do. They open a gap and slowly disappear into the distance. Now I'm fourth. I hear that the walker in fifth place is pretty far back. There are over a hundred athletes in the race. We reach Lake Locarno and continue along the shore.

Somewhere in the middle we have to turn around and go back the way we've come. Now I can see some of the walkers behind me. At kilometer 78 we turn right and make a long steep climb up Monte Ceneri in the Alps. Dale Hill on the way to Brighton looks like child's play in comparison. We ascend along the winding main road for about six kilometers to the top and then start down, although here it's not quite so steep. Just after I begin the descent, the West German Gerhard Weidner suddenly appears and overtakes me. He's an outstanding walker who would go on to take the world record for 50 kilometers on track. I finish fifth in excellent time: 10.01 hours. But I'm still a little disappointed. If it hadn't been for that reserve duty in the Jordan Valley, I could have devoted the time after the London to Brighton race to training in the cooler European climate, and then I just might have been able to win in Switzerland.

As soon as I crossed the finish line, the muscles throughout my body constricted and stiffened. I had to be helped back to the hotel. My assistant took his leave and hurried back to Zurich. I lay down on the bed, totally drained, with sharp pains in my legs and arms. The diagnosis was clear: lack of salt. I didn't have any more salt pills or table salt, and no aspirin to relieve the pain and relax the muscles. My legs were so stiff and painful that I couldn't even reach the door. I shouted for help, hoping that someone passing along the corridor could get me some salt and aspirin. No one seemed to hear me. I was writhing in pain, but nobody came to offer help. After about an hour of agony, I managed to make it to the door and ask a stranger passing by for what I needed. The salt worked wonders. In a matter of minutes, the pain was gone.

The victory celebration was held in a hall about two hundred yards from the hotel, and I made it there on my own power. I was limping a little and suffering from blisters on my feet, but I could see that the winner, Christophe Höhne, as well as Peter Selzer, who came in second, were limping just as badly. My trophy for fifth place was a large copper jug.

In the winter of 1970, Maccabi organized the traditional Hanukkah torch relay. This time it began in Modi'in, near the tombs of the Maccabees. I was given the honor of being the first to run with the torch. It was lit after a short impressive ceremony. The main speaker, the commander of the Central Command, Major General Rehavam Ze'evi (later murdered by Palestinian gunmen in October 2001 when he was serving as minister of tourism), known as "Gandhi," handed it to me, and as the first "runner," I started out at a walk. The mob of photographers urged me to stand still to have my picture taken with the various dignitaries and politicos, but I wanted to get started and kept moving. Not surprisingly, the group picture with me holding the torch in the middle didn't come out well. I maintained a fast pace.

The torch is made of wood with a metal holder on top for the kerosene and a kerosene-soaked wick. It's hard to hold it while you're walking. I had to switch hands constantly. Moreover, walking obviously requires moving the arms back and forth rapidly, and the flame kept going out. It was relit a few times, but when it continued to go out, I was told to go on without the flame. Nobody could see it anyway, so they'd just light it again before I passed it on. The kerosene was also dripping, splattering all over my arms, but at least now there was no danger of it catching fire and setting me alight. Each runner was to carry the torch for ½ to 1 kilometer. You need a lot of people for that, and it required intricate logistics to place them in the proper locations along the route and pick them up at the end of each sector.

I provided a solution for some of these problems, carrying the torch on my own, without passing it on, for the whole distance through Ben Shemen and Lod to Ramle. Although that arrangement had been made in advance, the total distance of around twelve and a half miles wasn't enough for my daily workout. So I walked from my home in Ramat Efal to Modi'in, and when I finished my stretch at Ramle, I walked back home again. The torch was carried as far as the President's House in Jerusalem. I was invited to take part in the final ceremony and "run" the last segment as well. I handed the torch, relit for the occasion, to Menachem Savidor, the chairman of Maccabi Israel (and later the Speaker of the Knesset), and he passed it on to President Shazar standing beside him. The president delivered a short, impassioned speech. I didn't understand a word he said. All I know is that he wasn't talking about the famous Israeli poet Rachel, his lover many years before, and that he sounded very eloquent.

I trained intensely during the winter, also coaching young race walkers from Ramat Efal, something I really enjoyed doing. Back in the summer of 1970 I had talked some fifteen kids between seven and fourteen into trying the sport. Twice a week they showed up in front of my house at the appointed time. After a short session of calisthenics, we walked to the National Park in Ramat Gan and continued training there. The littlest ones still didn't know how to tie their shoelaces, so when they came undone, I had to do it for them. It was all on a volunteer basis. Every time I went to a competition or a march, I crammed five to seven kids into the car with me. Every now and then I managed to persuade some of their parents to come along in their own cars, and then there would be room for the whole group. The kids had great fun, and especially enjoyed seeing the conspicuous and constant improvement in their abilities. They called me at all hours, but even though they often disturbed me while I was working, I loved every minute of the time I devoted to them. They were almost as gung-ho about race walking as I was.

Then I read in the British race-walking magazine about a group of walkers at the RAF base at Akrotiri in Cyprus, and got the idea of pitting them against the kids I was coaching. I ran it by the British military attaché during one of our encounters in the park, and he arranged it. I organized a meet in the National Park and a British military plane flew the RAF walkers over from Cyprus. It turned out that most of them weren't really dedicated to the sport and didn't train regularly. A lot of them had only taken up walking when they got word of the chance of a free trip to Israel. They weren't expecting serious competition from the Ramat Efal team consisting entirely of myself and a bunch of little kids. The results brought a broad smile to my face. Unfortunately, I got the flu and couldn't take part in the race, although I took a few aspirin tablets and came to officiate. One of the RAF team came in first, but Dror Adam, only eleven years old, astounded everyone there by doing the 20 kilometers in 1:59 and finishing second!

For the third consecutive year, the Three-Day March in the spring of 1971 was based at Beit El. It was my fifteenth straight year. I was now thirty-five years old. I finished first on each of the three days, and following the routine of the past few years, then turned around and did it all again in the opposite direction. Each day's official route was thirty-five to thirty-six kilometers, so in just three days I managed to get at least 210 kilometers of training under my belt. After the theft of my sleeping bag, I had stopped staying in the camp overnight. When I was through for the day, I drove back home and returned early the next morning just in time for the start. At the end of the event, in addition to the regular participant's medal I was awarded a gold-plated medal especially coined for those who had taken part in fifteen of the army's Three-Day or Four-Day Marches. I am one of the few individuals, if not the only one, ever to receive this honor.

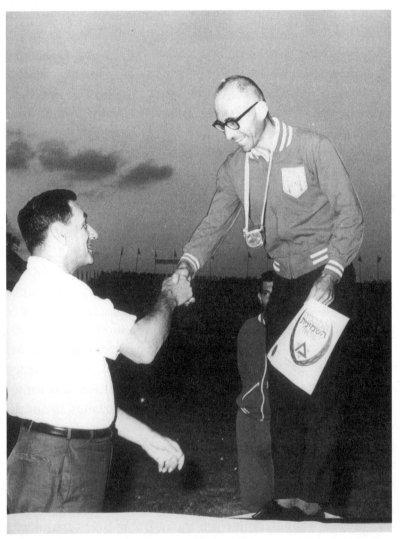

General Aharon Doron awarding me the winner's medal at the
Eighth Maccabiah, 1969

■ Chapter Thirteen | Fighting the Establishment

During the semester break in 1971, I was sent to Europe by the Track and Field Committee for a series of competitions, but this time they explicitly forbade me to add the American 50-mile championship to my itinerary. I couldn't fathom the reasons behind such small-mindedness! I stationed myself in Lausanne at an inexpensive hotel that might better be described as a no-frills youth hostel, located on Lake Geneva. The area is chock-full of excellent training routes, with water fountains and restrooms along the way. Above all, I could practice with other walkers.

The previous year I had made the acquaintance of two Swiss walkers, Paul Seifer and Alfred Badel, both of them policemen. As a rule, the Swiss are known not only for their attention to detail, industriousness, efficiency, and decorum, but also for their distaste for foreigners. During the five years they lived in the country, my sister Shosh and her husband never made a single Swiss friend and were never once invited to the home of a native Swiss family; this was par for the course. Americans are similarly known for not forming close personal ties, maybe because they are always moving away. What appear on the surface to be social relationships often turn out to be more like business contacts based on personal interest, and in most cases are short-lived.

But group dynamics in small populations do not always run along the same lines as in larger groups. There were only a limited number of race walkers in the US, and they were bound by a common interest. So, as a fellow athlete, I had been accepted almost immediately, becoming close friends with many of them and often welcomed into their homes. The same thing happened in Switzerland. Within a very short time, I received invitations from Paul and Alfred, both of whom later even offered to put me up.

My first race was the 50-kilometer Grand Prix de Gruyères, a traditional event whose course is actually only forty-eight kilometers. It begins and ends at the Gruyères Castle — in the town that gave its name to the cheese — after making a wide circle. For this kind of competition I need people to help me with beverages along the way. The year before, when I was arranging for army approval to leave the country, I ran into Ronny Kleiman, a cheerful guy who was studying in Lausanne and had just completed his reserve duty. He volunteered to help me out if I ever needed his assistance. I called him as soon as I got to Lausanne. He and his wife Alona lived in the Lausanne University married students' dorm in Vidy. Proud Israelis, they were well enough off to be able to maintain a large American car with Israeli plates. Together with another Israeli couple, they drove me to the competition early in the morning and kept me supplied with drinks, wet-downs, and encouragement throughout the race, providing some of the best assistance I have ever enjoyed.

My main rival, a man I had good reason to fear, was Manfred Eberhardt, the Swiss walker who had come in ahead of me in Mexico City. He had also beaten me out the year before in the 20-kilometer race in Zurich. This time Manfred kept ahead of me for the first twenty kilometers. For the next twenty, we were virtually shoulder to shoulder. The pace was too fast for me, but I refused to concede the battle. I pushed myself and stayed with him. At kilometer 40 I gave it all I had and stepped on the gas. Manfred tried to respond in kind, but he could only maintain the speed for about a hundred yards and then started to fall behind. That spurred me on to keep up the effort and not ease off the pace. Ronny held out cups of Coke and glucose the instant I asked for them, at the same time wetting my head with a sponge soaked in ice water and updating me constantly as to my progress.

By kilometer 44, Manfred was already out of sight somewhere behind me. Still worried that he might catch up, I didn't let myself slow down. I don't remember ever pushing myself so hard. To this day, I still consider that to be the greatest exertion I ever produced in a competitive event. I came in first, totally exhausted and on the verge of collapse. My time was 4:01. It's too bad the course wasn't a regulation 50 kilometers. Even if I had walked the last two kilometers in 5.5 minutes each (and my average time for the forty-eight was 5.01 min/km), I would have clocked in at 4:12, or maybe a little under. That would have placed me among the top walkers of the year. Regretfully, my effort went totally unappreciated in Israel.

The next stop on my itinerary was Sesto San Giovani, where the competition took the same form as the year before in terms of format, numbers, and the diversity of nations represented. I finished in twelfth place, and then went straight back to Israel in time for the Elijah Marathon organized by Braz. Although it was a running event, I walked. We took off from the Mukhraka, an ancient monastery on Mt. Carmel, and then followed the road along the mountain range to the Yemenite settlement of Elyakim. Staying in the mountains, we took the road crossing the Menashe Heights to Kibbutz Ramat Hashofet. I brought up the rear for the first seven miles, and then little by little began to overtake the slower runners.

It was a great training exercise for me. Whenever I caught sight of a runner up ahead, I would pick up the pace and make the effort to pass. Israel Assoulin served both as timekeeper and walking judge, and he kept me informed of my position. The weather changed and it started to get exceptionally hot and dry. The course descended from the heights, passing Juara to Kibbutz Mishmar Ha'emek in the valley. From there we turned right onto the road through the valley to the Megiddo junction. It was stifling hot. At Megiddo I heard that the favorite, Zion Hetzroni, had dropped out. We turned left onto what is known as the "ruler road," the straightest thoroughfare in the country. The extreme heat, more oppressive at the lower altitude, was almost unbearable. I was in third place. I spotted the runner ahead of me. In short order I had overtaken him. Not far in front I could see someone running languidly and then suddenly slowing to a walk. I picked up my speed. The heat was really getting to me. I caught up with him just before the turn to the Ta'anach settlements. It was Zvika Segal, an old friend. Zvika is an excellent runner, but he doesn't walk very fast. I left him behind and turned right onto the Ta'anach road, rushing forward.

The finish line was near Kibbutz Yizre'el. I came in first in 3:41, a fairly good time for a walker in my condition considering the heat. I had walked to first place in a marathon race. For several years this time appeared beside my name in the list of Israeli marathon winners, until someone apparently decided that it was embarrassing for the runners to have been beaten by a walker and arbitrarily deleted it on the grounds that my time had been achieved in a walk and not a marathon race. I fought hard for many years to have the win reinstated.

The Track and Field Committee accepted the invitation of the Greek Sports Federation to an international track and field meet scheduled for June 1971 in Athens. It was decided that the Israeli team would include anyone who had a chance, or who they hoped had a chance, of meeting the Olympic minimum. I was notified that I would be competing in the 20-kilometer walk. Two weeks later, I learned from the paper that I was not to be a member of the team. Lalkin, the general director of the Sports Federation, had erased my name from the list on the claim that my event was 50 kilometers and not 20. I knew that Lalkin had been out to get me ever since our run-in at Mexico City, but I couldn't understand how the chief Federation administrator could interfere with a professional decision over which he had no authority.

In the States I was accustomed to sports functionaries being elected by the athletes. It is not unusual for some to be themselves active in sports and to continue to compete even while performing their official functions. As a result, they have the athletes' best interests at heart; otherwise, they are simply removed from their posts by the people who elected them. I had naively thought the same to be true in Israel. Was I ever wrong! The Sports Federation is not a federation of sportsmen. It is an umbrella organization for the Hapoel, Maccabi, Elitzur, and ASA sports organizations, with the two latter groups carrying almost no weight at all. Hapoel and Maccabi (as well as Elitzur) are affiliated with political parties, and their officials are not chosen by the athletes.

At that time, the functionaries of Hapoel (associated with the Labor Party) were appointed by influential politicos in the Histadrut (the national labor union) and the local labor councils, who obliged their own supporters or people they owed favors to with these positions and all the perks they brought with them. The Liberal Party operated in the same manner in the case of Maccabi. Some of these officials had no connection to sports whatsoever, knew nothing about the various events and associations, and weren't even particularly interested in the subject. The only thing they cared about was securing the greatest possible personal benefit from their titles. There was nothing inherently wrong with their acting out of self-interest, as long as the results also furthered the overall interests of sports. But since the officials had no commitment to sports and were not responsible to the athletes, there was no pressure on them or control over their activities to ensure that this was indeed the case. Consequently, self-interest became their sole consideration.

The functionaries of the various arms of the Sports Federation, the Israeli Olympic Committee, and the other sports authorities are appointed by the national sports organizations in accordance with their relative power and the same extraneous considerations, so that none of them is in any way committed to or dependent on either the athletes or their performance in any given sport, or even on the success of Israeli sports as a whole. The professionals in the field are largely the employees of a certain club, and therefore owe their fealty to that club, its interests, and its political functionaries. This is the underlying reason for the fact that Israel lags far behind even smaller countries with considerably fewer facilities and resources to devote to sports, such as New Zealand and Luxembourg. It doesn't take an expert in organizational system analysis (like myself) to arrive at this conclusion.

I soon learned that I had no influence whatsoever over the sports establishment and no sword to hold over any of its functionaries. They were only interested in my athletic endeavors and performance — in fact in my very existence — insofar as I benefited them and justified their operations and the resources allocated to them. Since a large number of these functionaries were beholden to the general director of the Sports Federation, from whom they could expect favors in the form of free tickets and other perks, not one of them was willing to voice an objection to Lalkin's decision to exclude me.

In my case, even the interests of the professionals worked against me. Since I spoke so many languages and was personally acquainted with the people involved in my event the world over, there was no justification for paying the way for functionaries to accompany me to competitions abroad on the pretext that they were needed to mediate between me and the event organizers. Moreover, as I was known to train on my own, there was no need to include a coach in my entourage, ostensibly to devise a training program for me, especially since most of the coaches in the country knew nothing about race walking, and next to nothing about marathons as well. What I did need was people to clock me and psych me up, and assistants to keep me watered during the race, but these responsibilities demanded considerable time and my requests for this kind of help fell on deaf ears.

The major reason for my being ignored by the sports establishment and their disdain for my achievements, however, was the fact that I constituted a slap in the face for many of the coaches. Here I was, a man who, without any coaching, had produced impressive results in the international sports world, while their protégés could deliver little to be proud of. This fact painted the professional coaches as ineffectual and unknowledgeable at best, if not totally incompetent. The more they could do to belittle my achievements or stand in the way of my improving on them, the better they looked.

Lalkin, it seemed, wanted the delegation to Greece to include one of the junior officials of the federation who was presumably in line for a perk. No one on the Track and Field Committee was willing to fight my exclusion. I spoke to several newspapers which printed short items outlining my grievances against the Sports Federation and noting my intention to approach a number of Members of Knesset with the request that they present a formal question before the minister of education, sports and culture. I was also planning to apply to the High Court of Justice, and this too was reported. I did indeed speak to three Members of Knesset, Shulamit Aloni (later herself the education minister and afterward the minister for the arts), Yigael Horowitz (who was to become the finance minister), and Uri Avneri. All three presented the minister of education with parliamentary questions regarding my exclusion from the team.

Meanwhile, however, the publicity had made an impact, stirring up a fuss at the Sports Federation. To my regret, and that of many other people, General Doron had retired as chairman of the Track and Field Committee and was now chairman of the Sports Federation. He was a rare bird among the functionaries there. As the executive vice president and director general of Tel Aviv University, he wasn't looking to derive any personal benefit from the sports establishment. He had entered that realm purely out of his love for sports. I had a talk with him. He told me that the other members of the Federation directorate were very annoyed with the items in the press and angered by my threats, and although they knew I had been treated unfairly and that there was no justification in preventing me from competing in the 20-kilometer event, they had no intention of doing anything about it unless I apologized. As he saw it, since my goal was to compete in the Olympics, it was not to my advantage to tilt at windmills. It would be best for me to back down and apologize.

Following his advice, I wrote to Emanuel Gil, saying that I had not meant to offend them by going to the press, but merely to make them aware of the injustice done me and the need to rectify the situation. Furthermore, the legal action I had taken could not be considered a threat, since I was only invoking the right of any citizen. Doron later told me that the members of the directorate had complained that my letter did not constitute an apology. They were right; I'm not in the habit of backing down. Nevertheless, he persuaded them to settle for what I had written and to instruct Lalkin to reverse his decision and include me on the team. Doron soon tired of working with small-minded functionaries. A year later he retired from his post as chairman of the Sports Federation. I went to Athens as a member of the Israeli team at the international track and field meet and won the 20-kilometer walk, even though my training was focused on the 50-kilometer Olympic event. The competition also gave me the chance to meet up with Michael Igloi again; he was now the Greek national coach.

My next goal was the Belgian 50-kilometer championship, and Maccabi Tel Aviv agreed to cover my travel expenses. I'd been a member of the club since 1966 and had never before received any sort of financial support from them, neither in the form of equipment nor as a travel allotment for competitions or practice sessions in Israel. This was the first time they had agreed to underwrite a trip abroad for me, although admittedly it took a lot of nagging on my part, and it was also the last time I ever got anything from them. I was only going to be in Europe for the weekend. Shosh was in the last stages of her pregnancy, and I had to be back at the beginning of the week so as to make it in time to be with her on the date she was scheduled for a C-section.

The championship was held on Sunday, July 11, 1971, in Charleroi. The organizers located a captain in the Belgian navy who spoke English and was willing to assist me during the race. I was glad to be able to explain precisely what I wanted without having to break my teeth trying to make myself understood in broken French. The traditional course for the competition these many years ran from Charleroi to Beaumont and back the same way. I led the whole way. I had to push myself hard for the last ten kilometers, particularly the final one.

As always when I'm exerting myself, my facial muscles were taut and my breathing was rapid. The effort and the inner battle to overcome discomfort and pain could easily be read on my face. I won. I was the Belgian champion. Press photographers took pictures throughout the race and captured me crossing the finish line. The next day papers in Charleroi and Brussels carried the photo, with the supreme effort clearly written on my face. The caption read: "The smile of the victor." "What smile?" I thought to myself. "My expression obviously shows the effort of pushing myself to the limit."

As I crossed the finish line, I was handed a bouquet of flowers and the local beauty queen planted a kiss on my cheek. Other young women followed her example. The congratulatory kisses of the sixty-year-olds and up were somewhat less welcome, although they lasted longer... Several hours after the last of the competitors had completed the race, there was a banquet in a local restaurant. In true French fashion, spirits were high, in all senses of the word. The organizers, Monsieur and Madame Roger, who had been responsible for the championship for decades, were exceedingly convivial. I was the only one there who didn't drink any alcohol at all. It was nearly midnight before the celebrations broke up. The next morning I was back in Brussels for my flight home. The flight was delayed because of some technical glitch. I very nearly missed the birth of my daughter Danit!

I had become the American walkers' guru in all matters concerning long distances and regularly received letters from them asking for my advice on questions of training. Then I heard from Bob Henderson, a man I had never met, who wanted to know if he could come to Israel to train with me. Recalling the warmth and hospitality I had enjoyed throughout my stay in the States, I unhesitatingly invited him to be a guest in my home for three weeks. Maybe I should have thought twice before I did that. He arrived when Danit was only three weeks old and his visit was probably an unnecessary burden on Shosh. Moreover, Ray Posner, the Jewish walker from England who had competed against me at the Maccabiah Games in 1969, had just left, having wound up a visit to Israel during which he invited himself to stay with us for a few days right after Danit was born.

The Track and Field Committee decided to select four athletes with a chance of meeting the Olympic minimum and send them to Europe for the summer of 1971 to train and compete. I was chosen along with Hannah

Shezifi, Aviva Balas, and Esther Shahamorov. We were to be accompanied by the coach Avraham Green. The high point of our stay would be the pre-Olympic meet in Munich the second week of September.

Green convinced the committee it would be to our advantage to leave in early August to attend the European Track and Field Championship in Helsinki. It was obvious to me that he wanted the chance to attend the championship and to meet the who's who of European athletics, and that this was an important opportunity for him. But we weren't allowed to compete, nor would we be meeting and training with the foreign athletes. The stay in Helsinki would be of no value to us, except for giving us an opportunity to enjoy the pleasantly cool weather. Furthermore, I couldn't just get up and go away for seven weeks, leaving Shosh alone with two-week-old Danit.

Nevertheless, I did want to compete in the 50-kilometer pre-Olympic event in Munich, the Hastings-Brighton competition in the second week of August, and the London to Brighton Walk in early September. I asked to be permitted not to leave with the group for Helsinki. I wanted to go later, fly to England for the weekend for the Hastings-Brighton event, return to Israel, go back to England three weeks later for the London to Brighton Walk, and then meet up with the others in Munich and come back home with them. Permission was denied. I would have to go to Helsinki like everyone else. Begrudgingly, however, the committee agreed for me to go from Helsinki to England for Hastings-Brighton and then back to Israel for three weeks, at my own expense, after which I could fly back to England for the London to Brighton Walk, again at my own expense, and then rejoin the group in Munich.

I left for Helsinki in early August 1971 and took my leave from the others four days later. Since Green knew that I had justified my request to be exempted from the trip to Finland by invoking his egotistic reasons for wanting us to be there, he was less than pleased with me, to say the least. He had been entrusted with the funds to cover all our expenses abroad, and refused to give me what was coming to me to cover the cost of my trip from Helsinki to London and from London to Munich, as well as my living expenses for that period, even though the money had been promised me. I didn't even get the regular athlete's allowance of three dollars a day — and of course I never got any daily allowance when I traveled on my own. Either he wanted to boast to the committee that he had not exhausted the funds he was given, or he had some other use for the money.

I flew to London and from there to Hastings. Since I knew that Shmuel Benkler had left England meanwhile, I had written to Maccabi England requesting their help in finding me an assistant for the competition, but they were unable to locate anyone because the race was being held on the Sabbath. I then wrote to the offices of the Jewish Agency, and fortunately they found me a volunteer in the form of an Englishman, Joe Marx.

Hastings-Brighton is a long-standing 38-mile event. We start out in driving rain. Stretching and warming up before the start, I notice Ray Middleton. He catches sight of me and comes over, taunting me with: "Let's see what you can do now. This time you have to do it in our typical rainy weather without the advantage of your Israeli heat." I don't take the bait. The race is virtually a replay of the London to Brighton Walk of the previous year. As soon as the signal is given, I rush forward like the wind. Middleton catches up after ten miles and tries to overtake me. I respond by picking up the pace, not letting him get ahead of me. We keep up an evenly matched duel for ten miles. Finally, I step on the gas and Ray slowly begins to fall behind. The strong wind is hard to contend with, but I'm just glad it isn't hot.

The "assistance" I receive is far from optimal. For all his good intentions, Joe has no experience and no empathy with an athlete in need of his help. Furthermore, although Jewish, he is a typical Englishman, totally devoid of resourcefulness or chutzpah. He also has a hard time opening the cold box I packed with cans of Coke in a bed of ice cubes. He's afraid of breaking the lid. So all I have to drink is warm water and tepid Coke. Despite the rain and the wind, the exertion raises my body heat and I need a cold drink to cool myself down from inside. The route enters a road with a "No Entry" sign. All the other escort cars ignore it, but Joe is concerned about getting a ticket and looks for a way around. He loses contact with me for an hour. I nearly die of thirst.

Finally I see Brighton up ahead. I know the road. Here's the traffic circle. In front is the white building at the head of the pier. From there I have to turn left and the finish line is only a few dozen yards away. I'm panting. My whole body aches, even the palms of my hands and my fingers. I make a final effort, using the last bit of strength I have left. When I try to speed up I suddenly feel a sharp pain spreading out from the sole of my foot. A blister has burst. The pain is almost unbearable. I grit my teeth and lengthen my stride. The bobbies stop traffic, one of them badly confusing the drivers with his hand signals. Without warning, he stops directing traffic to applaud me! I give it that one last push. I'm on the verge of collapse, no strength left at all, but my body still responds, surprising even me. I reach the crossroads and turn left, picking up the pace even more. The final sprint, the finish. Every muscle is cramped.

There's a large crowd on both sides of the funnel to the finish line. "How much more, exactly how many more yards?" I wonder. "Can I hold out?" I don't know. I feel so bad I can barely stand it. "When will it finally be over? I can't go any further," I think. Twenty more yards — four seconds. "Is that the end?" "No." I estimate there are still ten yards to go. Someone shouts out "mazel tov" in Hebrew. I can hardly understand what he's saying in his thick accent. Applause. Over the loudspeakers I hear: "And the winner is — Dr. Ladany from Israel."

I spot the mayor of Brighton who presented me with the cup the year before. His wife, a Jewish woman, is standing beside him. Maurice Horton is also there. I'm very grateful to him for giving me a detailed description of the topographical layout of the route that morning before the start. He also advised me to plan my strategy "prudently," that is, not to take off like the wind. But now that he knew what I could do, he probably predicted I would win. Still five more yards. I can't feel my feet any more. The excitement of the crowd helps. One final effort. That's it. I pass the timekeepers. I'm finished, or so I think. But no. The tape across the finish line is still three yards up ahead. The momentum keeps me going. I finally reach the tape and it gives way.

I try to stop, but I can't. My muscles won't respond. I slow down, but I have to keep walking. Dozens of people are running toward me with their arms open, ready to embrace me. I wish they wouldn't. I'd rather they walked alongside me without touching or poking. I turn around and let out a deep sigh. Now I can feel the agonizing pain in my feet, but I'm thrilled. "I did it!" I congratulate myself. My face must bear an expression of joy mixed with pain, suffering, and exhaustion. My legs are starting to cramp up. Already there are new pains from the blisters on my feet. "It's a good thing they didn't bother me during the race," I think to myself, just as an "ouch" escapes from my lips as I move my arm and feel another pain in my armpit. "It must be chafed," I deduce. I completely forget that for hours I have been fighting the urge to stop and urinate. I no longer feel the need. What I do feel now is the cold. And I'm all sticky from the Coke that splattered on me when I drank it while keeping up a fast walk. Someone wraps a blanket around me. I'm starting to shiver.

I'm led to the mayor standing at the finish line to receive his congratulations. The press photographers are snapping pictures of me from all angles. I'm standing beside the mayor when one of the reporters asks, "What's your Christian name?" The announcer declared the winner only as "Dr. Ladany." I'm exhausted, but the phrasing of the question gets my goat. It was all I needed to let out with a cynical response. I'm aware he only wants to know my first name, but he could have asked for that or for my "given" name. He heard I'm from Israel, so why is he so insensitive, or so stupid, to imagine that everyone has been christened? So I spit back at him: "I don't have a Christian name, only a Jewish one. My first name is Shaul." He doesn't rise to the challenge, only writes down my name and asks how it's spelled. But there's a glint in the eye of the mayor's wife and a meaningful smile on her face. I sense she's proud of me not only for winning, but also for the way I answered him. An English Jew would never dare to respond as I had; it took the chutzpah of an Israeli.

I was led to the locker room. The gentleman in charge of the baths was the same man who had been there the year before at the end of the London to Brighton Walk. He had prepared bath number 1 for me again. I greeted him saying, "I remember that bath; I've missed it." With a smile he replied, "Congratulations! Bravo!" When I left the locker room I discovered that only a few competitors had finished the race while I was in the bath; the rest were still walking. Middleton came in second, eight minutes behind me, shook my hand, and congratulated me. I had convinced him that I didn't need hot weather to win.

At the medals ceremony I was presented with another large silver cup passed from one winner to the next. Wanting very much to hold on to it, if only for one year, and not being asked to leave it in England, I brought it back to Israel with me. The following year, when I had to return it to the organizers, I debated how to send such a large, heavy, valuable item to England without risking it getting damaged or going astray, heaven forbid. The solution grew out of my acquaintance with the British military attaché in Israel. Thanks to him, it went back to England in the diplomatic pouch.

As soon as the Hastings-Brighton race was over, I flew back to Israel. Danit was only three weeks old and I didn't want to be away from home for too long. Even so, my European "junkets" were more than most wives would be willing to accept with love and understanding. To her credit, Shosh didn't complain too much. She must have known how important it was to me, and how stubborn I could be. Sports activities are put on hold in Israel for the summer months. Braz's marches began in October and ended in May, and Hapoel crammed most of the marches it organized into the months of March and April. The summer is also downtime for track and field events. The midsummer heat is extremely oppressive if you plan to train.

But I couldn't give myself a rest — no way! I knew I would soon have to compete again in England against the same walkers, and this time they would all be fired with the desire to beat me. The London to Brighton Walk is an English event. A foreigner could only be allowed to win once. It had happened before, but never twice in a row. It was unheard of. And Ray Middleton was at the top of his form. I'd come in ahead of him again, but not by much this time. The final results are hard to predict at long distances. Anything could happen to any one of the competitors. In fact, that's what makes these races so fascinating. Ray had a good chance of improving during the three weeks before the walk, especially since he'd be training in the cool English climate. I was worried, but I didn't intend to throw in the towel. I decided to train as hard as possible, despite the temperatures in Israel, which can go as high as 101 degrees Fahrenheit in the shade! So in addition to my strenuous daily training sessions, two or three times a week I went out for super-long practices of extraordinary distances.

I would start out from my home in Ramat Efal at three in the morning, follow the inner road to the Tel Hashomer junction and then proceed south along the nearly empty Geha highway as far as the Palmachim junction, where I would enter the town of Rishon Le-Zion. A local grocery just getting its morning milk delivery would be my first watering station. Then I would go back as far as Beit Dagan, turn east onto the Jerusalem highway, and walk to the far end of Ramle. By this time, dawn would be breaking and I would make my second stop for a drink. Then I would turn left to Lod, climbing from the men's minimum security prison of Ma'asiyahu to the women's penal institution, Neve Tirza, and on to Ben Shemen.

I knew the area like the back of my hand, not only from the time I lived in

Lod, the hikes in high school, the Ramle March and the Four-Day March of 1959, part of which passed this way, but also from my regular 50-kilometer training route that also followed this road. My third stop was at the grocery opposite the youth village of Ben Shemen. Then on to Beit Nabala. The man who ran the lunch counter opposite the entrance to the army base had known me for years. Whenever he saw me approaching, he'd uncap two bottles of Coke and have them waiting for me with a cup, a salt shaker and a spoon. To the soldiers amazed to see me drinking salted Coke and walking in place so as to prevent my muscles from cramping, he'd explain: "That's Dr. Ladany, the walker. He's training for the Olympics."

I turned left toward Kfar Truman and the airport. There were orchards along both sides of the road between Beit Nabala and Kfar Truman. I could usually find an orange or grapefruit forgotten behind on a tree. There was a water fountain at the entrance to the airport. I turned right and continued northward. Past the gate to the Israel Aircraft Industries and the buildings on the right-hand side of the road that were once used to house new immigrants, there was a strip of vineyards stretching as far as the road to Tirat Yehuda. I could always find a few bunches of grapes hiding among the vine leaves. Ambrosia! I kept on to Petah Tikva. As I reached Feja on the left and Kfar Sirkin on the right, I could see to the east the whole line of hills where we trained in the officers' training course.

I continued from Petah Tikva through Ramatayim, passing the entrance to Kfar Saba and reaching the Ra'anana junction. At the kiosk on the left-hand corner I made a Coke stop. By now the sun was already high in the sky. I entered Ra'anana and crossed the city to Herzliya, then cut across the gravelly hills and descended to the coastal road near the entrance to Herzliya Pituach. There I turned left, again following the coastal road as far as the Country Club junction where I headed east. Passing through the Kfar Hayarok junction, I continued on to the Morasha junction and then turned south. There were a lot of orchards on the right-hand side of the road where I could easily find more oranges. The sun had passed its midpoint and was dropping to the west. Now I raced ahead like a horse who had caught the smell of the stable. Crossing the Petah Tikva road, I was back on the Geha highway. At last I was home again in Ramat Efal — three o'clock in the afternoon. It's not only this description of the route that was so lengthy — I had walked at least sixty-two miles, most of it in extreme heat under the broiling sun.

I went out for a practice walk like that every Friday. An hour after I got home, at four o'clock, the group of Ramat Efal children I coached showed up on my doorstep and I took them out to the National Park to train. That added another six to ten miles, done much faster than the long-distance walk I had just finished. It's the only way to forge steel. Bob Henderson arrived to spend three weeks with us at this time, now that I was back from the Hastings-Brighton walk, but since he hadn't been building up to long distances, there was no question of his joining me on my ultra-long training walks. He started out with me several times and made it nearly halfway. We chatted as we walked, and I learned that his father was an Illinois state senator. Unfortunately, this didn't give him any advantage when it came to race walking. Despite the intense training I was doing, I managed during this same period to write up a study I had conducted and submit it for publication.

In early September, after three weeks at home, I flew back to England for the London to Brighton Walk. It was only half an hour before the start when I got to the locker room and, to my great pleasure, found my American friends Elliott Denman, Don Johnson, and Paul Schell, who had also come to compete. There were over a hundred entrants, but Ray Middleton wasn't among them. Colin Young told me that Ray was out with an injury. I didn't believe that story. It sounded too much like an excuse, on the order of a tactical illness. Still, it made me very happy; I wasn't going to have any serious competition.

True, there was Don Thompson, Olympic gold medalist and eight-time winner of the London to Brighton Walk, but I didn't consider him too much of a threat. I knew I was much better than him. Shaun Lightman, whom I had met here the year before and had also been in Hastings-Brighton, didn't concern me either, even though he had finished among the leaders in both competitions. He was a very pleasant fellow who greeted me with a few words in Hebrew, which he had learned as part of his theological studies.

The seventh stroke of Big Ben was the starting signal, and again it took me by surprise. I was in the middle of a stretch, bending over with my head down. When I looked up, I saw the mass of walkers moving forward. I didn't let it upset me, just took off at a rapid pace. Within two minutes, even before crossing the Thames, I was in the lead. I knew I had to win, and I would.

And I did! In 7:52. I thought to myself that had I been a religious person I would thank God for putting the fear of Ladany into Ray Middleton and the other competitors so that no one gave me a real fight and I didn't have to push myself to the utter limit. By now I was very familiar with the route and the crossroads along the way. I was also on intimate terms with bath number 1. At the medals ceremony, I regained possession of the silver cup that the organizers had collected from the Israeli embassy. The moment it was handed to me, I proclaimed that it looked familiar and that I hoped to see it again in the future, a statement that won me loud applause from the other competitors and spectators. The mayor of Brighton also remarked jokingly that it had become a habit for him to see me standing in front of him waiting to receive the victor's trophy. I reported back to the Israeli press: "Veni, vidi, vici." They might not know Latin, but they'd all heard of Julius Caesar.

Joe Marx assisted me in this race, too. A public relations officer for the Jewish Agency, he was so impressed by the awards ceremony, the press coverage of my victory, and the favorable attitude to Israel that it generated, that at his own initiative he wrote to the Israeli Foreign Office and the Sports Authority claiming that there was no better way to gain positive publicity and spawn favorable public opinion for Israel than to send a goodwill ambassador like myself to major race-walking competitions. The letter, a copy of which I received from Yariv Oren, the director of the Sports Authority, several weeks after the competition, came as a surprise to me. From Yariv's cover letter, I gathered that he was also surprised by it, but remained doubtful that my competing had any effect on public opinion, or on other athletes either.

Six days later it was time to contend with walkers from all over the world in the 50-kilometer event at the pre-Olympic meet in Munich. By the time I flew in from London, I was coming down with the flu, probably the result of my prostration at the end of the London to Brighton Walk and the fact that the Coke I had drunk for the eight hours of that competition was too cold. It happens now and again, when overexertion lowers my resistance, that I catch the flu. My tongue can tell when it starts, even before the onset of the regular symptoms — hoarseness, cough, sore throat, headache, and fever. My upper lip gets a sharp unpleasant taste. I got progressively worse until the night before the race, when it hit me full force: fever, headache, and a runny nose.

When the meet doctor examined me, he didn't want to consent to my competing the next day. Avraham Green gave me pills to bring down the fever. I threw up before start time. That was a first for me, but I felt a little better afterwards. The night before the event, I arranged with Green to position himself at the watering station at kilometer 10 to make sure I got my Coke, with or without glucose as required.

We take off. I feel pretty good for the first six kilometers or so. Then I start getting hot and dried out, followed by cold shivers and a splitting headache. Green isn't at the watering station; I only get water. I feel terrible, stop, start up again, and stop once more. I can't compete when I'm feeling so bad. I move aside and lie down on the pavement. It's just like John Kelly in Mexico City. An ambulance appears and they lay me down inside. I have a raging fever. It's perfectly clear to all the other athletes in the walk, and the marathon taking place simultaneously, what's going on. It can happen to any athlete, and generally does from time to time, but the Israeli press presented it in a different light.

My success in the Hastings-Brighton and London to Brighton events, the most important race-walking competitions in the world, meant little to the Israeli sports writers. They only gave weight to the pre-Olympic meet. Thus they chose to write: "Ladany fails," "He fails in every major event," or "He came in among the last in Mexico City and probably won't do any better at the Olympics in Munich." I was angry and hurt by these totally spurious claims.

Most of the sports writers in Israel are total ignoramuses when it comes to any field outside of soccer or basketball. All of them ran 100 or 200 meters when they were young, not necessarily competitively, and that's more or less the extent of their knowledge of athletics. Their accounts of individual events almost invariably contain little more than the names of the winners of the first three places, their times, whether or not they broke any records, and any relevant anecdotes or scandals. The write-ups are dry and boring, with no background information, no analysis, and no description of the drama before and during the competition. This is, of course, merely the product of their lack of knowledge of the events and their unwillingness to bone up on them.

Although they reported on the walking competitions, on the whole they didn't know the rules governing the sport and had never even seen such an event, and certainly not a long-distance one. Once, when I showed an Israeli reporter an article about a race-walking competition that had appeared in the

British *Athletics Weekly*, he defended himself for not being able to write on that level by saying, "But that guy knows what he's talking about!" Furthermore, a lot of sports writers are dependent to some degree or another on the sports establishment, which feeds them information and free passes; and, as a result, their reports and analyses are often inaccurate because they come from an interested source. That also explains why it is so rare to find any criticism of the athletic establishment in the press.

It was a whole week before I was over the flu. I knew there was no one in Israel who would speak up for me in response to the criticism of the reporters, who didn't understand the circumstances. When I returned home I wrote a letter to the editor of one of the papers, refuting the facts contained in one particularly scathing article, but my letter was never published.

I kept up my training with the same intensity. For the third time I took part in Braz's 100-kilometer circuit of the Sea of Galilee, including the loop to Kibbutz Gesher and back, and again both finished first and was one of the few participants to complete the entire distance. The Track and Field Committee decided to send me to another competition abroad, the fourth time that year, in mid-October. I would be going only for the weekend, enough time to compete in the 100-kilometer world championship in Lugano.

Four days before I left, I tried to break my own Israeli record for 50 kilometers on track. I set it up on the cinder track at the Wingate Institute of Physical Education, arranging to make this attempt as close in time as possible to the Cento so that the 50-kilometer walk would work together with my high-carbohydrate diet to drain the glycogen from my muscles in preparation for the long-distance event in Switzerland. Dr. Oded Bar-Or, a physiologist of international repute at Wingate who gave his name to the army's fitness test, had meanwhile been elected chairman of the Track and Field Committee's professional subcommittee. He decided to assist me in my one-man endeavor. It was a hot, humid day and I felt like I was burning up. Not stopping, I requested ice water. Oded asked Dr. Gilad Weingarten, standing nearby, to assist me while he went to find ice. Gilad didn't have any interest in race walking, and I didn't get anything to drink for a long time until Oded got back. Although I completed the 50 kilometers, I wasn't able to break my record.

Shortly afterward, Oded resigned from his post on the Track and Field Committee, and when his advancement at Wingate was blocked, he left the country. I later heard that he had asked for modest compensation from the Israeli Olympic Committee for the extraordinary drain on his time demanded by his post as chairman of the professional subcommittee, a job he performed with utter conscientiousness. All he wanted was their assurance that he would be sent to the Olympics as a member of the Israeli delegation. The political functionaries on the Olympic Committee were clearly put out by this premature request, the granting of which would most likely come at the expense of one of their own, and they turned him down. Oded submitted his resignation. He was replaced as chairman by a man who knew less, devoted less of his time and energy to the job, and contributed less to Israeli athletics.

When I arrived in Lugano I found three other Israelis already there: the brothers Eli and Ben-Ami Shahar from the settlement of Tal-Shahar, and Shimon Shomroni. It was I who had originally encouraged them to take up race walking. This was their first experience of a competition abroad, and they were there to take part in the mixed-group relay race and the Nocturno, the 10-kilometer evening event. They knew a local jeweler by the name of Hirsch Galitzky, an ultra-religious Jew who sported the typical garb — a long black coat and large black hat — but was nevertheless an avid sports fan and supporter of the Lugano athletic club, SAL. Galitzky agreed to assist me during my race. The athletes made their way to Olivone on Saturday night, while Galitzky arrived just before the start early Sunday morning and assisted me faithfully throughout the Cento.

I moved rapidly, but this time I paced myself far more evenly. The East Germans Höhne and Selzer came in ahead of me. I was third, in 9:52, improving on my time from the year before and clocking in under the time set by Weidner when he had beat me then. I was totally exhausted. My feet hurt, apparently badly blistered. Eli, Ben-Ami, and Shimon helped me back to my hotel. I could deal with the muscle pain, even ignore it, but there was a surprise in store for me when I took off my shoes and carefully peeled off my socks. A strip of skin about 5 by 2 inches was hanging from the ball of my foot. When I stuck my foot up on the bed to look at it more closely, this piece of skin hung down like the tongue of a shoe, revealing a large hunk of raw flesh underneath.

I was dying to shower in order to cleanse my body of the salty perspiration and sticky soda all over me. I wouldn't have minded luxuriating in a warm bath to relax my muscles either. But I knew that if any water got on my torn foot it would be excruciating. I took a stab at crawling into the bath on my own power while keeping my left foot out of the water, but I couldn't do it. The few drops of water that splashed on the raw flesh were agony. I asked Eli and Ben-Ami to each take one of my legs while Shimon supported my back, and as I navigated with my hands, the three of them lowered me horizontally into the tub with my left leg sticking up in the air.

Half an hour later they covered the tear with a thick layer of salve as I instructed, then carefully realigned the strip of skin, added another layer of salve, and bandaged the foot. When they were done, I was at least able to walk. Two hours later I was at the medals ceremony — not even limping. When the torn strip dried up after about two weeks, I cut it off and pasted it in my scrapbook. Nobody paging through the album has ever guessed the identity of this item. I was presented with another copper trophy. It seems that the better you get, the smaller the trophy. The diameter of this cup for third place was considerably smaller than the one I had gotten for coming in fifth the previous year. But who cares; what mattered was that I had won the bronze medal in the world championship!

November 1971. Green called me a few weeks after I got home from Lugano. This was the first time he had ever done such a thing. He told me that I could earn him a monthly fee of eight hundred Israeli pounds. It had been decided that the coaches of all the candidates for the Israeli Olympic team would be entitled to this compensation from the athletic authorities. All I had to do was to notify the Track and Field Committee in writing that he was my personal coach. He didn't give the slightest indication that he would be willing to help me train. He was only interested in being a de jure coach for the money involved.

Even before I hung up, I realized that this was a golden opportunity to kill two birds with one stone. I could get myself some real help and at the same time give Green what was coming to him for refusing to turn over the money I had been promised to cover my travel expenses from Helsinki to England and from England to Munich. I always like to pay back my debts, whatever form they may take. I immediately called Edna Medalia, the veteran discus thrower who had in former days been the rival of the noted Olga Wittenberg. At that time she was working as a gym teacher and coach and was active on the Track and Field Committee. Although universally recognized as a genuinely nice person with integrity and a sense of responsibility who was always willing to help out and volunteer her time, she had never been afforded the honor or perks she deserved. I explained the situation to her.

She was hesitant, arguing that she knew nothing about race walking, but I insisted that none of the other coaches in the country did either, so she couldn't do any worse than anyone else. Furthermore, I needed someone to help me train, to time me, pump me up, and supply me with drinks during my super-long walks. She said she had to think about it. Two days later she informed me she had decided to accept my offer. I notified the Sports Federation, and Edna became my official coach. I wish I had seen Green's face when he heard the news. As only to be expected, Edna did an excellent job.

■ Chapter Fourteen | Setting the World Record

I trained intensively throughout the winter. Once or twice a week I went out for an ultra-long practice walk of a hundred kilometers, and two or three times a week completed fifty kilometers. The rest of the training sessions were short and quick paced. In order to get to the university on time in the morning, I would leave the house around 3:30 in the morning, do fifty kilometers, and be finished before 8:30. Towards the end of my route, I would be walking against the morning rush-hour traffic. Drivers who recognized me would honk their horns or flash their lights in greeting. Some of them were students of mine, and when I ran into them later that day at the university, I would invariably hear, "I saw you this morning on the road."

If there was no competition or march on a given Saturday, I used the opportunity for a super-long walk. Edna was there to assist me. I went out in all weather, even in the pouring rain. Edna followed me in her car, stopping every few miles to give me something to drink. Once she got a ticket for pulling up at a bus stop. Happily for me, and fortunately for her, the head of the traffic police was persuaded to tear up the ticket by a letter I wrote explaining the special circumstances.

The competitive events that did take place, mostly at the Wingate Institute, were good training sessions for me, walked at a faster pace than my other practices. I was preparing for The Event with a capital E — the Munich Olympics. Anything else was no more than a means of getting me in shape for that long-term goal. So I walked from my home to Wingate, about seventeen miles. While the added exertion had an inevitable effect on my performance in competitions, it improved my overall conditioning, which was much more important to me in the long run. And I was still winning the national events.

Menachem Nowitz, the treasurer of the Track and Field Committee who officiated at most competitions, was dumbstruck the first time he saw me arrive on foot. He responded to my explanation with a joke: "The favorite at a hot dog eating contest lost. Afterward, when they asked him why, he said he couldn't understand it. After all, he had practiced just before the contest, and downed eighty hot dogs." Presumably, this was the first time Nowitz had encountered an athlete with his sights set on a goal beyond the current competition. In contrast, after Avraham Paz interviewed me, he wrote an article in *Ha'aretz* stating that I was the only Israeli athlete who was systematically training for a long-term objective. Naturally, I walked home from the competitions too, an exercise that improved my endurance.

The Israeli Olympic Committee set the qualifying time for the 50-kilometer walk at 4:21, which in my opinion was a higher standard than required for the other track and field events, both in terms of the number of people anywhere in the world who were capable of meeting it, and in relation to the time set by the first, sixth, or even tenth in the world. But there was no point in arguing. I simply had to achieve this minimum. The Track and Field Committee gave its approval for a 50-kilometer competition, and I suggested it follow a circuit through the streets of Savion and Ganei Yehuda. A resident of the area and member of the local sports committee agreed to help map out, measure, and mark the route. It would be flat, with virtually no ascents.

The race was held in February 1972. It was a perfect day for it; we couldn't have asked for better weather conditions: around 50 degrees Fahrenheit, no wind, and overcast skies. For part of the competition there was a light rain, just enough to keep the body from overheating. I barely broke a sweat, didn't need a sponge dipped in ice water to cool myself down, and drank less than usual. I moved quickly, pushing myself but not feeling the effort and not exhausting myself. I finished first in 4:18. I'd met the minimum! Reuven Peleg, hoping to compete in the 20-kilometer walk at the Olympics, decided to try his hand at the 50-kilometer in order to improve his overall condition and stamina. He also recorded a fine time of 4:39.

The athletic coach Ilya Bar-Ze'ev, arguably the best coach in the country for middle- and long-distance runners, felt the need to make the relative time of his talented athlete Yuval Wishnitzer look better than it was. When he heard the times recorded by Reuven and myself, he immediately charged that there had been an error in measurement and the route wasn't a full 50 kilometers. About two weeks later a marathon was run on the same route, with the same turns, measured anew for the occasion. I came to watch. Yuval, the best 10,000-meter runner Israel has ever had, was in the lead. He could have been among the best in the world, and might have fulfilled this potential, especially in the marathon, with the right coach.

I was amazed to see that, although he was studying economics at Tel Aviv University and should have known enough to apply what he had learned in elementary school, he kept to one side of the winding road the whole way, instead of shortening the distance by cutting across the bends on a straight line. I suggested to Ilya, who was giving Yuval instructions during the race, that he explain to him how to save himself the effort of running more than he had to. Ilya's response was the same as Paul Schell's had been six years earlier: "It doesn't matter; it's only a difference of a few millimeters." It was a warm day, and the lap time of all the competition, including Yuval, was rather slow, causing Ilya to exclaim: "They measured it wrong. The route is too long!" His contradictory interpretations of a single verifiable fact reminded me of the saying "A person's view of an issue depends on which side of the table he's sitting."

As the Three-Day March in April 1972 drew near, I planned a special feat with the help of the daily paper *Ma'ariv*. I would do all three routes in one day. The route for each day started and ended at the Beit El camp, so that the three loops formed a pattern resembling a three-leaf clover. Edna Medalia followed me in my car, accompanied by a *Ma'ariv* reporter. Since there were places the car couldn't get through, every now and then I would have to proceed a good number of miles on my own before they met up with me again. On one such occasion, after I'd already covered around fifty miles, I passed a large group of Arab children and teenagers. It wasn't a pleasant experience. They tried to run alongside me — which can be very nice as long as the people doing so leave me alone. Finally, I picked up my pace, and when they couldn't keep up, they were left behind. I breathed a sigh of relief.

Another section of the route ran along a rough rocky road full of bumps and sharp jutting edges that descended in an arc down the northern slope of a hill. At the lowest point, the road rose, turning right up the southern slope of the next hill. It was a very difficult surface to walk on. I hoped my escorts would at least take pity on my car and wait somewhere further along the route where the drive was easier. As I started the climb up the southern slope of the second hill, I saw the car in the distance making the descent behind me, bumping up and down the whole way. I could also hear the squealing of the springs and the banging of the ruined shock absorbers. My worst fears were realized: as a result of this exploit, my car required drastic repairs. My body, on the other hand, was none the worse for the sixty-five miles I did in about eleven hours.

The Three-Day March took place three days later. I was participating for the sixteenth straight year. As things turned out, I was the only person to complete the whole route, thanks to my one-man endeavor sponsored by *Ma'ariv*. The route for the first day was twenty-two miles. I did it quickly, finished first, and repeated it in the opposite direction. But I wasn't done yet. The same day was the Tel Aviv University 10-kilometer race, with a concurrent walking competition that I'd won the year before. As soon as I completed the forty-four miles at the March, I drove to the university, arriving an hour before start time. I was so exhausted I could barely stand, let alone warm up. I spent the time resting on a bench. I knew how drained I was. Nevertheless, I fought like a tiger, even making the effort to take the lead.

We had to circle the campus four times. I held the lead for two laps, but then Reuven Peleg took it from me and I couldn't wrench it back. He won, coming in some twenty yards ahead of me. Everyone assumed he was the better walker, but I didn't care. Those fast-paced ten kilometers, coming on the heels of the demanding forty-four miles I had done only a few hours before, were an excellent opportunity for me to hone my abilities.

There was a rainstorm that night. Early in the morning I left for Beit El. The rain was still coming down hard. Although I didn't particularly enjoy that kind of weather, I was used to training in it. When I had completed the three routes in one day just a few days before, I had also had to walk in the rain for a few hours. When I got to Beit El I found the march commanders daunted by the rain and the fact that some of the tents had been flooded during the night. They cleared the entire camp, called off the rest of the march, and gave everyone a medal and a certificate proclaiming they had completed the Three-Day March, even though they'd only walked for one day. I was awarded the same trophies, but then I had actually done the whole route three days earlier. Later that morning the rain stopped and the sun came out.

In mid-April 1972 I went abroad, again at my own expense, to compete in several events. I had just celebrated my thirty-sixth birthday. First I flew to New York for the Eastern Regional AAU 50-Mile Championship, organized as usual by Elliott Denman. This year it was being held in a different town on the New Jersey shore, Ocean Township. Again I stayed with Don Johnson, and again his son Greg assisted me during the race. Everything went like clockwork — the preparations, the drinks in the cold box, the organization. This was the fifth time I had entered this competition, requiring two hundred laps around a standard stadium track. I won in 7:23:50.

All things considered, I felt very good, better than ever before after a 50-mile race. Incredibly, I had improved on the American record I myself had set in 1970 by twenty-nine minutes. Since 1966 I had shaved a full hour and twelve minutes off my time! Now in 1972 I had not only broken the American record once more, but had set a new world record as well! And it stands to this day. The American Augie Hirst missed it by twenty minutes in 1978, and Ray Middleton, the Englishman, by twelve minutes. Like all records, its time will come, too, someday. Reuters and UPI wired the news around the world, and the achievement earned modest mention in the Israeli papers.

The next day I was interviewed by the famous *New York Post* syndicated sports columnist, Al Zimmerman, whose articles appeared in hundreds of papers throughout the States. He was very impressed by my performance and the bonus of my being the only Israeli athlete who had already secured a place for himself on the Olympic team. The item he wrote was headed: "If you've seen one member of the Israeli team, you've seen them all. The entire Israeli Olympic men's athletic team entered my office. Its name is Dr. Shaul Ladany."

From New York, I went on to Mineola to stay with Henry and Hilda Laskau. Shosh sent a telegram to their home: "Congratulations! I can sit. Danit." In my egocentric mood, it took me a while to realize that the congratulations weren't for me, but for our nine-month-old daughter who had learned to sit up.

I gave myself a day off and then resumed my training regimen. A 20-kilometer walk was scheduled for the weekend on Long Island. I was feeling pretty good, but I knew my body hadn't fully recovered yet. Still, I managed to put in a tolerable performance. The race was won by Larry Young. From the States I flew to Germany for the Northern Germany 50-kilometer championship at Salzgitter. I was already on friendly terms with most of the top

German walkers, particularly those from the Quelle Fürt Club. We started out in the noon hours. Weidner came in first, while I took second, once again meeting the Olympic minimum.

The Israeli Olympic Committee had recently published new and stricter standards for making the team. Perhaps they had me in mind when they reached that decision. Athletes were now required either to meet the minimum twice, or to meet it at least once in the last six months before the games. I had already fulfilled both requirements. As soon as the awards ceremony was over, I took the train to Hanover where I switched to the night train for Milan. To save money, I didn't take a sleeper car. Instead, I did my best to doze off sitting up with my legs stretched out on the seat next to me. I arrived in Sesto San Giovani about two hours before start time for the international 32-kilometer (20-mile) walk. There were only eighteen hours between the end of the race at Salzgitter and the start of the one in Italy, and I hadn't gotten much rest in between.

Obviously, I couldn't expect to put in a good time. Most athletes need a long time to recover between long-distance competitions, which totally drain the body. Thanks to my training routine, I was able to bounce back fairly quickly, but I couldn't expect to return to top form after a mere eighteen hours. Nevertheless, since there are so few events in Israel and they didn't offer me any real challenge, I had an insatiable appetite to compete as often as possible during my short stay abroad. I didn't push myself in the race, justifying my reluctance to make any more of an effort by telling myself, "You already proved yourself yesterday." I was surprised to finish in sixteenth place, recording a good time against the who's who of international race walking at a distance which is relatively short for me.

The proximity of the two competitions was very good practice for me. The next day I went back to Lausanne, one of my favorite cities because it's so convenient for training. While there I competed in two small-scale events. Four weeks after I had left, I returned home. Danit hardly recognized me. Not one member of the Israeli sports establishment congratulated me on having set a new world record. Apparently, since they hadn't sponsored my trip, it didn't concern them. To this day, no mention is made of my record in a single official publication of any Israeli athletic body. (In 2007, my time result for the 100-kilometer as well as for the 50-mile were finally listed for the first time, but without mentioning that my 100-kilometer time was for first place in a world championship and that my 50-mile time was a world record.)

The Sports Federation refused to send me abroad for any more competitions. They claimed there was no need since I had already met the Olympic minimum and secured a place on the team. I can only guess at the name of the person or persons in charge who stonewalled my application. A good many other athletes were sent to Europe in the hope that they, too, would meet the minimum, even when their results indicated no realistic chance of their doing so. I kept the pressure on, arguing that I had not been sent abroad even once in 1972. Finally they relented, agreeing to finance a three-week trip to Europe, probably because they could no longer publicly justify shutting me out. I was joined for most of the trip by my friend Reuven Peleg, who had yet to meet the Olympic minimum.

We began in England for the 50-kilometer walk in Bradford, Yorkshire, held on May 30, 1972. Arriving only the night before, we were unable to make any private arrangements for assistance during the race. The route was the hardest I had ever competed on, alternately rising and falling, and that difficulty was just one in a long saga of problems, most of them avoidable. The organizers neglected to provide me with a personal assistant. Seeing this, prior to the start I asked the assistants of a British walker, people I didn't know at all, to lend me a hand as well, and turned over to them my bottles of Coke and paper cups. I never saw them again, and never got anything to drink the whole time. Fortunately, it wasn't too hot. After the race, these "assistants" offered me all sorts of bizarre explanations that clearly had no basis in fact.

The obstacles notwithstanding, I came in first, breaking the course record for this annual event then in its seventieth year. My speed threw the organizers' plans awry. By breaking the record, I reached the finish line before the honorable mayor of Bradford. She was supposed to present the trophy to the winner at the moment of victory. She arrived on time, that is, according to schedule; but meanwhile I was forced to wait, shivering in the cold. Once again I had met the Olympic minimum. Reuven Peleg was right behind me until around kilometer 20 when he was hit lightly by one of the escort cars. He was knocked down and suffered scratches, and either the blow he received or the scare it gave him convinced him to drop out. He wasn't seriously hurt, and felt a lot better by the awards ceremony; but the incident was blown out of proportion by the Israeli press, who billed it as an automobile accident, causing his family considerable distress and unwarranted concern.

From England we flew to Denmark, where we trained in Odense with a group of walkers who had gravitated to Christensen, the veteran athlete who had represented Denmark at the Olympics in London in 1948 and Helsinki in 1952. While there we competed in the annual 30-kilometer walk, which I also won, again breaking the event record. We then went on to Copenhagen for two days for a 20-kilometer competition. By now I had a terrible cold and a splitting headache, so I decided not to enter. After the race, Pale Lassen, the chairman of the IAAF Race-Walking Committee and a resident of Copenhagen, took us on a tour of the city as his personal guests.

Next we boarded the train to Lausanne, where Reuven and I trained intensely. Although I'd been there several times before, my training program had never left me enough time to visit Mont Blanc, whose peak I saw above the city every day. There was a 30-kilometer walk in Yverdon on the weekend. I came in second, with Reuven taking seventh. From there he went to Italy, while I flew to Athens for the international track and field meet, competing in the 20-kilometer walk I had won the previous year. Israel had sent a large team. I shared a room with Yuval Wishnitzer, who was also capping off a long tour of Europe. I finished my event in second place. For the last five kilometers I was moving much faster than the leader, but not enough to make up for the big gap he had opened in the first half of the race. If I had been told in time that I was closing on him steadily, I might have been able to overtake him. I only became aware of the situation in the very last stages of the competition, and by then, no matter how hard I pushed myself, it was too late to do more than reduce the gap to a mere few seconds. My three weeks were up and I returned home.

I continued to train rigorously, walking from 220 to 270 miles every week, the equivalent of 330 to 400 miles if you run at the same level of exertion. There are very few athletes in the world who come close to that much training. I wasn't doing anything else. I had arranged with the university to carry a double teaching load the first semester so that I wouldn't have to teach the second. My only responsibilities were to my research and to several students for whom I served as thesis advisor. I enjoy scientific activity, and I could occupy my mind with research questions during my long-distance training as well. I kept up the hard work during the summer, too, despite the obstacles at that time of year.

Not only were there the objective difficulties of the heat and the lack of competitions and competitors in Israel, but there were also subjective reasons. I find it very hard to push myself to train fast and effectively. I need competition and other walkers training alongside me to give me the motivation to make that extra effort. It was clear to me that without those conditions, I wouldn't be able to continue to improve during the few months remaining until the Olympics.

I asked the Sports Federation to send me to Europe again to compete in additional events. My request was denied on the grounds that I had been abroad more than any other Israeli athlete. That wasn't true; a lot of sportsmen had been sent abroad more times than I had. Moreover, it was like saying, "What's mine is mine and what's yours is mine." Of my two trips abroad that year, one had been paid for out of my own pocket after they refused funding, and now they were using that as an excuse not to send me again. It felt like the Federation was out to thwart my success at the Olympics, or at the very least was unwilling to take any steps to promote my chances. Since I had met the Olympic minimum three times, they had no choice but to include me on the team. Yet at the same time they wanted to make me stay in the country and train in the heat without any rivals or any opportunities to compete.

Simultaneously, they were making every effort to ensure that I did not remain the only athlete to meet the minimum. Even those who had no real chance of doing so were being sent to compete abroad time and again. I didn't envy them the adventure. It's no great pleasure for me to travel abroad or be away from home. I'm actually a homebody, and I'm happiest in Israel, but if I wanted to put in a good showing, I needed those trips, even if it meant putting up with the uncomfortable conditions and the nomadic existence they brought with them. I didn't believe I was the best Israeli athlete with the greatest chance of an Olympic medal, even though the British press — unlike their Israeli counterparts — regarded me as Israel's hope. What got my back up was that they were tying my hands and running interference despite what I had achieved and the effort I had put into it.

I appealed to Yitzhak Caspi, the chairman of Maccabi Israel and the co-chairman of the Olympic Committee, a post he enjoyed as part of the traditional horse trading between Hapoel and Maccabi. I asked him to help me convince Maccabi to finance a trip for me to compete abroad. Yitzhak was not blessed with an excess of patience, nor an excess of civility. He told me in no uncertain terms that the Israeli sports establishment had a lot of money to play around with, and they should be made to use some of it to pay for me to go abroad. He adamantly refused to dig into the "meager coffers" of Maccabi for that purpose. I realized that "should be made to use" and his promise to "look into it," uttered grudgingly, were mere lip service.

Now that I knew that my own sports club had no intention of helping me and was unwilling to lift a finger on my behalf, I wrote a letter to the editor of *Ma'ariv* detailing my grievances against the sports authorities for doing everything in their power to block my success at the Olympics. The letter was published, but made no waves whatsoever. As a result, I reached the inevitable conclusion that if I wanted to do well at the Olympics, considering the immense effort I had invested in training and the large amount of money I had already laid out, I would have to make additional financial sacrifices.

That spring, for the first time in my life (and what would prove to be the last), I had received a one-time grant equal to about a two-month salary that was given to all the Israeli athletes who had met the Olympic minimum. The check was placed in my hands by Yigal Allon, then minister of education. He declared that it was intended to cover the training expenses incurred by top athletes. At that very moment, the universities were on strike and the faculty had not been paid for over a month. When Allon shook my hand, I told him the check came just in time since our salaries had been stopped on his orders. He assured me I had nothing to worry about and that we would get our money in a couple of days. Had I been a reporter, I would have had a scoop on my hands. As it was, his comment only served to take a load off my mind. My source turned out to be reliable.

The money I spent in a year on track shoes and gym clothes, which wore out at a dizzying rate, along with the soda I drank when I trained, added up to about the same figure as the grant, but I considered them ordinary expenditures. So I had used the grant to cover part of my travel expenses when I went to the States and to Europe to compete in April. Now, I would have to pay for it all myself. Nevertheless, I decided to foot the bill for another trip to Europe.

I left in July 1972 to make the Belgian 50-kilometer championship held, as usual, in Charleroi. My sister Shosh and her family, who were living in Brussels at the time, came to assist me during the race. The same route was used every year, but this time the event headquarters had moved to a new café about two hundred yards from its previous home, and the start and finish lines had been adjusted accordingly. The turnaround point in Beaumont remained unchanged. As a result, the route had gained about 440 yards for a total of 50,400 meters, without the organizers taking note of the fact. I won the race, with the walker in second place over five kilometers back. Not only that, but I set another new event record, which in this case was nothing to sneeze at.

The previous record was held by the Englishman Don Thompson and the West German Nermerich, who also held the West German record for 50 kilometers. My official time was 4:17:03, but since the route was 50,400 meters, the time for 50 kilometers was actually 4:15:01. I had met the Olympic minimum for the fourth time, and won the Belgian title to boot. The time of 4:17:03 was my best official time for 50 kilometers on road. The Belgian press lauded my achievement, calling me "the little professor." The celebration party was again a joyous affair in typically French style.

I left Belgium, taking a train to Switzerland and again sparing myself the expense of a sleeper. The eight-day Tour de Romandie was on in Switzerland. It had begun on the day of the Charleroi race. I had had to choose between the two events, and opted for both, giving clear preference to the 50-kilometer competition in Belgium. In other words, I was planning to use the seven days remaining of the Tour de Romandie for training purposes.

At the end of an exhausting overnight train ride, I arrived in Yverdon early in the morning. The race, which had started in Geneva, was to reach the town by the middle of the first day. That morning, the second segment would start out from here. Not knowing where it would take off from, I sat down to wait on a bench outside the train station. Luckily, I spotted a car that appeared to be a race escort vehicle. I waved it down and caught a ride to the starting point, getting there just in time. I didn't want to tell the organizers that I had intentionally passed up the first leg of their competition in favor of a different event, so I made up a story about how my wife had suddenly fallen ill and I had had to stay with her, making me miss the first day. I asked to be allowed to take part outside the competition, and was very pleased when they agreed.

The second day consisted of a twenty-two-mile segment in the morning and a six-mile segment in the evening. I was walking very well, and finished the twenty-two miles first. Everyone assumed that my speed was possible because I had started out fresh on the second day while the other competitors were tired from the nineteen miles they had walked the day before. Not one of them had the slightest suspicion that I had actually put in a much greater effort than anyone else the previous day, and had hardly gotten any sleep sitting up on the train.

The Tour de Romandie wound through most of the French cantons of Switzerland. Arcing northward on a winding route, it circled Lake Geneva, passed through Neuchatel and Lausanne, and ended up in St. Maurice (not to be mistaken with St. Mauritz in the German-speaking part of the country), southeast of the lake. It followed the pattern of the Tour de France bicycle race. Escort vehicles equipped with loudspeakers shrieked news of the event wherever we went, announcing the names and results of the entrants, their overall placing, and their position that day. Special daily prizes were awarded, particularly to the winners of the short circuits inside the towns which were generally scheduled as the second part of the day's route in the afternoon or early evening hours. Simultaneously, everyone was competing for the best overall time. As a rule, we slept in army camps, although occasionally we were put up in hotels. We were given the whole of the fifth day to rest.

It was a fascinating experience, and great fun, creating a sense of fellowship among the competitors who came from all over Europe, most prominently from Italy, France, and Germany. The closeness we felt was so intense that on the eighth and final day we all "rebelled," walking the last segment bunched up together, at a slow pace, without anyone trying to get ahead of the others. At the medals ceremony I was awarded a small Neuchatel clock as a sign of appreciation. To this day I don't know if it works; I've never taken it out of the box it came in.

I stayed in Lausanne to train after the Tour de Romandie, going to France with my friend Alfred Badel for a competition a week later. It was a combination race: first a walk of about twelve miles ending with a sharp climb up one of the alpine ranges; then a run of around nine miles that began by descending the slope and continued on a level stretch; and finally another walk of about six miles. I was overtaken by a large number of competitors on the run down the slope along a twisting path studded with tree roots jutting up everywhere. The fear of bumping into one of them and falling, maybe even injuring myself, made me take that section at a very cautious slow run. It had been years since I'd last run. When we reached the straight, I started to pass the runners who had gotten ahead of me. It was very hard to switch back to a walk. My feet wanted to keep running. In the course of the final walk I overtook all the other athletes save for Alfred. He came in first, and I took second place.

From there I returned to Lausanne to train some more. A week later I was back on the night train, this time on my way to Holland. Traveling at night saved me the cost of a hotel. I was going for the Four-Day March in Nijmegen, an event generally known as "The Holland March."

The rules for entrants of my age called for us to walk fifty kilometers a day for four days. It was excellent training for me, especially because I ran into a friend, Hans Russ, a German walker from Hamburg, and we stuck close together as we moved ahead, each urging the other on. But we couldn't do the whole fifty kilometers at a fast pace. We took the first 49,950 meters at a speed of 6.8 miles an hour, and then fifty meters before the finish, sat down and waited so that we wouldn't get disqualified by completing the route faster than specified in the rule book. I didn't imagine then how I would come to fall in love with this march and its carnival atmosphere, reluctant to miss a single year.

In the middle of the first day, the weather suddenly heated up drastically, reaching 104 degrees Fahrenheit in the shade. Since I finished early, I hardly felt the heat, but the Dutch and the other Europeans were unaccustomed to such conditions. When one marcher died of dehydration, it was decided, for the first time in fifty-five years, to shorten the route on the next three days from fifty to forty kilometers. As I sped past groups of soldiers or civilian marchers in the early morning hours, the name "ISRAEL" on my shirt, I could hear people remarking or shouting out in English things like "That must be Ladany," or "See you on the way to Brighton." Obviously, English walkers had also come for the march and they recognized me. When it was over I returned to Israel, having been away for almost a month.

Back home I went on training like crazy. For the last six weeks before my Olympic event, I averaged fifty miles a day, every day! I shortened my super-long walks to fifty miles and went out for that practice twice a week. On other days, I started out in the morning by walking an easy thirty miles or so. In the afternoon I'd work on my speed: going back and forth and altering the pace for around twenty miles. Periodically I would shorten the morning practice to a fast twenty-five miles and then lengthen the afternoon speed training to twenty-five miles. Altogether, I was doing 350 miles a week, the equivalent of 525 miles for a runner. I received several letters from Belgians I had never met who wrote to congratulate me on my impressive performance in their national championship. I felt honored to hear from people who had no ulterior motives, but merely felt the urge to write and express their appreciation and admiration for what I had done.

The Israeli press quoted Lalkin's pronouncement that "this is Ladany's last Olympics." The International Olympic Committee was under constant pressure to add new events and was looking to get rid of existing ones so as not to extend the duration of the games inordinately. It had been suggested that the 50-kilometer walk be dropped, leaving only the 20-kilometer event in place. I don't know whether it was Lalkin himself, a lackey of his, or someone merely acting on his own initiative, but I do know that at one of the IOC subcommittee meetings, the Israeli representative voted in favor of eliminating the 50-kilometer walk from the Olympic program. The only logical justification for supporting that proposal would be if Israel were blessed with so many outstanding athletes that there was no need to enter an Israeli in the 50-kilometer walk.

Lalkin took great pleasure in informing me that the event would not be included in the Montreal games in 1976. Munich would apparently be my last Olympics. I guess I had stepped on too many toes. When I was in the States in early 1974, I joined an international committee set up to try to reinstate the 50-kilometer walk. Gary Westerfield and Ron Daniels were among the other members. My name appeared on the official letterhead printed for the occasion. We fought a successful battle. After Montreal, the 50-kilometer walk was reinstated as an Olympic event. We even managed to add another event to the program: the 10-kilometer walk for women athletes.

On the basis of past experience, I realized I had no chance of getting the assistance I needed at the Olympics from the delegation functionaries. I spoke to everyone whom I knew was going and asked if they would be willing to help out during my competition. I didn't have high hopes, so I wasn't excessively disappointed when they all turned me down for whatever reason. I was disappointed, however, by the response of my friend Uri Goldburt. I had arranged for him to be appointed as my research assistant at the university and had recommended him to General Doron because of the statistical data on Israeli athletics that he had collected. But when I approached him, he backed out diplomatically on the grounds that he wouldn't have the time to help me. The only person who didn't let me down was Edna Medalia, who announced that she was going to Munich at her own expense and would be there to assist me.

Then on top of everything, a few weeks before the Olympics there was an article in one of the daily papers written by an attorney by the name of Yoel Katz whom I had never heard of and whose knowledge of athletics clearly left much to be desired. He stated: "Ladany shouldn't be on the Olympic team. He never performs well." I wrote a letter to the editor in response, but it wasn't published.

The month before the Olympics, the Israeli public was made to witness a shrill, disgraceful sideshow. I had nothing to do with it. A number of outstanding swimmers who had been sent to train and compete in the States felt neglected and cheated when various promises that had been made to them were not kept. It was the same sort of thing that had happened to me four years earlier. They launched a harsh attack on the sports authorities, although they refrained from implicating the Swim Committee. Their spokesman, the Israeli Olympic swimmer Avraham Melamed, declared in the press, "The functionaries should know they owe their jobs to the athletes and not the other way around."

The politicos decided to show everyone just who was in charge. At an official trial swim meet organized by the Swim Committee of the Sports Federation, Melamed met the Olympic minimum. This would have been his third Olympics. The representatives of the Swim Committee hurried off to submit the results to the Olympic Committee then in session, arriving about an hour after the meeting had been called to order. The Committee claimed that the results were submitted after the deadline and refused to consider them. Avraham Melamed was not to be a member of the Olympic team. It's hard to tell whether their behavior came in response to Melamed's criticism or whether they had already decided which of them would be going to the games and if they included Melamed on the team, one of their own would have to be bumped.

After this shameful decision, Melamed and the general director of the Sports Federation, who was also the chairman of the Munich Committee, confronted each other in front of the TV cameras. The public had the chance to enjoy the spectacle of a member of the establishment trying to wriggle his way out of the situation by inventing flimsy excuses and twisting the truth. It being ungentlemanly to call someone a liar, allow me to invoke Winston Churchill's famous coinage as particularly fitting for the occasion: it was a case of "terminological inexactitude."

After fifty kilometers in the 100-km world championship, Lugano, 1970; from left to right: Luschke, Höhne, me, and the East German coach

Crossing the city of Bellinzona during the 100-kilometer world championship race, 1970

■ Chapter Fifteen | The Olympic Games in Munich

There were fifteen athletes on the Israeli team for the Munich Olympics: three wrestlers, three weightlifters, two sailboaters, two fencers, two marksmen, a woman swimmer, and two in track and field events — Esther Shahamorov-Rot, the hurdler, and myself. This time I was fitted out with a uniform, but was issued no sweat suit, the argument being that I had gotten one the year before as a member of the group traveling to Europe with Green. However, since "ISRAEL" did not appear on my sweat suit, when we got to Munich I had to fight with the delegation manager before I convinced him that I also deserved to have the name of my country on the back of my outfit.

With the image of the shirt I had worn for the race in Mexico City still fresh in my mind, I had bought myself a good number of specially printed shirts back in 1970 when I went abroad to compete. The word "ISRAEL" in large blue Latin letters was printed on the front and back of the shirts, which I used both for training and competitions. Thus, with the advantage of hindsight, I now had all the gear I needed. I also remembered the story of an athlete who had been unable to participate in her race after the airline lost the bags she had packed her running shoes in. So adopting my usual practice, I carried onto the plane in my hand luggage all the equipment essential for my event.

The head of our delegation was Joseph Inbar, the general manager of Hapoel and chairman of the Olympic Committee. Following established tradition, one man wore all three of these hats. Lalkin was the delegation manager. They were accompanied by a long line of other functionaries who had also met their own personal Olympic minimum. All in all, there were thirteen official escorts, nearly one per athlete. Two Israeli referees had also been invited to the Olympics: Joseph Gutfreund and Jacob Springer. Add to that several dozen more individuals sent to the games in some other official capacity at the direct or indirect expense of the government, albeit not out of the delegation budget.

About a week before we left, we were presented with a sheet of security regulations. They did little more than warn us to be leery of suspicious objects and not to accept any packages from strangers. For some reason I saved this document, and on the occasion of the twentieth anniversary of the massacre of the Israeli athletes in Munich, it was photographed by ABC, the German station STI, a French network, and Israeli television with considerable relish.

Our flight to Munich took much longer than necessary. The Olympic Committee, namely Globinsky, hadn't booked our seats in time, and by the time he got around to it, all the flights were full. As a result, we flew to Zurich, where we had a layover of five hours before the connection to Munich. The man in charge of the group in transit was Yitzhak Fuchs, an easygoing courteous gentleman under whose direction everything went smoothly. Yitzhak was in charge of operations for Hapoel. Several years later he changed his name to Ofek and took over from Inbar. I wanted to use the downtime at Kloten airport to train, and Yitzhak gave his approval, setting an hour for me to report back. Using the men's room, I changed into the training clothes in my bag and went out for a quick, valuable practice.

The flight to Munich was delayed. Finally, fourteen hours after leaving Israel, we landed in Germany. It was obvious that security at the airport was very tight in anticipation of our arrival. I was acutely aware of the fact that any Israelis who decided to board a plane could be putting themselves at risk. Ever since the terrorists had set their sights on Israeli flights, with skyjacking attempts, planting bombs on planes, and attacks on passengers at airports, I knew only too well that it could happen to me, too. I had flown several times just before or after a tragedy that had occurred on the same airline or at the same airport. It didn't deter me, but it did made me very conscious of the hazards and more sharply attuned to potential danger. Neither was I deterred nor alarmed by the news reports from Israeli sources warning of the possibility of an attack on the Olympic team.

At last we arrived in the Olympic Village. It was a strange feeling. I'd been in Germany several times since Bergen-Belsen and I had several young German friends, most of them born after the war. Yet whenever I was asked where I had learned German, I invariably answered pointedly, "In the Bergen-Belsen concentration camp." The Germans know the place, perhaps even better than Auschwitz, because the camp was in Germany proper, on the Lüneburg plain near Celle between Hanover and Hamburg. But this time I was a member of an official delegation of the State of Israel, with our team patch on my jacket displaying the blue and white of the national flag. It was the Star of David in the center that had the most meaning for me, maybe because of my childhood memories. Nazi Germany tried its best to exterminate the Jewish people, fearing our status as an eternal nation that had survived two thousand years of exile. Now we were marching on German soil, the proud, strong representatives of the independent sovereign State of Israel, and any Nazis still around would have living proof of our indestructibility.

The Olympic Village was flawlessly planned and run. Everything was clean, aesthetic, orderly, and efficient. German meticulousness — a trait I usually admire — was apparent wherever we went, unlike the situation in Mexico City. But as an Israeli with personal experience of the Holocaust, I found that the precise planning and organization brought to mind the precision and efficiency with which every detail of the "Final Solution" of the "Jewish problem" was devised and carried out, including the logistics of transport, selection, and deception. As an expert in production management, I was reminded of the trains routed to Maidanek, Treblinka, Sobibor, and Auschwitz, the victims tricked into believing they were being led into a shower room, then gassed and their corpses burned without a trace in the crematoria, the whole process humming efficiently like a well-oiled production line.

There was a convivial atmosphere in the village, with pretty flowers all around. The uniforms of the workers and officials, including the guards, were colorful and cheerful. Everyone was very polite, and the guards were unarmed. The German people had done everything in their power to present a friendly, welcoming, pleasant, and lighthearted Germany to the world — the "new Germany," with no reminders whatsoever of its dark, militaristic past. The *New York Times, International Herald Tribune*, and *Christian Science Monitor* all latched onto the singularity of my situation as a Holocaust survivor, the only one on the Israeli team, and printed long items under headlines such as "Israeli Race-Walking Champion Returns to Familiar Soil."

The Israeli delegation was assigned accommodations at 31 Connolly Street, named, like all the streets in the village, for a famous athlete. The complex was laid out so that the street level was reserved for pedestrians, while vehicular traffic moved along a lower level with parking facilities between the pillars under the buildings. We were allotted five adjacent units in a four-story building entered from the pedestrian walk. Each unit was actually a duplex, with a spiral staircase connecting the two floors. The doors to units 2 to 5 were about six meters apart. The first door on the left led to the stairs, which you could take to go up to the third floor or down to the basement garage.

The door to unit 1 was on street level and opened onto the stairwell. It was shared by the five coaches in the delegation — Amitzur Shapira, Tuvia Sokolsky, Kehat Shorr, Moshe Weinberg, and Andre Spitzer — and the two Israeli Olympic referees Yossef Gutfreund and Yakov Springer. Unit 2 originally had five occupants: the front bedroom on the second floor served the marksmen Zelig Stroch and Henry Hershkowitz; the back bedroom with a balcony was shared by the fencers Yehuda Weinstein and Dan Alon; and I was assigned the single room on the first floor, facing the rear of the building. A sliding glass door with a hinged glass door fitted into one of the panels opened onto a terrace. The three wrestlers, Eliezer Halfin, Gad Tsabari, and Mark Slavin, shared unit 3 with the three weightlifters, David Berger, Ze'ev Friedman, and Yossef Romano. The team doctor, Dr. Weigel, was assigned unit 4, and Shmuel Lalkin unit 5.

The two women on the team, the swimmer Shlomit Nir and the hurdler Esther Shahamorov, were accommodated in the separate women's dorms in the village. The two sailboaters and their coach were at some distance from the rest of the delegation, staying in the town of Kiel, the venue for their competition. The rest of the delegation officials had taken rooms in the finer Munich hotels. The Israeli liaison, Dr. Matti Kranz, welcomed us to the village. I wasn't entirely sure what his function was, except that he was obviously not an official member of the delegation. Nevertheless, he too was given a room in unit 4.

The daily paper *Ma'ariv*, which had followed Avraham Melamed's battle with the sports establishment sympathetically, presented him with a ticket to Munich by way of compensation for his exclusion from the team. He snuck into the Olympic Village, a routine operation. No one in training clothes was ever stopped at the gate, and if some overzealous guard did detain you, it was generally enough to say something like "it's okay" and to keep walking confidently, and you were in. On the rare occasions when people encountered a problem getting in through the entrance gate, all they had to do was to use the adjacent exit.

The Germans are a disciplined people. It is an extremely rare sight in Germany, unlike New York, for a person to cross the street against the light, even when there is no traffic at all. The German pedestrians wait patiently, like the good law-abiding citizens they are, for the light to change. Consequently, there were no guards at the exit gates, merely a sign reading "No Entry." So nobody entered that way, except for foreigners less in awe of rules and regulations. As a result, the Olympic Village was always crowded with visitors, most of whom had bluffed their way in.

Shlomit Nir didn't have a coach with her in Munich, and needed someone to time her during her training sessions. When Melamed showed up, she persuaded Lalkin to let him stay in unit 2 in exchange for helping her out. Thus he became my roommate, taking over the empty bed in my room. But he was never given a key to the front door. When he came back late and the door was already locked, he would enter our unit through an open window. This meant that every now and then he had to climb up to the second floor like a cat burglar until he found some way to get in. Since I only ate two meals a day, I gave him my extra meal coupons. Melamed thereby became a de facto resident of the Olympic Village, his presence there never officially reported.

My rigorous training continued without interruption, following the same routine of about fifty miles a day. I frequently practiced with the walkers from Italy, Luxembourg, and Canada, but I did most of my speed training with the Italians, coached by Pino Dordoni. He had taken Olympic gold for the walk in Helsinki in 1952, and was still in good condition. As a coach, he was unmatched for his dedication and the passion with which he promoted his athletes. Each time we did a quick four hundred meters around the track, he would click on his stopwatch, run across the field diagonally to give us our time after two hundred meters, and then race back to the starting point to time us at the end of the lap. When we did a thousand meters, he would start off with us at a walk, and then before we reached the two hundred-meter mark would run ahead to give us our time, cross the field to report our time at four hundred meters, and then run back and forth three more times to keep us apprised of our performance at six hundred, eight hundred, and a thousand meters. And all the while he would be spurring us on to greater effort and speed.

He treated me like all the rest of his athletes, although he had no obligation to do so. The same went for the Italian walkers themselves. I became very friendly with them, especially Vitorio Visini. We had first met in Mexico City, and renewed our acquaintance at the Sesto San Giovani competitions. Abdon Pamich, the gold medalist in Tokyo — who incidentally, as his name indicates, was Yugoslavian by birth, born in Trieste — was a lone wolf who rarely trained with the rest of the group, probably because of internal rivalries.

I was very pleased with myself at these speed sessions with the Italians, surprised to see how much my basic speed had improved with practice, although most of it had been long-distance endurance training. At four hundred meters, I managed to complete each lap in one minute twenty-one or twenty-two seconds, and could do a thousand meters in three minutes fifty seconds. Since I did most of the long distances of fify miles or so on my own, lapping the wide circle on which the 50-kilometer competition was to be held, I needed someone to help with my drinks during these sessions. Amitzur Shapira was the delegation's athletics coach. I'd known him from way back as a congenial character with a permanent smile on his face. But when I asked for his help, he turned me down politely on the grounds that he had to help Esther train. I knew that Esther had been his protégée ever since David Simhoni retired, and that as a rule he only worked with one athlete at a time. Accordingly, he considered her his only responsibility, even though his title was team athletics coach.

My appeal to Lalkin fell on deaf ears. I hadn't expected otherwise. I didn't even try to approach Dr. Weigel, although as I saw it he should have been available, since he was not occupied by any official duties. Shlomit Nir, who came from Kibbutz Ayelet Hashahar and had also been on the team with me in Mexico City, came up to me in tears one day. She was sick, a fact which was evident from the way she looked and sounded, and had been searching for the team doctor for days. When she finally located him, he brushed her off, saying that he didn't have time for her. I don't know the whole story. Maybe she caught him when he was late for an appointment or a meeting, but whatever the case, he didn't seem to see his function as team doctor the same way as we athletes understood it. Shlomit asked for my help. I explained what she already knew, that the "Dr." in my name had nothing to do with medicine. She asked if I had any painkillers or something to bring her fever down and I offered her some aspirin.

Eventually I solved my own problem the best way I could. At my own expense, naturally, I bought a large bottle of Coke at a pub, lugged it with me for the first two miles of my training until I reached the park where I did three-mile laps, and hid it under the bushes beside the path.

I ran into a lot of old friends at the Olympic Village. By now I knew most of the walkers and it was good to see them again. We all wanted to find out which of those from the previous games had made it here again and what had happened to the ones who didn't. We might all be rivals on the day, but there was a real sense of fellowship among us. My American friends, Larry Young, Tom Dooley, and Goetz Klopfer were there, and so was my fellow Long Island Track Club member, Steve Hayden. He had taken everyone by surprise by coming in third at the US Olympic trials, and in the 50-kilometer event, no less. Ron Laird was missing, which was an even greater surprise for me.

As usual, I was asked to translate. With me interpreting, the Americans congratulated Goloubniychyi, the veteran walker from the Soviet Union, for once more beating his rivals out for a place on the team. They also complemented him on his physique, still as muscular as ever without an ounce of fat. And muscles he did have. The others speculated that he must have been doing a lot of weightlifting. They asked Höhne how he trained, which is a very delicate question. A lot of athletes don't like to give away that sort of information. Höhne replied that he did three miles a day at a speed of 4 mph, a statement that brought a smile to everyone's face. With a regimen like that, he wouldn't be able to make a high school track team. You have to take information like that with more than a grain of salt, even when it appears in the papers or in some book. While training the day before, I'd seen Höhne doing speed work, a thousand meters around the track about forty times, clocking in at around four minutes each time.

Some time later I ran into Ron Laird. He'd put on a lot of weight. I found out he'd been in Germany for over a year, and as a veteran of three Olympics had decided not to compete for a place on the team for a fourth time. In Germany he was impersonating his twin brother and using his credentials to work as a draftsman. He had never been able to hold down a steady job, and instead of being proud of making a go at a field he hadn't even studied, he boasted that he had succeeded in putting one over on his employer, making him believe he was his brother.

He was in the Olympic Village to liaise with the athletes for one of the American TV networks, a job he was given because of his knowledge of sports and his acquaintance with so many of the sportsmen. As soon as he saw me he threw his arms around me, although I hardly recognized him. He arranged for his station to interview me. Those media people never imagined that after the murder of the Israeli athletes they would be re-airing that interview, this time as part of the news broadcast. Seeing Ron that way, I never believed he would ever get back to his former outstanding shape, but he eventually surprised us all by achieving the impossible. Four years later he was at the Olympic Games in Montreal, once again representing the USA. The layers of fat had vanished without a trace and he was back in top form. Justifiably, he was later admitted to the American Sports Hall of Fame.

What with my long training sessions, I hardly ever saw the other members of the Israeli team. I was told that one evening the delegation had been guests of the local Jewish community, and a few people showed me the sterling silver medal they had all been presented with on that occasion. I heard about their performances in the preliminary competitions and which ones made it to the next round. Henry Hershkowitz, who carried the Israeli flag in the opening ceremony, gloated that he was making good use of his time in Munich to earn some extra money. He was a watchmaker who had a shop in Tel Aviv, and since his training as a target shooter wasn't overly demanding, he was taking advantage of his free time to work in one of the local stores. Had it been me, I would have been ashamed to do anything like that, and even more ashamed to admit it.

One day I suddenly found the delegation in a frenzy. I learned that a few days before there had been a memorial service at the Dachau concentration camp, to which we Israelis had been invited. Hardly anyone from the Olympic delegation had gone. The town of Dachau is just outside Munich, virtually a suburb of the city. In fact, one of the main roads out of Munich is called Dachauer Strasse, and the concentration camp is along that road, about 3 miles from the Olympic Village. The absence of the Israeli delegation was reported in the press at home, raising a public outcry against the Olympic team and its officials for their failure to show their respect to the victims of the Holocaust by attending the ceremony. The media was flooded with harsh criticism of this insensitivity and demands that those responsible be made to pay for their lapse. The minister of education issued a statement in the same spirit. I got a letter from Shosh bawling me out for not having a modicum of feeling and being unwilling to give up any training time in order to honor the memory of the Jewish martyrs.

I was deeply hurt. I had known nothing about the ceremony, but even if I had, I would have chosen not to go, not because it would be at the expense of my training, but because it would bring back too many painful childhood memories. When we got the Israeli papers and read about the public outrage, which was undoubtedly also the subject of urgent telephone calls to delegation officials, it was decided to attempt to curb the damage by arranging another memorial service at the concentration camp. This time all the members of the delegation were notified in advance (something that obviously should have been done the first time around) and attendance was compulsory. Arrangements were also made for the participation of Jewish athletes from other countries, as well as Israeli youngsters attending various summer programs throughout Germany.

As the only Holocaust survivor in the delegation, I asked to be excused, so as not to have to relive my childhood experiences. My request was denied; I was informed that I was required to attend. I entered the camp through the gates and barbed wire fence and stood there alone, some distance from the others. After the service at the monument, there was a tour of the camp and the items on display in the barracks. I waited outside for the rest of the delegation. This second ceremony did little to make amends for the original blunder or appease the Israeli public's indignation and wrath. It's very likely that the removal of the delegation heads at the close of the games was forestalled by the imminent barbarous slaughter that was to silence criticism of the Olympic team.

Edna Medalia had no trouble stealing into the Olympic Village. I gave her my athlete's ID card, which entitled me to free use of public transportation. I hadn't yet been into the city, and didn't intend to go until after my event, whereas she was staying pretty far from the village. We arranged for her to position herself during the race at the official watering station and see to my drinks. I asked around again among the Israeli functionaries I ran into to see if anyone else was willing to help out, but nothing had changed. Several of them naively suggested I ask Lalkin.

All of a sudden the Israeli press discovered that I was training fifty miles a day — which came as news to them — and started calling me "the Israeli Stachanowitz." They were also stunned by the awe in which I was held by the British media.

In the three days before my race, I finally gave myself a respite from train-ing in order to raise the level of glycogen in my muscles. Following accepted wisdom, I limited my diet almost exclusively to carbohydrates, with the addi-tion of eggs and walnuts which Edna bought for me in town. I took advantage of this time to attend some of the other track and field events. I saw the preliminary heats for the 10-kilometer race, one of which included two of the greatest runners, Dave Bedford from the UK and Lasse Viren from Finland. Bedford was very full of himself and considered himself the best in the world. As soon as the gun went off, the two of them raced ahead, leaving the rest behind, and for the last few laps they had almost a half-lap lead over the runner in third place in their heat.

For the last lap, still going like the wind, they demonstrably carried on a conversation, turning to look at each other from time to time. They finished more or less together in fantastic time without giving it much effort — the only thing that mattered was making the final. When an interviewer asked them afterwards what they had been talking about, Bedford replied that they had discussed whether to break the world record in the preliminary round or to wait for the final.

I was in the stands for the final too. It was the kind of race you only get to see once in a lifetime. After the first turn on lap 1, one of the runners rammed his spikes into the heel of the man in front of him. They were both thrown off balance and landed on the ground. The competitors behind and beside them piled on top of them. The rest kept on running. The first one to get back on his feet got a look at the gap that had been opened between them and the others and decided to drop out. A couple more followed him onto the grass at the left of the track. The last man to get up was Lasse Viren. He looked from the men who had quit to the other runners several dozen yards up ahead and decided not to throw in the towel. He took off after them at full speed, to the noisy cheers of the crowd.

Running like mad, he quickly caught up with the tail end of the pack. The crowd kept up a roar. Viren didn't let up, and soon caught the runners in the lead. He had been going at such tremendous speed that we were all just waiting for him to collapse, but he still had a trick or two up his sleeve. He not only caught the leaders, but he left them behind, came in first, and set a new world record in the process. Who knows what time he might have recorded if he hadn't fallen and lost those precious seconds? When he went on to win the 5000-meter race, and then repeated his double victory in Montreal, he no longer raised any eyebrows. He retired from competition after 1976. I met him twenty years after Munich when he was visiting Israel, and he looked just the same as he had in his finest hour.

Along with this triumph, the worst screwup of the games also belonged to a track and field event. The three American sprinters made the final of the 100-meter dash. This may be the most prestigious race of all, but it's also the dullest. When all the competitors are more or less on the same level — and if they aren't, the results are a foregone conclusion — they take off together and remain in that formation until they cross the finish line in one body. The spectators see a line of runners sprinting shoulder to shoulder to the very end. Then all you can do is wait for the analysis of the photo finish to hear one of them declared the winner because his chest stuck out a quarter of an inch more, while one of the others, who seemed to break the tape at the exact same instant, is declared in last place.

The three Americans were the top sprinters in the world and were expected to take the three medals. The final was scheduled for 16:00, four o'clock in the afternoon. The Americans' chief athletic coach, unfamiliar with the twenty-four-hour clock, reported the time to his athletes as six p.m. They arrived at the track close to two hours early to warm up, and got there just in time to hear the start gun go off and watch the race run with five sprinters instead of eight. The coach became the laughingstock of the Olympics.

The next-best joke of the games was told about another American — Mark Spitz. He had finally lived up to his promise and shown the world what he could do, winning eight gold medals in swimming, seven in individual events and one in the relay race. The gag went like this: One athlete said to another: "Have you heard? Mark Spitz is third." "What?" exclaimed his friend in amazement. "He only came in third?" "No," replied the first, "he's third on the list of gold-medal-winning countries."

The 50-kilometer walk began at three o'clock on the afternoon of September 3. Shosh's cable wishing me luck came just in time. I was in great form, better than ever before, although I'd put on four pounds since Mexico City, weighing in at 130 pounds. I was convinced I could clock in at 4:06 to 4:12. According to my calculations, that would put me somewhere between sixth and twelfth place. An average of five minutes per kilometer (eight minutes per mile) would bring me in in 4:10. I knew my basic speed was faster than it had ever been, but I also knew that many of my competitors could top it.

My main edge was endurance and stamina, the ability to keep up a good pace for long distances. However, despite the stretching exercises and warm-ups I did before every race — doing an easy three miles interspersed with short segments at a quicker pace — I often got pains in my front lower leg muscles — shin splints in sports jargon — during the first few miles of a competition. The slower you go, the less the chance of this happening, and if it does, the pain is less fierce and goes away sooner. It usually takes three or four miles for it to disappear entirely. When I get these pains, it's hard for me to walk rapidly, and the faster I go the more it hurts. That's why I do such a long warm-up. I'm far from the only race walker with this problem, and I can never tell in advance when it's going to hit me.

Taking all this into consideration, I decided to start out at the relatively slow pace of five minutes per kilometer, figuring that if I got shin splints I might have to slow this down to five and a half minutes and might not be able to go any faster for as much as five kilometers until the pain passed. But even so, after a relatively slow five kilometers in twenty-seven and a half minutes I'd already be warmed up, and then I could bring my speed back to five minutes per kilometer and still finish in 4:12:30.

Amitzur Shapira accompanied me to the stadium, the first time he'd ever accompanied me anywhere. He told me he had to stay there, and would wait until I got back. "How nice of him," I thought, "but what I really need is help during the race!" The gun went off. About forty walkers moved forward. We were to lap the track twice, leave the stadium going west on a long service road that was closed to traffic, and then walk through a residential area to the huge park behind the Nymphenburg Palace. There were two large gates at some distance from each other at the entrance to the palace. There we would enter through the right-hand gate, circle the park, and leave through the gate on the left. The route made a small loop just before the palace. It was five kilometers from the start to this loop. After eight full circuits, we would go back more or less the way we had come, winding up with half a lap back in the stadium.

The whole pack rushes forward. I'm walking easily, but still, after around two hundred meters, I find myself in the lead. As soon as I become aware of that, I realize I'm moving too quickly and force myself to slow down. I let a few others get ahead of me, and by the time we leave the stadium I'm at the end of the second group, between fifteenth and twentieth position. Staying with this group, I'm walking comfortably, not really feeling the effort. I'm actually holding myself back, not letting myself progress any faster and making no attempt to overtake the athletes in front of me, even though I feel I could do it easily. I don't know exactly how fast I'm going, however, because unlike the rest of the competitors, I can't find a single member of my delegation willing to help out and give me my times. I hope I'm doing five minutes per kilometer as planned. Thankfully, I don't feel any pain in my legs.

At the five-kilometer mark there's a large clock (making it possible to list the five-kilometer times of all the walkers at the end of the race). I glance at it and my heart sinks. I'm not going too slowly; on the contrary, my time is twenty-three minutes five seconds. I can't believe it! That's thirty seconds faster than my personal best for a five-kilometer event! I have to pull back. I know I've been moving too fast and I may yet have to pay the price for stupidly allowing myself to be drawn forward at such a pace. The best tactic is to keep to a regular speed for the whole distance, assuming you know how to pace yourself, and not let yourself be affected by the psychological factor of where your rivals are at any given moment. I know I can't maintain this pace, which would amount to completing 50 kilometers in 3:50:50. I decide to hold myself in check even more, taking up position between the second and third groups. After the race I learned that the three Swedish walkers had kept together, their pace dictated by their coach from his seat on a bicycle behind the rows of spectators. They were the last to reach the five-kilometer mark, completing the distance in precisely twenty-five minutes.

Still holding back, I maintain my position, moving easily. At the ten-kilometer mark the clock reads forty-seven minutes thirty-four seconds, ten seconds faster than my Israeli record for this distance. I realize I'm still moving too rapidly, although at a slower pace than I took the initial five kilometers. The first watering station is positioned just after ten kilometers, outside the gate to the palace when we finish the wide circle in the park. It will also serve as the watering station for each of the next laps. I burned up a lot of calories in those first ten kilometers, particularly since I was going faster than usual. So as not to drain all the glycogen I've built up in my muscles, I need to take in sugar. Edna is supposed to be there, making sure that the officials pour out my Coke from the right thermos at the right time. I've prepared three — one with Coke alone, one with a little added glucose, and a third with a lot of glucose mixed in. I pass the table with the unmarked drinks and continue on to the one with the personalized cups. Just as I reach it I see Edna running up and shouting: "Dr. Ladany, I'm sorry, I was stuck in traffic..."

With no cups of Coke waiting for me, I don't stop. Not only don't I get the sugar I need, I don't even get the fluids so essential to replace some of what I lost in perspiration. The sponge table came before the watering station. As I passed it, I drenched myself liberally, but didn't squeeze any water into my mouth, assuming I'd soon get a drink. The second sponge table is positioned at twelve and a half kilometers. Here I suck the water in; it tastes atrocious. Despite these setbacks, I still feel in full command of my powers and I keep up a good pace. At fifteen kilometers I finally get to drink my Coke. Edna is standing by the table, directing the operation.

My time after twenty kilometers is 1:40, just as it should be for five minutes per kilometer. On the face of it, my average speed seems to be perfect, but I know I'm already paying for the lack of information that caused me to start out too fast. I actually did the second ten kilometers in fifty-two and a half minutes. At this point I'm overtaken by the three Swedes, their coach still pedaling his bicycle behind the spectators. They're maintaining the same pace they have from the start, twelve kilometers per hour, and I realize that as a result of my earlier mistake, I can't keep up with them. The fastest I can go is ten kilometers in fifty-three minutes. At the thirty-kilometer mark my time is 2:33. It seems I'm not the only one paying the price for the excessively quick pace of the first few kilometers. A lot of other competitors made the same mistake and now have to slow down even more than I do. A few are even forced to drop out. Thanks to my endurance, the product of my long-distance training, I can still keep up a reasonable pace, but it's a good bit slower than I could have done if I hadn't let myself get carried away at the beginning of the race.

I can see Elliott Denman in the park. He has his own special way of cheering his friends on: he leans forward, throwing his arms in the air, and moves his whole body in the direction I'm moving, as if he's trying to push me along. At the same time, he's clapping his hands and roaring out encouragement. He must be able to read what I'm feeling from my face and shouts out: "Hang on, don't give up." The next time around he does the same thing, and to pump me up even more he adds: "Pamich quit." Later I found out that Pamich, the gold medalist in Tokyo, didn't drop out of his own accord: he was disqualified. At forty kilometers, on top of the rest of my problems, I start to feel the effects of missing out on the glucose-enhanced Coke at the first watering station. Most of the glycogen has drained from my muscles. I feel fatigued, barely any spirit left in my body. It's an effort to keep up a respectable pace. I pass Kis, the Hungarian who finished second in Mexico City. He got even more carried away than I did at the beginning, and now it's taking a greater toll on him. I'm in nineteenth place. I can see the walker ahead of me, but I can't summon the energy to exert myself enough to catch up and overtake him.

The unique psychology of competitive athletes is well documented. When I'm in the lead and have a chance of winning or breaking a record, I can call up strength I didn't know I had, raising the level of my endurance enough to pick up the pace even more and make it happen. I can also find that extra ounce of energy to prevent a less capable rival from getting the better of me. By the same token, if I'm overtaken by someone I think is the better athlete, or if I don't feel that improving my placing at a given moment justifies the added effort, I just can't summon the motivation to push myself any harder. The same goes for all distance athletes. It happens when you're in contention for a medal or a trophy, or when two sworn rivals are fighting for position, even if it's only ninetieth place.

I had given my all for the whole race, so I persuaded myself that it wasn't worth it to me to stretch my endurance to a virtually intolerable level just to move up from nineteenth to eighteenth place. Had I known that Christophe

Höhne, the gold medalist in Mexico City, was just in front of me and on the verge of collapse from his frenzied pace for the first half of the race, had I known I had a chance of coming in ahead of him, it might have triggered the extra bit of will I needed. But unaware of these facts, I was happy enough to maintain my position and not let myself be overtaken. I described this to a reporter after the competition, but since he wasn't an athlete and couldn't understand what exertion means to us, he decided my whole psychological explanation of varying levels of motivation was a figment of my imagination and I was just using it as an excuse.

I finished in nineteenth place in 4:24. It was a good time and a respectable position, but I was sorry that the ignorance of my speed in the early stages and the mishap at the first watering station had prevented me from living up to my potential and doing better. The gold medal was won by the West German Bernhard Kanenberg in his inimitable classic style. Silver was taken by Venjamin Soldatenko from the USSR, and bronze by my American friend Larry Young, repeating his third-place win of four years before. He clocked in at a mere forty-six seconds over four hours. Visini finished fourth, and one of the Swedes came in sixth.

Breathing heavily, I was slowly making my way from the finish line toward the locker rooms under the bleachers when I found Amitzur Shapira waiting to congratulate me at the entrance to the tunnel. Seeing how exhausted I was, and undoubtedly having witnessed the state of those who had come in ahead of me, he remarked: "I never knew race walking was so hard." The Indians say: "You can't judge your neighbor until you've walked a few miles in his moccasins." I thought to myself that while Amitzur may not have tried on my moccasins yet, at least he'd finally seen them! In an interview that evening I was asked if I was planning to retire now that I was thrity-six. My spontaneous response was: "I've never been to Moscow," the venue for the 1980 Olympics.

The next day there was a long article in *Ha'aretz*, written by the same attorney, Yoel Katz, who had been so critical of me before the Olympics. "Bravo, Ladany," he wrote, lauding my very respectable nineteenth-place performance. It came as a surprise to him, as it did to me. Had things gone properly, had I gotten the right drink at the first watering station and been given my times and my position in relation to the other competitors, I would have had a chance of finishing somewhere between sixth and tenth.

■ Chapter Sixteen | The Massacre of Israeli Sportsmen in Munich

There was no reason for me to get up early and go out for a long training session the day after my race. But since habits are hard to break, I did do a short practice that day. Then, for the first time since we had landed in Munich, I went into town in search of souvenirs to bring home. I didn't actually buy much of anything, just looked around, noted the prices, and decided to do some comparative shopping before I came back and got what I wanted at some other opportunity. There was no way I could have known there would never be another opportunity. During the pre-Olympic meet the year before, I'd been ill and had hardly seen anything of the city. This time, too, I saw only a small part of Munich's lovely city center, the long pedestrian mall with its well-kept ancient churches and public buildings. I planned to visit the sites and tour other parts of the city another day. By the afternoon, I was back in the Olympic Village in time to watch the rest of the track and field events in the stadium from a seat in the athletes' section of the stands. The date was September 4, 1972.

That night the delegation was invited to the theater for a local production of *Fiddler on the Roof*, based on the book by Yiddish writer Shalom Aleichem. It was the first social activity or entertainment I'd allowed myself in Munich; it was also the last. During intermission, the delegation was invited backstage to meet Shmuel Rodensky, the Israeli actor playing the lead. The picture of us on stage with him is the last group photo ever taken of the delegation. Most of the men who were soon to lose their lives appear in that picture.

After the play, we went back to the village, getting in around midnight. Moshe Weinberg (known as Moony) asked to borrow my alarm clock. He had to be up at five in the morning to wake up his charge, the wrestler Mark Slavin, and take him to weigh in for his competition the following day. I promised Moony I'd bring him the clock after I got something to eat at the village restaurant. I finished my supper, got the clock from my room, and gave it to Moony in the unit next door. I warned him that it wasn't very accurate, but he said he always woke up early anyway and just wanted the clock to make sure he didn't oversleep. It didn't matter to him if it was as much as half an hour off. I set the alarm and left it with him.

By now it was close to 1:30 a.m. I sat down on my bed, leaned back on the pillow propped against the wall, and finally tackled the newspapers on the night table. They'd been piling up since my arrival in Munich, waiting for my race to be over when I would have time to look through them. I set about clipping out the articles I wanted to save for my scrapbook, either because they were about me or because they caught my interest for some other reason. My roommate Avraham Melamed was already asleep. It was after three o'clock when I finished the project, turned out the light, and went to sleep. I immediately fell into a deep, sound sleep, maybe because I was tired out from the effort of the race, because I rarely had trouble sleeping in any place at any time in any conditions, because it was so late, or because I had even learned to sleep through shelling in the army.

Suddenly something wakes me up. I open my eyes; Zelig Stroch is standing beside me. Avraham Melamed is sitting on his bed putting on his shoes. I hear Zelig say, "We've been attacked by Arabs." I shared a room with Zelig in Mexico City, and I know him to be a kidder. He has a strange look on his face now, too, an expression I try to interpret as the mark of someone playing a practical joke. But he sounds too serious to be pulling my leg. I also imagine I hear something like "they killed Moony," but I'm not quite sure what he's saying. Zelig leaves the room, Melamed stands up, and then I sit up, finally grasping that something is wrong. With studied calm, I put on my sneakers and throw my warm-up jacket over my pajamas.

Leaving the room, I walk along the corridor to the front door of our unit, crack it open and look out. I can't see any ominous or militant activity, or hear any of the sounds that would go along with it. But it's obvious that something has happened, although the scene is almost pastoral. About nine yards from the door to the stairwell that leads to unit 1, I can see four unarmed village guards lined up in their colorful uniforms. One is a woman. A dark-skinned man dressed in tan and wearing a hat is standing at the entrance to the stairwell. From where I am, leaning out of the doorway of unit 2, I can't see any more of the dark man's face than the truncated profile that extends beyond the wall of the building. The guards are talking to him in English, asking him to consent to letting the Red Cross in to see to the wounded man. The dark figure refuses. The guards try to persuade him to be a "humanitarian." He says that the Israelis aren't humanitarians.

From the window above my head, someone signals me to get back inside. I close the door behind me, but I still don't really understand what's going on. I am so oblivious to the gravity of the situation and the danger I'm in, that the first thing I do is the same thing I do every morning when I get up: I go into the bathroom to pee. Only after that do I climb the spiral staircase to the second floor, where I find the five other occupants of my unit in the front room belonging to the marksmen. Most of them are already dressed. When I ask what happened, they point to a dark stain on the ground in front of the door to the stairwell, telling me it is Moony's blood. The body has already been taken away. Everyone appears calm and rational and shows no signs of fear or panic. Everyone, that is, except for Henry Hershkowitz, who looks as white as a ghost and seems to be shaking in terror.

The six of us decided to get out of there. As little as three years later, in 1975, when we shared our recollections of these events, it turned out that our memories differ as to the order in which we left. Melamed was the first to go, followed, most likely, by Hershkowitz and Dan Alon, the fencer. Then it was probably Zelig Stroch, with me on his heels, and lastly the fencer Yehuda Weinstein. We went down to the first floor and into the back bedroom I shared with Avraham Melamed. Melamed pushed open the sliding door to the terrace on the same level as the lawn. Dividing walls separated our terrace from those of the adjacent units. Melamed moved to the wall on the left, peered around the edge, and checked out the area. Seeing that the coast was clear, he ran in a zigzag pattern across the lawn. The lawn sloped down from the building, meeting the vehicular traffic level on the far right.

It didn't occur to any of us that as we stood there out in the open on the terrace, we were in full view of anyone looking out of a second-story window. A man with a gun would have had a clear shot from any of the rear windows of the building. We were in the same danger when we stepped off the terrace and crossed the lawn. As Melamed, Hershkowitz, Alon, and Stroch followed each other across the grass, I pulled my sweatpants on over my pajamas. I was convinced that inching over to the wall in a crouch and fleeing from the building in zigzags was a sign of spinelessness; I could do it just as well like a man, with my head held high and without panicking. Needless to say, I was unaware of the full extent of the threat.

By the time I finished dressing, those who had left before me had disappeared. Believing I was the last to leave the unit, I went out to the terrace, standing tall, and then realized that I couldn't flee the building without warning Lalkin, the manager of the delegation, despite our strained relations. I turned right and walked erect close to the edge of the terraces for the length of the building until I reached what I imagined to be unit 5. I went up to the sliding door and tapped on the glass. No response. I knocked again. Suddenly it dawned on me that I had counted five terraces along the way, so was actually in back of unit 6. I retraced my steps and rapped on the glass door of unit 5.

A few seconds later the drapes moved slightly and I could see Lalkin's face. He recognized me, opened the door and let me in. "Listen…" I started, but he cut me off: "I know." He was dressed in the delegation uniform. His wife and son, whom I had seen several times staying overnight with him in the unit, were nowhere in sight. Lalkin was as composed as I was, showing no sign of distress. "Wait a minute," he said. "I have a few things to take care of." Picking up the phone, he went back to what he had been doing, alerting the delegation officials in the city hotels to what was going on.

While he was on the phone, there was another knock on the sliding door. I pulled the drapes aside and saw Yehuda Weinstein in full uniform. I let him in. He had lingered in his second-floor room long enough to put on the suit, and was still inside when I left the unit, believing it to be empty save for me. He had also had the same idea of warning Lalkin. He may have been only eighteen years old, but he was utterly levelheaded, apparently a basic feature of his personality; in fact, he was to go on to become an Air Force fighter pilot.

Lalkin finished calling all the people on the list in front of him, and then announced: "Give me another minute. I have one more call to make." From where I was standing across the desk from him, I saw him take out a sheet of paper headed: "Israeli journalists in Munich." He looked down the list trying to select one reporter to notify of the attack. There was no trace of agitation in his behavior or his voice, nor in mine for that matter. I noticed the name of a reporter I liked and suggested that Lalkin call him, pointing to his number.

Lalkin made no reply, but simply continued to review the list, his finger finally stopping by the name of a different newspaperman. He made his call and delivered the news. The three of us went out to the terrace, and with straight backs and confident steps we crossed the lawn and left the building behind.

Arcing across the grass to the right, we reached the lower traffic level, turned right, and were under the building. Immediately we could see armed German policemen covering the area. They had taken up positions next to the pillars. The first one we encountered led us to his commanding officer who ascertained who we were and had us taken to village headquarters. Yehuda Weinstein and I were placed in a room with the other four occupants of our unit and told to wait to be interviewed by the police.

All of a sudden, someone remembered that we hadn't warned the people in unit 3. Someone else said he was sure they had already gotten the message because he had seen a light on in the second-story rear window of their unit when he was leaving the building. We compared notes as to what we had seen and heard that night. I was the only one who had nothing to contribute; I'd been sleeping like a baby until Stroch woke me up.

All the others had heard sounds in their sleep, as if they were dreaming: the noise of doors slamming, shouts, and something like shots. A few had awakened, but had assumed the noise was coming from our neighbors, the Uruguayan athletes, who often celebrated in inimitable South American style. Ten minutes later the sounds came again, but the possibility that the Israeli delegation was being attacked by terrorists didn't cross anyone's mind. No one had checked his watch, but we figured it must have been between 4:30 and 4:45. Henry Hershkowitz and Zelig Stroch had woken up when the police arrived and gone to look out their front window. Three years later, Zelig remembered it this way:

> I told Henry I was going outside to see what was going on. I put on my sweat suit and went out. A plainclothes cop came up to me and asked if I had heard anything. I said to him in English, "Yes, but I don't know where it was coming from." I was standing out there when I suddenly saw a dark-skinned figure in a cap stick his head out of Gutfreund's room in unit 1. Meanwhile, uniformed village guards

showed up and the figure spoke to them in German. I heard the word "Palestine."

Hershkowitz signaled to me from the window to come back inside. Before that, I saw drops of blood leading from outside into unit 3. I went back into unit 2, went up to my room and saw Shmuel Lalkin looking out of the window of unit 5. [The village guards had contacted him by phone.] I also saw the guy in the cap toss a bunch of papers out of unit 1 [supposedly the terrorists' ultimatum], and shout in German: "You have till twelve o'clock — *und alle polizei weg* [and all policemen stay away]." I stayed by the window and saw Moony Weinberg's body, covered in blood, carried out of unit 1. Some guy outside in civilian clothes checked his pulse and pronounced him dead.

When I saw that, I ran to wake up Dan Alon and Yehuda Weinstein in the room across the hall from me, and then I went downstairs to Ladany and Melamed's room. When I went in, Melamed was already awake. I told him to get up, that something was going on. He said he had also heard noises. Meanwhile, Dr. Ladany, who was sleeping in the next bed, woke up and asked what was going on. I told him that we were being attacked by Arabs. He told me to stop fooling around.

While we were waiting to be called in to be questioned, Tuvia Sokolsky, one of the coaches assigned to unit 1, came into the room. We were very glad to see him. The police had just finished with him. We showered him with questions, hungry to know the fate of the other coaches in his unit. Tuvia told us he had been awakened by the wrestling referee Yossef Gutfreund shouting, "Guys, get out of here fast!" as he tried to use his mammoth size to hold the terrorists at bay (many published accounts later incorrectly claimed it had been Moony Weinberg who yelled this). Tuvia went on to relate that when he heard shots coming from Gutfreund's direction, he jumped out of bed and ran from his first-floor room to the sliding door (one of whose panels could be opened like an ordinary hinged door), broke the glass and rushed out onto the terrace. From there he raced to the building where some other delegation was staying and took cover there. He calculated that the time must have been around 4:30.

Now, some four hours later, he was still befuddled and in shock. He was also annoyed by our attempts to find out from him exactly what had happened in unit 1 and how he had managed to get away dressed in sneakers and long pants. We realized that he had been terrified, and that the state of shock he was in and the fact that he spoke no foreign language had caused him to hide in the quarters of another delegation for at least two hours without reporting the attack to the authorities. Although we were willing to allow that some people react that way to pressure or danger, we couldn't rely on the accuracy of his story.

Indeed, two days later, when those of us who had survived the attack returned to 31 Connolly Street to pack our belongings and those of the victims, we found that Tuvia hadn't broken the glass door as he said, but had twisted the handle out of shape in his frantic attempt to force it open. Neither were there any bullet holes in the front door that Gutfreund had supposedly been blocking with his body. Consequently, there is no way of knowing precisely when unit 1 was attacked.

Meanwhile, we were informed that the terrorists were holed up in unit 1 and were holding hostage all the occupants of units 1 and 3, save for Moony who was dead and whose body had been removed from the scene. After a while, Tsabari emerged from the interrogation room. We pounced on him, thirsty for knowledge of the other occupants of unit 3. Tsabari told us that both he and his second-floor roommate David Berger had been awakened by the noise. He thought it must have been 4:55, but we eventually learned that it was earlier. The noise was followed by someone ringing the front doorbell. He put on his pants and found himself face to face with a terrorist aiming a submachine gun at him.

Mark Slavin and Eliezer Halfin had already been seized by the same terrorist. It all happened very quietly, without a word being uttered. When Berger came out of his room to see what was going on, he was also taken prisoner. The terrorist told the four of them to descend the spiral staircase to the first floor and stand by the alcove under the stairs. Yossef Romano and Ze'ev Friedman were already there. Except for Tsabari, the others were all in their underwear or shorts. Moony was there too, a handkerchief wrapped around his wounded jaw. Two more terrorists had submachine guns trained on them.

Tsabari went on to relate that the terrorists asked them, in English, where the rest of the Israelis were, but since he didn't know any English, it is impossible to tell if that was indeed what was said. In any case, as Tsabari told it, David Berger whispered in Hebrew: "Come on, let's jump them. We've got nothing to lose." The terrorists heard them talking, and before they had a chance to work out a plan, they were ordered to line up in single file and marched out the front door where they turned right, passed the door to unit 2, entered the stairwell and descended to the lower level.

Tsabari was first in line. Another masked terrorist was waiting for them at the bottom of the stairs. He gestured with his weapon toward the wall, ordering Tsabari to move toward it. Tsabari took advantage of the split-second when the gun was turned away from him and fled through the stairwell door, running in zigzags between the pillars of the parking garage and out onto the street. Hearing shots being fired in his direction, he raced as fast as he could to the fence around the Olympic Village, about a hundred yards from the building, and climbed over.

He reached the information booth, and using his hands and broken German, he managed to make himself understood to the guards, explaining that Arab terrorists had attacked members of the Israeli delegation in unit 3. Since none of the village guards were armed, these local sentries called the cops and then got in touch with Shmuel Lalkin in unit 5. Thus Gad Tsabari was the first to alert the security forces as to what was going on in the Olympic Village.

I knew that the occupants of unit 3 were now being held hostage together with the coaches from unit 1, but from what Tsabari said, it seemed that the terrorists had made an attempt to take them out of the village, probably by car. "Why else would they lead them down to the lower parking garage unless they intended to drive them somewhere?" I thought, concluding that Tsabari's escape had upset their plans and forced them to barricade themselves in unit 1.

Without waiting to be called, I went into the interrogation room and presented the surprised investigator with my deductions and the suggestion that they search the village for accomplices in vehicles that could be used to transport the athletes out of the village. The cop was very civil, but unimpressed. I insisted that it was imperative that he take immediate action because these accomplices could disappear without a trace. He replied with total serenity that he would make note of my suggestion and pass it on to his superiors. At no time did I hear that this possibility was ever investigated, not then and not later.

When the village guards called out by Tsabari arrived at 31 Connolly Street at around 4:30 a.m., the terrorists and eleven hostages were already entrenched in unit 1. No one saw how it went down. By the time Henry Hershkowitz and Zelig Stroch, the first occupants of my unit to wake up, looked out the window not long afterwards, the terrorists had already taken up position.

Since neither Sokolsky nor Tsabari could be relied on to estimate the time precisely, we will never know the exact order of events. I managed to come up with three possible scenarios, but they can be no more than conjecture.

(1) The terrorists ring the doorbell of unit 1. After gaining control of the occupants, they force Moony Weinberg to show them to the quarters of the other Israelis. Since Moony works with the wrestlers and weightlifters, the strongest members of the Israeli team and the ones who might be able to get a jump on their attackers, he leads the terrorists to unit 3.

(2) Moony gets out of bed to wake up Mark Slavin, who has to weigh in that morning, gets dressed and exits unit 1. He leaves the door ajar, intending to return in a minute or two, goes out to the street and rings the bell to unit 3. As he walks from unit 1 to 3, he is easily identifiable as an Israeli by his uniform. He is attacked by the terrorists, either as he waits outside the door to unit 3 or when one of the athletes inside opens the door and lets him in.

The terrorists most likely planned to whisk the six occupants of unit 3, along with Moony, out of the Olympic Village with the help of cohorts waiting in a parked vehicle downstairs. This is the only logical explanation for their dragging the Israelis down to the lower level. Gad Tsabari's escape and the shots fired at him fouled up their plans. (When we returned to the building two days later, there were no signs of shots being fired, but the shell casings may have been collected by then.) Not wanting to encounter resistance as they make their escape from the village, and assuming the police have been alerted, they decide to take up a position inside the building. As they retrace their steps up the stairs, they notice that the door to unit 1 is ajar and decide spontaneously to attack the coaches' quarters as well.

Gutfreund in unit 1 is awakened by the shots fired at Gad, gets up and maybe tries to lock the door, but he is too late. The terrorists burst in.

(3) Unit 1 is attacked at or near the same time as unit 3, when Moony is already in unit 3 and the door to unit 1 is open. The plan is to take the occupants of both units out of the village by car in two consecutive groups. When Tsabari's escape upsets this plan, the terrorists decide to entrench themselves in unit 1.

In my opinion, the second and third scenarios seem more likely since there is no other way to account for their forcing the Israelis down to the lower level.

Another question is why they ignored unit 2, a surprising circumstance considering that it was situated between the two units they did attack. They had to pass it, and there was no light on inside that might have deterred them. Was it merely blind luck that saved its six occupants? I considered this for quite a while before reaching the conclusion that avoiding unit 2 was an integral part of their scheme. Subsequent investigation revealed that the attack was carefully planned out in advance, aided by two members of the gang who were employed in the Olympic Village, affording them the opportunity to observe village routine. Maps of the village, with the quarters of each delegation clearly marked, were readily available. The maps indicated that 31 Connolly Street was occupied by the delegations from Uruguay, Hong Kong, and Israel. A large white sign on the door to each unit bore the names of all its occupants, and was in clear view of anyone passing along the street. Names like Dan Alon, Yehuda Weinstein, etc., obviously didn't belong to sportsmen from Uruguay or Hong Kong.

Furthermore, a free computerized information service was available for the use of any visitor. All you had to do was key in the name of an athlete to receive a computer printout containing his or her particulars, including biographical data, event, and personal record. If the terrorists had obtained this information for the five occupants of unit 2 (remembering that Melamed's presence was never officially reported), they would have learned that two of them were marksmen who would not only know how to use a gun, but could be expected to keep their weapons and ammunition in their personal residence. Knowing this in advance, and not wanting to encounter armed resistance, the terrorists probably decided from the word go to stay away from unit 2. These facts, along with my deductions, were published in September 1982 in an article I wrote for the weekend supplement of the prestigious Israeli daily *Ha'aretz* in memory of the tenth anniversary of the massacre.

After we had all been questioned, we were transferred under armed guard to a secure hall in the basement of village headquarters. The women athletes Esther Shahamorov and Shlomit Nir were also put in with us, along with the sprinters Hannah Shezifi and Aviva Balas, who had snuck into the village and needed a safe place to stay. We were all pretty self-absorbed, with Henry Hershkowitz and some of the women still looking pale. I didn't see any good reason to stay there, and there was no one to stop me from leaving. I went out and walked around. The games had been suspended, so that the village was filled with the athletes who weren't out training or whose events were already over.

As I wandered around, I ran into my American friends, Steve Hayden and Goetz Klopfer, who threw their arms around me as soon as they caught sight of me. News of the attack on the Israeli quarters had spread quickly and by now was common knowledge. Steve and Goetz took me to their room to shave and shower. Another friend, Bruce MacDonald, the manager of the American walking team, asked if I needed anything, even money. Since I happened to have a few ten-deutsche mark bills in the pocket of my sweatpants, I didn't have to take him up on his generous offer.

I tried to call Shosh, but for a long time all the lines to Israel were engaged. The delegation officials had already taken phone numbers from the surviving athletes and had promised to get in touch with our families through the foreign office to assure them that we were safe and sound, but I didn't want to count on them to do that. I later discovered that my name was missing from all the lists of survivors put out by the media. Shosh was working as a researcher at the Weizmann Institute of Science at the time. When Israel radio reported the attack, without giving the names of the hostages or survivors, one of the women in the office ran to give Shosh the news. With a heavy heart, Shosh went on with her work. When she got home at the end of the day, our good friends Uri and Michal Raudenitz came to take her and one-year-old Danit to their house so that she wouldn't be alone at such a time. The names of the survivors were read out on the evening TV news, but mine wasn't mentioned. Shosh was seized with fear.

It was after midnight by the time I got through to her and she was finally able to breathe easy. I told her that someone was supposed to have called her. The next morning she asked the babysitter who watched Danit during the day if she had heard anything. The woman — who was not unduly burdened by intelligence — admitted that someone had called to say that I was fine, but she didn't think it was important enough to mention. As soon as I hung up, Shosh got a call from Noah Gurock, a friend of ours from the States who was now working as a reporter. He got himself a phone interview with Shosh as the wife of a survivor, a real scoop for his paper, *The Hartford Times*.

I was still wandering around outside. Everyone had been evacuated from the area of our residence on Connolly Street and the adjacent buildings, which were now occupied by armed security forces, including police snipers dressed in sweat suits. The terrorists had barricaded themselves in unit 1 with their hostages, and from there they delivered their ultimatum: the hostages would be killed unless the State of Israel released hundreds of convicted terrorists from prison. I got as far as the police barrier blocking off our building. A large crowd had gathered. A lot of people recognized me and embraced me, among them the English walkers. Others who didn't know me but saw the name "ISRAEL" on my jacket shook my hand and wished me well.

I was surrounded by reporters, including Al Zimmerman whom I had met in New York. I told them everything I knew or had heard from the other Israeli athletes, offering my three alternative theories as to how the attack on units 1 and 3 might have gone down. Most of them adopted the first explanation and published it as confirmed fact. The idea of Moony leading the terrorists to unit 3 in the hope that the delegation strongmen could overpower them sounded like a good juicy story for their readers or listeners.

Everyone wanted to know if the Israeli government would give in to the terrorists' ultimatum. Even though I hadn't been asked or authorized to do so, I took on the job of Israeli information officer, explaining that the government would never allow itself to be blackmailed, a situation that could only lead to further terrorist actions and more demands. I repeated that statement not only to every reporter I met, but also to any of the athletes I spoke to.

At noon we learned that Yossef Romano had also been killed, either in the attack or directly afterwards. He was carrying a training injury that made him use crutches. In fact, he was supposed to fly back to Israel that day for an operation on his knee. Even injured and walking with a limp, his size and strength could be very intimidating. No one can say for sure if he was murdered because he put up resistance, but it is a definite possibility. Not only did he speak Arabic, but, although generally a very sweet guy, he had a short fuse. It is only too likely that he was wounded and then died a slow death before the eyes of his nine companions on the upper floor of unit 1.

In addition to the nine hostages, the delegation doctor, Dr. Weigel, remained inside the building, cut off in unit 4. There would have been no shame in admitting that he was afraid to step outside and preferred the relative safety of his room, even considering the risk of the evacuated building being damaged in an attempt to rescue the hostages. He, however, claimed that he didn't leave his unit for nearly a whole day because he felt he had to maintain telephone contact with the authorities. Bravo, courageous telephone monitor!

I was sure that some sort of rescue operation was in the cards. It was very quiet in the village that whole day, despite the presence of hundreds, maybe thousands, of armed security officers. In the evening, after being out all day, I rejoined the rest of the surviving members of the delegation ensconced at headquarters. We were transferred to a higher floor of that well-guarded building. There we waited. Only the following day did we find out what had happened. Israel had demanded that as the host of the Olympics responsible for the safety of foreign athletes, Germany take action to secure the release of the hostages. The Germans accepted this position. First, German agents tried to buy the lives of the hostages in exchange for a sum in the neighborhood of a million deutsche marks. When that didn't work, they decided they would have to use force.

Operationally, the best strategy was to attack the terrorists where they were holed up, either immediately or after placing them under siege for a while. But that would interfere with the continuation of the Olympic Games and — which was worse in the eyes of the Germans — would involve taking military action in public, under the watchful eyes of the huge corps of reporters, broadcasters, and TV cameras. Germany's whole intention in organizing the Olympics had been to show the world that it was no longer a Nazi war machine, and as a result, the authorities were loath to do anything that might rekindle memories of its past, such as launching a military operation against the terrorists in full view of the media.

Accordingly, the Germans decided to play both hands. Publicly, they reached a compromise with the terrorists, agreeing to allow them to leave Germany with the hostages and promising to fly them to an Arab country from an isolated military airfield at some distance from the Olympic Village. At the same time, they made preparations to secure the release of the hostages by force before they boarded the plane.

In general terms, the plan appeared reasonable and feasible. By all indications, it was also approved in principle by the Israeli authorities. After dark, the terrorists and hostages were to be taken in two buses from Connolly Street to the courtyard outside village headquarters. Two helicopters would be waiting there to fly them to the airport. The copters would land at a distance from the waiting plane. Commando soldiers would be positioned in the plane, with snipers lying in wait along the dark path they would have to cross to get from the helicopters to the plane.

We all remembered Germany as a mighty military power with the prodigious operational skills that had enabled it to occupy large parts of the world thirty years before. We were unaware that in the Germany of the seventies, the armed forces had lost their aura and appeal, and no longer attracted the finest of the country's sons, who now preferred careers in other endeavors. Consequently, it never occurred to us that execution of the plan would be anything less than perfect — that is, up to the accepted standards of the Israel Defense Forces.

But in point of fact, the operation was carried out in a shabby and amateurish manner. From the reports of the survivors and observation of the building, the number of terrorists was estimated as three or four. No one thought to count them as they boarded the helicopters, although there was plenty of light. The entire village had been plunged in darkness, except for two bright spotlights aimed at the courtyard outside headquarters. The two helicopters landed there and waited. The buses carrying the terrorists and hostages pulled up. Together with the rest of the Israeli delegation, I could see them very clearly from our position at the window of a high dark office.

We saw both the terrorists and the nine hostages in their official uniforms, their hands tied behind their backs as they were led to the helicopters and climbed in. Zelig Stroch remarked that from where he was standing, he alone could take out several of the terrorists with his rifle. Even if some member of the rescue team did make a count and discover, as we did, that there were eight of them, this information was never relayed to the snipers at the airfield. Five volunteer snipers were lying in wait, stretched out on the ground with their rifles, which were not equipped with night sights. Neither had any armored vehicles been positioned as backup.

On top of that, the commandos placed in the empty plane to surprise the terrorists decided to take independent action. Whether out of "overzealousness" or a reluctance to incur undue risk just to save a few Jewish hostages, they abandoned the plane and took off, without telling anyone. In sharp contrast, the terrorists behaved like true professionals. When the copters landed, two of them went to check out the plane while the other six remained in or near the copters. They found the plane totally deserted. Unaware that the commandos who were supposed to take them out had absconded, they started back toward the copters.

Meanwhile, believing that they had half or two-thirds of the terrorist gang in their sights, the snipers along their path opened fire. Only one terrorist was wounded. The snipers called for reinforcements, but several hours passed until the arrival of armored troops from a distant camp. All the hostages tied up in the helicopters lost their lives, either murdered by the terrorists during this waiting period or killed in the firefight that ensued once the troops showed up. Five terrorists were killed and three taken alive.

Back in the Olympic Village, we had no inkling of the rescue plan or the drama unfolding far away. We were hoping that some kind of rescue operation was being planned and would be successful according to the norms we were accustomed to for IDF operations. We were stuck in the office in village headquarters, waiting tensely. Around two o'clock on the morning of September 6, the German radio announced that all the hostages had been released. We leapt up and threw our arms around each other, celebrating joyously. We could finally relax and get some sleep. I was awakened at six o'clock by Zelig

Stroch, sobbing bitterly as he mouthed, "They're all dead." It was only then that we learned the calamitous outcome of the botched rescue operation.

The "fearlessness" of the commandos who abandoned their posts was only discovered by an investigation conducted twenty years later. Understandably, the German authorities, none too proud of their "courageous" soldiers, were not eager to volunteer this information. Whether the nine hostages were murdered in cold blood by their captors or shot down by their rescuers — a fact of interest especially to the victims' families — is not known to this day.

The Olympic Committee decided to suspend the games on September 6 as well. Everyone soon learned the tragic news. An official memorial service was held in the Olympic stadium during which we, the surviving members of the Israeli delegation, stood in the middle of the field, as speeches, some in Hebrew, were delivered condemning the massacre of eleven innocent athletes. Even the president of Germany was there to denounce the murder, the criminals perpetrating it, and the agents behind them. But he was only a paper tiger with no political or executive authority. I wondered whether the German government would actually take any action in line with his statement. Hundreds of foreign athletes and delegation officials came to shake our hands and offer their condolences. A good many women athletes were in tears. The whole modern world was in shock that the Olympic Games had become the scene of such a violent act of terrorism. For over two thousand years, the Olympics had been a symbol of peace and brotherhood, with all acts of hostility suspended for their duration even in ancient times.

There was a touch of irony in the fact that the massacre was perpetrated by members of the terrorist organization known as Black September. The Palestinian organizations based in Jordan had grown so strong that they had established their own private army, defying the law of the land and constituting a threat to the reign of King Hussein. Determined to nip this opposition in the bud, in September 1970, the King ordered the Jordanian army to mercilessly annihilate the Palestinian militants in his country. Thousands of their members were killed. Many thousands of others crossed the border with Israel and surrendered to the IDF, choosing to submit to their sworn enemy, whose destruction was the very cause for which their organizations were founded. They preferred judgment in an enlightened country with, in effect, no death penalty and relatively better prison conditions, than to face certain death at the hands of their fellow Arabs. Black September was founded in memory of those events in Jordan in September 1970, but the target of its present flamboyant action was, of course, the State of Israel.

I heard that the prime minister, Golda Meir, had demanded cancellation of the Olympic Games. It was obvious to me that this was a political act aimed at strengthening the position of Israel, censuring terrorism, and pressuring the international community to ensure the safety of Israeli citizens anywhere in the world. I didn't think her demand was appropriate. Acceding would turn all the world's athletes against Israel, despite their sympathy for the country and the victims and despite their abhorrence of the terrorists and their masters. I also believed that the eleven victims, all sportsmen to the core who understood the mentality of the athlete, would not have wanted their personal sacrifice to earn Israel the antipathy of the sports world or to damage the unbroken tradition of the Olympic Games.

The International Olympic Committee did not acquiesce to Israel's demand to halt the games, declaring that competition would resume after being suspended for two days. In response, Golda ordered the Israeli delegation to return home immediately. It was hard to accept this position, which, uncharacteristically, stemmed from emotional rather than purely rational considerations. It was said that she wanted to provoke the Swedish secretary general of the UN, Dag Hammarskjold, who was far from being a friend to Israel. Knowing he was a bachelor and said to be homosexual, she supposedly remarked at one of their meetings: "Why don't you find yourself a nice girl and settle down?"

The Israeli government had no legal authority to force the national Olympic Committee to do anything, its only redress being its control of the budget, so it is unclear why the committee acceded to Golda's demand. Either they were afraid of being accused of not taking appropriate security measures, were reluctant to defy the prime minister, or were in full agreement with her stance. Whatever the case, the delegation officials consented, voting for the remaining members to return to Israel en masse the following day. When I heard this, I tried to persuade any official I could find, as well as the members of the team, that this was the wrong decision and would not serve Israel's interests. I did my best to convince them to reconsider the steps they should take and not blindly follow Golda's instructions, arguing that for years the Arab nations had been making vain efforts to exclude Israel from international forums, including the Olympics, and to prevent us from leading a normal life.

Now, after the painful carnage, the murder of eleven of our brothers, we would be handing them two additional victories, abandoning the Olympic arena and interrupting our routine. I also insisted that even if we went straight back to Israel, we had to leave someone there to carry the flag, draped in black, in the closing ceremony. But the decision makers of Israeli sports were unable, or unwilling, to comprehend what I was saying. The Olympic Games proceeded as planned and the closing ceremony followed long-established tradition, with a single exception: there was no trace of the Israeli delegation. It later became known that certain members of the Olympic Committee objected to the decision, and in fact, several of them only paid it lip service. Chaim Globinsky, the honorary chairman of the committee, and Yitzhak Caspi, its vice chairman, left their wives in Munich, came back with the delegation, attended the funerals of the victims, and then rejoined their wives in Germany the next day.

After the memorial service in Munich, we were taken to our quarters on Connolly Street to pack our things and those of the victims. We were under heavy guard the whole time, surrounded by armed police both during the ride and in the building itself. We were joined by several Israeli athletes who had bluffed their way into the village but were not members of the team. They were given the task of collecting the belongings of the victims while we members of the delegation packed our own bags. A large group of us was sitting in my room waiting until everyone was finished, when we heard our guards arguing with a crowd of curiosity seekers that had gathered.

"Those cops are real squares," someone remarked. We had come to know the virtually blind obedience to authority that was the product of a German upbringing, causing most of the country's citizens to uphold the letter, although not necessarily the spirit, of the law. It was unusual for anyone to take the initiative, even to achieve a cherished goal, or to do something they had not been explicitly ordered to do. The same person added, "I bet their commanding officer ordered them to watch us and place guards out front, and none of them had enough enterprise to understand that to mean there should be guards at the back of the building too." He had barely finished his sentence when an Israeli athlete who had snuck into the village came in through the rear terrace. He told us the front door was heavily guarded to keep people away from the building, but there wasn't a single cop in the rear.

The arguments at the front entrance got louder, and I could even hear the sound of crying. I opened the door and went out, and who should I see but my Swiss friend Alfred Badel. The sobbing was coming from him. The cops refused to let him through. As soon as he saw me, he fell silent, staring at me with an expression halfway between astonishment and joy. Then he ran forward, hugging and kissing me. With tears streaming down his cheeks, he held me in a tight embrace, touching me to be sure I was real flesh and blood and not a figment of his imagination, as he explained in a choked voice that he had been sure I was killed.

Apparently, a good many items in the German, French, and Danish press had listed me among the victims. For Alfred, it was as if I had come back from the dead. Some time later I saw a headline that read "Ladany could not escape his fate in Germany for a second time," over an article which included the fact that I was a Holocaust survivor. Another paper went even further, illustrating the report of my death with an "artistic" photograph. Like many other works of art, this was no thing of beauty; in fact, it was downright disgusting. The photographer had used a wide-angle lens so that my body looked badly distorted, with the limbs all out of proportion, like the subject of one of Dr. Mengele's experiments at Auschwitz. It was supposed to bring home the message that I was a Holocaust survivor.

A while later Don Johnson told me that he and a group of other veteran athletes were competing in a major event in Denmark when they got word of the massacre in Munich, with my name mentioned as one of the victims. They lit candles and observed a minute of silence in my memory. A lot of people suggested I offer up a prayer of thanksgiving.

We didn't sleep in our official quarters that night either, but were put up elsewhere, still under heavy guard, until we were driven to the airport in the morning. Eleven coffins draped in the national flag sat on the tarmac beside the plane. We lined up in our uniforms facing the ramp, with the caskets on our left. I was suddenly struck by how few of us were left. Of the eleven male athletes in Munich, only six had survived; of the eleven athletes and coaches listed on the same collective passport with me, only two were still alive. The German foreign minister, Walter Schell, later to become president of West Germany, officially took leave of us in the name of the government. He walked down the line, shaking each of us by the hand as a gesture of condolence; it didn't take him long.

An official ceremony awaited us at Lod airport, with a somber memorial service held on the runway. The huge asphalt expanse between the terminal and tarmac was crowded with thousands of people. The service was broadcast live over radio and TV. Eleven military command cars were lined up beside the plane, each carrying a single flag-draped casket. The ten surviving team members, out of the original fifteen athletes, stood alongside the vehicles — not even enough for one for each car. I was standing beside Amitzur's coffin. The crowd received us as if we had risen from the dead. Thousands came to kiss and embrace me, among them friends, acquaintances, and fellow marchers I hadn't seen in years.

It was a regular workday, yet when news of the ceremony was broadcast over the radio, scores of people left their jobs to demonstrate their solidarity with the horrendous loss suffered by Israeli sports. As the airport service ended, the funeral processions set out. I formed part of an honor guard for the five national burial rites at the Tel Aviv cemetery of Kiryat Shaul. The service, attended by thousands, was somber and imposing. Five adjacent graves gaped opened in the first row off the main path. Ever since, whenever I am in Israel on the anniversary of the massacre, I take part in the modest graveside memorial service. My father is buried in the same cemetery, and each time I come to visit his grave or attend a funeral there, I stop by the five Olympic graves as well. The memory remains fresh; it will never go away.

It goes without saying that when I finally got home, Shosh kissed me with the same intensity as when I had returned from the Six-Day War. She'd been at the airport with Danit in her arms, but I had barely gotten a chance to exchange a word with her. Hearing I was coming home, hundreds of friends and neighbors came to greet me the day I arrived, expressing their thanks that I was safe and sound. I was most moved by the uncoordinated appearance of each and every one of the Ramat Efal kids I had coached.

In the days following, I was flooded with letters, some from friends and acquaintances and others from people I didn't even know. A number of them were addressed solely to "Dr. Shaul Ladany, Israel," several with the addition of "Olympic race walker," but nothing more. All of them bore congratulations on my having survived the massacre. The Rogers sent a telegram from Belgium. I received numerous letters expressing shock at the massacre and joy at my survival from old friends, like Don Spiro, the world rowing champion; George Latarulo, a fellow competitor in many US competitions; and Professor Richmond, the acting dean of the Graduate School of Business Administration at Columbia. It was a good feeling to know that all these people were thinking of me.

A number of inventive books were written about the events in Munich. In 1975 I received a request from Neil Amdur, a sportswriter for the *New York Times*, who wanted my opinion on a book translated from the French that was about to appear in English. Neil didn't trust its authenticity. The author, Serge Groussard, claimed in the introduction that it was the product of exhaustive research, based entirely on official documents and personal interviews he himself had conducted. As soon as I opened it, I realized it was the work of a charlatan. I later had occasion to say as much to Groussard himself, in front of witnesses. Despite the author's claims, the book, although admittedly well written, was full of wholesale fabrications constructed around a few commonly known facts.

Among other fictions, it states — perhaps inspired by the grotesque news photo — that I woke up at the start of the attack on the building, grasped what was happening, and fled. When my roommates asked me what was going on, I didn't answer and didn't warn them. The author goes on to invent a story whereby I escaped by leaping from the balcony of my second-story room and thereby survived. When the publisher refused my demand to correct the lies depicting me as a coward before the book came out, I took him to court. I managed to have distribution of the hardcover English version stopped at a very early stage, and to prevent its printing in paperback. I also got Paramount to expunge the scene of an athlete leaping from a second-story balcony from a movie based on the book.

I was utterly astounded when a number of sports officials and two of the other survivors put pressure on me to drop the suit. Whether or not I cleared my name was of no interest to them; the survivors had been bought off by the promise of proceeds from, or a part in, the film. As for the officials, I discovered that Groussard's wife was the secretary of the International Olympic Committee and had helped to correct lapses resulting from the inefficiency of the Israeli committee, such as agreeing to accept the list of members of the Olympic delegation although it was submitted after the deadline. They preferred to keep on her good side rather than amend the slanderous depiction of an independent athlete unafraid to take on the establishment.

The three terrorists captured alive by the German forces at the airport were imprisoned, but spent only a short time in a German jail. Their cohorts hijacked a German passenger plane over Yugoslavia, and they were set free as part of the deal struck with the skyjackers in exchange for the release of the plane and the hostages. They were welcomed as heroes in Libya where they were granted asylum. It is said that each of them received a million-dollar reward from Gaddafi himself.

But things were different in other parts of the world. Many of the leaders of Black September and other terrorist organizations that acted against Jewish or Israeli targets were mysteriously taken out around the world, with no clue as to the perpetrators, save for the tragic case of mistaken identity in the northern Norwegian town of Lillehammer. Conventional wisdom has it that they were stricken down by the long arm of the Mossad on Golda Meir's orders, a warning to other terrorist groups that they could not escape Israeli justice.

An article published in late 1977 claimed that one of the terrorists responsible for the massacre in Munich was living the good life in Lebanon. I sent the clipping to Ezer Weizmann, then defense minister, along with a letter stating that I felt it was in Israel's interest to show all the terrorists involved in the massacre, wherever they might be, that they would eventually have to pay for what they did. Only in this way could future attacks be prevented. Weizmann wrote back that he had "relayed my message to the proper channels." My scrapbook of the Munich Olympics slowly filled with clippings reporting the mysterious slayings of the assassins and the masterminds behind the carnage, until it became clear that the chapter was closed. There was nothing more to add.

Part IV

Life After the Olympics

■ Chapter Seventeen | The World Title

Two weeks after I returned home from Munich, it was time for Braz's 100-kilometer march around the Sea of Galilee. It began, as usual, on a Friday at four in the afternoon. Braz had prepared black bands for us to pin to our shirts in memory of the eleven murdered athletes. The route, making a full circle of the lake plus the loop from Zemach to Gesher, was already a matter of established routine. I walked the loop late in the evening, when there was a lot of traffic, making it a dangerous stretch of road, particularly between Zemach and Ashdot Ya'akov. Fortunately, a bicycle path ran parallel and to the west of the road between Zemach and Kibbutz Afikim, separated from the traffic by a drainage ditch.

Not having to worry about the cars, I took the path blithely, confident I was safe. My complacency turned out to be misplaced. Not far from Afikim I suddenly struck my foot badly. The "guilty party" was a pipe laid across the path to keep cars off. I hadn't seen it in the dark. My foot hurt like hell, but I kept going. On the way back I knew what to look out for and exercised extreme caution, saving my other foot from suffering the same fate. As always, I finished first, having walked for ten and a half hours. The swim across the Sea of Galilee was a week later. Shosh came along too. It was the fourth time for her and the sixth for me. The swim itself was as boring as ever, but it was worth enduring the tedium to feel such joy when we made it to the other side.

Long before Munich, I knew that taking part in the Olympics — even for the second time — would be the fulfillment of my greatest dream. Nevertheless, I didn't consider it the end of my athletic career. Training, marches, and competitions were a way of life for me. Therefore, at the end of the Olympics I intended to ask to compete in my third London to Brighton Walk, scheduled for a few days after the closing ceremony in Munich, and the 100-kilometer world championship in Lugano in early November. Obviously, the terrorist

327

attack and our immediate return to Israel made London to Brighton out of the question. Still, I was reluctant to give up the Cento. I knew I was in the best form ever for ultra-long distances, and I wanted to take advantage of it to set new personal records.

I submitted a request to the Track and Field Committee for funding from the Sports Federation for participation in the world championship. The Committee seconded my request, but the answer that came back from the Federation was "No." After the events in Munich, the sports officials sensed they could be charged with not ensuring adequate security arrangements, and as a result they decided not to send any athletes to competitions abroad until the security authorities issued instructions as to how to guarantee their safety. I wasn't prepared to be a party to this evasion and their do-nothing policy, aimed solely at shielding them from possible future accusations. I thus decided to go anyway, and continued to train for it. The only question left to answer was who would cover my travel expenses.

Zvi Galitzky called from Lugano and I told him the Sports Federation had refused to pay for the trip. He tried hard to persuade me to come, relaying the news that the East Germans were not going to be there, and, in his opinion, this meant I had a good chance of winning the title this time. Needless to say, that drove me to train even harder. I had already been determined to compete; his call merely served to reinforce my belief that the financial sacrifice was worthwhile. I reported Galitzky's assessment to the Track and Field Committee, but they replied that the chance of my winning the world championship was not enough to alter the Federation's decision.

Galitzky called again a few days later, and when he heard that nothing had changed, he declared himself ready to commit to procuring a thousand Swiss francs to cover part of my expenses. That was about half of the actual cost. I submitted another request to the Sports Federation, outlining Galitzky's offer and asking them to match his contribution. The answer was still no.

I flew to Switzerland for the weekend, knowing full well that if Galitzky couldn't make good on his promise — and after all, he was only acting out of a love for sports and a desire to promote Israeli athletes — I would have to bear the full cost myself. Zvi proved to be not only a devoted fan of sports and Israel, but a reliable, trustworthy person as well. He was also aware of the potential risk to my safety. By now the whole world was in a panic over security. He arranged for an armed plainclothes cop to be assigned to protect me, in addition to the regular security arrangements being made for the championship. Galitzky also carried a gun.

On Saturday night we set out for the trip from Lugano to Olivone in two cars. I was in one car with the bodyguard; he didn't let me out of his sight for a second. I registered at the hotel in Olivone under a false name. No one even knew I was there. There had been no mention in the press that I would be coming. The cop slept in my room; actually, he sat up most of the night with the gun in his hand. I spotted a second gun strapped to his leg under his pants. During the race, he and Galitzky kept close to me in their cars. Ignoring the warnings, the shirt I wore proudly displayed the name "ISRAEL" in Latin letters. There may not have been any advance notice of my participation, making it impossible to plot an attack, but anyone driving past on the road could easily see there was an Israeli in the race. What was undoubtedly an even odder sight, however, was Galitzky in his long black coat sticking to me and faithfully handing me drinks, reporting my times, and calculating my lead.

After the Olympics, I had heard about a new version of the high-carbohydrate diet used to temporarily raise the level of glycogen in the muscles. Apparently, most of the other walkers had already applied this regimen in Munich. The difference was reflected in almost total abstinence from proteins and fats in the last three days before an event. In the past, we had been told to eat mainly carbohydrates and limit our intake of proteins. I had tried the variation for Braz's 100-kilometer march, eliminating the eggs and nuts from my diet the last three days and eating only jam on bread (which looked more like bread on jam), macaroni and potatoes without any sauce, and fresh fruits and vegetables. The system worked wonders. I was able to walk the whole distance at full speed without any sense of heaviness or fatigue.

Years later, it became customary to eat pasta the night before a marathon as part of the high-carbohydrate diet. But those who organize the dinners for the participants generally evidence dogmatic compliance without the benefit of understanding. The pasta is usually swimming in fatty sauce, as is the lettuce served alongside, which may make the food taste better but defeats its purpose. When I saw the results of the new diet at the Sea of Galilee March, I adopted it for the Cento as well. It worked this time too, and everybody knows that nothing succeeds like success.

I came in first in 9:38, better than Höhne's time when he took the title in each of the two preceding years. I was the 1972 world champion for the 100-kilometer walk, making me the first Israeli ever to win a world title in any track and field event. Toward the end of the race, when I had already entered Lugano a few kilometers ahead of my closest rival, I could hear the announcement over the loudspeakers at the finish line beside the lake in the center of town: "Dr. Ladany of Israel is coming and he's going to win the world championship!" Thousands of people were crowded around the finish line, applauding and shouting congratulations. Despite my excellent time, I was not as exhausted as I had been the two previous times I competed, probably thanks to the modification of the high-carbohydrate diet.

I was presented with a trophy truly worthy of the world champion, a glorious bronze statuette on a green Italian marble base. The medal I received along with it had been specially coined for the championship, with the number 1 in relief, rather than embossed or engraved as usual. Oddly enough, I had competed in this championship three times, and the better I did — moving up from fifth to third to first — the smaller the trophy I was awarded. Maybe the organizers were trying to make it easy for me to cart my prize back home to Israel! After the ceremony, Galitzky took me and the two Shahar brothers, again in Lugano for race-walking week, for a panoramic view of the beautiful city as seen from the mountains above it. It was an incredible sight. I am truly in love with this city, and not just because it is the site of my greatest victory.

The achievement earned me a great deal of publicity in the Swiss and Italian media. Reuven Peleg, who frequently visited Italy, where he had been hidden by an Italian family during World War II, was competing around the same time in a walking event in Castelgandolfo, the home of the papal summer palace outside Rome. Fluent in Italian, he immediately spied an item on the Cento in the popular sports magazine *Corriera dela Sport*, reporting that the Israeli Dr. Ladany had won the world championship. The news agencies wired the item to Israel as well, where it received modest mention in several papers.

On my return to Israel after the championship, I naturally expected representatives of the sports establishment to be on hand to congratulate me on my triumph, but I was in for a bitter disappointment. It goes without saying that no one was there to greet me at the airport. In fact, the only time I had ever been honored by an official reception was when I accompanied the caskets of the murdered sportsmen home from Munich. In place of words of greeting or a congratulatory note, I was met with sobering news that soon brought me back down to earth. The bearer of these tidings was the border policeman who checked my passport and recognized my name. He had read in the paper that the Sports Federation was preparing to bring me up on charges for defying them and competing abroad against their will. A quick glance at the paper confirmed what he said. The report, prominently headlined, made no mention whatsoever of my having won the world title. A few days later I received a summons to appear at the disciplinary board of the Sports Federation.

I arrived at the hearing well prepared. To my surprise, I found Reuven Peleg there, charged with the same infringement for competing in Italy. "He has to suffer," I thought to myself, "just because these blowhards want to get at me. They had no choice but to file charges against him too." Reuven sat down beside me, congratulating me on my victory, which he had read about in Italy. The "trial" was called to order. The "prosecutor" was the very same underling whom Lalkin had wanted to send to Greece instead of me. He was far from a genius — in fact, very far. The tables were arranged in the shape of a large square. The presiding judge sat in the center on the right-hand side, with the prosecutor at the corner opposite us and to our left. When he stood up, he was facing both us and the judge.

He began with me: "Ladany, you are charged with traveling without permission. How do you plead?" If I had entertained any doubt as to his intelligence, he had now laid it to rest. "Not guilty," I replied, "I don't need anyone's permission to travel. I didn't get permission to come here today, either." The prosecutor amended his question: "Do you admit to the charge of traveling abroad without permission?" "Not guilty," I repeated. "Israeli citizens with valid passports are entitled to go abroad at their own discretion, without the need for permission of any kind, except for the consent of the army, which I have here."

The prosecutor mulled over that, scratching his head, and finally came out with: "Do you admit to the charge of going to a competition abroad without permission?" "Not guilty," I said for the third time. "As an Israeli citizen I do not require permission to attend a competition abroad." By this point, the prosecutor had run out of ideas, and even scratching his head didn't seem to help. I decided to come to his aid: "Charge me with entering the competition." His face lit up as he began again: "Do you admit to the charge of competing abroad without permission?" "Not guilty," I said, this time addressing the court. "There's no specific charge here, it's too general."

The judge instructed the prosecutor: "You have to charge him with competing in a specific event without permission." I'm not sure the prosecutor understood the meaning of that big word "specific," but he seemed to grasp that he would have to mention the name of the event. He looked down at the papers in front of him, turning them this way and that, and finally blurted: "You know which event you competed in." It was hard to keep myself from laughing out loud. I made do with a smile as I answered: "I know what I know, but it's you who has to spell out the charges against me." Lost again, he pleaded with me: "Ladany, tell us which competition it was." I knew that if I kept quiet they would simply adjourn the meeting and I would just have to do it all over again at a later date, by which time they would have found someone with a higher IQ to serve as prosecutor. So I helped him out for the second time: "Charge me with competing in, and winning by the way, the 100-kilometer world championship in Lugano, Switzerland."

This breathed new life into the prosecutor. "Do you admit to competing without permission in the 100-kilometer event?" I had no intention of making things so easy for him. "Not guilty! You have to include the full name of this prestigious event in the charges. Charge me with competing in the 100-kilometer world race-walking championship in Lugano." It took him a while to get it all down. Finally, having gotten himself organized, he tried again: "Do you admit to competing without permission in the 100-kilometer world race-walking championship in Lugano?" he declared with a triumphant smile on his face. My answer was terse: "Not guilty."

By now the judge knew who he had for a prosecutor, and decided to address me directly: "You do not admit to competing in this event?" "I admit I competed in the world championship," I explained, "but I do not admit to competing without permission." The judge wasn't going to let me go so easily: "Do you have any proof that you had permission to compete?"

According to an old Arab proverb, he who is bitten by a snake is afraid of ropes. I had learned my lesson from the affair of Greece in 1965, when I was prevented from participating in the marathon because I didn't have an official certificate from the Sports Federation attesting to my amateur status. Every year since, before my first trip abroad, I made sure to obtain this certificate, which entitled me to take part in any and all competitions without restriction. It was a routine procedure, and I never had any trouble getting the necessary document. I had kept them all and brought them with me to the hearing, but I wanted to enjoy the fun a little more, even though I already knew how it was going to end. I handed the judge the certificate I had been issued in 1965 before I went to the States for my doctorate. It bore Lalkin's signature.

The judge examined it, proclaimed: "It's from 1965," and passed it on to the prosecutor, who looked it over and parroted the same words. "Yes, it's from 1965, but there's no time limit," I replied. I let the judge chew over that for a minute or so and then handed him the next document from 1966, which I had obtained when I was in Israel for the Four-Day March that year. One after the other, the judge and the prosecutor declared that this paper was from 1966, and again I explained that it was valid indefinitely. I let another minute pass before remarking that if the judge and the prosecutor enjoyed reading documents, I could offer them another one, even though those I had already presented were still valid. The same procedure was repeated over and over again — and I savored every minute of it — as one by one I presented my certificates of amateur standing from 1967, 1968, 1970, 1971, and finally 1972. When I handed the judge the document from 1972, he turned to the prosecutor: "I would suggest that you drop the charges." Miserably, the prosecutor mouthed: "I hereby drop the charges."

It was now Reuven Peleg's turn. He also had certificates of amateur standing from each year, but he wasn't in the mood for games. When the prosecutor read out the charges, Reuven didn't make him squirm and didn't correct him. He merely stated right away that he was not guilty and handed the judge his latest document from 1972. The judge again recommended that the charges be dropped. With the wisdom of past experience, the prosecutor accepted his advice. The press contained no hint of the Sports Federation's resounding achievement in time wasting and no mention of the results of the proceedings.

Three days letter I received a registered letter informing me that the

Sports Federation had rescinded my credentials and demanded the return of all my documents. I knew they had no legal recourse to compel me to hand them over. I still have them. I cherish them as a reminder of how I tilted at windmills and won. Nevertheless, the sports institutions also flexed their muscles. I was a loose cannon who was not dependent on the Israeli athletic establishment, of which I was contemptuous and against which I repeatedly rebelled. In consequence, my triumph in the 100-kilometer world championship, along with my world record for 50 miles, have never appeared in an official publication of any Israeli athletic authority as a triumph of Israeli sports. Maybe they are right. They were not triumphs of Israeli sports; they were the triumphs of an Israeli athlete who displayed the name of his country with pride, honor, and outstanding success.

During the semester break in February 1973, I was invited by the Zionist Organization of America to give a four-week lecture tour in the States. The idea certainly didn't come from the Sports Federation, which would never have given them my name. Had it been up to them, the ZOA would have used some yes-man who didn't speak a word of English and could thus be counted on not to embarrass them. The ZOA wanted me to talk, in English naturally, about the massacre in Munich. Since I was an unknown quantity to them, they first gave me a "dry run" by simulating a press conference. When I proved that I could reply clearly and coherently even to unexpected questions and could elaborate on my comments, they arranged for my first trial by fire: a television interview. As soon as I passed that test, they kept me busy from early morning to late at night.

There was a press conference, TV or radio interview every day, as well as a talk, whether in the morning, at a luncheon, in the afternoon, or at a dinner affair. My audiences ranged from sympathetic Jewish communities, through cross sections of the American population, to university students. The day I took off from New York at five in the morning, gave a breakfast talk to a small group in Rochester, a luncheon speech to a larger audience in Buffalo, and addressed a dinner function in Cleveland, I began to understand what it means to campaign for president. In those four weeks I spoke in twenty different states, from Florida in the south to New York, Massachusetts, and Illinois in the north, and as far west as Iowa, Missouri and New Mexico.

I was usually accompanied by a ZOA press officer who was highly professional, virtually a master at his job. After viewing my first simulated press conference, he prepared dozens of articles about me, all illustrated with photographs, and each different. He didn't even use the same picture twice. Wherever I appeared, he shoved the articles into the hands of reporters. All they had to do was affix their name and collect their fee without any effort or footwork on their part. I wish the large public affairs division of my university had a fraction of that press officer's enterprise and success in getting its write-ups into the press. Thanks to him, I was the subject of hundreds of different items, and a good many others he had nothing to do with that were generated by the dynamics of the media industry and the competition between rival papers. The press dubbed me "survivor" or "witness," and referred to Israel as "a country maintaining its involvement in sports in memory of the slain athletes."

In all my talks I made a point of asserting that our departure from Munich was a psychological victory for the terrorists, the product of emotion triumphing over logic, and that we should have remained in Munich to maintain a symbolic presence at the games. I spoke of my impression of the amateurish efforts of the German police and the lack of initiative that results from instilling blind obedience in its citizens. I suggested imposing an international embargo on Libya and Syria, which had given refuge to the assassins taken alive after the massacre, and recommended their banishment from the Olympic movement.

In the midst of my lecture tour, the Israeli Air Force brought down a Libyan plane that had entered Israeli air space and refused to respond to instructions. I conscientiously defended Israel's position, although I had no inkling of the official government or foreign office line. I explained, debating Jewish Americans unfamiliar with Israel's security problems, that we could not afford to take the sort of risks that a world power like the US could incur. I must have been pretty persuasive. The Chicago press adopted my position in their reports of the interception of the Libyan plane. I felt very like an Israeli ambassador or information officer, helping them to understand our fight for survival as an independent sovereign state aspiring to live in peace with its neighbors.

Telegrams arrived from Globinsky and the US Committee for Sports in Israel threatening to "take action" against me for my remarks regarding our departure from Munich and demanding that I leave reference to the affair to the officials "authorized to comment on it." Long before I considered Globinsky senile, I never believed him capable of rational analysis even stone sober. Moreover, I did not believe that political foot soldiers rewarded with posts in the sports institutions were the only people authorized to express a personal opinion. Needless to say, I continued to present my own views in public.

On one occasion I did verbal battle with a New York rabbi who disagreed with my sentiments on sports and attacked my view that the German government had acknowledged its responsibility for the security of the Israeli hostages in Munich and made sincere efforts to attain their release, including its duplicitous negotiations with the terrorists.

Every now and then someone would approach me before or after my talk and tell me they had seen me walking in Israel or competing in the States or in Munich. Invariably, they shook my hand, congratulating me on coming through the massacre alive and wishing me luck in my future athletic endeavors. It was very heartwarming.

The frenzy over security and fear for my safety were strongly in evidence throughout the tour. There was considerable concern that I might be attacked while addressing a mass audience at Illinois University with its several hundred Arab students. Both during that talk and everywhere I went, I was under heavy guard: uniformed policemen, plainclothes cops, university guards, activists from the Jewish Defense League, and members of the ZOA. The German students were also offended by my portrayal and assessment of the affair, and protesting loudly. In fact, security officers were present at all times and whenever I appeared.

With so much traveling and speaking, I had almost no time to train, and actually felt physically ill from the lack of exercise. I tried hard to convince the organizers to give me a little time "to breathe" — in my terms, to train. Finally, I got a few free hours in Philadelphia. I went out walking on the bank of the Schuylkill River, along the boardwalk between the Vester Boat Club and the second rail bridge. I had competed on the same route several times when I was at Columbia. In lieu of a locker room, we had changed in the shed of the Vester Rowing Club, whose president was the brother of Princess

Grace of Monaco and later the head of the American Olympic Committee. After two hours or so, my police bodyguards asked me to stop; the engine of their car had overheated because they had to drive so slowly.

Landing in New Orleans was a particularly disconcerting experience. The plane was taxiing on the ground when it came to a halt before it reached the gate where the sleeve to the terminal could be hooked up. A convoy of police cars with flashing lights drove up and came to a stop by the plane. Steps were rolled up to the door and a local sheriff in full uniform, including revolver and handcuffs, stepped inside and demanded. "Which one of you is Dr. Ladany?" I raised my hand. The eyes of every single passenger turned to stare at me. They must have thought I was some criminal who was going to be arrested, or at the very least a stool pigeon about to give state's evidence in a Mafia trial. The sheriff ordered me roughly, "Get your things and come with me!" I got into the police car.

The regional ZOA point man was already inside. He was an Israeli, and it was he who had organized this "reception" to ensure my safety. I was assigned three cops, two of them in plainclothes, who did not leave my side for the whole time I was in the city. When I had a free hour, I got their consent to go out for some exercise. I was guarded by two police cars, one in front and one behind. Afterwards, the cops complained to the ZOA official. At one point I had passed through a park and gone behind a tree to relieve myself, but given the circumstances they had been forced to turn a blind eye and not ticket me for this act, illegal in New Orleans. Now they were afraid of being reprimanded for that dereliction of duty.

South Africa, fearing it would be banned from the Olympic games and other international athletic forums for maintaining its policy of apartheid even in sports, decided to organize a large-scale athletic display arranged by event. The track and field events were scheduled for April 1973 in the capital of Pretoria. Athletes and influential officials from all over the world were invited, regardless of race or color. For the first time, non-white South Africans would be allowed to compete and to share accommodations with white athletes. They were hoping to create the impression that there was no racial discrimination in South African sports, an attempt to forestall their expulsion from the international arena.

Three Israelis were invited to attend: the hurdler Esther Shahamorov, myself for the 20-kilometer walk, and an escort. I had become friendly with the outstanding black South African race walker Eddy Michael when he took second place at the London to Brighton Walk. He had told me how hard it was to be a black athlete under apartheid. Even without this advance knowledge, the diffidence of the nonwhite South African athletes quartered with the whites for the duration of the games made it obvious that this "equality" was only temporary camouflage and not a customary practice.

I was in poor form. The lecture tour in the States had had extremely adverse effects on my physical condition. I had also been training less and devoting more time to research at the university. The day after my picture appeared in the local papers in Pretoria and Johannesburg, I received a visit from the British military attaché in South Africa, who came to wish me well. He was the same man who had once been posted to Israel and used to go horseback riding in the National Park in Ramat Gan with Chief of Staff General Haim Bar-Lev when I was training there. Reluctantly, he conceded that I moved faster than his horse. I was dying to remark that horseback riding was excellent exercise — for the horse — but I used restraint and kept my thoughts to myself. Still, it was very nice to see him again, a man whose stay in Israel had made him a true friend of the country.

Pretoria is over 7000 feet above sea level, generating the same problems encountered at the Mexico City Olympics. I trained hard, but I knew I had no chance of putting in a good performance; my poor conditioning, the altitude, and the relatively short distance of 20 kilometers would all be working against me. Following instructions, I did most of my training in an isolated park. Here I could be closely guarded, and it was the assessment of the local police that there was less chance of my coming to harm in the park than in the city. A plainclothes detective drove behind me in an unmarked car, and another one, with a gun hanging from his waist, ran alongside me. Every few minutes the two of them switched places; neither could run for very long at the pace I was walking.

Their presence impeded my training, forcing me to go more slowly than I would have liked. At one point, when the cop running with me started to lag behind and the car was a little farther back than usual, I seized the opportunity to pick up the pace and give them the slip. I was finally free, and convinced that my best protection was my speed. Eventually the two detectives found me on a side road in the same large park. Despite their relief at finding me safe and sound, they were furious. I could understand how they felt, but for a while there I had enjoyed our game of hide and seek.

Bernhard Kanenberg, the winner of the 50-kilometer walk in Munich, was also there. As soon as we saw each other, we gave one another a bear hug; it's so good to run into old friends. He won the competition in South Africa, too, while I came in seventh, better than I had expected, all things considered. As I was waiting to board the plane back home, I noticed that Krugerrands were being sold freely at the Jan Smuts Airport in Johannesburg. The one-ounce gold coins cost thirty-eight dollars, whereas the price of an ounce of gold at the time was thirty-five dollars. I weighed the idea of buying one as a souvenir, but finally decided that it wasn't worth the 10 percent premium. I've always been aware that real estate prices, exchange rates, and the price of precious metals are unpredictable, but this was really brought home to me when the international price of gold soared to three hundred dollars an ounce not long afterwards.

After my return to Israel in April 1973, I continued my light training routine, with most of my time occupied by the university. The Three-Day March was generally held during the Passover vacation in the spring, and 1973 would have been my seventeenth straight year. However, in view of the fact that the march had been rained out the year before, the army decided to reschedule the event for the Succoth holiday in the early autumn. Meanwhile, my friend and rival Reuven Peleg beat me out in two events in the Hefer Valley near the kibbutz where he lived, causing a sensation trumpeted in eye-catching headlines in the Israeli press. The blow to my ego drove me to start training seriously again.

The next Maccabiah Games, slated for July 1973, were already on the horizon. After two months of rigorous training, including distance walks of up to fifty kilometers as well as speed work, I was back in top form. In fact, I even won the Israeli 50-kilometer championship in better time than my result

at the Olympics. I avoided Reuven during training, and he didn't compete in
the 50-kilometer championship.

The next time we met up was at a 20-kilometer event. Leery of what he
could do, I let him take the lead. That turned out to be a wise move. About
halfway through, I picked up the pace, summoning the last of my strength to
catch up with him. Within a short while, I had pulled in front, building up a
one-minute lead. I knew I had to lengthen that gap to prevent Reuven from
getting the better of me in the final sprint to the finish line. But I had no
power left. As a matter of fact, I even considered quitting, but I couldn't let
myself do that; I was determined not to throw in the towel. I managed to
stretch my lead to two and a half minutes. The route described a rectangle
around the town hall, a circuit we repeated over and over again, giving me the
chance to watch Reuven out of the corner of my eye and remain constantly
aware of our relative positions. I could see he was also tiring. He gave it one
last supreme effort and started to close the gap between us, but I wouldn't let
him catch me. I gritted my teeth and kept pushing. I came in first, with
Reuven two minutes behind. My self-confidence was restored.

My battle to convince the steering committee of the Maccabiah Games to
include the Olympic race-walking events would surely have failed had Itzhak
Braz not joined forces with me. Thanks to his consent to take charge of organization, and even more so, his distinguished status in the Maccabi movement, substantially bolstered by the popularity of the marches he arranged,
the games would now include 20- and 50-kilometer walks. Braz and I went
off to locate and measure out an appropriate route through Yarkon Park.

July 1973. This was to be my third straight time in the Maccabiah Games.
Tal Brody, a prominent basketball player, was given the honor of carrying the
torch at the opening ceremony and lighting the flame. Since Israeli sports
were still overshadowed by the massacre in Munich, it was decided that he
would be accompanied by two survivors who would run alongside him in
memory of the eleven who had lost their lives. Esther Shahamorov and I were
selected. I was warned to run, not walk, and I promised to comply. Esther and
I entered the stadium with Brody, keeping by his side until he reached the
bottom of the stairs leading up to the flame.

The 50-kilometer race was the first walking event. It began at 1:30 in the
afternoon in blazing heat. I had arranged for several friends and the kids
from Ramat Efal to help all the competitors by handing out drinks and

sponges throughout the race. My sister Marta and her daughter Irit assisted me, while Shosh watched Danit and Marta's two sons. We started out at the Maccabiah stadium in Ramat Gan, and then followed the road until we entered Yarkon Park, where we lapped the circuit over and over again. The assistants were spread out along the course, offering ice cold drinks and sponges soaked in ice water every few yards. The ice water helped to make the extreme heat and high humidity more tolerable. I led from the word go, and never looked back.

The British walker Roy Posner was behind me. Steadily, I increased my lead until I finished as the unrivaled winner in 4:23, despite the hellish heat. Under better conditions, I would have clocked in much faster. Roy took second place, over twenty minutes behind me. My resounding victory made a strong impression on both the spectators and the press.

My triumph in the 50-kilometer walk frightened off a number of rivals who withdrew from the 20-kilometer event scheduled for three days later. This is exactly what is meant by the term "psychological victory." Reuven Peleg, however, had not entered the 50-kilometer event, so he was still fresh. He hadn't perspired like I had, hadn't lost the huge quantity of salts that are so hard to replace in just three days. He was also the favorite going in. Everyone, including all the reporters and sports officials, was betting on him to win. Still, I decided to put on a good show and prove who had the upper hand.

The route was the same as for the 50-kilometer event, except that we had to do fewer laps in the park. This time we took off around five in the afternoon. It was still hot, but not so blazingly unbearable. Again we began in the stadium. Reuven took the lead, without any interference from me. Toward the end of the second lap around the stadium, before we left for the long leg of the race outside, I picked up my pace and reversed the order. Now I had the lead, and I held on to it to the finish line. By the time we were on our way back from the park, I knew I was already a few hundred yards in front. Nevertheless, I didn't want any surprises at the very end, so I pushed even harder and increased my lead.

Back in the stadium, we had to complete less than two laps. As the first to reenter the stadium, I belied all predictions. I started the first lap with no rivals in sight, not even Reuven. The crowd roared encouragement. I was sopping wet from the water I'd splashed over my body, making my wet bloomers glisten. Although I had sweated profusely and could certainly feel it, that wasn't what the spectators saw. Still, they mistakenly assumed that I was soaked in perspiration, and cheered even louder. By the time Reuven entered the stadium, I had almost reached the finish line.

I was thirty-seven years old, and heard the announcer declare: "Ladany is always Ladany. Age doesn't make any difference to him." The evening TV news that night included a long piece reviewing my triumphs. A week later I was the subject of a special edition of "Outstanding Maccabiah Games Achievements." An article on the games in one of the papers stated: "We are looking forward to seeing 'young' Dr. Ladany do even better in the next Maccabiah Games." I remembered that statement when I brought home a gold medal in the 1977 games as well.

I'm not the one to say how successful my ZOA lecture tour of the States was, but in the summer of 1973 I was approached by Israel Bonds and asked to come to New York for three days on short notice. I accepted their offer. I was to address two groups of businesspeople in different fields in an effort to get them to buy Israel development bonds. The first group was in the underwear and brassiere trade, and the second in wine and alcoholic beverages. The organizers knew I had no specialist knowledge of panties or bras, except for my wife's, but they were concerned that I might say something damaging to the second forum. They made it very clear to me that it was nobody's business if I abstained from liquor, just as long as I didn't even hint at that fact in front of the honorable members of the industry. I kept my part of the bargain.

The Tel Aviv University School of Business Administration where I had been teaching for five years was home to a diverse collection of individuals. The founder of the school and its first dean was Yair Aharoni, who had been my professor in a graduate course in cost accounting at the Hebrew University. He was a dynamic, efficient man, and it was generally believed that the full professorship he was awarded was not in recognition of his research, which is usually the case, but of the excellent job he did in setting up the school.

When I joined the faculty, I was pleasantly surprised to find Pini Shwinger, an old high school classmate, already on the staff. I had attended a farewell party for him in 1957 before he left for the States to study either medicine or mechanical engineering. Now I discovered that he had a PhD in business administration. Pini was a fine teacher and an outstanding adminis-trator/entrepreneur, with little interest in research or publications. He claimed that "one hundred people see a research paper, ten read it, and two understand it." We became close friends and collaborated on consulting jobs.

Teddy Weinshal was the oldest member of the faculty, an exceptional lecturer and popular teacher. There's something intriguing about the fact that with a degree in mechanical engineering and experience as a production engineer, he eventually opted for the field of organizational behavior and became a harsh critic of the whole quantitative realm he started out in. Beyond this, however, he was often charged by fellow members of his new field with living up to the old college joke about the way conclusions are drawn and theories developed, sometimes on the basis of a single observa-tion. A researcher wanted to study the behavior of the grasshopper. "Jump," he said to the grasshopper, and the grasshopper jumped. The scientist noted in his log book: "A six-legged grasshopper can jump." Then he pulled one leg off the insect and again instructed him to jump. The grasshopper jumped. The scientist noted: "A five-legged grasshopper can jump." The researcher pulled off another leg and again ordered it: "Jump!" The grasshopper jumped. The scientist noted: "A four-legged grasshopper can jump." He continued to remove the grasshopper's legs one by one and the grasshopper continued to jump, even with only two legs left. When the scientist broke off the fifth leg and repeated his instruction, the bug did not respond. The scientist wrote down his conclusion: "A one-legged grasshopper loses its sense of hearing." Sad to say, this is a very good illustration of how conclusions are drawn in a great many studies, although it is a well-known fact that grasshoppers do hear through their legs.

One member of the faculty towered over the others in terms of intelli-gence and analytic ability. He was Avraham Beja, who had also started out as a mechanical engineer, and via statistics and operations research became an expert on theoretical models of finance. Any conversation with him brought to mind the story about how President Truman wanted his aides to find him a one-armed financial advisor. When asked why he needed a crippled advisor, he explained that he was tired of people always saying "on the one hand" and gesturing with their right hand, and then "on the other hand," gesturing with their left. Beja exemplified this sort of behavior. Whatever the subject of discussion, he invariably spelled out convincing arguments for one course of action, and then in the same breath and with the same fervor, supplied the equally convincing arguments for doing exactly the opposite. Despite his genius, he had the habits of an unweaned baby, always holding a handkerchief which he sucked on periodically as he talked.

The publicity I enjoyed as a result of my athletic activities was a thorn in the side of many of my colleagues. I could sense they were envious. Ze'ev Hirsch, the dean who replaced Yair Aharoni, was a classic economist. He informed me I would have to decide which I liked better, sports or the academic world. I gathered he was referring to how I spent my time and not my likes and dislikes. I told him it was a choice I had made long ago: "I like sports better, but I do everything in my power to fulfill all the commitments of my academic career." He couldn't hide his envy when he related what his son had said: "Daddy, you may be Ladany's boss, but I think Ladany's more important than you." I had to smile at his pronouncement that "Patents do not indicate creativity and innovation." Supposedly, he was trying to imply that the height of creativity and innovation was the "extraordinary" work he did by applying routine regression analysis to the export figures of different countries, systematically repeating the same standard calculations over and over again.

During my five years at Tel Aviv University, fourteen of my articles appeared in distinguished scientific journals, I was granted four American patents, edited two dictionaries of statistical terms published by the Institute for Productivity, and published ten additional studies in professional journals. Presumably, it had all been done as a "hobby" in the free time I had left over from sports. Quite satisfied with my scientific output, I decided to take a sabbatical.

Before I left, I wanted to find a good home for the Ramat Efal boys I had nurtured. I appealed to nearly every track and field coach in the center of the country, explaining that these were talented kids with tremendous enthusiasm for the sport who were willing to devote considerable time and effort to training and competition. Nearly all of them could be champions when they grew up, if their potential were properly developed. To my surprise, my request fell on deaf ears. No one was interested. Some of the coaches claimed to have enough athletes to look out for and didn't want any more, while others responded that coaching race walkers demanded a great deal of time and attention and they weren't looking for youngsters who required so much work. I couldn't find a single coach willing to take them under his wing.

As a result, when I went on sabbatical, the children were left with no guiding hand and no moving spirit, and they simply stopped training. Not only did none of them ever become an active athlete, but Israel lost a reserve of potential race-walking champions. Every now and then I run into one of them at some short march or other, and it always warms my heart to see that he still carries a tiny spark of the love for walking. It was hard to say good-bye to them. I was very touched when they gave me a pen with my name engraved on it as a farewell gift.

Thanks to my impressive victories at the Maccabiah Games, the Track and Field Committee decided to send me to the 50-kilometer walk in Norway at the end of August 1973. They even approved travel expenses for the London to Brighton Walk to be held a few days later. Reuven was also sent to Europe to compete. Since it was common knowledge that I was going to the States for a sabbatical in September, I was notified that they would only cover the cost of the stopover in Norway between Israel and London, as I would be flying to the US through London anyway. That decision might have been justified had they covered my previous travel expenses, but it was no secret that in former years about half the cost of my trips to foreign competitions had come out of my own pocket.

Consequently, I unhesitatingly told them a bare-faced lie, claiming that after these events I would be returning to Israel to collect Shosh and Danit and only then flying to the States. They had no choice but to take me at my word and agree to cover the full cost of the trip, as they were doing for Reuven. Thus I was able to recoup a small part of the huge expenses I had incurred by competing abroad all those years.

I still had one more thing to take care of before I left. I had resolved to do it a long time before, in the Olympic year when I was so offended by the treatment I received from my own club and its refusal to help me. The regulations of the Sports Federation contain a de facto ban on resigning from a club without first getting that club's permission. Otherwise, the athlete is interdicted for two years. This means not only being forbidden to join any other club for

that period of time, but also being forbidden to enter any competition organized by the Sports Federation or held under its aegis. In practical terms,
interdiction means that an athlete cannot compete in any event for two years,
including the national championships. Obviously, no athlete who remains
idle for so long can be expected to return to competition. Therefore, for most
people this regulation connotes a choice between maintaining membership
in a club with which they are dissatisfied or retiring from sports. But I am not
most people.

I knew that while I was on sabbatical I would join the AAU and one of the
American sports clubs, which would entitle me to enter any competition in
the world, notwithstanding the interdiction of the Israeli Sports Federation.
So I decided to give Maccabi Tel Aviv a very public, demonstrative slap in the
face. In the six and a half years I had been a member of the club, I had represented Israel in two Olympics, set a new world record, won the world championship, won the national titles of Belgium, Switzerland, and the US, as well
as Israel, and garnered four gold medals at the Maccabiah Games. In that
whole time, all I had gotten from them was one trip to a European competition, one sweat suit, one shirt, and twenty dollars in living expenses. Exactly
one day before I left the country, I submitted my resignation and incurred
interdiction. It would take effect two weeks later. By that time, the European
competitions I was about to enter would already be over.

I flew to Bergen, Norway. The name bothered me a little, sounding too
much like Bergen-Belsen, but the place was exquisite, a real gem. Reuven
Peleg arrived and we shared a room in a small hotel. I didn't get a lot of training in, but I was still in fine shape from the run-up to the Maccabiah Games.
We both competed in the 50-kilometer walk; I took gold. Our official host
was Kjell Lund, a race walker himself who trained along with us, taking us to
places where we could enjoy the beautiful views of Bergen. One day we
climbed a steep path into the high mountains north of Bergen Bay. Normal
people take the funicular railway. For us, that climb was just the start. We kept
going until we reached a large anchor high in the mountains.

During World War II, a German ship used to transport heavy water had
been anchored in Bergen harbor and was blown up by the Norwegian underground in an attempt to sabotage the Nazi nuclear weapon program. To ward
off this very possibility, the Germans had demonstrably filled the ship with
Norwegian citizens who were then killed in the explosion. It must have been

a tremendous blast for the anchor to be thrown so high and to have cost so many lives. I saw the Hollywood version of the incident, too. When I visited Bergen twenty-two years later and wanted to show Shosh the anchor, I had trouble finding anyone who had ever heard of it or could tell me where in the mountains it was located. I guess the Norwegians would prefer to forget the whole controversial affair.

I parted company with Reuven and flew to London. The London to Brighton Walk took place on the first weekend in September. I had arranged for assistance from Nissim Kiviti, a sportscaster with the Israel Broadcasting Authority who was posted in England for a year. He was as bald as me; he too combed his hair with a towel. The format of the race, as well as the start signal, remained unchanged, as did the route. By now it was an old friend, and I knew how to save steps. Nissim did an excellent job, assisting me efficiently and wholeheartedly. Although this was his first experience of a long-distance race-walking competition, he understood what an athlete needs.

The race also had a familiar ending: veni, vidi, vici! I had the good fortune to score a psychological victory as soon as I appeared at the starting line. Since my rivals already knew what I could do at such long distances, no one fought me for the lead. Out in front on my own, I finished far ahead of the second-place winner without having to grit my teeth and dig in too deep. The lack of pressure also told in my time: it was excellent — under eight hours — albeit two minutes slower than the year before. I enjoyed the chance to renew my acquaintance with bath number 1. By this time, the British walkers were accustomed to watching as I was handed the winner's trophy.

The Longest Day:

From the 100-Mile Championship to the Yom Kippur War

When I arrived in New York for the start of my sabbatical year in early September 1973, there was a surprise waiting for me at customs. The insulated jug I was holding caught the eye of the customs officer, who wanted to know the nature of this strange article, not the sort of thing people ordinarily carry with them off a plane. I explained I used it for cold water and ice during a race. He asked to see the customs declaration I had filled out. After glancing through it and noting the items I had listed, he scrutinized my face. Finally, he asked: "Aren't you the race walker who set the world record for 50 miles?" I was astounded. Scores of people knew me in Israel, or had at least heard my name, but I hadn't expected anyone to recognize me in New York. It turned out he was a devoted fan of athletics who had read about my achievements and remembered my name.

By now I was very familiar with New York, and knew exactly where I wanted to live. I had already looked into the possibilities during my short trip to the States for Israel Bonds just over a month earlier. By chance, on that occasion I had run into my friend and colleague at Tel Aviv University, Micha Perry, who was also coming to New York on sabbatical, and we had gone together to check out a large apartment house in Riverdale. Riverdale is part of the Bronx, just over the bridge from Manhattan. Situated between Van Cortland Park — where I had often trained and competed — and the Hudson River, it was isolated from the rest of the Bronx with its seedy reputation. As a result, most of the residents listed their address as "Riverdale, New York," preferring to omit the designation "Bronx."

I rented an apartment on the sixteenth floor in one of the three buildings in the Skyview complex. The twenty-two-story building stood on a hill near the river, so that one window offered a view of the imposing Palisades cliffs across the river, and another looked out on the stately George Washington Bridge linking Manhattan and New Jersey. I had to wait two days before I could move in, so in the meantime I was the guest of Hilde and Henry Laskau. Hilde had never competed in a race-walking event, but her whole life centered around the sport. She accompanied Henry to every single race, even in pouring rain and wind, and often served as an official. Even on those occasions when only Henry was an officially accredited judge, she never made any secret of her opinion as to who deserved a warning or who should be disqualified. In fact, she had acquired such expertise in the sport that a lot of people addressed her as "chief judge," whether out of respect for her skills or in jest I couldn't say.

Within two days I had the whole apartment furnished. Micha Perry lent a hand, helping me to cart a large sofa inside. He had taken an apartment two floors above us. By the time Shosh arrived with Danit, everything was in place. Shosh didn't waste any time getting started on her endocrinological research at the Columbia University School of Medicine, in the same lab where she had worked before. I was in a new environment at the Baruch College of the City University of New York, but there were two old friends there who had done their doctorates at Columbia at the same time as I had, and I collaborated on two new studies with one of them.

I renewed my membership in the Long Island Athletic Club, the new name of Howie Jacobson's Long Island Track Club which I had joined in the summer of 1970. Howie must have had some good reason for changing the name, although I can't imagine what it was, since everything else remained the same. The club was still home to the same race walkers I remembered. On Sundays when there was no competition, we trained together at Kings Point or somewhere else on Long Island. On Saturdays, I went out for distance training with John Markon. Both of us were hoping to compete in the 100-mile walk that had officially been named the US championship several years before. I was all fired up with the passion to become a Centurion, especially with the memory of my abortive attempt at the honor in 1967 still very fresh in my mind.

John and I followed our old familiar route north along the Hudson, but since we were now starting out in Riverdale, we made it a good bit farther than Tarrytown. The first time we went out, I stopped to buy a Coke from the machine at a gas station. When the manager saw me, he came over. "It's been a while since I've seen you training out here," he said. I didn't bother to explain where I'd been for the three years since I'd last walked this route in the summer of 1970, but merely announced, "I'm back." Within two weeks, we had lengthened our distance to around sixty miles. I managed to get another long-distance practice in during the week as well. On other days, I only did ten miles or so. In terms of speed, I was far from the level I had achieved that summer, only a few months before, but the ultra-long-distance training did wonders for my stamina and endurance.

The 100-mile championship traditionally takes place in Columbia, Missouri, from noon Saturday to noon Sunday. Monday was Columbus Day, a holiday in New York, so I planned to leave on Friday, October 4, 1973, and get back the following Monday, October 7. I left my car at LaGuardia, and after changing planes in St. Louis, arrived in Columbia early Friday evening. John Markon was with me. From New York I had called Joe Duncan, the inveterate organizer of the competition, from New York about a place to stay and he had referred me to my friend Larry Young who was in Columbia for a while. As soon as we landed I got in touch with him.

Larry was from Kansas and was studying sculpture. He would soon be leaving for Italy to continue his studies, but meanwhile he was working as the superintendent of a complex of buildings with apartments for rent. We hadn't seen each other since Munich. He looked just the same, although he claimed he didn't do much training. That didn't surprise me. It had taken a lot out of him in terms of self-sacrifice and time to reach the stage where he took the bronze at Mexico City and Munich. He assured me that, although he would be entering the competition and starting out with everyone else, he would only walk the first ten miles.

Larry gave us the use of one of the empty apartments in his charge and promised to pick us up the next morning at eleven o'clock to drive us to the starting line. He told us he was putting other walkers up too. That apartment was among the most pleasant accommodations I had ever enjoyed, and it didn't even cost me anything. John and I each had our own room, so we didn't have to alter our pre-competition routine or stay up late chatting with hosts. My alarm went off at 7:30 Saturday morning so I could eat my last meal four hours before the competition and give my body enough time to digest it.

John and I were in place by 11:30. It was the same stadium that had been used for the race six years before. I made last-minute arrangements with the officials, asking them to hand me the food and drinks I had prepared the next lap after I signaled for them. This was the first time in my life that I would be walking 100 miles — about 161 kilometers, more than three times as long as my usual event. Obviously, for such a distance I would have to ingest some solid food and couldn't rely solely on liquids, so in addition to my regular repertoire of drinks and glucose, I had brought along slices of bread spread thickly with jam and sandwiches with thick slices of boiled potatoes stuck between the bread. As a matter of course, everything was generously laced with salt.

I also took into account that I might have to change my shirt, shoes, or socks, and might have to rub more Vaseline on myself in the sensitive places. Accordingly, I had prepared a bag with a change of clothes and all the other equipment I might need. I left it by the side of the track and explained to the officials the sort of odd requests I might be expected to make. My requirements neither surprised nor alarmed them. In the six years that John Duncan and his group of volunteers had been organizing this twenty-four-hour event, they had encountered most of the problems and idiosyncratic demands that were likely to arise.

There were about forty of us at the starting line. It was perfectly clear to everyone there that only a very few would actually complete four hundred laps of the track in twenty-four hours and be declared Centurions. To this day, only nine men in the United States have ever won that title, and only six of them are still alive. A lot of the contenders were not experienced walkers and were only there for the challenge. I didn't expect them to go the distance, despite the slow pace; they would probably quit after twenty or thirty miles. The large majority of competitors, including the experienced race walkers, would drop out somewhere between fifty and a hundred miles.

As for me, I was not only in better shape than when I had made my previous attempt in 1967, but I was also older and wiser. I could easily figure that a pace of twelve minutes a mile, the equivalent of five miles an hour, would mean that I would complete the hundred miles in twenty hours. I hoped to be able to keep up that level of exertion, or maybe even do it in less than twenty hours. I also knew it didn't matter whether or not I did the first fifty miles in good time. On the contrary, if I took the first half too fast, it might hurt my chances of becoming a Centurion. Taking all this into consideration, I decided to start out at a speed of eleven and a half minutes a mile. If I could maintain that pace, I would finish in 19:10.

A good many others did the same calculations and set themselves the goal of 14.24 minutes a mile or a little under that, the average speed needed to complete the distance in precisely twenty-four hours. Others, less experienced, rushed forward from the start when they were still feeling fresh. I wasn't intimidated by any of my rivals. Larry Young, who was already a Centurion, might have been a cause for concern, but I knew that despite his fast start he would be dropping out after ten miles. He is a very decent man, and I had no fear that he was trying to pull a fast one on me, nor had I ever encountered deceit of that kind among race walkers.

For the first three hours it was very hot. I kept up the pace I had set for myself. Larry withdrew from the arena after an hour and a half. The younger inexperienced walkers who had started out fast had had to slow down, and, in fact, were already going even slower than I was. Despite my low speed, I was now the fastest one on the track, still moving at the pace I had decided on in advance. I kept overtaking slower competitors, gaining as much as a lap or more on some of them. Each time I went by, they told me how many times I had already passed them. A couple were holding small transistors and listening to music. I can't concentrate with the sound of music buzzing in my ear all the time, but there are a lot of athletes who enjoy the diversion of songs or any other kind of entertainment they can catch on the radio.

About three hours from the start, when I passed John Markon, he told me he had heard on someone else's radio that there was fighting in Israel. He didn't know the details. A half hour or so later, I caught up with one of the walkers carrying a radio. I slowed down and asked him what he had heard. He didn't know anything more. I resumed my steady pace. Thirty minutes later I was alongside the other man with a radio. He hadn't heard anything at all. An hour went by, and I had again caught up with the first of the radio owners. He hadn't heard anything new in the meantime. I figured he must have misunderstood the original news item. An hour later, I was alongside him for the third time. He told me a war had broken out in Israel. I assumed it was a border skirmish like many others before it, and the local radio station just didn't understand the difference between that kind of engagement and a real war. Only a week before, the Israeli Air Force had downed six Syrian fighter planes in a similar border incident. I slowed down and kept pace with him, but for as long as I was there, the radio station chose to play music.

When I had had enough, I picked up the pace again. The next time I was alongside him an hour later, he told me he had again heard the report of a war in Israel. Again I slowed down, hoping they would repeat the item so I could "read between the lines" of the rural broadcast and get some idea of what was really going on. But it was only music for now. I left behind the slow-moving radio and resumed my pace. When I passed the second radio owner again, he told me he had also heard brief mention of a war in Israel. Although I was still convinced the small-town station was just blowing a border skirmish out of proportion, a tiny doubt was beginning to seep in.

After considering the possibilities for some time as I completed several more laps, I imagined I had a certain take on the situation. If war had actually broken out without warning, it must have happened on Yom Kippur, the holiest day in the Jewish calendar, when the Israeli radio and television were off the air. That would make it hard to mobilize the reserves, who constituted the lion's share of IDF troops, and the country might be in very serious trouble. I needed more information.

Not trusting the small-town radio station, I stopped beside an official and asked him to make a collect call to Shosh in New York, giving him the number of our apartment in Riverdale. It was two hours before he got back. His repeated attempts to reach Shosh had failed. I guess the radio report had really gotten to me. I had given him the wrong number. It was new to me, so I couldn't yet recite it off automatically, and now I was too upset to remember it at all. I asked him to please go back to the pay phone and get the number from information in New York. Luckily, it wasn't unlisted.

Knowing I was an Israeli and understanding my concern, he agreed graciously. Maybe he was also influenced by the fact that I was leading the competition. I kept walking as if nothing was going on. An hour later he was back. He told me he had spoken to Shosh who had asked him to give me this message: "Everything's under control. Keep walking!" I don't know whether Shosh was not yet aware of the true situation, and like every other Israeli she dismissed the reports from Egypt as wild exaggerations, or whether she was remembering the two weeks during the Six-Day War when she didn't know if I was alive or dead. Whichever it was, her message put my worst fears to rest and I continued the race untroubled.

Around dusk, it started to rain. The heat that had built up inside my body from the effort offset the cold, and although the rain itself was driving and unpleasant, it didn't interfere with the race. The officials pulled tarps over our bags beside the track to keep them dry. However, we were walking on a cinder track, and it didn't take long until lane 1, the inside lane, and then 2 and part of 3, were under two to three inches of water. Either there were no drain pipes, or they were clogged. There was no way we could use lanes 1 and 2, so we all had to take 3 and 4. That meant that each lap was at least eleven and a half yards longer. Not only that, but the lanes that weren't under water also presented a good many difficulties. The cinder track was old, so that the rain turned the top layer of cinders and dust into slippery mud. With every step, my foot slipped backwards a little, and the thick mud seeped into my shoe and splattered on the back of my leg.

I was also having the same problem you get when you drive in the rain. The front of my leg — right up to the pelvis — was soon covered in the mud tossed up by the walkers in front of me. After less than thirty minutes in these conditions, my legs were completely black from the thick layer of goo that had been splashed on them, and my shoes looked like clods of mud themselves. I could feel the thick wet muck oozing between my toes and under my feet, and I kept having to wipe it off my glasses with my shirt so I could see where I was going.

The rain kept up for several hours with varying intensity, only letting up after midnight. It took a few more hours for the wind to dry the water from the outer lanes. The mud hardening inside my shoes gradually went from being a plain nuisance to being an intolerable nuisance, as the pain in the soles of my feet got worse and worse until it was so sharp I couldn't take it any more. As I passed the tables of food and drinks, I asked the officials to place my bag on the bench nearby, parallel to the track, and to get me two buckets of water. By the time I completed another lap, everything I had asked for was waiting for me. I angled off the track, sat down on the bench, and stuck one foot, with the shoe still on, into a bucket so I could get my shoe and sock off. Then I washed the whole leg down. I used the other bucket to rinse off the finer dirt, and then changed my shoe. Within a few short minutes I had repeated the process on the second leg and changed my clothes as well.

When I changed my shoes, I noticed the large number of great big blisters, some of them bloody, for which the mud was wholly, or at least partly, to blame. As soon as I changed clothes, they really started to hurt. But I felt much better when I got back on the track. I had rid myself of the extra weight of the mud, and was floating on air, although maintaining a legal walking style. For the first time in my life, I thoroughly appreciated the story of the rabbi who told the poor man who griped to him about his cramped living conditions to bring a goat into the house. When the man came back to complain that the goat had only made matters worse, the rabbi told him to take the animal back outside. Suddenly the house seemed much more roomy.

The event was a tremendous strain on the muscles. By around three-quarters of the distance, every single muscle in my body ached. The discomfort caused by the blisters was also getting worse, so that the saying: "a long-distance walker needs good teeth — so he can grit them" was proving very true. I was in the lead, miles ahead of the contender in second place. A lot of walkers had already dropped out, leaving about fifteen of us still in the race. I didn't only want to complete the distance, I wanted to do it as fast as possible so I could find out what was really going on back in Israel. At seven in the morning I had less than four miles left to go. I picked up the pace, taking the last mile in only nine minutes.

Larry Young cheered me on; he knew from personal experience just what I was feeling. He called out that he would do the last two laps alongside me to pull me along. Nobody complained that it was illegal, and in fact, the same thing usually happens, in one form or another, at every event, including the Olympics. I increased my speed even more. It was surprisingly easy. The quicker pace must have called into play new muscles that weren't exhausted yet, and altered the position of my foot so that it was pressing on different blisters. There were two laps left to go. Larry Young was keeping pace with me on my right. He didn't make any attempt to demonstrate what he could do; he was only there to pull me ahead to a better time.

We did the penultimate lap in two minutes two seconds, a good lap time even for a 50-kilometer event. I moved into a sprint. I could hardly believe it when my body responded and I was able to maintain the faster speed for the whole of the last lap. Finally, we were at the finish line, and I broke the tape. I had done the last lap in one minute fifty-two seconds, an incredible feat after 399 laps. I took first place, clocking in at 19:38, an extraordinary time. If it hadn't been for the rain that made me walk further and slower, my time might have been even better. I was thrilled. I was both the 1973 US 100-mile champion and the tenth American Centurion.

As soon as I stopped walking, all my muscles seized up. If I had thought they were sore before, it was nothing compared to what I felt now. I also began to suffer the full brunt of the blisters. Breaking with my usual practice, and with sports etiquette, I had no desire to stay there and watch the rest of the event, cheering on the other competitors. The officials empathized with me; they handed me the winner's trophy and championship medal right there on the spot. I asked Larry to take me back to the apartment to shower and then drive me straight to the bus terminal. Despite the terrible pain and my body's obvious need for rest, I decided to change my plans and go back to New York immediately. I had to wait almost two hours for the bus to the Saint Louis airport. I finally got there close to two in the afternoon, and found a seat on the next plane out.

On the flight home, I read the *New York Times*, my favorite paper and the one I consider the best and most reliable in the world. Only then did I realize that a full-scale war had broken out at home and that things were not going well at all. My car flew from La Guardia to Riverdale like a horse with the smell of the stable in its nostrils. It was after dark by the time I got home.

Thoroughly drained and exhausted, with painfully cramped muscles and agonizing blisters on my feet, I was barely able to drag myself limply through the door. My first question to Shosh was a blunt "How does it look?" She understood what I was asking. The radio was tuned to a news station, her only source of information. "It's bad, but under control," she answered. I called the Israeli embassy in Washington. My experience of the Six-Day War had taught me there was no point in talking to the consulate in New York; it would just be a waste of time.

The embassy put me through to the office of the military attaché. I identified myself and asked if the army had need of my services. I was told the army only needed three types of reserve soldiers: armored corps soldiers,

paratroopers, and artillery officers. I explained I belonged to the third category. They wanted to know the date of my last reserve duty. "Two months
ago," I answered. Apparently, I met the qualifications. "If you're willing to fly
back to Israel at your own expense," the embassy official informed me, "we'll
make sure there's a seat waiting for you on the next plane." "I'll be there," I
replied unhesitatingly. "I have an open ticket." I was told to be at the El Al
terminal at Kennedy airport by ten o'clock that night. They would be holding
a place for me. All service to Israel had been halted immediately at the
outbreak of the war. This was to be the first flight from the States since then,
and would be operated by El Al at the behest of the Ministry of Defense in
response to the emergency.

Shosh was standing next to me and listening to my end of the conversation. As I hung up, I announced, "I'm going back for the war." Shosh tried her
best to dissuade me. "The army doesn't need you. You don't enjoy reserve
duty, and you always try to wriggle out of it any way you can. You just want to
prove how important you are. Don't you remember that when you got back
after the Six-Day War you said they didn't need you and they would have won
without you?" I knew she was right. I really didn't like my annual reserve
duty. I also knew she had selfish reasons for not wanting me to go, and must
have been thinking of how worried she had been when I went back for the
Six-Day War and she didn't hear from me for so long. Not only that, but the
memory of her fears for my safety during the massacre in Munich were still
fresh in her mind.

At the same time, however, I knew I would never be able to forgive myself
if I didn't go, notwithstanding the fact that I had just completed the 100-mile
championship and was a helpless invalid at the moment. I repeated my decision, and Shosh made no further attempts to convince me otherwise. My
duffel bag was full of filthy, sweaty track clothes. Shosh repacked it with the
gear I always took with me to the army, including sandwiches. I didn't have
time now to buy myself a gun as I had six years earlier, and in any case, the
sporting goods stores were already closed. Shosh didn't drive, and I had to get
to the airport fast. I called Yoram Yogev, who lived a few floors below us with
his wife Sarah. Unapologetically, I asked him to give me a lift to the airport,
something I would never dare to do under ordinary circumstances.

Yoram was an Israeli who had come to New York to study, with the dream
of returning to Israel with a PhD in communications. It didn't look like that

was ever going to happen, but he didn't stop talking about it. Meanwhile, he had opened a chain of boutiques and become an American citizen. I can't say whether or not Yoram was taken aback by my request, but the fact is that he could easily have simply told me to call a cab. Instead, he voiced no objections whatsoever and agreed to take me. Shosh came with us.

The El Al terminal was crammed with young men escorted by family members and friends. To my dismay, I wasn't on the list of passengers for whom the embassy had reserved seats, and the plane was full. Fortunately, however, I was recognized by one of the El Al officials — I have no idea who — and he arranged to get me on it. Paula, a colleague of Shosh's who had called us just before we left for the airport, was also there. She was amazed by the general cheerfulness. It wasn't how she had imagined the mood of people going off to war. Takeoff was delayed three times, for reasons of which we were not informed. Finally, we were instructed to board and I had to part from Shosh. By the time we took off, it was the middle of the night. We later found out that the delays had been designed to ensure that we landed in Israel after dark.

We were in a jumbo jet crammed to the gills with over four hundred people, but not your typical cross-section of El Al passengers. I saw no one dressed in traditional religious garb, no pairs of yeshiva students coming back loaded down with clothes from a shopping spree in New York, no one who looked like he was planning to smuggle commercial quantities of electronic equipment past customs, not even any rank-and-file citizens who had stocked up on liquor and cigarettes in the duty-free shops. My fellow passengers were all reserve army soldiers dressed simply and functionally in jeans or khaki. Most of them were equipped with only a duffel bag or gym bag. I didn't know anyone there.

Spirits were high throughout the flight. Everyone was keenly aware of why we were there. People chatted with their neighbors and strolled the aisles looking for old friends and acquaintances. The PA system played music the whole time, interrupted periodically by news broadcast live from the Israeli radio stations, during which the whole plane fell silent and drank in every word. Afterwards, we tried to analyze the real meaning behind what we had heard. I hadn't slept in forty-eight hours, twenty of which I had spent walking, but I couldn't fall asleep in this atmosphere. I waited expectantly for each newscast. Our nonstop flight approached Israel after dark. We were instructed to draw the curtains and all lights were extinguished. I could feel the plane losing altitude, and through a chink in the curtain could see the coastline in the moonlight, and then Tel Aviv below us, no lights anywhere. We landed at Lod in total darkness. It was after eight on the evening of Monday, October 8, 1973.

The plane taxied right up to the terminal building. There didn't seem to be any activity at the airport. We deplaned and entered the arrivals terminal. A girl soldier stood at the entrance ordering: "Armored corps to the right; trucks are waiting for you. Everyone else call your liaison office." Dozens of telephones were positioned on the tourism ministry counters. At any other time, they would have been concealed behind the counter, reserved for the exclusive use of the clerks. It looked like extra lines had been added, too. They were ordinary phones, not pay phones; all we had to do was dial. I called my reserve unit liaison office. The officer in charge, Captain Hugi, answered the phone. I gave him my name. He knew me from years back, and declared: "It's a good thing you're here. Your regiment has just taken up position in the same sector where you served in the reserves two months ago. They need a gun position officer. Get going!" To my question as to how I was supposed to get there, he replied, "Hitch a ride." I now knew I had to make my way to somewhere in the Jordan Valley near the Sartaba.

I called my sister Marta, who lived in the city of Lod. She was overjoyed to hear my voice: "I knew you'd come. I told Mama you would, but she said you had enough sense to stay in the States." I was happy and proud not to have let her down, and as for my mother, I couldn't fault her maternal instincts. I wouldn't have expected her to say anything else. I arranged for Marta to pick me up at the airport. In normal times, it would have taken her ten minutes. Now, in the pitch black with her headlights painted over, it would probably take longer. A fellow passenger from the flight was standing next to me and recognized me. He told me he came from the settlement of Bnei Atarot, about three miles from the airport, was also in the artillery corps, and had to get to Jerusalem. We made arrangements for Marta to drive him home. I would then wait at my sister's house while he got his gear together and he would take me as far as Jerusalem.

While we waited for Marta, I used the time to call Shosh's parents. My mother didn't have a telephone at home, only at the pharmacy. Shosh's father picked up the phone. He was so thrilled and excited that he choked up as soon as he recognized my voice and heard I was calling from Lod. I asked him to inform my mother and Shosh that I had arrived safely. Marta barely recognized me standing outside the terminal in the dark. We made the detour through Bnei Atarot and got to her house in half an hour. She gave me the army clothes her husband Shmuel had left behind when he went to join his armored corps unit two days before. A little while later my "ride" showed up in uniform, and I realized he was a lieutenant colonel. On the way, I used a ballpoint pen to draw my first lieutenant's stripes on the epaulets of my shirt. When we got to Jerusalem, he dropped me at the soldier's hitchhiking station east of the Lions Gate before going on to Central Command Headquarters. The IDF had stormed through this gate in the Six-Day War to take the Old City of Jerusalem and liberate the Western Wall.

By now, it was after eleven o'clock at night. I was all alone in the street. The city lay in total darkness and silence, not a single car on the road. After about an hour, an army car came by, made me out in the moonlight, and stopped. They took me as far as the police station at the southern entrance to Jericho. I knew the building well. I had rested there in the middle of the third day of my attempt at a solo walk from Metulla to Eilat three and a half years before. I waited across the street in the dark for another ride. It was 12:30.

Thirty minutes or so later, a jeep pulled out of the police station heading north and picked me up. They were going to the settlement of Gilgal in the Jordan Valley. We proceeded slowly, not glimpsing a single light the whole way. It was lucky there weren't any other cars on the road or we would have seriously risked an accident driving in the dark with shaded headlights that could only be seen from a few yards away. We reached Gilgal sometime after 1:30. It looked more like an army post than an agricultural settlement. I was informed an incoming fire alert had been ordered for two a.m.; in other words, they were expecting a Jordanian artillery barrage on that and other Jordan Valley positions. Anyone without specific duties to perform was ordered into the shelters which, hopefully, could sustain a direct hit.

A sergeant at the settlement command post put me in touch with Jordan Valley battalion headquarters. I asked to speak with my regiment commander. Eventually, they tracked him down. I told him I had come from the States and had just gotten to Gilgal. He was happy to hear that: "I'm glad you're here. Your battery doesn't have a gun position officer. The battery commander is filling in, meanwhile. They just took up position in the same spot where you did reserve duty a couple of months ago. Get over there and assume command!" I knew exactly where he meant, the track leading to the foot of the Sartaba where I had done ultra-long-distance training in the fall of 1970 during the run-up to the world 100-kilometer championship. It was over ten miles away from Gilgal.

I asked the regiment commander how he expected me to get there, assuming he would send a car. But he remembered my eccentric method of setting up gun positions, running along the gun convoy and fixing their positions, which got them fire-ready faster than if I had adopted the customary practice of using a military vehicle. Now he had his own eccentric suggestion for me: "Ladany," he said, "you're a race walker so it's no trouble for you to walk. You can make it to your battery on foot." I was all cramped up and my whole body ached. The worst muscle pain always comes two days after any supreme effort, which meant right then. The blisters on my feet were also tormenting me. After the 100-mile championship, I not only couldn't walk, I could barely hobble. I also had to carry my gear. Still, ashamed to admit to my pitiful condition, I said okay, and, even before the defensive alert went into effect, set out from Gilgal, limping slowly down the half-mile access road to the highway.

It was past two o'clock in the morning. Except for the moon, there was no light whatsoever. Nor was there any sign of a Jordanian bombardment. The Jordan Valley road was empty. After about an hour, a truck finally drove by, its headlights dimmed as expected. The driver made out my hand signal and pulled up. There were three people in the cab. I told the driver I had to go ten miles to a track on the left where my unit was positioned, and that I would signal him when to stop. I climbed into the back of the truck. When we reached the track, I rapped on the rear window of the cab. The truck stopped and the driver asked me if I wanted him to take me up the track. I could barely walk, and I was also afraid that if I came up on the battery on foot in the dark, the guards might shoot first and ask questions later. "I'd be most grateful," I said.

The truck took a left, making its way eastward along the twisting track for two or three miles. Then, instead of arcing right, the track ended at the foot of the Sartaba. Obviously, we had turned off in the wrong place. I signaled the driver to stop and told him I had made a mistake; the track I was looking for must be a couple of miles further north. We went back to the highway. There was another track leading off to the left a little way up ahead. The two of them look exactly the same even in broad daylight. The driver turned left for a second time. This time the track twisted to the right, and as soon as the incline started to get sharper, I recognized the outline of the gun position and could see the guard aiming his rifle at the truck. I had made it, no question. This was my unit.

I climbed down from the truck. Four a.m. The guard recognized my face and welcomed me. I thanked the driver and he went back the way he had come. Three years later, a march participant informed me that it was he who had driven me to the battery position that night. He had recognized me when I was talking to him on the road outside Gilgal, and as a result he wasn't at all reluctant to make a detour onto a lonely track in the middle of the night. My familiar face may have saved me a few unwelcome holes in various parts of my body.

I made my way to the command post. A technical assistant was leaning over an artillery board, positioning targets and calculating the firing data. As soon as he saw me, his jaw fell open and he threw his arms around me. Then he woke up the other technical assistant and exclaimed, "Look, Ladany's back from the States." I learned the battery had only taken up position three hours earlier, after a series of delays. I checked the situation at the command post, received a report of our orders and mission, and went out to review the battery, gun by gun. There was at least one guard posted at each gun position. The same scenario I witnessed when I appeared without warning at the command post played out again and again. The guards couldn't restrain themselves from waking up the other members of the team to give them the news that I had arrived from the States. I don't know who was more thrilled, the soldiers who discovered I had not abandoned them, or me, made to feel I had certainly made the right decision.

When I had finished checking out the positions, I went back to the command post. By now it was five a.m. The effect of the caffeine in the huge quantities of Coke I had drunk during the long 100-mile walk was finally wearing off. After nearly three days with no sleep, nineteen and a half hours of which I had spent walking, I couldn't stay awake any longer. I lay down on a flat rock outside the command post, using my duffel bag for a pillow, and immediately fell asleep. At ten o'clock I was awakened by the blazing desert sun. The guys told me I had been sleeping out there in the sun without moving a muscle, dead to the world.

Two days later, my battery sergeant major, Shmuel Miller, arrived. The war had caught him by surprise in South Africa. He might not have been in a 100-mile event, but he wasn't as fast a walker as I was either. He had flown home through London. On the tenth day of the war, another member of the unit who had been touring Romania also showed up. Unlike the Six-Day War, in the course of which only six reserve soldiers made it back from abroad, in the Yom Kippur War over sixteen thousand reserves voluntarily joined their units. Many of their names are engraved on the monuments to the fallen.

Everything was quiet on our front; no shots fired at all. But the situation was far from encouraging. Along the entire border with Jordan, from the Beit She'an Valley to the Dead Sea, there were only two tanks left, and they were old Sherman tanks, to boot. Not only were no additional tanks brought in, but all the armored equipment in the sector, save for those two old Shermans, had been transferred to the north to beat back the Syrian incursion on the Golan Heights, or to the south to hold back the Egyptian offensive in the Sinai. Moshe Dayan, the minister of defense, elected to take the risk of leaving the eastern front exposed, but chose not to inform King Hussein of this strategic decision. On the contrary! The two tanks moved from place to place, performing flamboyant maneuvers under the watchful eyes of the Jordanian observation posts in order to give the impression that the sector was jam-packed with tanks.

Israeli propaganda was enlisted simultaneously as a strategic measure to deter Jordan from entering the war against Israel and opening a third front close to the center of the country and its densest population. The Kingdom of Transjordan had occupied the West Bank in the War of Independence, annexing the territory and making its point by changing the name of the country to the Kingdom of Jordan. In the Six-Day War, the king had been taken in by Egyptian and Syrian propaganda — a fine example of the vivid Arab imagination — and believed he could extend his kingdom as far as the Mediterranean. Despite Israeli warnings conveyed through the offices of the United States, Jordan entered the war against Israel, and lost the whole of the

West Bank it had annexed nineteen years earlier. This time Israeli propaganda was at work, cautioning Hussein that if he again bought into the Egyptian and Syrian lies and was tempted to throw his troops into the battle, he could count on losing the other half of his kingdom.

We fervently hoped the ruse would work. However, two days after I arrived at the battery, when the sad truth about the battles in the Sinai and the Golan Heights became known, along with the extent of losses in men and equipment, the commander of the Jordan Valley decided to modify the strategic deployment of the troops in the sector. With such sparse forces at his disposal, and the prospect of reinforcements still a long way off at best, he abandoned the idea of repulsing a Jordanian attack at the border along the Jordan River. Instead, he ordered the troops to prevent the Jordanians from crossing the valley and seizing the heights of the Judea and Sumeria hills that ran the length of the valley to the west. If we were unable to push them back, we were to attempt, at least, to impede their advance.

Israeli forces were redeployed accordingly. The fortified outposts along the river were left manned, but the rest of the troops took up positions on the mountain range. My battery was transferred to a site behind a rise high in the hills. It was the first time I was ordered to devise a plan to provide cover for a possible retreat. It didn't feel good at all. Wherever vehicles, especially tanks, could cross the valley into the hills, resistance was planned and obstacles thrown up. Light anti-tank guns, presumably purchased in Nicaragua during the War of Independence, were brought in. I hadn't seen anything like them since 1951 when I joined the artillery army training group in high school. Apparently Israel hadn't been able to sell them off, not even to some third world country.

Taken out of mothballs from the self-defense armories of small settlements and towed by light farm tractors on wheels, they were positioned so that two guns were aimed on each bend in any track the enemy might be able to use. They were operated by two-man teams and were well camouflaged, but we all knew they couldn't fire more than one, at most two, shells at an advancing tank. If our soldiers didn't manage to disable it, the tank would take them out. On every narrow pass, whether a road or a dirt track, groups of deep holes were drilled and covered with wooden or tin boards. Explosives were piled up nearby ready to be inserted into the holes, and teams of soldiers were positioned to wait for the order to set the charges.

Naturally, I hadn't brought a rifle with me. The battery was equipped with two machine guns, but most of the soldiers had been issued Czech rifles, and just a few lucky ones had gotten Uzi sub-machine guns. The Czech guns might be highly accurate and reliable, but they were designed in 1898, which means they are very low on firepower. Single-action rifles, the clip holds a mere five rounds, with another in the breech. Even worse was the fact that only five rounds were issued with each Czech rifle, and twenty with each Uzi; that was all the ammunition we had. It was obvious to us all that the battery could be attacked by infantry soldiers — usually the job of commando units — and that virtually the only means of defense available to us was to aim our Russian cannons directly at them, a process that took a long time and wasn't an easy thing to do considering how heavy and unwieldy they were.

It was two days before I got my own rifle, a Czech gun with no strap, a problem I solved by hooking up a long flannel cleaning rag. When I was summoned to headquarters for a staff meeting, the regiment commander was put off by the sight of the rag gracing my chest and suggested I switch guns with one of the guys who had been given an Uzi, all of which were equipped with straps. I told him I wouldn't use my authority to take away the rifle that was providing a soldier with a modicum of confidence in his ability to defend himself, and compel him to carry an inferior weapon instead. I don't know whether or not it was because my commander couldn't stand the sight of the rag anymore, but a week later I was given a strap and we were all issued a sufficient supply of ammunition. A few days later we received enough Uzis to go around.

At the end of one long day, Shmuel Miller and I were lounging on our backs on the slope near the command post. Having heard of the appalling losses suffered in the Sinai, we were carrying on an academic discussion: did it hurt more to lose a child if you only had one. As the father of a single daughter, I naturally claimed that there was nothing worse than the death of an only child. On the other hand, Shmuel, who had a son and daughter, argued that it didn't matter how many children there were in the family, the intensity of the grief would always be the same. The next day, Shmuel was summoned to the regiment commander. I next saw him an hour later, supported by two soldiers and weeping uncontrollably. He had been notified that his son, a lieutenant in the paratroop corps, had fallen in battle at the

Chinese farm in the Sinai. I packed his things for him. The two soldiers took him home in a state of utter collapse.

A good many years have passed since then. In German, old soldiers are known as "AK," — *Alte Krieger*, or old warriors. We're still AK — *Alte Kakkers*, decrepit old fogies. We've both been discharged from reserve duty, meanwhile. Shmuel never liked to walk. Still, every year I meet him and his whole family at the Kfar Shmariyahu Sons March, held by his town in memory of the local citizens who fell in Israel's many wars.

When it became clear that Jordan was unlikely to enter the war, I finally found time to train on the paved road outside the battery that sloped down to the Jordan Valley. By now the muscle cramps and blisters from the 100-mile championship were all gone. It felt good to be able to work up a real sweat at last. It also felt good to hear one soldier call out to another as I went by: "Look, it's Ladany. He's back from the States," and then yell out "Way to go!" in my direction. When the war was over, I found out that a couple of days after I got to Israel, one of the papers had printed a short item about my winning the 100-mile championship just before I decided to come back and rejoin my unit. Whatever paper it was, it must have found its way to the units on the Jordanian front, probably distributed by the culture officers.

A cease-fire was declared on all fronts. Every now and then, each of the guys in my unit made it to the settlement of Argaman in the valley where he could call home. I hadn't exchanged a single word with Shosh for three weeks. The regiment commander promised to find a way for me to contact her, and the communications officer pulled every string in the book so he could keep that promise. After devoting four whole hours to setting it up, the communications officer finally gave me the signal. It was two a.m. I was sitting in the large tarp-covered foxhole in the middle of the battery that served as our command post. I cranked up the battery-operated field telephone and got the regiment operator. He connected me with the battalion operator, who passed me on to the sector headquarters operator.

All these connections were made through the telephone lines laid over the tracks we ourselves had leveled. From there I was transferred to the Central Command exchange which connected me with the all-army exchange. Every single operator along the way had been briefed in advance and knew I had permission to call the States. Before passing me on, one of them mentioned that he had been a student of mine. From the all-army exchange, I was connected, after a short delay, with the civilian international operator. I recited the number I was trying to reach in New York, and within a minute or so I heard a phone ringing and Shosh answered.

There I was in a field in the middle of nowhere holding the receiver of a cumbersome field telephone in a leather pouch, so primitive it only had a crank handle, not even a dial, and I was speaking directly with the US! I can't remember whether I was shouting because I was so excited or because I couldn't hear Shosh very well, but the next day the guys told me I had woken them up and they heard every word I said. I was ecstatic, only disappointed that Danit was asleep so I couldn't talk to her too.

A few days later I also got a chance to get to Argaman for a shower. Before I went in to clean myself off, I decided to try my luck at telecommunications. There was a pay phone at the settlement. I don't know who was responsible, the signal corps, the postal service who operated the phones, or the ingenuity of some soldier, but it didn't cost anything to use the phone. That didn't surprise me; it had been the same every time I was in the reserves in the Jordan Valley area. But this time we didn't even have to put in a token to dial, we just picked up the receiver and we had a line. The only problem was the traffic on the lines in the sector, so heavy that service had to be "rationed." Periodically, the line would go dead and you had to wait until service was reinstated. The guys in my unit told me there was invariably a long line for the phone at all hours of the day or night.

It was no different when I got there. I took my place and waited patiently, moving up slowly. When I was next, I witnessed the vain attempt of the soldier in front of me to contact his daughter in Netanya. Even when the phone showed signs of life, all the lines to the city were engaged. Then it was my turn. The phone was working. I dialed 18 for the international operator and she came on immediately. I told her I wanted to call the States and gave her Shosh's number, and within a few short seconds I was talking to her. I was thrilled. I asked her to put Danit on and Shosh handed her the receiver. Danit was now two years and three months old. "Danit, this is Daddy. How are you, honey?" I said, tickled pink that I was finally able to talk to her.

The guy ahead of me had gone back to the end of the line to take a second stab at phoning his daughter in Netanya. When he saw how easily I got through to the States — apparently I was so excited I was shouting again — he remarked wryly that it might be a good idea to try to reach Netanya by dialing the international operator and routing his call through the States. About twenty years later, Professor Ze'ev Tzahor from Ben-Gurion University told me he had been standing behind me in that same line. When he heard me call the States, his initial reaction had been to berate me for making social calls at the expense of the State of Israel, but then he realized from my conversation with Danit that I had come back for the war and my family was still overseas, and he regretted his unkind thoughts. Several days later, I got my first letter from Shosh. She apologized for trying to persuade me to stay in the States. I was vindicated; Shosh admitted I had only done what was to be expected from a man who loved his country.

After I had been with my unit for four weeks, the regiment commander released me to return home to my family. Unlike the situation in Israel, Social Security in the States doesn't pay your salary when you do reserve duty, and certainly not reserve duty in the Israeli army. I was also worried that CUNY might decide to cancel my appointment after I had disappeared on them for the duration of the war, neglecting the duties I had undertaken to perform.

As soon as I was released, I went straight to the reserve unit liaison office to get the army consent form I needed to leave the country, but there was a surprise in store for me. The chief artillery officer had issued orders not to allow any artillery officer to leave the country until the requirements of the corps had become absolutely clear. Considerable losses had been incurred, and the precise nature of the reorganization that would be necessary at the end of the fighting had not yet been determined. I had now acquired a very bizarre status: I had been discharged from the army and was officially a civilian again, but I wasn't free to return to the States. I called a few friends to see how they were. The men were all still in the army, but I was overjoyed to hear that they had all come through the war safe and sound.

I also called the Sports Federation to find out if any of my fellow athletes were among the casualties. The response I got was unexpected: "It's great you're here and you've already been discharged, because we've been invited to take part in the Asian Track and Field Championships in Manila and we've got no one to send. You can enter the 20-kilometer walk." The fact that I was still officially under interdiction didn't seem to bother anyone. I would have to leave in a week. The 20-kilometer event would be held right at the beginning of the games, but the Israeli delegation would be staying for three weeks. I had never been in the Philippines, or anywhere else in Asia, apart from Israel, for that matter. Moreover, I was a sucker for competitions, and it was a real honor to compete in the Asian championships. There was even a chance I was still in good enough shape, despite the war, to take the gold, and I believed the worst I could do was second or third place.

The only problem was time. I had to be back in New York as soon as possible if I didn't want to jeopardize my appointment. I was willing to take the risk of extending my absence for a few days for the sake of the Asian games, but there was no way I could delay my return until the Israeli delegation left Manila. I explained all this to the Sports Federation, asking them to fly me straight from the Philippines to the States immediately after my event. I also made it clear that I wasn't willing to bear any greater expense than the price of a ticket from Israel to New York. They promised to look into the feasibility of my demands, and in the meantime urged me to take advantage of the facilities of the Wingate Institute for some intense training, as if I ever needed urging to train!

I did use the Wingate facilities, where I met my protégé, Shimon Shomroni, who was about to be inducted into the army. We trained together a few times, but I knew that if I wanted to be ready for a 20-kilometer event, I needed speed work, and Shimon was a lot slower than me. Consequently, I followed the same routine I had used with John Markon. I started out behind Shimon, caught up to him, and continued on for twenty or thirty yards. Then I turned around and went back in the opposite direction until I was more or less the same distance behind him, repeating the pattern over and over again. After three days of rigorous training, I was convinced I was back in top form and as fast as ever.

Around the same time, I learned that the chief artillery officer had finally given permission to issue consent forms for the corps reserve officers to leave the country. I also read in the papers that the Ministry of Defense had promised to pay for the flight home for all those soldiers who had come from abroad at their own expense to join their units during the war. It was time for a decision. I called the Sports Federation to get their answer. They told me I could leave Manila directly after my event, but I would have to bear the full cost of the flight to the States, about four times higher than the fare from Tel

Aviv to New York. Full-fare tickets, I was told, are much more expensive than the round-trip group rates they were paying, and I would have to make up the difference. There was no question in my mind as to what I was going to do. I thanked the sports official politely, and then added, "I'm not some cow you can milk all the time!" That was the end of that conversation.

I got my consent form and went straight to the Ministry of Defense where I was handed a coupon for a free flight to New York on the spot. Within twenty-four hours, I was back in Riverdale. I have no idea how or when the Sports Federation found out I had left, or what the reaction of the officials was to the act of an obstinate athlete who wouldn't compromise his principles. Nor do I know how they solved the problem of not having any athletes to enter in the Asian games. Furthermore, to this day I don't know who won the 20-kilometer walk or in what time. I never made the slightest effort to find out.

ZIONIST ORGANIZATION OF AMERICA – DETROIT DISTRICT

proudly presents

DR. SHAUL P. LADANY

Professor at Tel-Aviv University
Member of Israel Olympic Team

Dr. Ladany is scheduled to tour the United States under the auspices of the Zionist Organization of America. He witnessed the tragic massacre of the Israeli athletes in Munich; participated in the Six-Day War; received his Ph.D. at Columbia University and has been visiting professor and lecturer at numerous universities both in Israel and in this country.

THURSDAY, FEBRUARY 15, 1973   ZIONIST CULTURAL CENTER
8:30 P.M.   18451 WEST 10 MILE ROAD, SOUTHFIELD

INTERESTING AND INFORMATIVE!   **INVITE YOUR FAMILY AND FRIENDS!**   **SOCIAL HOUR!**

No Admission Charge!

JACK R. GREENBERG, M.D.   SANFORD A. BENNETT, M.D.
President   Program Chairman

Invitation from the Zionist Organization of America for my lecture in Detroit, 1972

The Big Bang

When I got back to New York in early November 1973, I found I had arrived in the nick of time. If I had stayed away any longer, the university would have given me my walking papers. I threw myself into my research, completing a study every three or four weeks, writing it up, and submitting it for publication in an appropriate scientific journal. At the same time, I was also working on ideas for new inventions and formal requests for US patents. By the spring of 1974, I had eight patents registered or pending, all of which were eventually approved.

I kept up my training throughout the winter as well, but nowhere near as much as in the past. My academic activities demanded too much of my time, and I was badly put off by the biting cold of the New York winter. I sorely missed the Columbia University gym. On two particularly cold weekends, I trained with Howie Jacobson in the parking garage under the housing complex in Riverdale. It provided shelter from the wind and wasn't quite as cold as it was outside, but the air was heavy with exhaust fumes, and being cooped up for so long in such an enclosed inhospitable space was grimly depressing. Twice was more than enough.

I resumed serious training in February 1974, having decided to prepare for the 100-kilometer American championship scheduled for mid-March. There had been no official championships for such long distances when I was studying for my doctorate, but things had changed since then. With my experience and skill at events of this kind, I welcomed these changes happily. The 100-kilometer championship was to be held in Des Moines, Iowa. Naturally, I had to fly. The course for the race was flat, no climbs to contend with, repeatedly lapping around, and sometimes cutting across, the local exhibition grounds. I hadn't returned to top form, but since I was the only one who knew that, I was deemed the favorite to win and the man to fear. I led the whole way, without a single rival making so much as a token attempt to catch me.

We had fine weather for the race, pleasantly mild, but I still perspired a lot from the exertion. One of the organizers kept me supplied with drinks. I had also given him a few salt pills. Starting at kilometer 40, he handed me one pill every twenty kilometers, as per my instructions. I would split the pill with my teeth and grind it up so that the salt could be absorbed as quickly as possible. At kilometer 80, as I was trying to bite down on the pill, I broke a tooth. I realized what I'd done the instant it happened, and could feel the fragment of tooth on my tongue. I managed to fish it out with my fingertips and handed it to the next official I passed, asking him to hold on to it until the competition was over.

I couldn't blame anyone but myself for my reluctance to endure the taste of the salt on my tongue for longer than necessary, a finickiness that caused me to grind it with my teeth rather than let it dissolve in my mouth. Had I not done that, my tooth would undoubtedly still have been in one piece. But I couldn't indulge in self-accusation for too long; I had to concentrate on the race. I won the championship, finishing fifteen minutes before the contender in second place. I had now claimed the American title for the second time.

As a registered member of the AAU, I was automatically entitled to medical insurance for any accident incurred in the course of competition. Aware of this right, I asked the championship organizers for an official letter stating that one of my teeth had broken while biting down on a salt pill during the race. I had the tooth repaired and filed a claim with the insurance company for reimbursement of the dental bill, enclosing the letter I had been given at the end of the event and detailing my claim. But it seems that insurance companies are the same the world over: first they say no, and then they ask, "What's your problem?" My claim was rejected on the grounds that the insurance didn't cover dental care.

I was only asking for the measly sum of thirty dollars, but I'm a stubborn guy. I wrote back explaining — as I had in my original claim — that the "dental care" involved was in fact a repair job on a tooth accidentally damaged during a race, and that the policy did, in fact, cover that sort of work. When they realized they couldn't just brush me off, they paid. Not surprisingly, they didn't happen to mention in the letter that came with the check that they had tried to cheat me the first time and only honored their policy when they found they couldn't pull the wool over my eyes so easily. Instead, in eloquently polished phrases, they apologized for not noticing that in the case of a competition accident, dental care was indeed covered. I wonder how much harder they would have fought if I had been demanding a larger sum of money.

On Sunday, April 21, 1974, three weeks after the 100-kilometer race, the American 75-kilometer championship was held at Long Branch, New Jersey. The event replaced the Eastern Regional 50-mile championship, but it was still organized by Elliott Denman and followed the same format as the previous distance, run on a quarter-mile stadium track to facilitate the setting of a new record. In fact, it was the same race, only about five and a half kilometers shorter. I had put on some weight and was not in the same form I had been in two years before when I set the world record for 50 miles. But I was still in good enough condition to win the event hands down and set a new American record for 75 kilometers.

This was not only the third time I won an American title, but on this, the sixth time I entered the event — the 50-mile championship introduced in 1966 and its "successor" the 75-kilometer — it was my sixth win and the sixth time I set or improved on the American record. It goes without saying that I could feel every muscle in my body when it was over, but it wasn't too bad. I could still walk and see to my own needs.

The following day, a Monday, I flew to Boston for the joint biannual conference of the Operations Research Society of America and the Institute of Management Sciences, where I presented two papers. On Wednesday, back home in Riverdale, I was surprised to receive a telegram from the French Sports Federation inviting me to take part in the two-day Tour du Var starting on the following Saturday in Toulon.

The Tour du Var is off and running. I've done twenty kilometers and I'm in the lead, far ahead of the pack behind. We're walking on local roads, passing through towns and villages, and the excitement in the air reminds me of the Tour de Romandie in Switzerland in July 1972. Loudspeakers have been mounted on several of the official cars, and everywhere they go they call out the names of the contenders and the leaders and the length of their lead. The announcements start as soon as we enter the outskirts of some town and then the cars take up position in the town center and keep up the commentary.

The citizens line up in droves on both sides of the road to watch us pass, cheering and urging us on. They know my name, that I come from Israel, and what my more outstanding achievements are. They got it all from the sound trucks, repeating it over and over again wherever we go. It's like a public holiday, and the atmosphere pumps me up and helps me forget the effort.

There's just one procedure here I've never seen in a race before, a special checkpoint set up every twenty-five or thirty kilometers in the center of town with a list of all the entrants spread out on a table. As I pass, I have to stop and put my signature next to my name. The officials want to make sure that no competitor sends in a fresh imposter in his place when he gets tired, so they don't want to rely solely on a number on a shirt. In other words, this French tradition is not just an attempt to collect autographs, but a means of comparing signatures to prevent cheating.

After sixty kilometers I'm told I have a twelve-minute lead over the walker in second place. I have to save my strength for the second day of competition, and I figure this is a big enough lead, so I don't push myself to pick up the speed. Maybe I'm even a little too complacent. After eighty kilometers I'm warned that my rival is steadily closing the gap and is now only four minutes back. I'm very conscious of the effort awaiting me tomorrow, but I don't want to lose the advantage I still have, so I speed up just a bit. I finish the first day's walk of ninety-eight kilometers in first place, maintaining the four-minute lead over second place.

I'm tired out and ache all over, and unfortunately I've gotten blisters on my feet again as well. Not wasting any time, I drain them and lie down to get some rest. I'm worried my rival might be faster than me tomorrow, especially in the third leg of the race, which is just twenty kilometers, a distance at which a walker's basic speed can make a big, maybe even crucial, difference. We start out at six a.m. All my muscles are sore, but from the expressions on the faces of the others, I don't think they're feeling any better right now. I'm hoping that the last two long-distance events I entered and won, the 100-kilometer in Des Moines and the 75-kilometer in Long Branch, have put me in better shape for this race than whatever my rivals have been up to. But I can only hope; I don't have any information to base a reasoned assessment on. The second leg is sixty-five kilometers.

Once we get started, my body begins to warm up and I slip into a quick pace, as if I hadn't been feeling the effects of the first day's exertion before we took off. Every now and then I ask my escorts where my rival of yesterday is at the moment. He's the only one I'm at all concerned about. They calm my fears, assuring me he's way back and that I'm steadily increasing my lead over him. He must have drained every last bit of energy on the first day and has to go slower today. I can't say I'm sorry. By the end of the morning segment on this, the second day, I've opened a gap of twenty-five minutes. My confidence is back. I now have two and a half hours to lie down before the start of the last stage — twenty kilometers. The ones who finish behind me don't have as much time to rest.

Waiting to start on the third and last leg, I'm feeling very tired. There's no real chance of my losing the whole of my twenty-five-minute lead, but if I want to be on the safe side, I'll have to make a real effort. So that's what I do. I push myself, but I don't squeeze myself dry. Nobody overtakes me on this segment either, but a few contenders come in right behind me. My overall lead over second place still stands at twenty-five minutes. I've won. Naturally, as soon as the end was in sight I stepped on the gas so that I'd reach the finish line in Toulon not only as the winner of the event, but as the victor in the third leg as well.

My achievement made a big impression on a lot of people. Afterward, the French sports papers declared that "Ladany is undoubtedly the best race walker in the world at 100 kilometers." I felt that I had now closed the circle: my victory completed the "grand slam," the "big bang" — I had won every major long-distance event there is.

The awards ceremony was held that evening after the race. I was handed a large cup and a beautifully embroidered pennant as mementos of the event. After the ceremony, Monsieur Genevien, the potentate of French race walking — with a smile and a physique big enough to suit the grandeur of his status — informed me that the Tour du Var had also served as the international trial for the Strasbourg to Paris competition. I already knew that, but it didn't affect me. I'd heard a lot about that 520-kilometer event, and I knew that a while ago, two compulsory one-hour rest periods had been introduced after 160 and 320 kilometers. I'd even read a book about it, and was very well aware of the sort of effort and agony the serious contenders had to endure. So when Monsieur Genevien went on to say that as the winner of the international trial, the French Sports Federation was ready to pay my way to participate in Strasbourg to Paris, and would even cover travel expenses for an escort of my choosing, I just smiled and said, "All long-distance walkers are crazy, but I'm not crazy enough yet to enter the Strasbourg to Paris race." He smiled back, not at all offended. He understood what I was talking about. If he had asked me again a few days later, when the pain was gone, leaving only the pleasant memories of the Tour du Var, my answer might have been completely different.

Beginning of the second day portion of the Tour du Var, 1974; Charles Sowa behind me

Postscript

I went on to repeat my victory in the American 75-kilometer championship in 1975, 1976, and 1977. Each time I not only took first place, but systematically broke the American record I myself had set the year before. When I went to the States to take part in this competition in 1976, I was already living in the Negev in the south of Israel. Don Johnson put me up for the weekend while I was in the States. But the most unusual aspect of my achievement was that I had now turned forty, making this the first time that the winner in the seniors category was also the overall winner of the open championship. I repeated that feat in 1977: same competition, same host, same startling result.

In the fall of 1975, I was a guest of Cape Town University for six weeks. I didn't fly home before taking part in the South African 50-kilometer championship in the town of Stellenbosch. I won that race too, in the second-best time ever recorded in that country, and thus I was dubbed a "Springbok," the nickname of South African champions. In July 1977 I won my fifth Maccabiah Games gold medal in the 50-kilometer walk held in the middle of the day in the broiling heat. A month later I entered the world seniors championship in Göteborg, Sweden and took first place in the 5-kilometer walk on track in twenty-three minutes fifteen seconds and in the 20-kilometer event in 1:38:07, in both cases breaking the championship record.

In 1981, when I was forty-five and on sabbatical in the States for the second time, I entered the 100-kilometer American championship now held in Washington, DC, and I won it again. Naturally, I was the winner in the seniors category as well, but after the precedent I had set in 1976, there was no longer anything sensational about this accomplishment, except for the fact that I was five years older.

I also routinely won the Israeli title for a variety of distances. The last time was at the 50-kilometer event in August 1996, the year I turned sixty. At the time of writing, my world record for 50 miles has yet to be broken, although it goes without saying that my condition today is far from what it was in my days of glory. Yet to this day I still compete and continue to employ the same strategy I always did when it comes to dividing my effort between flat segments and ascents. On a straight I go at full speed, calling on every last ounce of strength I've got, until I'm utterly squeezed dry, gritting my teeth in agony and absolutely incapable of going any faster — and then when I reach a climb, I put some more effort into it.

Over the years, I have written and published thirteen books and some 110 scientific papers, and I still have more up my sleeve. In addition, I hold eight patents. For the past thirty-three years I have been at Ben-Gurion University, where among other positions I held an endowed chair and was chairman of the university entrepreneurial center, now as professor emeritus. In 2007 the Council of the Olympic Committee in Lausanne, Switzerland, awarded me the Pierre de Coubertin Medal for outstanding service to the Olympic Movement. As a testimony to the double life I lived, just a few months later, on March 10, 2008, at the Israeli bi-annual Industrial Engineering Conference I was awarded a Life-Achievement Award for my contribution to the field of Industrial Engineering.

I still take part in almost all the marches held in Israel and in some of the major marches around the world. In May 2006, in an event organized by Ron Laird in Ashtabula, Ohio, I walked 100 miles in 21:45:34, the fastest time ever recorded by a person over age seventy. Moreover, I still train every day, although I'm not so fanatical about it anymore. I hereby invite everyone, including you, my readers, to celebrate my birthday with me. Ever since I turned fifty, I mark the day by walking a kilometer for each year of my life. Even in Singapore, just a hop, skip and a jump from the equator, where the humidity is unbearable and the heat oppressive, I managed to celebrate my fifty-ninth birthday by walking 59 kilometers. Last year, for my seventy-first birthday, walking on a five-kilometer loop, I failed to complete the event as initially planned: the brakes in my legs failed to function properly, and I managed to stop only after seventy-five kilometers. How long will I be able to keep up the tradition? I can't say; I don't have a crystal ball.